COVID-19's Impact on the Cryptocurrency Market and the Digital Economy

Nadia Mansour
University of Sousse, Tunisia & University of Salamanca, Spain

Salha Ben Salem
University of Monastir, Tunisia

A volume in the Advances in Finance, Accounting, and Economics (AFAE) Book Series

IGI Global
PUBLISHER of TIMELY KNOWLEDGE

Published in the United States of America by
IGI Global
Business Science Reference (an imprint of IGI Global)
701 E. Chocolate Avenue
Hershey PA, USA 17033
Tel: 717-533-8845
Fax: 717-533-8661
E-mail: cust@igi-global.com
Web site: http://www.igi-global.com

Library of Congress Cataloging-in-Publication Data

Names: Mansour, Nadia, 1984- editor. | Salem, Salha Ben, 1992- editor.
Title: COVID-19's impact on the cryptocurrency market and the digital economy / Nadia Mansour, and Salha Ben Salem, editor.
Description: Hershey, PA : Business Science Reference, [2022] | Includes bibliographical references and index. | Summary: "This book provides theoretical and empirical frameworks in the field of finance and technology for professionals who want to improve their understanding of the importance of blockchain, bitcoin, and the digital transformation in business"-- Provided by publisher.
Identifiers: LCCN 2021038880 (print) | LCCN 2021038881 (ebook) | ISBN 9781799891178 (hardcover) | ISBN 9781799891185 (paperback) | ISBN 9781799891192 (ebook)
Subjects: LCSH: Electronic commerce. | Cryptocurrencies. | Blockchains (Databases) | COVID-19 (Disease)
Classification: LCC HF5548.32 .C685 2022 (print) | LCC HF5548.32 (ebook) | DDC 332.4--dc23/eng/20211007
LC record available at https://lccn.loc.gov/2021038880
LC ebook record available at https://lccn.loc.gov/2021038881

This book is published in the IGI Global book series Advances in Finance, Accounting, and Economics (AFAE) (ISSN: 2327-5677; eISSN: 2327-5685)

British Cataloguing in Publication Data
A Cataloguing in Publication record for this book is available from the British Library.

Advances in Finance, Accounting, and Economics (AFAE) Book Series

ISSN:2327-5677
EISSN:2327-5685

MISSION

In our changing economic and business environment, it is important to consider the financial changes occurring internationally as well as within individual organizations and business environments. Understanding these changes as well as the factors that influence them is crucial in preparing for our financial future and ensuring economic sustainability and growth.

The **Advances in Finance, Accounting, and Economics (AFAE)** book series aims to publish comprehensive and informative titles in all areas of economics and economic theory, finance, and accounting to assist in advancing the available knowledge and providing for further research development in these dynamic fields.

COVERAGE

- E-finance
- Economics of Risks, Uncertainty, Ambiguity, and Insurance
- Field Research
- Managerial Accounting
- E-Accounting
- Economic Downturn
- Health Economics
- Accounting information systems
- Applied Accounting
- Banking

IGI Global is currently accepting manuscripts for publication within this series. To submit a proposal for a volume in this series, please contact our Acquisition Editors at Acquisitions@igi-global.com or visit: http://www.igi-global.com/publish/.

The Advances in Finance, Accounting, and Economics (AFAE) Book Series (ISSN 2327-5677) is published by IGI Global, 701 E. Chocolate Avenue, Hershey, PA 17033-1240, USA, www.igi-global.com. This series is composed of titles available for purchase individually; each title is edited to be contextually exclusive from any other title within the series. For pricing and ordering information please visit http://www.igi-global.com/book-series/advances-finance-accounting-economics/73685. Postmaster: Send all address changes to above address.

Titles in this Series

For a list of additional titles in this series, please visit:
www.igi-global.com/book-series/advances-finance-accounting-economics/73685

Modern Regulations and Practices for Social and Environmental Accounting
Teresa Eugénio (Centre of Applied Research in Management and Economics (CARME), School of Technology and Management, Polytechnic Institute of Leiria, Portugal) Graça Azevedo (University of Aveiro, Portugal) and Ana Fialho (CEFAGE, University of Évora, Portugal)
Business Science Reference • © 2022 • 345pp • H/C (ISBN: 9781799894100) • US $215.00

Impact of Open Innovation on the World Economy
Orlando Lima Rua (Polytechnic of Porto, Portugal)
Business Science Reference • © 2022 • 306pp • H/C (ISBN: 9781799886655) • US $225.00

Handbook of Research on Challenges in Public Economics in the Era of Globalization
Şahin Akkaya (Istanbul University, Turkey) and Başak Ergüder (Istanbul University, Turkey)
Business Science Reference • © 2022 • 480pp • H/C (ISBN: 9781799890836) • US $295.00

Handbook of Research on Green, Circular, and Digital Economies as Tools for Recovery and Sustainability
Patricia Ordóñez de Pablos (The University of Oviedo, Spain) Xi Zhang (Tianjin University, China) and Mohammad Nabil Almunawar (Universiti Brunei Darussalam, Brunei)
Business Science Reference • © 2022 • 418pp • H/C (ISBN: 9781799896647) • US $295.00

Handbook of Research on the Significance of Forensic Accounting Techniques in Corporate Governance
Suleman Sherali Kamwani (A'Sharqiyah University, Oman) Elisabete S. Vieira (University of Aveiro, Portugal) Mara Madaleno (University of Aveiro, Portugal) and Graça Azevedo (University of Aveiro, Portugal)
Business Science Reference • © 2022 • 417pp • H/C (ISBN: 9781799887546) • US $265.00

Handbook of Research on Energy and Environmental Finance 4.0
Abdul Rafay (University of Management and Technology, Pakistan)
Business Science Reference • © 2022 • 545pp • H/C (ISBN: 9781799882107) • US $295.00

IGI Global
PUBLISHER of TIMELY KNOWLEDGE

701 East Chocolate Avenue, Hershey, PA 17033, USA
Tel: 717-533-8845 x100 • Fax: 717-533-8661
E-Mail: cust@igi-global.com • www.igi-global.com

Table of Contents

Foreword xii

Preface xiv

Acknowledgment xx

Introduction xxi

Chapter 1
The Degito-Financial Movement's Impact of Digital Transformation on Financial Services 1
Nadia Mansour, University of Sousse, Tunisia & University of Salamanca, Spain
Salha Ben Salem, University of Monastir, Tunisia

Chapter 2
Blockchain and Cryptocurrency Development Without Regulation 13
Bechir Chenguel, University of Kairouan, Tunisia

Chapter 3
Digital Transformation: Opportunities and Challenges 33
Ahmed Chemseddine Bouarar, University of Medea, Algeria
Smail Mouloudj, University of Medea, Algeria
Kamel Mouloudj, University of Medea, Algeria

Chapter 4
COVID-19: The Pandemic's Outcome on Cryptocurrency-Bitcoin Futures....... 53
Sumi K. V., IMK, India

Chapter 5
Examining the Impact of COVID-19 on Cryptocurrency Enforcement in the United States 65
Leo S. F. Lin, The University of Southern Mississippi, USA

Chapter 6
Principal Components Analysis: Impact on Alternative Crypto-Currencies 82
Nabiha Haouas, University of Sousse, Tunisia
Asma Sghaier, University of Sousse, Tunisia

Chapter 7
Cyber Regulations and Access to Justice During COVID-19 107
Eltjon Mirashi, University of Salamanca, Spain

Chapter 8
Coalescing Skills of Gig Players and Fervor of Entrepreneurial Leaders to Provide Resilience Strategies During Global Economic Crises 118
Manpreet Arora, Central University of Himachal Pradesh, India
Roshan Lal Sharma, Central University of Himachal Pradesh, India

Chapter 9
The Impact of COVID-19 on Volatility Spillover Between Bitcoin and Turkish Financial Markets 141
Yakup Ari, Alanya Alaaddin Keykubat University, Turkey
Esin Yelgen, Alanya Alaaddin Keykubat University, Turkey
Harun Uçak, Alanya Alaaddin Keykubat University, Turkey

Chapter 10
The Importance of Partnership for the Public and Private Sectors in the Renewable Energy Technology Industry in Algeria 166
Hadda Rebbouh, Independent Researcher, Algeria
Mekhelfi Amina, Technologic Institut, Algeria

Glossary 185

Compilation of References 192

Related References 215

About the Contributors 246

Index 249

Detailed Table of Contents

Foreword xii

Preface xiv

Acknowledgment xx

Introduction xxi

Chapter 1
The Degito-Financial Movement's Impact of Digital Transformation on Financial Services 1
Nadia Mansour, University of Sousse, Tunisia & University of Salamanca, Spain
Salha Ben Salem, University of Monastir, Tunisia

The digital revolution and big data are improving the real-time analysis capacity of organizations, allowing them to optimize their tools and processes and to confront the available data with greater efficiency. In this context, where the time spent on data collection is decreasing, many functions in the company see their missions evolve towards more analysis and communication to help decision making. The COVID-19 pandemic has given a tremendous boost to the development of digitalization in the world. How then will the digitalization of financial services in Africa consolidate after this pandemic and what are its challenges?

Chapter 2
Blockchain and Cryptocurrency Development Without Regulation 13
Bechir Chenguel, University of Kairouan, Tunisia

Blockchain is a technology based on a chain of interconnected blocks containing transaction history and user data. Blockchain permitted the creation of cryptocurrency. Among its advantages are decentralization, transparency, and integrity. This technology has increased with COVID-19 with the accentuation of the wave of digitalization. Classic finance systems felt overwhelmed by events and tried to catch up with this new wave by creating their cryptocurrency and embarking on this new world of digital finance where regulation and control are nonexistent. Many central banks see the introduction of central bank digital currencies. But the expansion of these cryptocurrencies could present risks in terms of transmission of monetary policy, monetary creation, and financial stability. In this work, the authors present the evolution of cryptocurrency and the reaction of classic finance systems to this wave of digitalization of transactions and especially to an absence of regulation.

Chapter 3
Digital Transformation: Opportunities and Challenges..33
Ahmed Chemseddine Bouarar, University of Medea, Algeria
Smail Mouloudj, University of Medea, Algeria
Kamel Mouloudj, University of Medea, Algeria

Digital literature has provided significant insights into how digital transformation contributes to improving business performance. This research departs from these studies by focusing on driving factors of digital transformation and digital transformation strategies. Moreover, the authors determine the impact of digital transformation on firm performance and identify the challenges of adopting digital transformation. The results show that successful digital transformation can speed up the pace of innovation, increase productivity, improve customer experiences and satisfaction, reduce costs, and improve business performance. The results also revealed that major barriers to digital transformation include lack of knowledge, lack of digital expertise, poor digital leadership, resistance to change, inflexible culture, unclear vision and objective, lack of collaboration and alignment. These results will help to illuminate the complex issue of how to set an effective digital transformation.

Chapter 4
COVID-19: The Pandemic's Outcome on Cryptocurrency-Bitcoin Futures.......53
Sumi K. V., IMK, India

The SARS-CoV-19 coronavirus pandemic has had a huge economic impact around the world. As a result, the behaviour of all financial instruments, including cryptocurrencies, was significantly affected. Following the COVID-19 market crash, cryptocurrency derivative markets have seen a massive increase in popularity as speculators try to profit from the price and trading volume instability. The fluctuations in the virtual currency market during this time span seem to be a reflection of shifts in other capital and commodity markets. During this challenging era, the demand has remained relatively stable. It's yet another example of how cryptocurrencies can be viewed as a fully developed financial tool. Despite mediocre trade volume, the number of markets available increased significantly in the run-up to this case.

Chapter 5
Examining the Impact of COVID-19 on Cryptocurrency Enforcement in the United States 65
Leo S. F. Lin, The University of Southern Mississippi, USA

This chapter examines how COVID-19 has impacted cryptocurrency enforcement at the state level. This author employs a qualitative single case study method and investigates the cryptocurrency enforcement actions of the United States Securities and Exchange Commission (SEC) in 2020. The data were collected from SEC cryptocurrency press releases and public statements. The US Securities and Exchange Commission (SEC) has brought 28 enforcement actions against companies and individuals in the crypto industry in 2020 regarding the three types of cryptocurrency enforcement actions and trading suspensions (trading suspension, litigation, and administrative proceeding). Among them, litigation is the most common type of cryptocurrency enforcement action taken by the SEC. This author concludes that the law enforcement agencies in the United States faced several challenges before and during the pandemic. Finally, the author suggests some measures that law enforcement agencies can take to address the above challenges.

Chapter 6
Principal Components Analysis: Impact on Alternative Crypto-Currencies.......82
Nabiha Haouas, University of Sousse, Tunisia
Asma Sghaier, University of Sousse, Tunisia

Today, cryptocurrencies are rapidly gaining popularity and sweeping all the economies of the world, but the bulk of the literature is devoted to a few cryptocurrencies only. The purpose of this chapter is to analyze of the cryptocurrency market. More than 2000 cryptocurrencies are examined, and a set of 70 cryptocurrencies were recovered for a sample spanning 2015-2018. The degree of relationship between the variables was then investigated. The PCA was performed. This analysis allows the initial variables to be replaced by five factors that retain almost all of the information (91.028% of the total information) and have the advantage of being uncorrelated. Therefore, the authors have concluded that the first factor corresponds to the cci30 index used by the crypto funds while the rest of the factors can be distinguished according to some variants.

Chapter 7
Cyber Regulations and Access to Justice During COVID-19 107
Eltjon Mirashi, University of Salamanca, Spain

This chapter aims to study the initiatives to regulate cybersecurity with non-binding norms and the impact of COVID-19 on access to justice. It mentions the principal initiatives to create resilience to cybersecurity and build digital trust. The pandemic situation related to COVID-19 has put in real difficulty the access to justice as a fundamental right. In this chapter, the intention is to expose these initiatives and create an awareness to the related topics, as well to propose possible solutions.

Chapter 8
Coalescing Skills of Gig Players and Fervor of Entrepreneurial Leaders to Provide Resilience Strategies During Global Economic Crises 118
Manpreet Arora, Central University of Himachal Pradesh, India
Roshan Lal Sharma, Central University of Himachal Pradesh, India

The COVID-19 pandemic has caused diverse sorts of disruption across the globe. The pandemic has drastically impacted the economies of almost every country of the world. The international economic scenario is full of despair as the entrepreneurs and business leaders find it hard to come to terms with the extent of damage caused by the pandemic. In view of largely prevalent gloom and despair, it is imperative that certain resilience strategies are worked out so that global economic crisis can be stemmed from further escalation. The gig economy has been viewed as a powerful resilience mechanism to tide over the economic crisis caused the world over by COVID-19. Entrepreneurial leadership can also make significant difference in providing a paddle-push to the pandemic-struck world by reactivating the engines of economic growth. The nature of this chapter is qualitative, and it seeks to theoretically work out certain strategies that can help various economies of the world to stand up and be resilient in the face of complex challenges that the pandemic has thrown before us.

Chapter 9
The Impact of COVID-19 on Volatility Spillover Between Bitcoin and Turkish Financial Markets 141
Yakup Ari, Alanya Alaaddin Keykubat University, Turkey
Esin Yelgen, Alanya Alaaddin Keykubat University, Turkey
Harun Uçak, Alanya Alaaddin Keykubat University, Turkey

The aim of this study is to examine the volatility spillover between bitcoin and Turkish financial markets for the pre-COVID-19 and COVID-19 periods. Using GARCH-based volatility spillover indices, the authors find that BTC-USD was a volatility transmitter in the pre-COVID-19 period but has become the main volatility receiver in the COVID-19 period, and its net volatility transmission fell from 0.7% to -10.84%. Moreover, they concluded that the total spillover index increased from 12.49% to 15.25% indicates a low connectedness between the markets in both periods and the error variance in markets is on average 15.25% originated from other markets in the COVID-19 period.

Chapter 10
The Importance of Partnership for the Public and Private Sectors in the Renewable Energy Technology Industry in Algeria 166
Hadda Rebbouh, Independent Researcher, Algeria
Mekhelfi Amina, Technologic Institut, Algeria

The aim of this study is to show the importance of partnership in developing renewable energy technology in Algeria by focusing on Algeria's renewable resources and addressing the incentive mechanisms adopted by Algeria in the field of encouraging partnership with renewable energy and diagnosing the most important projects resulting from the partnership between the public and private sectors (domestic and foreign). The study concluded that there is a cooperation as many institutions and renewable energy production stations appeared in the Algerian market resulting from the partnership, but this cooperation is insufficient and is limited by many obstacles, the most important of which are monopoly and lack of experience in the field.

Glossary 185

Compilation of References 192

Related References 215

About the Contributors 246

Index 249

Foreword

The digital transformation that began decades ago was accelerated by the outbreak of the COVID-19 health crisis. To stay in business, many companies were forced to adopt new business models based on digital and data-driven chain value. To preserve their jobs, employees around the world had turned to telework. Moreover, millions of students had experienced distance learning for the first time during the COVID-19 pandemic.

Without a doubt, the pandemic had unveiled the potential impact of digitalization in future societies and economies and has been a catalyst for cultural and structural change. In 2022, global internet traffic had exceeded all the internet traffic up to 2016. However, the pandemic had also highlighted the disparities between economies in access to technology and the opportunities offered by digital transformation.

Digital transformation is a multi-dimensional phenomenon whose effects cannot be limited to technical aspects. Socio-economic, regulatory, cultural, and institutional considerations make the issue of digital transformation increasingly complex and require the mobilization of multidisciplinary approaches and methods.

This book entitled *COVID-19's Impact on the Cryptocurrency Market and the Digital Economy* fits perfectly into this holistic, transversal, and multidisciplinary approach to the digitalization of organizations, markets, economies, and societies.

Indeed, one of the strengths of the book is to give an overview of the challenges and opportunities of big data, digitalization, blockchain technology, and crypto-assets. A key challenge is how to govern the digital era for humanity's well-being. At the microeconomic level, data is a strategic asset that allows optimizing the decision-making process and creating added value. On the macroeconomic level, data affect the achievement of public policies and the implementation of sustainable development goals.

Digitalization is also a source of risks. Responses are needed to mitigate emergent risks mainly cyber risks but, also environmental, natural risks, and pandemic risks. All the relevant stakeholders, public and private actors, or non-government organizations are implicated in the digitalization process. "COVID-19's Impact on the Cryptocurrency Market and the Digital Economy" is a book accessible to all concerned parties.

Readers, regardless of their profile, whether they are beginners or experts, will have the curiosity and pleasure of discovering the many facets of digitalization and the various issues related to processing automation, artificial intelligence, or blockchain technology.

The book calls for innovative approaches to analyzing digitalization and its multiple interlinked dimensions. By balancing digitalization advantages to its inherent risks, the path of inclusive and sustainable development may be possible.

I commend the book to a wide global audience interested in a data-driven digital economy.

Wissem Ajili Ben Youssef
Eslsca Paris Business School, France

Preface

The digital revolution is impacting not only organizations but all areas of society. No sector of activity has been spared, and the survival of many organizations depends on their ability to transform and reinvent themselves in a new digital paradigm that is still very uncertain and relatively anxiety-provoking. Before tackling technological issues, it is important to ask the right questions and to acquire a minimum of digital culture that will enable the implementation of a transformation strategy and the use of appropriate technological tools.

COVID-19's Impact on the Cryptocurrency Market and the Digital Economy proposes a dive into the digital ecosystem through a historical, sociological, political, and economic approach that supplies readers with a foundation they can build their future digital skills on. Covering topics such as cryptocurrency and economic resiliency, it is ideal for industry professionals, researchers, practitioners, scholars, academicians, and students.

The book contains the following chapters:

CHAPTER 1: THE DEGITO-FINANCIAL MOVEMENT IMPACT OF DIGITAL TRANSFORMATION ON FINANCIAL SERVICES

Nadia Mansour, Salha Ben Salem

The digital revolution and big data are improving the real-time analysis capacity of organizations, allowing them to optimize their tools and processes, and to confront the available data with greater efficiency. In this context where the time spent on data collection is decreasing, many functions in the company see their missions evolve towards more analysis and communication to help decision making. The COVID-19 pandemic has given a tremendous boost to the development of digitalization in the world. How then will the digitalization of financial services in Africa consolidate after this pandemic and what are its challenges?

CHAPTER 2: BLOCKCHAIN AND CRYPTOCURRENCY DEVELOPMENT WITHOUT REGULATION

Bechir Chenguel

Blockchain is a technology based on a chain of interconnected blocks containing transaction history and user data. Blockchain permitted the creation of cryptocurrency. Among its advantages: decentralization, transparency, and integrity. This technology has increased with the covid19 with the accentuation of the wave of digitalization. Classic finance systems felt overwhelmed by events and tried to catch up with this new wave, by creating their cryptocurrency, and embarking on this new world of digital finance where regulation and control are nonexistent. Many central banks see the introduction of central bank digital currencies. But the expansion of these cryptocurrencies could present risks in terms of transmission of monetary policy, monetary creation, and financial stability. In this work, we will present the evolution of cryptocurrency, and the reaction classic finance systems to this wave of digitalization of transactions, and especially to an absence of regulation.

CHAPTER 3: DIGITAL TRANSFORMATION – OPPORTUNITIES AND CHALLENGES

Ahmed Chemseddine Bouarar, Smail Mouloudj, Kamel Mouloudj

Digital literature has provided significant insights into how digital transformation contributes to improving business performance. Our research departs from these studies by focusing on driving factors of digital transformation and digital transformation strategies. Moreover, we determine the impact of digital transformation on firm performance and identify the challenges of adopting digital transformation. The results show that successful digital transformation can speed up the pace of innovation, increase productivity, improve customer experiences and satisfaction, reduce costs, and improve business performance. The results also revealed that Major barriers to digital transformation include lack of knowledge, lack of digital expertise, poor digital leadership, resistance to change, inflexible culture, unclear vision and objective, lack of collaboration and alignment. We think that these results will help to illuminate the complex issue of how to set an effective digital transformation.

CHAPTER 4: COVID-19 THE PANDEMIC'S OUTCOME ON CRYPTOCURRENCY – BITCOIN FUTURES

Sumi K. V.

The SARS-CoV-19 coronavirus pandemic has had a huge economic impact around the world. As a result, the behaviour of all financial instruments, including cryptocurrencies, was significantly affected. Following the Covid-19 market crash, cryptocurrency derivative markets have seen a massive increase in popularity as speculators try to profit from the price and trading volume instability. The fluctuations in the virtual currency market during this time span seem to be a reflection of shifts in other capital and commodity markets. During this challenging era, the demand has remained relatively stable. It's yet another example of how cryptocurrencies can be viewed as a fully developed financial tool. Despite mediocre trade volume, the number of markets available increased significantly in the run-up to this case.

CHAPTER 5: EXAMINING THE IMPACT OF COVID-19 ON CRYPTOCURRENCY ENFORCEMENT IN THE UNITED STATES

Leo S. F. Lin

This chapter examines how COVID-19 has impacted cryptocurrency enforcement at the state level. This author employs a qualitative single case study method and investigates the cryptocurrency enforcement actions of the United States Securities and Exchange Commission (SEC) in 2020. The data were collected from SEC cryptocurrency press releases and public statements. The US Securities and Exchange Commission (SEC) has brought 28 enforcement actions against companies and individuals in the crypto industry in 2020. Regarding the three types of cryptocurrency enforcement actions and trading suspensions (trading suspension, litigation, and administrative proceeding). Among them, litigation is the most common type of cryptocurrency enforcement action taken by the SEC. This author concludes that the law enforcement agencies in the United States faced several challenges before and during the pandemic. Finally, the author suggests some measures that law enforcement agencies can take to address the above challenges.

CHAPTER 6: PRINCIPAL COMPONENTS ANALYSIS IMPACT ON ALTERNATIVE CRYPTO-CURRENCIES

Nabiha Haouas, Asma Sghaier

Today, crypto-currencies are rapidly gaining popularity and sweeping all the economies of the world, but the bulk of the literature devoted to a few crypto-currencies only. The purpose of this paper is to analyze of the cryptocurrency market. More than 2000 cryptocurrencies are examined and a set of 70 crypto-currencies were recovered for a sample spanning 2015-2018. The degree of relationship between the variables is then investigated. The PCA was performed. This analysis allows the initial variables to be replaced by five factors that retain almost all of the information (91.028% of the total information) and have the advantage of being uncorrelated. Therefore we have concluded that the first factor corresponds to the cci30 index used by the Crypto funds. While the rest of the factors can be distinguished according to some variants.

CHAPTER 7: CYBER REGULATIONS AND ACCESS TO JUSTICE DURING COVID-19

Eltjon Mirashi

This article aims to study the initiatives to regulate cybersecurity with non-binding norms and the impact of Covid-19 on access to justice. It mentions the principal initiatives to create resilience to cybersecurity and build digital trust. The pandemic situation related to Covid-19 has put in real difficulty the access to justice as a fundamental right. In this article the intention to expose these initiatives and create an awareness to the related topics, as well to propose possible solutions.

CHAPTER 8: COALESCING SKILLS OF GIG PLAYERS AND FERVOR OF ENTREPRENEURIAL LEADERS TO PROVIDE RESILIENCE STRATEGIES DURING GLOBAL ECONOMIC CRISIS

Manpreet Arora, Roshan Sharma

COVID-19 pandemic has caused diverse sorts of disruption across the globe. The pandemic has drastically impacted the economies of almost every country of the world. The international economic scenario is full of despair as the entrepreneurs and business leaders find it hard to come to terms with the extent of damage caused by the pandemic. In view of largely prevalent gloom and despair, it is imperative that certain resilience strategies are worked out so that global economic crisis can be stemmed from further escalation. Gig economy has been viewed as a powerful resilience mechanism to tide over the economic crisis caused the world over by COVID-19. Entrepreneurial leadership can also make significant difference in providing a paddle-push to the pandemic-struck world by reactivating the engines of economic growth. The nature of this chapter is qualitative and it seeks to theoretically work out certain strategies that can help various economies of the world to stand up and be resilient in the face of complex challenges that the pandemic has thrown before us.

CHAPTER 9: THE IMPACT OF COVID-19 ON VOLATILITY SPILLOVER BETWEEN BITCOIN AND TURKISH FINANCIAL MARKETS

Yakup Ari, Esin Yelgen, Harun Uçak

The aim of this study is to examine the volatility spillover between Bitcoin and Turkish financial markets for the pre-Covid-19 and Covid-19 periods. Using GARCH-based volatility spillover indices, we find that BTC-USD was a volatility transmitter in the pre-Covid-19 period but has become the main volatility receiver in the Covid-19 period, and its net volatility transmission fell from 0.7% to -10.84%. Moreover, we concluded that the total spillover index increased from 12.49% to 15.25% indicates a low connectedness between the markets in both periods and the error variance in markets is on average 15.25% originated from other markets in the Covid-19 period.

CHAPTER 10: THE IMPORTANCE OF PARTNERSHIP FOR THE PUBLIC AND PRIVATE SECTOR IN THE RENEWABLE ENERGY TECHNOLOGY INDUSTRY IN ALGERIA

Hadda Rebbouh, Mekhelfi Amina

The aim of this study is to show the importance of partnership in developing renewable energy technology in Algeria by focusing on Algeria's renewable resources and addressing the incentive mechanisms adopted by Algeria in the field of encouraging partnership with renewable energy and diagnosing the most important projects resulting from the partnership between the public and private sectors (domestic and foreign).The study concluded that there is a cooperation as many institutions and renewable energy production stations appeared in the Algerian market resulting from the partnership, but this cooperation is insufficient and is limited by many obstacles, the most important of which are monopoly and lack of experience in the field.

So, despite all the negative aspects of the spread of the coronavirus across all industries, it is safe to say that many markets will be able to survive and even benefit from this difficult period. There is no doubt that a global recession looms in these uncertain times.

In the long run, the cryptocurrency market may not be affected by these upheavals, but it will not be completely spared, especially shortly.

Nevertheless, the confinement imposed in many countries around the world has paradoxically generated a bullish effect on the crypto-currency market unlike the rest of the stock market, according to financial experts.

While many experts describe the cryptocurrency market as "more than safe", they also pointed out that it can be identified as a good option for long-term investments, as its value continues to grow.

Nadia Mansour
University of Sousse, Tunisia & University of Salamanca, Spain

Salha Ben Salem
University of Monastir, Tunisia

Acknowledgment

We would like to thank all the contributors to this book on a topical subject, the reviewers, and the readers for the attention given to this work.

Introduction

With the latest pandemic "Covid-19", schools, tourism, transportation, public events, sports, elections ... almost everything is disrupted, which has inevitably affected the social and economic life of everyone. Thousands of cases of contagion and deaths have been registered all over the world, and the stock markets are suffering strong shocks, recording very low levels, which had not been known for years.

Despite all the negative aspects of the spread of the coronavirus across all industries, it is safe to say that many markets will be able to survive and even benefit from this difficult period. And in this context, we can mention cryptocurrency.

In the long run, the cryptocurrency market might not be affected by these upheavals, though it might not be completely spared, especially soon.

Nevertheless, the confinement imposed in many countries around the world is having a generated a bullish effect on the cryptocurrency market unlike the rest of the stock market, according to financial experts.

While many experts describe the cryptocurrency market as "more than safe", they also pointed out that it can be identified as a good option for long-term investments, as its value continues to grow.

So, it will be worth checking if these analyses come to fruition in the coming months and what impact the Covid-19 crisis will have on the cryptocurrency market.

Chapter 1
The Degito-Financial Movement's Impact of Digital Transformation on Financial Services

Nadia Mansour
https://orcid.org/0000-0001-7690-7096
University of Sousse, Tunisia & University of Salamanca, Spain

Salha Ben Salem
https://orcid.org/0000-0002-4946-7782
University of Monastir, Tunisia

ABSTRACT

The digital revolution and big data are improving the real-time analysis capacity of organizations, allowing them to optimize their tools and processes and to confront the available data with greater efficiency. In this context, where the time spent on data collection is decreasing, many functions in the company see their missions evolve towards more analysis and communication to help decision making. The COVID-19 pandemic has given a tremendous boost to the development of digitalization in the world. How then will the digitalization of financial services in Africa consolidate after this pandemic and what are its challenges?

INTRODUCTION

For more than three decades, we have witnessed a strong incentive for the most

DOI: 10.4018/978-1-7998-9117-8.ch001

advanced economies to create new businesses and the growing emergence of start-ups in the digital economy or the creative industries. Thus, the establishment of an ecosystem favorable to their expansion has become imperative for economic competitiveness. We have gone from technological and innovative startups to startups more oriented towards 3D, augmented reality, the Internet of Things, etc.

The digital transformation is affecting the whole economy, and new industrial policies are being implemented in several countries. Growth, employment, and attractiveness depend on it. A new economic vision is needed.

Entire sectors of the economy are undergoing a profound transformation, with some sectors are disappearing and others will follow, while new ones are emerging. The majority of professions are changing, and more than 60% of tomorrow's jobs are not yet defined today.

At the conference organized by the World Economic Forum in (2016), Klaus Schwab defined the fourth industrial revolution.

This revolution is characterized by technologies that merge the physical-digital and biological spheres. In other words, this revolution is based on new technological advances (sensors, robotics, artificial intelligence...) that are coming together to define the next wave of progress and that will require progress and will force companies to re-examine how they operate.

This new wave of technical progress allows computers and robots to match or even exceed the cognitive abilities of humans. All sectors will benefit directly or indirectly directly or indirectly from this technological revolution in the medium and long term.

China, the first country affected by Covid 19, is a living laboratory of the measures against the coronavirus. Extraordinary containment measures, forced use of masks, spraying of disinfectants in the streets, closing of factories... The country also mobilized all the technological means to contain the pandemic, like Alibaba and Tencent, which have developed a QR code system with a three-level color code to track the health status of its citizens.

The Chinese government has called for the withdrawal of cash in circulation for 14 days and disinfected or even destruction of some of it. To maximize the impact of the measures, the government has been able to rely on the enthusiasm of the Chinese people for mobile payments.

Small vendors, street stalls, large international brands in China, all businesses are using mobile payment and since the emergence of this virus online sales and payments have increased dramatically in China, and Alibaba has reportedly added 10 new servers to meet the demand.

Alipay (Alibaba) and WeChat (Tencent) provide merchants and citizens with electronic payment solutions for merchants and citizens that are adapted to the current situation to limit the risk of exposure to the virus. With the use of these two applications, the Chinese can pay in a fully automatic way via a QR code that is displayed on the checkout system, thus limiting the physical exchanges between the buyer and the seller.

Hence, this chapter will be divided into two parts. We will start with a literature review to define the different concepts related to the subject. The second part will be devoted to digitalization in Tunisia.

POST-FINANCIAL CRISIS PERIOD: NEW ERA FOR FINANCIAL DIGITAL TRANSFORMATION

The boom of the financial crisis in 2008 in the financial and real estate market showed that people's lives were gradually being networked and digitized due to the development of digital transformation, Shao et al. (2020). A review of the literature reveals the blurred nature of the contours of the digital economy. Digital transformation, sometimes called digital transformation, refers to the process that consists of an organization fully integrating digital technologies into all of its activities.

Digital transformation or digitalization implies the transition from a state of face-to-face relationships to virtual or more precisely digital relationships. A transition during which the company evolves its business processes, but also its global strategy both internally and externally, its organization, as well as its products and interactions with its customers. This process takes place both upstream (suppliers, service providers, partners, production chain, etc.) and downstream (prospects, customers, competitors, etc.), which implies a change in the way the company operates.

All the players are concerned, these real revolutions profoundly change the way we understand the banking business (Nicolas DENIS, 2019). Consumers have been offered a new choice and have profoundly and have profoundly changed their approach and expectations. The product alone is no longer enough, and this will pave the way for the emergence of a new form of "intelligent service" (Allmendinger and Lombreglia. 2005; Wuenderlich et al., 2015). In sum, digital, to define it simply, has led banks to enrich their value propositions. To this end, banks must transform themselves to satisfy customer desires (Sajić et al. 2018).

According to (Ettien, Peron, 2018) "Transformation involves a pathway that serves to identify, mobilize, and organize resources to start from one point and go to another"; it is also seen as "the adoption of readily available technological skills that transforms the organization's responsiveness to changes in market" (Bos, 2018).

From these definition we can agree that "Digital transformation can be defined as a revolution of practices, automation, and simplification of processes: towards acceleration and optimization of the flow of internal exchanges and those between the bank and its customer or partners. Digitization is a vector of value creation and commercial opportunities.

The risks to the traditional banking model are so high that some economists are talking about the disappearance of banks. Economists do not hesitate to speak of the disappearance of banks.

With the introduction of new technologies, the rules of competition are being transformed in the banking industry. Certainly, the effects of digital technology contribute, on the one hand, to the intensification of competition in the banking market, and on the other hand, they offer new opportunities to diversify the range of services available to customers (Berdi & Sebbar, 2018; Daley, 2003). Many banks that could be described as historical, very solidly anchored in their markets, have been attacked by the emergence of new non-banking players who seek to develop internet-banking services, and who by placing digital technology at the heart of their business model propose new offers and new services.

Fintech, participatory finance, the era of Big Data, the emergence of block chain and many others. Another area invested by the new technology is that of Crowdfunding, and it is here that the new technology players have and it is here too that innovation is highlighted.

Big Data is important for financial institutions, its integration into the information system of the system of the banking system has been achieved thanks to digital technology and the exponential development of real-time processing and storage capacities, to be valued. The data must be carried out in such a way as to allow a better collection of intelligent data on the clientele following the example of "positive files " that allow banks to develop their offers and to propose new develop their offers and propose new services and non-banking activities to the behavior of their customers and their aspirations.

In addition, Big Data technology allows targeting the most appropriate channel to anticipate customer's future actions and serve them to facilitate access to the real-time goods and services in real-time, while enriching the proximity and permanence of the link between the bank and its customers (Alain B., 2018).

This technological manna is nothing without competence and human intelligence, and this will lead to the employment of competent profiles that have not been used until now (mathematicians, statisticians, psychologists and statisticians, psychologists and similar). Big Data technology has demonstrated all its capabilities and is the subject of innovative approaches from banks that are looking for and developing concrete applications to both develop their activities and their business of control and risk.

DIGITAL CURRENCY: IMPORTANCE AND RESEARCH ISSUES

With the development of information over the past few years, many electronic money has developed very rapidly. Digital currencies such as Alipay, Bitcoin, and Libra Coins have emerged and are highly exploited by large investors, Tan and Xue (2020). The digital currency market, led by Bitcoin, has become active yet. Among the top 50 important digital assets by market prices, 14 currencies have overstated Bitcoin. Among them, the largest raises reached 440%, which is 3.4 times the rise of Bitcoin, Shoa and al (2020). This proves the gain that investors can produced with these currency and also the importance of volatilities that can be supported.

The report of the Cap Gemini World Payment in 2019 proves that world non-cash transactions are widely increased. during 2013and 2017, the non-cash transactions in developing economies grew by 22.6% on average, while in Europe, America and other Developed markets grow by 7%. The report shows that world noncash transactions scope 1.046 billion dollars in 2020, with an annual growth rate of 14%, see below figure. The global development of digital currency is speeded by the confinement measures taken by governments following the Coronavirus pandemic.

Furthermore, the speed of development of digital currency and its possible crucial impact have attracted the preoccupation of several monetary authorities around the world. Federal Reserve Chair, Jerome Powell, continuing its study into whether to implement its own digital currency is important. in a short document that he had published recently, he declared that" I think it's important that we get to a place where we can make an informed decision about this and do so expeditiously," and he continued "I don't think we're behind. I think it's more important to do this right than to do it fast.", Jeff Cox (2021).

Despite the strong preoccupation of central banks on its technological transformation at the currency level, several problems remain unanswered.

The first major problem is the difference in national conditions, the level of development, and the knowledge of the people. A Libra coin will replace the functioning of a large amount of currency could have a significant impact on the value of national currency issued by the monetary authority of the economy in question. This will surely affect the level of surety and the regulations of legal tender.

Second, the problem may lie in surveillance. The sharp increase in currency trend, as shown in figure 1, may weaken the government's ability to control and oversee. This can impacts the performance of the monetary policy since it can issue currencies excessively.

In Sum, with the crussy development of private digital currency, several short-term issues can occur and they can be difficult to be solved. The main elements proposed by Tan and Xue (2021) to improve the performance of central bank digital currency is strength the financial technical and reliable hardware system and the national credits

Figure 1.

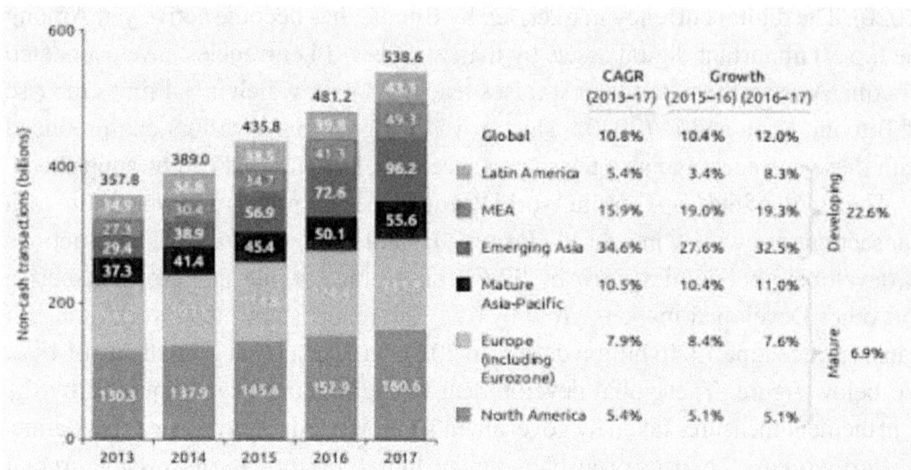

GLOBAL DIGITAL CURRENCY REGULATION IN THE PERIOD OF CORONAVIRUS PANDEMIC

Since the emergence of the coronavirus and with containment procedures in all countries of the world, digital currencies and associated services and products have greatly increased. In addition, the interconnection of these products with the regulated banking sector has also increased. This speed decreases the power of policymakers to monitor and evaluate the risks associated with these products. With a market capitalization close to 2.5 trillion dollars, which is an alarming value, the sharp increase in these products could have a mass in an environment of uncertainty. The world shows that the appearance of a new variant of the coronavirus is associated with a massive sale of digital currencies. Adrian and al (2021) note that primary reactions to the Omicron variant are associated with a significant crypto selloff.

The bellow graph shows that during the Coronavirus period investors on digital assets like bitcoin and crypto money, have had crazy gains but also high price volatility. Bitcoin's volatility, for example, increased tenfold between April and October 2021.

The notion of credibility is very important in the market for these products. Credibility is often backed by a certain basket of currencies like the classic fiduciary currency which is certainly seen as credible as Bitcoin. However, this does not prevent that it will have great problems at the level of the government if a private

Figure 2.

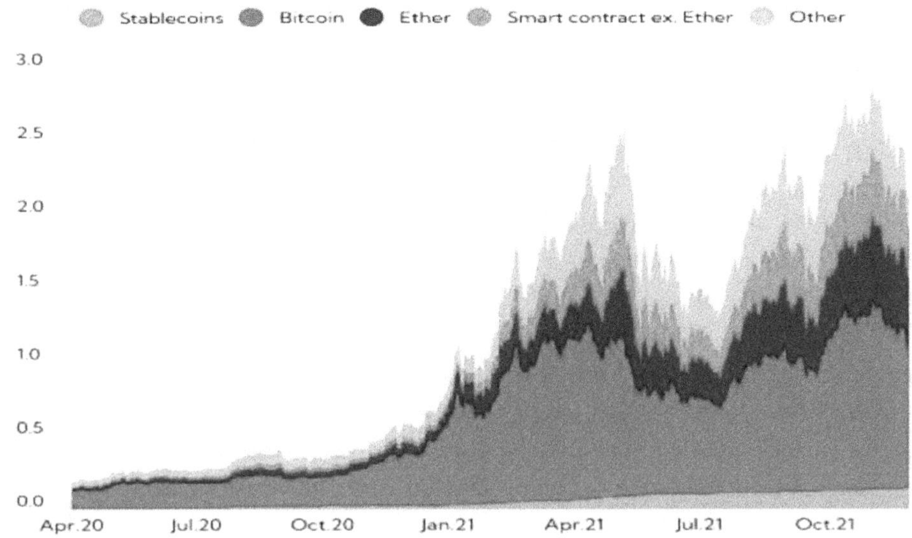

unit, which has its own currency, puts its power on the market. Caractens (2021) shows that private currency, even if it is stable, cannot become the basis for a healthy monetary system. Thus, to remain credible, it is necessary to rely on strict and supervised regulations. Here the confidence of the financial institution and the monetary authority is fundamental and very important.

To define the regulations for investors and companies it is not enough to assess the degree of risk-taking but it takes a complete ecosystem including identification and control. The regulation should be focused on operational and financial integrity risks from digital currencies investor security, and inadequate reserves, and inaccurate deviation for some stable coins. In developing markets and emerging economies, "the advent of crypto can accelerate what we have called a crypto nation". In these economies, digital assets replace local currency and circumvent exchange limitss and capital account management measures.

EVIDENCE OF THE CENTRAL BANK DIGITAL CURRENCY IN AFRICA AND TUNISIA

Digitalization is remodeling economic activity, reducing the role of cash, and enhancing new digital kinds of money. Many Central banks have been considering whether and how to exploit. One opportunity is central bank digital currency

(CBDC)—a broadly available digital shape of fiat cash that might be legal tender. Despite various central banks having analyzed the feature of CBDC, many have now no longer actively explored it and stayed skeptical. Many narratives suggested that the most effective cryptocurrencies could be used for bills in the future. While this will be wishful thinking, the destiny of cash is certainly going to be disrupted, Ledger Insights (2021). It is important to note that the effect of digital currency introduction will depend on its design and country-specific features. Critical characterizes will be anonymity such as" the traceability of transactions", security, transaction contracts, and interest earned.

Digital financial services could also be a weapon in the fight against the progression of COVID 19 and for economic resilience. Indeed, to fight against the spread of the corona virus, countries must accompany measures to reduce proximity between people, as long as the technologies are available and efficient. Digital finance in African countries is still mainly used to effect (electronic) money transfers, immediately followed by re-transformation into trust money (to carry out current transactions). The current crisis should be the opportunity to go further in the use of digital finance. The main objective of electronic money is to have a comprehensive analytical framework with a built-in set of complementary measures to achieve large-scale adoption of this form of money, Deloitte (2020).

Within the Global Information Technology Report 2016, which covers 139 countries, Tunisia achieved a score of 3.9 on a scale ranging from 1 to 7 which allowed it to ranked 81st in the world and second rank in North Africa just after Morocco and 7th place in Arab countries.

In 2020, the BCT launched its "regulatory sandbox" to test technological innovations in the banking and financial sector. "Ledger", a Tunisian fintech startup labeled Startup Act specializing in payments, has been selected by the BCT as part of the first cohort of the regulatory sandbox to carry out tests with voluntary clients to experiment with a Proof of Concept on the "Digital Currency of the Central Bank", CBDC. This experiment is being carried out to identify how innovative technologies could improve the efficiency and fluidity of payment systems and financial infrastructures.

Ledger Insights provide the bank the possibility to identified the date of publication even by phone or email and does not receive any definitive response. After publication, the Central Bank of Tunisia refuted that the e-dinar was an official test initiate and fixed that a Central Bank Digital Currency was only at the examination level, Wood (2019). As such, the" Société Tunisienne de Banques" (STB) is the first Tunisian bank to integrate the Dinar Digital network, object of the "Digital Currency of the Central Bank" project to participate in this testing phase, which is spread over a limited period by the sandbox access guide. Other banks will also join this network.

E-dinars are now accessible to exchange between individuals, with cafes, and restaurants that accept the currency in many months. The central bank announced also to utilize it in cross-border payments, avoiding the need for united state dollars. The CBDC will be transferred to consumers online and through two thousand kiosks, which will be installed in Tunisia. Hear, they can attach funds to a digital portfolio through a browser application or, why not in the future, a mobile application. Exchange are finished between individuals and firms by "scanning a QR code", Wood (2019).

The Digital Dinar network is an interoperable money transfer and payments network of member financial institutions. This network is operated on block chain technology with digitalization of fiat currency (cash) which will improve efficiency and reduce the costs of financial transactions for individuals. Once the tests are conclusive within the framework of the BCT sandbox, these new digital payments infrastructure will be set up in Tunisia by the regulations in force, and will offer citizens and financial institutions a complementary solution to the payment networks. Already existing, namely electronic banking transfers and checks.

Digital currency has been the exposed of challenges and opportunities for policymakers, entrepreneurs, consumers, and economists since its start. It is represented to be separate from any other money or equities in the financial market. It provides further opportunities for stakeholders in terms of portfolio testing, risk analyze, and consumer sense test (Dyhrberg, 2016). Several literature compare the Bitcoin with gold because it has many similarities points. None of them is national or surveilled by the government, and many independent operators and firms are extracting them.

Digital Dinar could improve profitability and decrease the cost and probability of risks borne by the payment system and could help reinforce financial inclusion, IMF (2018). However, demand could not automatically be important and could depend on the attractiveness of option types of money. Furthermore, there are other payments form to facilitate the monetary authorities to complete its objective relative to money. CBDC could supply various level varying of dependence and immediate settlement. It could thus curtail the emerge of private forms of anonymous payment but could amplify volatility in the financial market.

Cryptocurrencies or digital currency are highly considered as touriblem innovations that lift both anticipations and concerns in the minds of many teams of economic stakeholders. In reality, digital currency hand over a range of potential opportunities as an digital and flexible payment channel, while at the same time analyzing future risks that could impact investors, consumers, firms, banking sector and even country security (Guesmi et al., 2019).

This does not prevent that there are costs to bear derail the use of this payment solution. The digital currency will have to contend with operational risks arising from disruptions and cyber attacks. Several authors like Selmi et al. (2018), Symitsi and Chalvatzi (2019), and Baur and Hoang (2020) showed that digital currency presents as a very volatile asset since a small deterioration or increase in its value can amplify the economic and financial risk.

Despite being a small country, Tunisia could be a good testing ground for a CBDC. She followed several major countries such as Argentina, Brazil, and China on the crypto currency emission.

CONCLUSION

The conclusion is that the overall net effect of technical progress depends on three parameters: the rate of destruction of automatable jobs, the extent of job transformation and the rate of new job creation.

The digitalization is disrupting the business model of established companies in fundamental ways; It disrupts the way products are marketed, knowing that no established company is immune to these changes; and requires reforming the organization and the culture of the company's personnel.

The effects of the arrival of new digital waves on industrial sectors will be significant and will lead to major transformations in the Tunisian economic landscape: erasing sectoral barriers, changing the nature of services, the emergence of a new range of goods and services, redistribution of value added between players ...

Tunisian companies seem to be aware of the challenges of digital and its impact on their activities without fearing it.

An industrial policy to guide companies through this digital transformation process is strongly recommended. Its objectives will be to accelerate the economic transformation of the most exposed sectors and to be able to position certain firms in the high value-added segments.

In Tunisia as elsewhere, new sectors will also emerge and will require specific skills. The challenge will be the ability of the country to accelerate the training of new digital jobs and especially to disseminate widely the digital culture.

FUNDING AGENCY

This research received no specific grant from any funding agency in the public, commercial, or not-for-profit sectors.

REFERENCES

Alain B. (2018). Transforming the bank. In *Banking strategy in the digital age*. Dunod.

Allmendinger, G., & Lombreglia, R. (2005). Four strategies for the age of smart services. *Harvard Business Review*, *83*(10), 131–145.

Berdi & Sebbar. (2018). Contribution to the study of the strategic nature of information and communication technologies (ICT) for the organization: case of the Moroccan banking sector. *Moroccan Review of Research in Management and Marketing, 18.*

Bos. (2018). Digital transformation, towards increased strategic management? Céline Bos, Ea Conseil & formation, DIF 2018.

Carstens, A. (2021). *Digital currencies and the future of the monetary system.* Working Paper. Bank for International Settlements.

CoxJ. (2021). https://www.cnbc.com/2021/09/22/the-fed-is-evaluating-whether-to-launch-a-digital-currency-and-in-what-form-powell-says.htm

Daley, N. (2003). ICTs and retail banking: Prospects and challenges. Digital Notebooks, 4.

Daley, N., & Dyhrberg, A. H. (2016). Hedging capabilities of Bitcoin. Is it the virtual gold? *Finance Research Letters*, *16*, 139–144.

Deloitte. (2020). *Digital financial services: Weapon in the fight against the progression of COVID 19 and for the resilience of African economies.* Author.

Guesmi, K., Saadi, S., Abid, I., & Ftiti, Z. (2019). Portfolio diversification with virtual currency: Evidence from bitcoin. *International Review of Financial Analysis*, *63*, 431–437.

Lin & Xue. (2020). Research on the Development of Digital Currencies under the COVID-19 Epidemic. *Procedia Computer Science, 187*, 89–96.

Sajić, M., Bundalo, D., Bundalo, Z., & Pašalić, D. (2018). Digital technologies in transformation of classical retail bank into digital bank. *2017 25th Telecommun. Forum, TELFOR 2017- Proc.*, 1–4. doi:10.1109/TELFOR.2017.8249404

Selmi, R., Mensi, W., Hammoudeh, S., & Bouoiyour, J. (2018). Is Bitcoin a hedge, a safe haven or a diversifier for oil price movements? A comparison with gold. *Energy Econ.*, *74*, 787–801.

Shao, Nib, Wanga, & Wang. (2020). Research on venture capital based on information entropy. *Procedia Computer Science, 187*, 278-283.

Symitsi, E., & Chalvatzis, K. J. (2019). The economic value of Bitcoin: A portfolio analysis of currencies, gold, oil and stocks. *Research in International Business and Finance*, *48*, 97–110.

Wood. (2019). Tunisia issues central bank digital currency. *Ledger Insights*.

ADDITIONAL READING

Salha Ben Salem, P. (2020). Empirical Evidence on Non-Performing Loans and Credit Frictions: Banking sector in Tunisia. *International Journal of Financial, Accounting, and Management*, *2*(3), 171–183. doi:10.35912/ijfam.v2i3.191

KEY TERMS AND DEFINITIONS

Bitcoin: It's a type of digital currency in which a record of transactions is maintained, and new units of currency are generated by the computational solution of mathematical problems, and which operates independently of a central bank.

Digital Currency: Digital currency is a form of currency that is available only in digital or electronic form. It is also called digital money, electronic money, electronic currency, or cybercash. Digital currencies are currencies that are only accessible with computers or mobile phones because they only exist in electronic form.

Digital Transformation: Is the process of using digital technologies to create new—or modify existing—business processes, culture, and customer experiences to meet changing business and market requirements. This reimagining of business in the digital age is digital transformation.

Typical Digital Currencies: Do not require intermediaries and are often the cheapest method for trading currencies. All cryptocurrencies are digital currencies, but not all digital currencies are cryptocurrencies.

Chapter 2
Blockchain and Cryptocurrency Development Without Regulation

Bechir Chenguel
University of Kairouan, Tunisia

ABSTRACT

Blockchain is a technology based on a chain of interconnected blocks containing transaction history and user data. Blockchain permitted the creation of cryptocurrency. Among its advantages are decentralization, transparency, and integrity. This technology has increased with COVID-19 with the accentuation of the wave of digitalization. Classic finance systems felt overwhelmed by events and tried to catch up with this new wave by creating their cryptocurrency and embarking on this new world of digital finance where regulation and control are nonexistent. Many central banks see the introduction of central bank digital currencies. But the expansion of these cryptocurrencies could present risks in terms of transmission of monetary policy, monetary creation, and financial stability. In this work, the authors present the evolution of cryptocurrency and the reaction of classic finance systems to this wave of digitalization of transactions and especially to an absence of regulation.

INTRODUCTION

The global financial crisis contributed to the advent of cryptocurrencies which challenged the paradigm of state-guaranteed currencies and the dominant role of central banks and other mainstream financial institutions; Nakamoto s. (2008). These virtual assets have become new means of payment, even units of account,

DOI: 10.4018/978-1-7998-9117-8.ch002

thus reducing the demand for fiduciary currencies. But currently, cryptocurrencies are too volatile and even risky. For some, they inspire less confidence and can be entangled in cases of fraud, security breaches, breakdowns, and links to illicit activities. However, continuous technological innovation has addressed some of these shortcomings. To counter the potential competition from cryptocurrencies, central banks need to implement effective monetary policies too. They can take inspiration from the characteristics of cryptocurrencies and the technology they use to bring fiduciary currencies more in step with the digital age. Cryptocurrencies are pure blockchain products and a real advance in cryptography and distributed ledger technology. Cryptocurrencies are digital representations of value. They are denominated in their units of account and are traded peer to peer, without intermediaries S Wen, W Xiong, J Tan, S Chen, Q Li (2021). The market value of these assets is that they can be exchanged for other currencies and used for payments or as a store of value. Unlike fiduciary currencies, whose value is inseparable from monetary policy and their status as legal tender, crypto-assets are only worth the anticipation that other agents will value them and will use them Piera Ca, Roberto C b, Emilio Ea, Eugenio O a (2021). The fact that their valuation is based on convictions not firmly anchored in real assets, explains the high price volatility observed. With some cryptocurrencies like bitcoin, the risk of inflation is limited because the supply is also limited. However, these assets do not perform three essential functions that stable monetary regimes which are: protection against the risk of structural deflation, ability to adapt flexibly to temporary shocks in demand for money (thus impacting the economic cycle), and finally, the ability to act as a lender of last resort. several questions arise about the future of the use of these cryptocurrencies. For the volatile side, admittedly with maturity, the volatility could subside, encouraging more people to adopt them in their financial transactions and uses. By introducing new issuance rules, such as rules-based on artificial intelligence, the valuation of this virtual currency could become more stable. To remedy this, there has been the creation of new "stable" cryptocurrencies the Stablecoins; JB Abdo, S Zeadally (2020). The term stable has its origin because some virtual currencies are linked to existing fiduciary currencies. Used as a medium of exchange, cryptocurrencies have certain advantages. While offering roughly the same anonymity as cash, cryptocurrencies allow transactions to be made between operators neglecting the unit of transaction. These properties make crypto-assets particularly attractive for small payments made in the new digital economy based on sharing and services. In addition, unlike bank transfers, the clearing and settlement of transactions are fast and unmediated, which is particularly beneficial for international payments, which are expensive, complicated, and opaque. By increasing the number of correspondent banking networks, new services using blockchain technology and crypto-assets have shortened the times for international payments, since cryptocurrency reaches its destination in seconds instead of days. Thus, some cryptocurrencies will be more widely used and will have more monetary functions in certain regions or certain private digital commerce networks. More generally, the rise of cryptocurrencies and blockchain technology could herald the transition from an account-based payment system to a value-based or token-based system; Ali s. T., Clarke d. and McCorryP. (2015). In the traditional monetary system, the transfer of receivables is recorded in an account managed by an intermediary, usually a bank. In addition, the second system provides for the transfer of a payment object.If the value of the object is verifiable, the transaction can take place, regardless of the trust placed in the intermediary or the counterparty. In the digital age, this shift could also affect money creation itself: from scriptural money to commodity money.In the nineteenth and twentieth centuries, money was essentially based on credit relationships: central money represents a credit relationship between the central bank and citizens (in the case of cash) and between the central bank and commercial banks (in the case of reserves). And demand deposits from commercial banks represent a credit relationship between these banks and their customers. Moreover, cryptocurrency is not based on any credit relationship; it does not represent any debt, and is more like commodity money. This is how economists continue to debate the origins and use of this type of currency and to wonder why monetary systems have always alternated between cryptocurrency and cashless money, despite the absence of regulation and the risks that can arise there. Through our work, we will want to focus on the spectacular development of the use of this digital currency, despite almost no regulation on this type of currency. We have also focused on the reactions of traditional financial institutions in the world of finance, and more precisely their reactions to this competing phenomenon, especially with calls for digitization of services and the emergence of artificial intelligence. Our work will be organized as follows: first, we will present and define the blockchain, present cryptocurrencies. Then, we will present the evolution of the uses of digital currencies, and the risks that can result from it. In a third part, we will present the reaction of the world of classical finance to the emergence of the use of virtual currencies, and the future it holds for us.

DEFINITION SECTION

Blockchain and Cryptocurrency

1. Blockchain Definition

Blockchain is a technology for storing and transmitting information, transparent, secure, and operating without a central control body. This is the platform on which cryptocurrencies are based. A blockchain is a database that contains the history of all exchanges between its users since its creation. This database is secure and distributed: it is shared by its various users, without an intermediary, which allows everyone to check the validity of the chain. There are two types of blockchains: public and private ones. Public blockchains, as the name suggests, are open to all users, while private blockchains are limited to several actors for access and use. A public blockchain can be likened to a public accounting ledger, anonymous and tamper-proof; H Albayati, SK Kim, JJ Rho (2020). Itis like the ledger, which anyone can read freely and for free, and which anyone can write about, but which is unbreakable and indestructible. The operation of the blockchain is based on majority control, it is an accounting entry of digital operations, shared between multiple stakeholders P Martino, KJ Wang, C Bellavitis (2020). It can only be updated by consensus between a majority of participants in the system. And, once entered, information can never be overwritten. Thus, the cryptocurrency blockchain contains a record of all transactions carried out by cryptocurrencies without exceptions. Beyond its monetary aspect, this decentralized information storage technology could have multiple applications, such as applications based on smart contracts, allowing the exchange of all kinds of goods or services; and also ways to reduce payment costs and transaction costs.

2. Cryptocurrency Definition

Technological developments have led to the creation and emergence of a new form of currencies:virtual or digital currency or also cryptocurrency or synthetic commodity currency (Selgin, 2013).These electronic currencies are created using a peer-to-peer cryptographic protocol, therefore without a central bank (Narayan et al., 2016).The first cryptocurrency is bitcoin, created in 2009 by one or more computer programmers using the pseudonym "Satoshi Nakamoto".Bitcoin is exchanged peer to peer (individual or company) on the Internet against other monetary currencies (Euro, Dollar, Yen ...), outside of traditional banking networks, and it is accepted as a medium by some physical and online merchants. But cryptocurrency has no legal framework unlike other monetary currencies.In fact, cryptocurrency is not legal course, and its value is not regulated by a central bank.Today,internet trade relies almost exclusively on financial institutions that serve as a trusted medium for processing electronic payments.While this system works well for most transactions, it still contains weaknesses to its trust-based model.Completely irreversible transactions are not possible there, since financial institutions must manage conflict mediation ButerinV. (2015). The cost of this mediation increases transaction costs, effectively limiting the minimum size of a transaction and preventing the possibility of having small, inexpensive transactions.The impossibility of having non-reversible payments for non-reversible services results in an even greater cost.With the ability to reverse transactions, the need for trust increases.Merchants should be wary of their customers, harassing them for more information than necessary.A certain amount of fraud is accepted as inevitable.All these costs and uncertainties of payment can be avoided by the use of a physical currency, but no mechanism exists to make payments through a communication system without having recourse to a trusted third party Böhme r., Christin n ., edelman b. And Moore t. (2015). A cryptocurrency wallet is software where virtual currency is stored.This is because cryptocurrency is not stored anywhere, and there is a private key for each cryptocurrency address that is stored in the wallet of the person who owns the balance S Corbet (2020).Cryptocurrency wallets make it easy to send and receive cryptocurrency. Thecryptocurrency wallet can be in different forms, the smart phone, the web, it is a digital wallet. Cryptocurrencies are the digital equivalent of cash; a cryptocurrency wallet is analogous to a physical wallet. But instead of storing cryptocurrency, what's stored is a lot of important information like the secure private key used to access cryptocurrency addresses and to make transactions.

a. First-generation cryptocurrency (Bitcoin)

First-generation cryptocurrencies are digital assets with no intrinsic value. Their real value stems from the trust their user's place in them. This trust does not guarantee the sustainability of the value over time Dwyer g. (2014). And their relative scarcity is not a condition for keeping their value within a sufficiently narrow range to ensure relative price stability. Thus, the drop in demand for bitcoin in 2018 led to a sharp collapse in prices. In addition, this type of digital currency does not constitute a claim of its holder towards its issuer, unlike the official currency which is a claim on the central bank (assets of commercial banks in the central bank, fiat money) or the issuing credit institution (bank deposits). Conventional money is backed by bank balance sheet assets, and also exhibits liquidity characteristics according to the balance sheet of the central bank or the commercial bank that issued it; IMF International Monetary Fund) (2016).In the case of a commercial bank, bank assets are, on average, much less liquid than bank deposits are to their holders. Prudential rules, therefore, oblige the bank to build up reserves with the central bank in a certain proportion of customer deposits (1% in the Eurozone since 2012).

b. The Stablecoins

Stable coins were issued by official or unofficial financial institutions or entities, which back then, to assets usually issued by central banks. For example, the JPM coin, issued by US bank JP Morgan in February 2020, falls into this category. It is a "wholesale" crypto-asset (that is to say for financial institutions that want to participate in its blockchain. This currency would be exchangeable at parity against the dollar and accompanied by the guarantee of the issuing bank. Other stable coins will emerge such as the Libra project initiated by Facebook, which will be accepted by central banks promoting the issuance of stable coins. It is a paperless payment method backed by a basket of safe assets denominated in major currencies. By construction, parity will be maintained between each unit of Libra and the safe asset mix, of which the basket is multiple. Thus, the issuance of any additional libra will result in the purchase of the complementary safe asset mix for an amount corresponding to the parity. The first limitation of libra is that sellers of safe assets can agree to be paid in libra. What these stablecoins have in common with official currencies is that these currencies are claims on their issuers, whose balance sheet quality depends on a basket of more or less secure assets. This virtual currency is therefore considered as part of the shares of its funds. In addition, issuers of this currency generally belong to the institutional sector of financial and monetary institutions (MFI) in the same way as credit institutions. So stablecoins are distinguished by two aspects. First, their issuers are not necessarily money market funds and are therefore not subject to the same regulations as the latter JB Abdo, S Zeadally (2020). Then, stablecoins are designed to be mobilized as a means of settlement (at least vis-à-vis those who accept them), to settle a transaction, or to repay a debt.

c. The special case of tokens

Another innovation in crypto-assets lies in the digitization of certain tangible (work of art) or intangible (patents, copyright) assets in the form of tokens. These are digital assets representing a right to a future service (native token) or an existing thing (non-native token). According to the same principle as that of crypto "currencies", these tokens can be redeemed without third-party intervention over the internet Hm Kim, M Laskowski, M Zargham, H Turesson (2021). The register of each protocol can operate independently of the tokens while the primary crypto-assets (bitcoin, ether, ripple, etc.) are inseparable from it. One particular operation, the public offering of tokens "(Initial Coin Offering, ICO) allows fundraising in crypto" currency ". In Europe and France in particular, the Financial Markets Authority (FMA) defines this operation as "a fundraising operation carried out through a blockchain device, which gives rise to the issuance of tokens that can then be used to obtain products or services. Similar to a fundraiser, these transactions allow a business to raise funds at an early stage of development. However, they differ from IPOs (initial public offering, IPO), to which they are often compared. Indeed, unlike shares, tokens do not give their holders rights to the share capital but to products or services that will subsequently be marketed by the company. They are thus akin to an early sale, or pre-financing.

They allow a company to build up cash flow before a project comes to fruition and to the subscriber, confident of being allocated, under attractive conditions, rights to products or services developed by the company. While it has so far been mainly used by start-ups, this solution is potential of interest to any company planning to market a new product or service. Tokens therefore present as wide a variety as that of "digitized" assets, or that of pre-financed projects, which in essence makes the market narrower and less liquid than that of "coins".

To a New Economy with Cryptocurrency?

The emergence of cryptocurrency and the associated digital asset ecosystem, have made debates at several economic and societal levels, and in particular in economic and financial circles M Shaker, FS Aliee, R Fotohi (2021). And the big question is: is Cryptocurrency money or not? Money is classically defined as a medium of exchange, a store of value, and a unit of account.

Is Cryptocurrency a Medium of Exchange?

In the digital entrepreneurial environment, a business owner can pay his teams residing in other countries in Bitcoin for their services provided. Likewise, a person in any country can order different technology products by paying in Bitcoin rather than local currency or dollars and receive them by conventional international delivery services thereafter. This is a reality that is starting to consolidate in some economies. Not to mention instant currency transfers internationally, to relatives, cross-border, wherever you are connected to the Internet on our planet, and at an unbeatable cost. The digital economy has now accepted the use of cryptocurrency as a means of payment and as a tool for the exchange of services and products.

Is Cryptocurrency a Reserve of Value?

Cryptocurrency is a reserve of value when its value is deeply appreciated, and on the other hand, other traditional reserves of value, such as life insurance, savings funds, can be devalued by inflation or management fees. Cryptocurrency is certainly a volatile reserve of value, but over the medium to long term, it has been able to prove to be a real store of value.

Is Cryptocurrency a Unit of Account?

Certainly, the volatility is quite high, but over the years the price of Digital Gold may be more stable to become a Digital Gold standard. However, it should be noted that the creation of stable coins backed by the Dollar or Euro will strengthen the stability and unity of account of the cryptocurrency. Thus, the cryptocurrency and the ecosystem of associated crypto-assets, appear as an emerging currency, in full expansion, which presents strong characteristics of a currency of more and more common use, despite its imperfect character from an economic point of view on the medium and long term.

MAIN FOCUS OF THE CHAPTER

Evolution of Cryptocurrencies and the Blockchain

The various factors suggest that virtual currency will soon be part of our daily means of payment and also for the investor who will benefit from this major turning point in the history of money. Currently, virtual currencies are multiplying, and traditional currencies are going through a period of crisis, which means that the democratization of cryptocurrencies is starting to be confirmed on the economic level (I Cioroianu, S Corbet, C Larkin 2021). The next few years could mark an intensification of the diffusion of cryptocurrencies observed in recent years. Therefore, the spread of this new form of money in everyday life could lead to particularly interesting economic and financial reactions.

Virtual Currency: The Multiplication of Flows and Global Users

According to Monetary and Financial Control in France (2021) in 2018, the number of cryptocurrency users was estimated at 35 million worldwide. And it is estimated that there would be nearly 100 million crypto holders worldwide in the first half of 2020, an increase of almost 185% despite the fall in the prices of major cryptocurrencies over this period. These figures are found in the capitalization of the main cryptocurrencies. Bitcoin represented a total of $ 15 billion in December 2016 against $ 290 billion currently in March 2021. The resulting multiplication of global flows can be explained by the great interest shown by financial institutions in cryptocurrencies. Added to this is the emergence of a distinction between customary money and save money and above all the emergence of a growing need for decentralization. Negative rates have the effect of accentuating the difference between the currency of use and currency of savings, and above all to implicitly increase the risk-taking of the agents. The use of cryptocurrencies is favored due to independence from central banks and also for the global and decentralized nature (where the law of each state does not apply directly).

Paypal has Adopted the Use of Cryptocurrencies to Pay for Purchase Transactions

PayPal has joined the cryptocurrency market by allowing customers to buy, sell and hold bitcoin and other digital assets, using the company's online wallet accounts. This new option on the PayPal platform came into effect in the first half of 2021. In addition, PayPal intends to eventually distribute the main cryptocurrencies for its 346 million active PayPal accounts (accounts that have traded for more than $ 220 billion in transactions in the second quarter of 2020). Thus in the long term, the potential number of cryptocurrency users will be up to 3 times greater than the current number of users with the sole decision of PayPal. This is why the PayPal cryptocurrency project is very ambitious and plans to work with central banks to find the maximum means so that PayPal can impose itself in this matter.PayPal's decision to view this new form of currency as an opportunity created a veritable euphoria behind the scenes in the markets, and many institutions immediately revised their positioning. Facebook should also soon make it possible to pay with its cryptocurrency.

Central Banks Issue Their Tokens

The proliferation of private cryptocurrencies, in a digital world where the free choice of one's currency would become the norm, encourages central banks (and States in terms of regulation) to enter the game so as not to get caught in the trap. Many central banks were considering creating their digital currencies known as CBDC (Central Bank Digital Currency). The reduction in cash exchanges and the multiplication of exchanges in private currencies are pushing institutions like the Central Bank to launch their tokens.

How to Profit from the Multiplication of Virtual Currencies?

The increase in users leads to an increase in the price of cryptocurrency, indeed, the democratization of cryptocurrencies is a factor in the rise of the prices of currencies like Bitcoin. Another effect of the democratization of cryptocurrencies is the development of real industry in this area: the emergence of Decentralized Finance (DeFi) of which ChainLink, Wrapped Bitcoin, Dai or Aave are the main players. In addition, there are also positive effects for all platforms that allow crypto investments. The fact that cryptos become widespread at the transaction level should systematically translate into democratization at the level of savings. We will mention platforms like Binance, CoinBase, which are seeing their number of users, grow. So, just like traditional currencies that are linked to the banking industry, virtual currencies are linked to the crypto industry. It is therefore particularly appropriate to focus on companies with the greatest potential to become in the face of the massification of cryptos. Cryptocurrencies have the advantage of being able to develop a fast payment system that can be used in a very large part of the countries of the world, which does not allow a traditional national currency which remains, in comparison, a brake on world trade.

The COVID-19 Crisis: A Major Factor in the Democratization of Cryptocurrencies?

The Covid-19 crisis would have been a real opportunity for cryptocurrencies. The spectacular development of this type of currency in recent years has convinced many institutions and companies like Facebook, certain central banks, and more recently PayPalto take the plunge to enter the game and create their cryptocurrencies. So, for the next few years, the use of these virtual currencies will certainly be higher than it has been in recent years. Cryptocurrencies, after having established themselves in the financial landscape in recent years, is now expected to enter the economic landscape.Cryptos, therefore, appear as an everyday means of payment (or even investment/savings). The pandemic has accelerated the development of monetary solutions responding to the digitalization of the economy. Overall, cryptocurrencies fell sharply at the start of the global phase of the pandemic, from February to March, and then experienced a phenomenal rebound. Bitcoin has seen dramatic swings and volatility, already approaching $ 20,000 in 2018 before collapsing to around $ 3,000, to more than quadruple after the pandemic. These uncontrollable variations are the typical characteristics of these cryptocurrencies. The phenomenon of rising to these spectacular levels is fueled by the pace of creation (or “mining”). On the demand side, global investor demand has been greatly bolstered in recent months by support from PayPal, which has announced that it is integrating several cryptocurrencies into its payment solutions. The idea of a decentralized data architecture has many advantages, first of all when no centralized instance can manage it or when there is a problem of trust between participants in the system. But, in monetary and financial terms, many considered bitcoin as the new “digital gold”, but the fundamental elements of its architecture were often ignored. Cryptocurrencies of this type have no real backing, and their risks, such as the risk of a crypto breach, cannot be ignored. For their part, “stable coins” type cryptocurrencies, which promise a stable value against benchmark currencies, avoid certain obvious pitfalls. However, apart from central bank digital currency projects, which should be equivalent to cash, stable coins are the subject of financial engineering that returns them to the status of the synthetic financial product rather than currency, this is notably the case with Facebook’s libra project.

The Acceleration of the Economic Digitization by the Pandemic, Changed the Cryptocurrency Market and Public Digital Currency Projects?

The covid19 pandemic has accelerated digitization with phenomena as diverse as teleworking or e-commerce. We are therefore observing the development of solutions based on adaptation to digital life, particularly in monetary terms. Cryptocurrencies have an important aspect and their integration into real life as a means of payment gives them more credibility and practicality. In addition, the accumulation of public debts following the pandemic and the resulting financing by central banks translates into additional amounts of liquidity to finance sectors in distress I Cioroianu, S Corbet, C Larkin (2021). That's why. Cryptocurrency prices benefit greatly from this situation. The massive use of cryptocurrencies and the digital currency projects of private companies have also encouraged the digital currency projects of central banks, which have the potential to revolutionize the relationship between economic agents and the new currency that will be at stake. both digital and backed by the central bank. Regardless of the interest in blockchain and its less decentralized derivatives, it is difficult to see a stable and beneficial role in the potentially widespread use of digital currencies globally. The danger can arise when the use of almost all currencies does not rely on the real economy and its use without geographical limits can have disastrous consequences if that currency is used for money laundering and financing terrorism.

IS CRYPTOCURRENCIES A THREAT TO TRADITIONAL FINANCIAL INSTITUTIONS?

Financial institutions around the world are worried about the growing success of cryptocurrencies. These financial institutions are trying to regulate them or create their national digital cryptocurrencies. There are hundreds of digital currencies (Ether, Ripple, LiteCoin, etc.). The most famous of these, Bitcoin, has become the main and booming cryptocurrency with both individuals and large private investors.

There are two categories of digital currencies:

The first is made up of Bitcoin-type currencies which can be private or even public if they emerge from central banks. Monetary and Financial Control in France defines blockchain in its article Article L54-10-1 as any digital representation of a value that is not issued or guaranteed by a central bank or by a public authority that is not necessarily attached to a currency which is legal tender, but which is accepted by natural or legal persons as a medium of exchange and which can be transferred, stored or exchanged electronically. The second category of digital currency consists of tokens that are assimilated into financial instruments. Article L552-2 of Monetary and Financial Control defines this second category as a token, any intangible asset representing, in digital form, one or more rights, which can be issued, registered, stored, or transferred using a recording device. A shared electronic system allowing the identification, directly or indirectly, of the owner of the said property. The crisis of confidence is particularly affecting the banking sector and it is little wonder that Bitcoin and Ethereum, which are cryptocurrencies based on Blockchain technology, are giving rise to true monetary systems that are independent and parallel to each other. to state monetary and banking systems Y Hu, YG Hou, L Oxley, S Corbet (2021). In addition, cryptocurrencies are no longer objects of mere speculation but are increasingly becoming real currencies and long-term investments. This situation seems to worry high financial circles such as central banks and multinationals.

Cryptocurrencies Risks and the Regulation

Due to the anonymous transactions, bitcoin is considered one of the preferred means of payment for acquiring illegal goods and services (drugs, identity papers, arms trafficking, murder, prostitution, etc.), but also as a means to promote the financing of terrorism, tax evasion or money laundering. These problems were particularly revealed during the closure of the Silk Road site by the American authorities (Christin, 2013). The Cypriot and Greek crises also showed that bitcoin made it possible to bypass regulations on the movement of capital. In the Cypriot case, in 2013, holders of a deposit account over 100,000 euros, especially Russians, turned to bitcoin to avoid participating in the rescue. In Greece, in July 2015, bitcoin transactions increased by 300% to bypass bank withdrawal regulations. Bitcoin can thus appear as a haven to the point of making it a kind of digital gold S Shanaev, S Sharma, B Ghimire (2020). However, many states warn of the dangers of using virtual currencies Y Hu, YG Hou, L Oxley, S Corbet (2021). This is the case of France (ACPR report, Prudential Supervisory Authority, and Regulation, 2014) or China. For the European Central Bank (ECB, 2015), bitcoin is not legal money and does not plan to regulate it at this time. Countries such as Germany treat it as a private currency, which helps to tax transactions. The United States and Japan regard it as a commodity to tax capital gains. In addition to the benefits of using blockchains for financial transactions, there are several obstacles, both technical and legal; AM Sharma (2021). We start with operational risks. They manifest themselves in the first place by the risk of blocking transactions. Currently, the number of transactions that the blockchain can validate is limited to seven per second. But this technical characteristic is incompatible with the financial markets where saturation effects could lead to a blockage. But solutions are proposed and tested to allow the blockchain to process the volumes of the financial markets. The status of minors could be problematic if they operated in the financial markets. Currently, there are no regulations or oversight imposed on them, as is the case with financial intermediaries TK Siu (2021).

Therefore, there is no guarantee that investors will trust the miners in the settlement of transactions. The governance of the blockchain should also be a matter of concern. Indeed, it has no owner or regulatory authority, since the founding principle of the blockchain is: "Code is the law. It is considered a decentralized organization, its openness and flexible governance mean that future problems may not be properly anticipated; Committee on Payments and Market Infrastructures (CPMI, 2015). Conflict resolution is a central problem in the absence of regulatory authority, laws, and jurisdiction. One solution, currently being tested by financial institutions (R3 project), consists of setting up their blockchains, and minors are then approved beforehand. Thus, the validation of transactions is the responsibility of a set of nodes and not of all certifiers, which should contribute to a greater fluidity of transactions compared to a public blockchain.

When the blockchain is private, only approved members can carry out transactions on it for their account and/or for that of third parties. It can be semi-private if operations can be started by any agent, but certified by certified members. Regulators will need to monitor the authenticity of the channels. According to Emmet Rennick (2015), the generalization of chains would save banks up to $ 20 billion per year.

FUTURE RESEARCH DIRECTIONS

Crypto Currencies Regulation

Among the unique characteristics of these cryptocurrencies are the decentralized aspect, and the lack of regulation and control. Several supporters and users of virtual currency see the regulation of cryptocurrencies as a threat to the freedom and independence of this medium of transaction type of cryptocurrencies HAlbayati, SK Kim, JJ Rho (2020). But the advantage of regulation is an advantage for cryptocurrencies that must be well regulated so that the new means of transactions are robust in the event of shocks or financial crisis. The regulation aims at protecting transactions, ensuring security, and also protecting personal data, and especially regulation acts to fight against money laundering SP Yadav, KK Agrawal, BS Bhati, F Al-Turjman (2020). The supervision of cryptocurrencies is essential since it is a speculative asset and is used in business and money laundering activities as well. It must therefore have regulations. And it has to be applied globally because if there are loopholes or weaknesses in the system, it will be used fraudulently. This new highly innovative market has currently absent or poorly designed regulation, which risks harming the innovation. According to V Ferrari 2020) in Europe, the Monetary and

Financial Code indicates that the only legal tender currency in France is the Euro. As a result, cryptocurrencies cannot be used in payments and it is possible to refuse them without violating Article R162-2 of the Monetary and Financial Code. Crypto currency is used to purchase goods and services from professionals who accept it. One of the outstanding features of cryptocurrencies is that they allow transactions to be carried out anonymously. With a traditional currency, transactions must go through a bank that knows the name and contact details of its customers as well as the people and organizations with which they carry out transactions. On the contrary, cryptocurrencies work according to a decentralized system thanks to encryption keys (blockchain principle) which do not require any identification. It is therefore impossible today to regulate its emission. Thus, the use of cryptocurrency like Bitcoin currently poses a challenge for legislators and other regulatory authorities, which fought against money laundering and tax evasion.

On the other hand, banking and financial regulations have clearly defined all the traditional means of payment, and even the category of financial instruments is grouped in assets related to personal rights such as equity securities, debt securities, and financial contracts. While cryptocurrencies and their related activities are neither regulated nor well understood. Like, for example, Bitcoin, which does not correspond to any of these classic notions of finance. This is because it is generated by a computer program and does not give rights to anyone in particular. As a result, the lack of regulation allows the different parties to the contract to accept or refuse to be remunerated by cryptocurrency. Indeed, since the latter is not a currency like other regulated currencies such as the euro or the dollar, a party to the contract cannot require the other party to accept payment by cryptocurrency. This lack of regulation could be a danger to contractual relations R Kher, S Terjesen, C Liu (2020). Several central banks presented the different dangers associated with the use of cryptocurrencies, because it is a virtual value, and it is not backed by any real activity. Characterized by high volatility, long transaction times, and above all a legal risk linked to the status of an unregulated currency resulting in the fact that it presented no legal guarantee of repayment at any time and face value. Another danger arising from the use of cryptocurrency is that no authority ensures the security of electronic safes, the guarantor of the security of holders, and which has no guarantee in the event of theft following hacking operations. Finally, another danger arises from the random nature of the convertibility of cryptocurrencies into legal tender because based on the principle of supply and demand and therefore the risk of blockage and collapse of the system in the event of absence or insufficiency of buyers to redeem cryptocurrencies against currencies. Currently, it is impossible to regulate the issuance, and the challenge for lawmakers and other regulators for cryptocurrencies is the fight against money laundering and tax evasion. This is due to the use of this innovation which does not identify the different parties of the transaction. However, several platforms for the use of cryptocurrency, have expressed their dissatisfaction with the plans to regulate these cryptocurrencies, and find that these regulations are an infringement of the freedom to conduct online transactions privately and an attempt to extend the scope of financial supervision of banking institutions to cryptocurrencies. And the financial records that will now have to be revealed contain a lot of sensitive information about people's lives, their beliefs, and affiliations.

The Creation of Competing for Virtual Currencies

This situation leads national financial institutions to set up projects to create virtual currencies as a response. And in many countries, their financial bodies are working on launching their public digital currencies, like the digital euro project. Cryptocurrency is a form of virtual and digital currency that does not need to exist physically to be of value. Cryptocurrencies have become increasingly popular thanks to the decentralized peer-to-peer exchanges that have developed. In January 2021, India paved the way for cryptocurrency regulation, which could go as far as a ban on private cryptocurrencies. A decision that would be taken in parallel with the establishment of national electronic money, backed and managed by the Central Bank of India. The E-euro would be issued by the ECB, would trade at 1 to 1 parity with the Euro, and would complement or even substitute for cash. A public cryptocurrency, regulated by a central bank, backed by a currency, is of course more secure than a private cryptocurrency. Moreover, the digitization of central bank money will, in countries where cash is in decline, guarantee citizens' access to central bank money. Thus, having a Central Bank Digital Currency would allow preserving confidence in the financial system which results in part from the possibility of exchanging one's assets for legal tender. In Russia, the Central Bank announced in October 2020 that it was evaluating the possibility of creating a digital version of the Ruble. China embarked on the creation of a national cryptocurrency in 2014. A project that would be very ambitious, to ban Bitcoin on its territory. Finally, it must be said that cryptocurrencies are a major issue for the financial system facing public authorities, central banks, regulatory authorities, credit institutions, and citizens. However, regulation is the majority proposition. We note that the majority of authorities have warned and are proposing framework conditions to protect the market and investors.

CONCLUSION

Cryptocurrency can only perform perfectly the classic functions of a real currency. But currently, everyone uses them as a medium of exchange despite the risk of their true nature. To minimize the risk relating to this category of currencies, other cryptocurrencies have emerged, called stable coins, which have the particularity of being backed by baskets of safe assets, and unlike first-generation cryptocurrencies, they have intrinsic value, which will help make their prices less volatile. Thus, backing to official currencies moves stable coins away from the free and volatile side that characterizes the first generation of cryptocurrencies. Thoughts in favor of the creation of digital central bank currencies called stable coins have been fostered by the perception of a threat to the monetary sovereignty of each conventional currency. The new stable coins are not simple official alternatives to crypto "currencies" from private networks, but they also allow access to stable private or individual corners called retail CBDC (Central Bank Digital Currency), in the form of accounts, or to open access to non-bank intermediaries (wholesale CBDC). These new private or wholesale creations will certainly structurally modify the process of monetary creation (in the true sense and not of cryptocurrency) and even the channels of transmission of monetary policy. Importantly, a retail CDBC introduces "digital" banking risk, the effect of which can be significant financial stability. These reasons alone justify slowly deepening the reflection on the creation of this type of cryptocurrency. This race for power in a new mode of financing has a neglected point but whose impact is consistent, it is the energy-intensive nature of this blockchain and crypto currencies, for future research, we must study and see the impact of the development of these crypto currencies on the ecological cost

REFERENCES

Abdo & Zeadally. (2020). Multi-utility framework: blockchain exchange platform for sustainable development. *International Journal of Pervasive Computing*.

Albayati, H., Kim, S. K., & Rho, J. J. (2020). Accepting financial transactions using blockchain technology and cryptocurrency: A customer perspective approach. *Technology in Society*.

Ali, T., Clarke, D., & McCorry, P. (2015). Bitcoin: Perils of an unregulated global p2p currency. Newcastle University, Technical Report Series, no 1470.

Böhme, R., Christin, N., Edelman, B., & Moore, T. (2015). Bitcoin: Economics, technology and governance. *Journal of Economic Perspectives, 29*(2), 213-238.

Buterin, V. (2015). *On public and private blockchains*. Blog Ethereum. https://blog.ethereum.org/ 2015/08/07/on-public-and-private-blockchains/

Ca, P. (2021, April). Surfing blockchain wave, or drowning? Shaping the future of distributed ledgers and decentralized technologies. *Technological Forecasting and Social ChangeVolume*, *165*, 120463.

Christin, N., & Moore, T. (2013). Beware the middleman: empirical analysis of bitcoin-exchange risk. In *Financial cryptography and data security*. Springer.

Cioroianu, I., Corbet, S., & Larkin, C. (2021). The differential impact of corporate blockchain-development as conditioned by sentiment and financial desperation. *Journal of Corporate Finance*.

CMF (2019) Contrôle Monétaire et Financier article L552-2 du Création LOI n°2019-486 du 22 mai 2019 - art. 85,

CMF (2021) Contrôle Monétaire et Financier en France L'article L54-10-1(2021) https://www.legifrance.gouv.fr/codes/article_lc/LEGIARTI000038509570/

Corbet. (2020). Evaluating a decade of cryptocurrency development: Navigating financial progress through technological and regulatory ambiguity. *Cryptocurrency and Blockchain Technology*.

CPMI. (2015). *Digital currencies*. Committee on Payments and Market Infrastructures, Bank of International Settlement.

Dupré, D., Ponsot, J-F., & Servet, J-M. (2015). *Le bitcoin contre la révolution des communs* (5th ed.). Congrès de l'Afep.

Dwyer, G. (2014). *The economics of bitcoin and similar private digital currencies*. MPRA Paper, No 57360.

FE (Federal Reserve). (2015). *Strategies for improving the US payment system*. Author.

Ferrari. (2020). *The regulation of crypto-assets in the EU–investment and payment tokens under the radar*. Academic Press.

FerrariV. (2020). Maastricht Journal of European and Comparative. journals.sagepub.com

FMI (Fonds Monétaire International). (2016). *Virtual currencies and beyond: initial considerations*. Staff Discussion Note, No 3.

Hu, Hou, Oxley, & Corbet. (2021). Does blockchain patent-development influence Bitcoin risk? *Journal of International Financial*.

Hu, Y., Hou, Y. G., Oxley, L., & Corbet, S. (2021). Does blockchain patent-development influence Bitcoin risk? *Journal of International Financial Markets, Institutions and Money*.

Kher, R., Terjesen, S., & Liu, C. (2020). Blockchain, Bitcoin, and ICOs: A review and research agenda. *Small Business Economics*.

Kim, H. M., Laskowski, M., Zargham, M., & Turesson, H. (2021). *Token Economics in Real Life: Cryptocurrency and Incentives Design for Insolar's Blockchain Network*. IEEE Computer Society. ieeexplore.ieee.org

Martino, Wang, & Bellavitis. (2020). *An introduction to blockchain, cryptocurrency and initial coin offerings*. Academic Press.

Martino, Wang, & Bellavitis. (2019). *New Frontiers in Entrepreneurial Finance Research*. World Scientific.

Nakamoto, S. (2008). Bitcoin: A peer-to-peer electronic cash system. *Consulted, 1*, 28.

Narayanan, A., Bonneau, J., Felten, E., Miller, A., & Goldfeder, S. (2016). *Bitcoin and Cryptocurrency Technologies*. Princeton University Press.

Rennick, E. (2015). *The Fintech 2.0 Paper: rebooting financial services*. Santander InnoVentures.

Revue de l'ACPR. (2014). https://acpr.banque-france.fr/publications/revue-de-lacpr/revue-de-lacpr-2014

Selgin, G. (2013). *Synthetic Commodity Money*. University of Georgia, Working Paper.

Shaker, M., Aliee, F. S., & Fotohi, R. (2021). Online rating system development using blockchain-based distributed ledger technology. *Wireless Networks*.

Shanaev, S., Sharma, S., & Ghimire, B. (2020). Taming the blockchain beast? Regulatory implications for the cryptocurrency market. *Research in International Business and Finance*.

Sharma, A. M. (2021). *Cryptocurrency and Financial Risks*. digitalcommons.liberty.edu

Siu, T. K. (2021). The risks of cryptocurrencies with long memory in volatility, non-normality and behavioural insights. *Applied Economics*.

Wen, S., Xiong, W., Tan, J., Chen, S., & Li, Q. (2021). Blockchain enhanced price incentive demand response for building user energy network in sustainable society. *Sustainable Cities and Society*.

Yadav, S. P., Agrawal, K. K., Bhati, B. S., & Al-Turjman, F. (2020). *Blockchain-Based Cryptocurrency Regulation: An Overview. In Computational Economics*. Springer.

KEY TERMS AND DEFINITIONS

Blockchain: A blockchain is a distributed database that is shared among the nodes of a computer network. As a database, a blockchain stores information electronically in digital format. Blockchains are best known for their crucial role in cryptocurrency systems, such as bitcoin, for maintaining a secure and decentralized record of transactions. The innovation with a blockchain is that it guarantees the fidelity and security of a record of data and generates trust without the need for a trusted third party. One key difference between a typical database and a blockchain is how the data is structured. A blockchain collects information together in groups, known as blocks, that hold sets of information. Blocks have certain storage capacities and, when filled, are closed and linked to the previously filled block, forming a chain of data known as the blockchain. All new information that follows that freshly added block is compiled into a newly formed block that will then also be added to the chain once filled. A database usually structures its data into tables, whereas a blockchain, like its name implies, structures its data into chunks (blocks) that are strung together. This data structure inherently makes an irreversible timeline of data when implemented in a decentralized nature. When a block is filled, it is set in stone and becomes a part of this timeline. Each block in the chain is given an exact time stamp when it is added to the chain.

Cryptocurrency: Sometimes called crypto-currency or crypto, is any form of currency that exists digitally or virtually and uses cryptography to secure transactions. Cryptocurrencies don't have a central issuing or regulating authority, instead using a decentralized system to record transactions and issue new units. Cryptocurrency is a digital payment system that doesn't rely on banks to verify transactions. It's a peer-to-peer system that can enable anyone anywhere to send and receive payments. Instead of being physical money carried around and exchanged in the real world, cryptocurrency payments exist purely as digital entries to an online database describing specific transactions. When you transfer cryptocurrency funds, the transactions are recorded in a public ledger. Cryptocurrency is stored in digital wallets. Cryptocurrency received its name because it uses encryption to verify transactions. This means advanced coding is involved in storing and transmitting cryptocurrency data between wallets and to public ledgers. The aim of encryption is to provide security and safety. The first cryptocurrency was bitcoin, which was founded in 2009 and remains the best known today. Much of the interest in cryptocurrencies is to trade for profit, with speculators at times driving prices skyward.

Chapter 3
Digital Transformation:
Opportunities and Challenges

Ahmed Chemseddine Bouarar
University of Medea, Algeria

Smail Mouloudj
University of Medea, Algeria

Kamel Mouloudj
University of Medea, Algeria

ABSTRACT

Digital literature has provided significant insights into how digital transformation contributes to improving business performance. This research departs from these studies by focusing on driving factors of digital transformation and digital transformation strategies. Moreover, the authors determine the impact of digital transformation on firm performance and identify the challenges of adopting digital transformation. The results show that successful digital transformation can speed up the pace of innovation, increase productivity, improve customer experiences and satisfaction, reduce costs, and improve business performance. The results also revealed that major barriers to digital transformation include lack of knowledge, lack of digital expertise, poor digital leadership, resistance to change, inflexible culture, unclear vision and objective, lack of collaboration and alignment. These results will help to illuminate the complex issue of how to set an effective digital transformation.

DOI: 10.4018/978-1-7998-9117-8.ch003

INTRODUCTION

Technology is the main story in business today, plain and simple (Westerman, Bonnet, & McAfee, 2014). The technology is advancing rapidly and prompted companies to adapt to the changes it has brought about, not just to take benefits of the enormous opportunities it supplies but even to stay relevant in this rapid, uncertain, complex, and opaque world (Kraus, Jones, Kailer, Weinmann, Chaparro-Banegas, & Roig-Tierno, 2021; Shahi & Sinha, 2021). The Internet-based digital or electronic business (e-business) is considered one of the most significant information technology innovations over the last decade (Geoffrion & Krishnan, 2003). Thence, digitalization isn't a new obligation for business, but COVID-19 has made it more urgent and it is expected that the post-COVID-19 era will engender new challenges and opportunities and rapid trend for digitalization. For example, the increased fear of contracting COVID-19 virus brought about major changes in food service delivery and shoppers' behaviors (Bouarar, Mouloudj, & Mouloudj, 2021), and COVID-19 obliged universities to close their doors and compelled the the transition toward online education system (Alarabiat, Hujran, Soares, & Tarhini, 2021; Mouloudj, Bouarar, & Stojczew, 2021).

Reis, Amorim, Melão, & Matos (2018, p.411) state in their literature review that "the society as a whole is facing a fast and radical change due to the maturation of digital technologies and their ubiquitous penetration of all markets". Recently, firms in almost all sectors have taken many steps to explore new digital technologies and take advantage of their merits (Matt, Hess, & Benlian, 2015). The current technological evolution helps us to access more information more easily and promptly, computing capacity, communication, and connectivity, in addition to providing new forms of collaboration between different networks and actors (Pereira, Durão, Fonseca, Ferreira, & Moreira, 2020).

Digital transformation refers to the integration of digital technology into all sectors of a business, fundamentally altering how you perform and bring value to customers (Gebayew, Hardini, Panjaitan, Kurniawan, & Suhardi, 2018). Accordingly, digital transformation does not only mean the shift towards using technology within the borders of a firm, but rather it is a comprehensive program that involves a firm as a whole, primarily in terms of working methods internally, and externally in terms of providing services to the targeted public to bring about services accessibly, and quickly. Digital transformation is pushing companies to alter their business models and cope with the new market reality. Westerman et al. (2014) note that "executives are digitally transforming three key areas of their enterprises: customer experience, operational processes, and business models".

Digital Transformation hovers around technologies that create cross-functional value generation and significantly impact the way of doing business (Vogelsang,

Liere-Netheler, Packmohr, & Hoppe, 2019). Companies aspire for considerable gains in terms of efficiency and productivity by moving forward digital transformation (Schwab, 2017). The digital transformation of organizations is mandatory due to the expanding global population. However, the transformation processes have costs and consequences. (Heavin & Power, 2018). Manufacturing companies encounter barriers in changing traditional routines and work processes to adopt the digital transformation (Sjödin, Parida, Leksell, & Petrovic, 2018). Organizations have experienced major difficulties in applying digital transformation due to several reasons, including a lack of standardized implementation protocols, focusing on applying of new technologies rather than assessing their role within the business, the compartmentalization of digital initiatives from the rest of the business, and the huge implementation of digitalization in the light of an absence of a realistic view of return on investment (Butt, 2020).

We try through our research paper to answer the following questions: Q1: Why do companies digitally transform? Q2: How do companies formulate and implement their digital business transformation strategies? Q3: What is the impact of adopting digital transformation on business performance? Q4: What are the challenges of adopting digital transformation? Therefore, the aim of our study is: (1) Identifying the compelling reasons, motivations, and incentives to adopt digital transformation; (2) Shedding light on the formulation and implementation strategy framework of digital transformation; (3) Determining the impact of digital transformation on firm's performance; and (4) Identifying the main challenges and obstacles that could stymie digital transformation. Finally, we provide some recommendations that may help companies transition smoothly and successfully towards digital transformation; to this end, a literature review has been conducted on the most recent available references on digital transformation published in indexed journals and research papers discussed at international scientific conferences. The rest of the paper is divided as follows. Section 2 presents the theoretical development, including the concept, motivation, and goals for embracing digital transformation. Section 3 describes the formulation and implementation of digital transformation strategies. Section 4 analyses the impact of digital transformation on business performance. Section 5 discusses the main barriers to digital transformation. The paper closes with a discussion of major findings, limitations and implications for both research and management.

DEFINITION OF DIGITAL BUSINESS TRANSFORMATION

Digital transformation covers several functional areas, like marketing, information technology, innovations, strategic and operations management, as a result, the concept of digital transformation is multidimensional and includes a wide range of subjects and activities (Ahmad, Alshurideh, Al Kurdi, Aburayya, & Hamadneh, 2021). Before defining the digital transformation, it is important to understand exactly what the "digital" means. We define digitization from a business perspective as "being a set of operations that integrate and incorporate digitalization across all functions of a business in order to serve customers with electronic products or services".

One of the digital transformation definitions is from Westerman, Calméjane, Bonnet, Ferraris, & McAfee (2011, p.5): digital transformation is "the use of technology to radically improve performance or reach of enterprises". Similarly, Fitzgerald, Kruschwitz, Bonnet, & Welch (2014, p.2) defined digital transformation as follows: "the use of new digital technologies, such as social media, mobile, analytics or embedded devices, in order to enable major business improvements like enhancing customer experience, streamlining operations or creating new business models". According to Stolterman & Forst (2006, p.689), digital transformation can be understood as "the changes that the digital technology causes or influences in all aspects of human life". For Henriette, Feki, & Boughzala (2016, p.3), the digital transformation is "a disruptive or incremental change process. It starts with the adoption and use of digital technologies, then evolving into an implicit holistic transformation of an organization, or deliberate to pursue value creation".

Another definition is from Morakanyane, Grace, & O'Reilly (2017, p.11), where the digital transformation of the organizations is "an evolutionary process that leverages digital capabilities and technologies to enable business models, operational processes and customer experiences to create value". Accordingly, we define digital transformation as "a process of changing and substituting traditional working methods and processes with more developed and newfangled technologies in order to maximize customer's value". From a strategic perspective, digital transformation refers to "moving forward digitalizing all aspects of a business through implementing digital technologies according to a strategic plan".

The different definitions for digital transformation may be categorized into three distinct elements (Reis et al., 2018, pp.417-418): (1) Technological: digital transformation is based on the use of new digital technologies such as the Internet of Things (IoT), Cloud Computing, and Cyber-physical systems (CPS); (2) Organizational: digital transformation requires a change of organizational culture, structure, operations, policies, procedures, and strategy, or creating and implementing a new business model; (3) Social: digital transformation is a phenomenon that is permeating every aspect of human life by, e.g., enhancing customers experience.

According to Ulas (2019), driving factors expediting digital transformation are (1) Advancement of technology and innovation, sensor technology, (2) Change of business practices with internet economy, electronic commerce, social media, (3) Globalization, (4) industry 4.0, (5) Artificial Intelligence, (6) Internet of things (IoT), (7) As new consumers, Generation Z's expectations affecting market, (8) Blockchain,

Figure 1. Internal and external factors affecting digital transformation
Source: Tarutė et al. (2018, p.377).

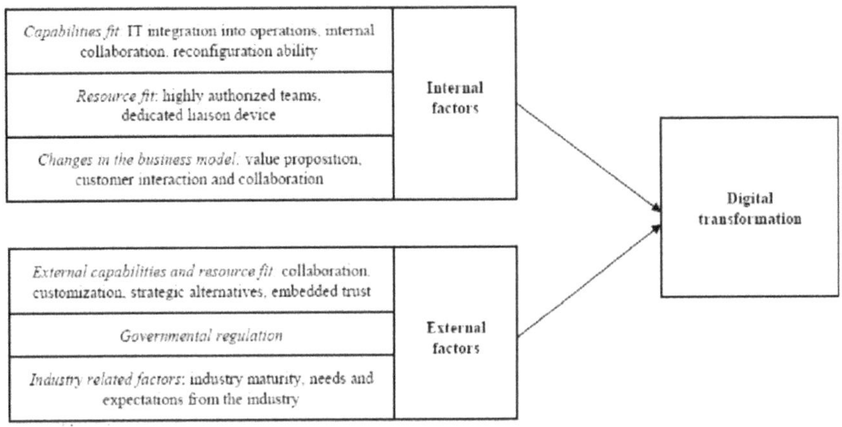

(9) Cloud computing, (10) Increase in the use of Smartphones, (11) 3D printers, (12) Chatbots (software applications), (13) Big data, (14) Augmented reality, (15) Developing of sharing economy, (16) Nanotechnology, (17) Digital supply chain, (18) Robotics, and (19) Advanced manufacturing technologies.

According to Henriette et al. (2016) digital transformation has two main dimensions: (1) the digital technologies, such as Internet technologies, analytical technologies, and mobile technologies; and (2) the user experience, such as customers, internal users (collaborators or employees). Digital transformation encompasses more than using technology. It also includes the alignment to the organization and the environment (Matt et al., 2015). However, moving forward solely to technology forward is insufficient to harvest the benefits from digital transformation (Vogelsang et al., 2019).

Many studies indicate that many factors are affecting digital transformation in companies. For example, Tarutė, Duobienė, Klovienė, Vitkauskaitė, & Varaniūtė (2018) categorized factors affecting the digital transformation of SME into two categories: (1) internal factors include capabilities fit, resource fit, and changes in the business model; and (2) external factors are external capabilities and resource fit, governmental regulation, and industry-related factors (see Fig. 1).

According to Winarsih, Indriastuti, & Fuad (2021), there are three things related to digital adoption: (1) Digital transformation is not confined solely to technology, but rather more about how businesses can compete more effectively because as it can shrink costs in many areas; (2) Increasing digital knowledge and skills related to business. Lack of understanding often makes digital transformation undertaken decision less beneficial to the needs of the business itself; and (3) Using integrated e-wallet services.

DIGITAL BUSINESS TRANSFORMATION STRATEGIES

To compete and survive, most organizations ought to implement appropriate digital transformation as a key strategy (Heavin & Power, 2018). Digital transformation represents a crucial strategic decision (Henriette et al., 2016). For this reason, strategy is an action plan formulated and developed by an organization in order to achieve long-term objectives. Bharadwaj, El Sawy, Pavlou, & Venkatraman (2013, p.472) define digital business strategy as "an organizational strategy formulated and executed by leveraging digital resources to create differential value". Strategic management functions must take into account digital transformation technologies and their impact on assets and resources (Vogelsang et al., 2019).

The effects of digital transformation in the world are conspicuous and they confer significant benefits for entrepreneurs, consumers, and society in general (Llopis-Albert, Rubio, & Valero, 2021). However, Digital transformation remains a difficult task starting with strategic leadership and a digital organization strategy (Heavin & Power, 2018). Henriette et al. (2016) found that digitalization represents strategic, organizational, and cultural stakes for the company and requires the commitment and involvement of top management. Companies must understand what is paramount for the successful implementation of digital transformation to be able to aim at a strategic transformation (Vogelsang et al., 2019).

Power (2017) pinpointing a strategic vision for digital transformation is beneficial; however, vision must be oriented towards customer needs and technology possibilities. In order to successfully applying the process of digital transformation, it requires a skilled, qualified, highly motivated person with leadership skills that lead employees through a process of change based on the use of digital technology (Popović-Pantić, Semenčenko, & Vasilić, 2019). However, Heavin & Power (2018) contends that while technology is the most significant factor of any digital transformation program, it is only one element of any digital transformation strategy. According to Winarsih et al. (2021), four things can be implemented for digital transformation: (1) ensuring companies to remain more competitive, (2) bringing effectiveness and efficiency in business processes, (3) improving customer satisfaction, and (4) improving strategic decisions making. In addition, Vogelsang et al. (2019) found that digital transformation can only be successful if companies collaborate with customers, suppliers, and also other firms from the branch.

Parviainen, Tihinen, Kääriäinen, & Teppola (2017) provide a good approach by proposing four necessary steps to benefit from DT. First, a company should analyze recent trends to take decision regarding the position to take toward the change impact of digitalization. Second, the current position regarding the desired positioning and digitalization impact is also analyzied. As a third step, the authors propose defining concrete actions to heal the gap between the current state and desired position of the organization. The fourth step seeks to implement and validate the actions with technical support. In addition, Hess, Benlian, Matt, & Wiesböck (2016), develop the digital transformation framework that identifies four key dimensions for a company-wide digital transformation strategy formulation: the use of technologies, changes in value creation, structural changes, and how to finance digital transformation.

Chanias, Myers, & Hess (2019) summarized the seven main phases of digital transformation strategy formulation and implementation:

- Phase 0: recognizing the need for digital transformation
- Phase 1: setting the stage
- Phase 2: initially formulating the digital transformation strategy;
- Phase 3: preparing for digital transformation strategy implementation;
- Phase 4: starting digital transformation strategy implementation;
- Phase 5: finding a working mode;
- Phase 6: enhancing the digital transformation strategy.

According to Tekic & Koroteev (2019), there are four generic digital transformation strategies: disruptive, business model led, technology led, and proud to be analog. Tekic & Koroteev (2019) posit that digital transformation strategies can be characterized in terms of two dimensions: (1) level of mastery of digital technologies relevant to the sector in which the company competes (high or low) and (2) level of business model readiness for digital operation (high or low). The main characteristics of the four types of digital transformation strategies are summarized in Table 1.

THE IMPACT OF ADOPTING DIGITAL TRANSFORMATION ON FIRM PERFORMANCE

Firm performance is a measure of the extent of how well a firm is able to achieve its goals and objectives compared with rivals (Cao & Zhang 2011). Dimensions of firm performance include profitability, revenue growth, customer satisfaction, employee satisfaction, social performance, market value, and environmental performance. In recent years much attention has been directed towards understanding the relations between digital transformation and firm performance. Previous studies posited that digital transformation has a positive effect on business performance (Dalenogare, Benitez, Ayala, & Frank, 2018). The impact of Industry 4.0 allows technologies in

Table 1. Main characteristics of digital transformation strategies

Main characteristics	Types of digital transformation strategies			
	Disruptive	**Business model led**	**Technology led**	**Proud to be analog**
Primary target of transformation	Substantial change of the value proposition	Exploration of new opportunities	Optimization and cost reduction	Identification of parts of a business that could and should be digitalized
Leadership type	Vision led	Vision led	Risk avoidance led	Risk avoidance led
Creativity and entrepreneurial spirit among employees	Crucial for success and main fuel of the company	In high demand, but typically not available inside the company	Typically underutilized, sometimes even counterproductive	Not in high demand as all innovation steps are done with extreme caution
Typical risks and challenges	Failing with experiments slowly; scaling up too early	Recognizing which parts of firm's knowledge base are useful and needed, and which are not	Using individual digital technologies to solve discrete business problems	Transiting from predigital generation of users to digital native users
Consequences of the failure	Minimal	Very high, may be fatal	Medium	Low to medium
Tactics for improvement	Fail fast and fail cheap	Copy from the disruptor as much and as quickly as possible	Allow and promote bottom-up approach in selected cases	Experiment through partnering with digital native companies
Companies pursuing this strategy	Dominantly startups from B2C sector	Dominantly from B2C sector (e.g., consumer financial and insurance services, retail, telecom, media)	Dominantly from B2B sector (e.g., oil and mineral extraction companies, heavy machinery, legal services, healthcare)	Exclusively from B2C sector (e.g., producers of the finest luxury watches, jewelry, suits, shoes, porcelain, cars)

Source: Tekic & Korotee, (2019, p.688).

the manufacturing sector, and their perfect use provides benefits such as enhanced productivity and asset performance, lower inefficiencies, reduced production and maintenance costs while improving system agility and flexibility (Butt, 2020). Further, Llopis-Albert et al. (2021) contends that digitization confer major improvements to the value chain by enhancing efficiencies, reducing costs, and bringing about greater collaboration and innovation.

The impact of digital transformation is associated with the merits of digital transformation; it has impacted business and the principle of the organization.

Among the merits of digital transformation for business are (Gebayew et al., 2018): (1) increase customer satisfaction; (2) increase customer experience; (3) improvement in productivity; (4) increase revenue from products and services; and (5) cost reduction. Therefore, digital transformation confers innumerable benefits, which are not confined only to customers and the public but involves governments institutions and firms as well, among these benefits is that it significantly reduce costs and efforts, which ultimately ensue improved operational efficiency, it can also upgrade the quality and facilitate procedures in providing services, it creates opportunities for a providing more creative and innovative services compared to conventional methods, digital transformation also helps government institutions and firms expand their span of services to reach as much as possible of customers and public.

Previous studies have pointed out that business model innovation can creates a competitive advantage and improve business performance (Latifi, Nikou, & Bouwman, 2021). Nwankpa & Roumani (2016) reported that digital transformation mediates the positive influence of IT capability on firm performance. Furthermore, the results show that digital transformation has a significant positive influence on both innovation and firm performance. A new study by Zhai, Yang, & Chan (2022) concluded that digital transformation enhances a firm's performance. Chen, Jaw, & Wu (2016) found that the service-oriented portal function dimension (portal maintenance service, B2B function, and cloud computing) significantly influences SMEs organizational performance. Popović-Pantić et al. (2019) showed that digital transformation has a significant, positive, and strong impact on business performance (financial and non-financial). Mubarak, Shaikh, Mubarik, Samo, & Mastoi (2019) discovered that big data, cyber-physical systems, and interoperability have a significant positive impact to improve business performance, while the insignificant effect of the internet of things was revealed. Abou-Foul, Ruiz-Alba, & Soares (2021) found that digitalization and servitization has exerted a positive and significant impact on a company's financial performance. In addition, Sousa-Zomer, Neely, & Martinez, (2020) showed that the building blocks of the digital transforming capability (digital-savvy skills, digital intensity, and context for action and interaction) lead to sustained business performance in a digital economy environment.

Didenko, Skripnuk, Kikkas, Kalinina, & Kosinski (2021) discovered that digital transformation affects the indicators of a logistic system, and the open innovation. Guo & Xu (2021) concluded that mechanisms of digital transformation have significant effect on both operating performance and financial performance. Zhai et al. (2022) argue that "digital transformation is most helpful for firms in the mature stage of their product life cycle". Hanelt, Firk, Hildebrandt, & Kolbe (2021) showed that digital transformation enhances a firm's performance. Jafari-Sadeghi, Garcia-Perez, Candelo, & Couturier (2021) reported that digital transformation has positive impacts on value creation. However, Aral & Weill (2007) found that firms' total IT investment is not associated with performance. Also, Koski (2010) suggests that mobile connectivity does not significantly contribute to the firms' growth and profitability. In addition, Popović-Pantić, Semenčenko, & Vasilić (2020) found that digital technology has no direct influence on financial performance, and that product innovation mediates the relationship between digital technology and financial performance.

The controversy regarding the outcomes of the relationship between digital transformation and firms' performance could be attributed to the inability of some firms to adopt a sound digital transformation. Some managers, for instance, believe that mere possession of new digital technologies guarantees a firm's performance enhancement, is completely incorrect because failing in implementing digital transformations is associated with several factors, such as employees' inability to understand new technology's contents and functions or their resistance to any new working patterns.

CHALLENGES OF ADOPTING DIGITAL TRANSFORMATION

There have been many studies reported in management literature on factors that contribute to the success or failure of the adoption of digital transformation (Jonathan, 2020; Martin, 2018; Vogelsang et al., 2019). Critical success factors (CSFs) are "those few things that must go well to ensure success for a manager or an organization" (Boyton & Zmud, 1984, p.17). The knowledge of the potential factors that may impact digital transformation positively may facilitate a realization of gains due to digital transformation (Vogelsang et al., 2019).

Many researchers have attempted to identify the key factors of successful digital transformation. Martin (2018) discovered that the successful digital transformation is affected by having the right digital-savvy leaders in place, building capabilities for the workforce of the future, empowering people to work in new ways, giving day-to-day tools a digital upgrade, and frequently connecting to traditional and digital methods (see Tab.2).

There are very significant factors that are directly related to digital transformation. Most of the success factors relate to the organizational dimension which represents the challenge, but also to the opportunity for companies to implement their own digital transformation (Vogelsang et al., 2019). Henriette et al. (2016) found that digital transformation involves fundamental changes in a company's business model, which may influence processes, resources, operational methods, or culture. Moreover, according to Berman, (2012) to succeed in digital transformation, pioneering companies pay close attention to two additional activities: recreating customer value

Table 2. Critical success factors for digital transformation in companies

Dimensions	Success factors
Organizational success factors	- Pilot projects (it implies a stepwise introduction of digital integration instead of a complete rollout for whole sites). - Prepare for future (includes the ability to set up roadmaps and strategic as well as operational goals). - Ability to understand customer needs. - Higher autonomy of machines. - Employee qualification (the staff must be trained and prepared). - Culture (*Culture tells us what to do when the CEO isn't in the room*). - (Big) Data use (the ability to use and to collect lots of data and provide these). - Management support (includes the provision of projects with the resources, knowledge, and time needed). - Usability (ensures the fit between technologies and tasks). - Interdisciplinary working environment (interdisciplinary team work).
Environmental success factors	- Connectivity (includes the seamless data exchange within the/ a network). - The high degree of transparency (requires trust into the data exchange). - Collaboration across company borders (is necessary because tasks are not solvable alone due to complexity). - Hybrid value creation (*the process of generating additional value by innovatively combining products (tangible component) and services (intangible component)*). - Standards (need to be established by international bodies).
Technical success factors	- Infrastructure (provide a useful infrastructure). - Reliability (the system guarantees the right data). - Relevance (data delivers the right data for the right user). - Adaptability (means a flexible system which can adjust to new information needs and the company using the system). - Security (is the base for the exchange of information). - Completeness (information needs to cover different aspects and alternatives). -Availability (secures the access to the system). - Real-Time Data (have to be available without delay).

Source: Vogelsang et al. (2018, p.11).

propositions and transforming their operations using digital technologies for more customer interaction and collaboration.

On the other hand, and according to Gupta (2018), major barriers to digital transformation regarding organizational are: Unclear vision and objective of the digital transformation; lack of management understanding, knowledge and experience in digital transformation; lack of organizational agility; lack of digital leadership skills (forward-looking, understanding of technology, open-mind, collaboration); inflexible organizational culture; rewards and incentives are not aligned to digital transformation; unclear measurement and rewarding systems; lack of employee involvement and engagement; and employee' resistance to change.

It has been reported that senior leadership teams lacking digitalization experience represents a major obstacle to business transformation (Sawy, Amsinck, Kræmmergaard, & Vinther, 2016). Therefore, managers with the know-how and experience of digital are likely more apt to perform the constant renewal required in the digital era (Sousa-Zomer et al., 2020). According to Machado et al. (2020), the lack of knowledge among manufacturing companies is the main obstacle in the transition to Industry 4.0 in Sweden. Sari, Güleş, & Yiğitol (2020) think that the biggest obstacle to the successful implementation of Industry 4.0 in the Turkish manufacturing industry is the lack of a collaborative strategy of digitalization.

Vogelsang et al. (2019, pp.16-17) suggest three propositions about digital transformation success, are: (1) a dynamic and flexible organization is pivotal for digital transformation. The organization has boost improvement, technical capabilities, and resources. The better the organization is attuned to change, the more likely the success of digital transformation; (2) the company's environment also influences digital transformation success. Enterprises need to cooperate to bring about stronger value chains for digital transformation; and (3) technology is pivotal for digital transformation. Without (secure and reliable) technological innovations, digital transformation is of little avail. However, driving only technology forward is insufficient to draw benefits from digital transformation.

FUTURE RESEARCH DIRECTIONS

In general, the authors hope that the study findings may help managers and decision-makers to design effective programs, policies, and strategies that would illuminate and pave the way for firms to adopt digital transformation. Hence, we believe that it would be beneficial for futures studies to address the following topics, determinants of adoption of digital transformation; evaluating challenges to adoption of digital transformation; the impact of digital transformation on improving the performance of companies; the impact of digital transformation on supply chain performance; challenges of implementation of the digital transformation strategy.

CONCLUSION

The aim o the study is to explore what are the impetuses that prompt organizations to adopt digital transformation, to address digital transformation strategies, and to identify the impact of digital transformation on performance. We found that several factors stimulate organizations to urgently adopt digital transformation; among these factors are globalization, the increasing use of smart devices, rivalry pressure, and customer awareness. We have also found that that digital transformation decisions are strategic crucial and challenging decisions that essentially requires providing a whole set of the necessary ingredients and a sound ground, most notably with respect to persuading, commitment, higher management involvements, having a clear strategic vision, determining major digital transformation objectives, selecting the best possible strategic alternative, and perfectly implement digital transformation strategy.

Additionally, it appeared that firms engaged in digital transformation may gain several advantages such as improving efficiency and effectiveness, enhancing environmental performance, boosting creativity, increasing customer satisfaction, reducing cost, increasing profitability, and improving the overall firm performance strategy. Arguably digital transformation however may engender some demerits as well, such as getting rid of several traditional functions which ultimately eventuate in increasing unemployment rate among the less-skilled workforce. On the other hand, it effectively increases digital job opportunities (such as information technologies security jobs) which in turn requires more expenditure on training and skills developments. Moreover, firms that failed to acclimate to the digital economy in the upcoming near future will inevitably incur significant losses before deciding to withdraw from the market.

Moreover, among the most important objective of the study was to identify the hurdles that stymie adopting digital transformation. We found that there are several obstacles such as managers lack of knowledge, experience, the necessary digital skills, the existence of an obscure vision and objectives of adopting digital transformation, lack of awareness of the advantages and benefits of the digital transformation, resource shortages in some firms, the emphasis on bringing technology and neglecting organizational aspects such as not performing the necessary changes in the organizational structure and organizational culture, employees resistance to digital transformation, and poor training programs.

Based on the obtained results, we present the following recommendations for firms willing to move towards digital transformation, which may effectively help to perform smooth digital transformation: (1) providing all digital capabilities such as new technologies, the appropriate technology, the appropriate organizational culture, and the necessary financing, (2) modernizing digital technology infrastructure, (3) adopt 'customer-first' approach in order to guarantee a better understanding of customers preferences, boosts customer engagement, providing personalized products, and benefiting from data to strengthen the relationship with customers; and (4) improve employees' skills to meet new technologies job's requirements through investing in effective training.

This research received no specific grant from any funding agency in the public, commercial, or not-for-profit sectors.

REFERENCES

Abou-Foul, M., Ruiz-Alba, J. L., & Soares, A. (2021). The impact of digitalization and servitization on the financial performance of a firm: An empirical analysis. *Production Planning and Control, 32*(12), 975–989. doi:10.1080/09537287.2020.1780508

Ahmad, A., Alshurideh, M., Al Kurdi, B., Aburayya, A., & Hamadneh, S. (2021). Digital transformation metrics: A conceptual view. *Journal of management Information and Decision Sciences, 24*(7), 1-18.

Alarabiat, A., Hujran, O., Soares, D., & Tarhini, A. (2021). Examining students' continuous use of online learning in the post-COVID-19 era: an application of the process virtualization theory. Information Technology & People. doi:10.1108/ITP-02-2021-0142

Aral, S., & Weill, P. D. (2007). IT assets, organizational capabilities, and firm performance: How resource allocations and organizational differences explain performance variation. *Organization Science, 18*(5), 763–780. doi:10.1287/orsc.1070.0306

Berman, S. J. (2012). Digital transformation: Opportunities to create new business models. *Strategy and Leadership, 40*(2), 16–24. doi:10.1108/10878571211209314

Bharadwaj, A., El Sawy, O., Pavlou, P., & Venkatraman, N. (2013). Digital business strategy: Toward a next generation of insights. *Management Information Systems Quarterly, 37*(2), 471–482. doi:10.25300/MISQ/2013/37:2.3

Bouarar, A. C., Mouloudj, S., & Mouloudj, K. (2021). Extending the theory of planned behavior to explain intention to use online food delivery services in the context of COVID -19 pandemic. In C. Cobanoglu & V. Della Corte (Eds.), *Advances in global services and retail management* (pp. 1–16). USF M3 Publishing. https://www.doi.org/10.5038/9781955833035

Boyton, A. C., & Zmud, R. W. (1984). An assessment of critical success factors. *Sloan Management Review, 25*, 17–27.

Butt, J. (2020). A conceptual framework to support digital transformation in manufacturing using an integrated business process management approach. *Designs, 4*(3), 1–39. doi:10.3390/designs4030017

Cao, M., & Zhang, Q. (2011). Supply chain collaboration: Impact on collaborative advantage and firm performance. *Journal of Operations Management, 29*(3), 163–180. doi:10.1016/j.jom.2010.12.008

Chanias, S., Myers, M. D., & Hess, T. (2019). Digital transformation strategy making in pre-digital organizations: The case of a financial services provider. *The Journal of Strategic Information Systems*, *28*(1), 17–33. doi:10.1016/j.jsis.2018.11.003

Chen, Y.-Y. K., Jaw, Y.-L., & Wu, B.-L. (2016). Effect of digital transformation on organisational performance of SMEs: Evidence from the Taiwanese textile industry's web portal. *Internet Research*, *26*(1), 186–212. doi:10.1108/IntR-12-2013-0265

Dalenogare, L. S., Benitez, G. B., Ayala, N. F., & Frank, A. G. (2018). The expected contribution of Industry 4.0 technologies for industrial performance. *International Journal of Production Economics*, *204*, 383–394. doi:10.1016/j.ijpe.2018.08.019

Didenko, N., Skripnuk, D., Kikkas, K., Kalinina, O., & Kosinski, E. (2021). The impact of digital transformation on the micrologistic system, and the open innovation in logistics. *Journal of Open Innovation*, *7*(2), 115. doi:10.3390/joitmc7020115

Fitzgerald, M., Kruschwitz, N., Bonnet, D., & Welch, M. (2014). Embracing digital technology: A new strategic imperative. *MIT Sloan Management Review*, *55*(2), 1–12.

Gebayew, C., Hardini, I. R., Panjaitan, G. H. A., & Kurniawan, N. B., & Suhardi, (2018). A systematic literature review on digital transformation. In *International Conference on Information Technology Systems and Innovation* (pp. 260-265). 10.1109/ICITSI.2018.8695912

Geoffrion, A. M., & Krishnan, R. (2003). E-business and management science: Mutual impacts (Part 1 of 2). *Management Science*, *49*(10), 1275–1286. doi:10.1287/mnsc.49.10.1275.17311

Guo, L., & Xu, L. (2021). The Effects of Digital Transformation on Firm Performance: Evidence from China's Manufacturing Sector. *Sustainability*, *13*(22), 12844. doi:10.3390u132212844

Gupta, S. (2018). *Organizational barriers to digital transformation. KTH Royal Institute of Technology*. School of Industrial Engineering and Management.

Hanelt, A., Firk, S., Hildebrandt, B., & Kolbe, L. M. (2021). Digital M&A, digital innovation, and firm performance: An empirical investigation. *European Journal of Information Systems*, *30*(1), 3–26. doi:10.1080/0960085X.2020.1747365

Heavin, C., & Power, D. J. (2018). Challenges for digital transformation – towards a conceptual decision support guide for managers. *Journal of Decision Systems*, *27*(1), 38–45. doi:10.1080/12460125.2018.1468697

Henriette, E., Feki, M., & Boughzala, I. (2016). Digital transformation challenges. In *Proceedings of the 10th Mediterranean Conference on Information Systems* (pp. 1-8). Academic Press.

Hess, T., Benlian, A., Matt, C., & Wiesböck, F. (2016). Options for formulating a digital transformation strategy. *MIS Quarterly Executive*, *15*(2), 123–139. doi:10.7892/boris.105447

Jafari-Sadeghi, V., Garcia-Perez, A., Candelo, E., & Couturier, J. (2021). Exploring the impact of digital transformation on technology entrepreneurship and technological market expansion: The role of technology readiness, exploration and exploitation. *Journal of Business Research*, *124*, 100–111. doi:10.1016/j.jbusres.2020.11.020

Jonathan, G. M. (2020). Digital transformation in the public sector: Identifying critical success factors. In M. Themistocleous & M. Papadaki (Eds.), *Information Systems. EMCIS 2019. Lecture Notes in Business Information Processing* (Vol. 381). Springer. doi:10.1007/978-3-030-44322-1_17

Koski, H. (2010). *Firm growth and profitability: The role of mobile IT and organizational practices.* Discussion Paper No. 1222. Available at: https://www.etla.fi/wp-content/uploads/2012/09/dp1222.pdf

Kraus, S., Jones, P., Kailer, N., Weinmann, A., Chaparro-Banegas, N., & Roig-Tierno, N. (2021). Digital transformation: An overview of the current state of the art of research. *SAGE Open*, *11*(3). doi:10.1177/21582440211047576

Latifi, M. A., Nikou, S., & Bouwman, H. (2021). Business model innovation and firm performance: Exploring causal mechanisms in SMEs. *Technovation*, *107*, 102274. doi:10.1016/j.technovation.2021.102274

Llopis-Albert, C., Rubio, F., & Valero, F. (2021). Impact of digital transformation on the automotive industry. *Technological Forecasting and Social Change*, *162*, 120343. doi:10.1016/j.techfore.2020.120343 PMID:33052150

Machado, C. G., Winroth, M., Carlsson, D., Almström, P., Centerholt, V., & Hallin, M. (2019). Industry 4.0 readiness in manufacturing companies: Challenges and enablers towards increased digitalization. *Procedia CIRP*, *81*, 1113–1118. doi:10.1016/j.procir.2019.03.262

Martin, J. F. (2018). *Unlocking success in digital transformations*. McKinsey & Company.

Matt, C., Hess, T., & Benlian, A. (2015). Digital transformation strategies. *Business & Information Systems Engineering*, *57*(5), 339–343. doi:10.100712599-015-0401-5

Morakanyane, R., Grace, A., & O'Reilly, P. (2017). Conceptualizing digital transformation in business organizations: A systematic review of literature. In *Proceedings of the 30th Bled EConference on Digital Transformation – From Connecting Things to Transforming Our Lives* (pp. 427–443). 10.18690/978-961-286-043-1.30

Mouloudj, K., Bouarar, A. C., & Stojczew, K. (2021). Analyzing the students' intention to use online learning system in the context of COVID-19 pandemic: A theory of planned behavior approach. In W. B. James, C. Cobanoglu, & M. Cavusoglu (Eds.), *Advances in global education and research* (Vol. 4, pp. 1–17). USF M3 Publishing. https://www.doi.org/10.5038/9781955833042

Mubarak, M. F., Shaikh, F. A., Mubarik, M., Samo, K. A., & Mastoi, S. (2019). The impact of digital transformation on business performance: A study of Pakistani SMEs. *Engineering, Technology &. Applied Scientific Research*, *9*(6), 5056–5061. doi:10.48084/etasr.3201

Nwankpa, J. K., & Roumani, Y. (2016). IT capability and digital transformation: A firm performance perspective. In *Proceedings of the 37th International Conference on Information Systems* (vol. 5, pp. 3839-3854). Academic Press.

Parviainen, P., Tihinen, M., Kääriäinen, J., & Teppola, S. (2017). Tackling the digitalisation challenge: How to benefit from digitalisation in practice. *International Journal of Information Systems and Project Management*, *5*(1), 63–77. doi:10.12821/ijispm050104

Pereira, C. S., Durão, N., Fonseca, D., Ferreira, M. J., & Moreira, F. (2020). An educational approach for present and future of digital transformation in Portuguese organizations. *Applied Sciences (Basel, Switzerland)*, *10*(3), 1–22. doi:10.3390/app10030757

Popović-Pantić, S., Semenčenko, D., & Vasilić, N. (2019). The influence of digital transformation on business performance: Evidence of the women-owned companies. *Ekonomika Preduzeća*, *67*(7-8), 397–414. doi:10.5937/EKOPRE1908397P

Popović-Pantić, S., Semenčenko, D., & Vasilić, N. (2020). Digital technologies and the financial performance of female SMES in Serbia: The mediating role of innovation. *Economic Annals*, *65*(224), 53–81. doi:10.2298/EKA2024053P

Reis, J., Amorim, M., Melão, N., & Matos, P. (2018). Digital transformation: A literature review and guidelines for future research. In Trends and Advances in Information Systems and Technologies. Springer International Publishing. doi:10.1007/978-3-319-77703-0_41

Sari, T., Güleş, H. K., & Yiğitol, B. (2020). Awareness and readiness of industry 4.0: The case of Turkish manufacturing industry. *Advances in Production Engineering & Management, 15*(1), 57–68. doi:10.14743/apem2020.1.349

Sawy, O. A. E., Amsinck, H., Kræmmergaard, P., & Vinther, A. L. (2016). How LEGO built the foundations and enterprise capabilities for digital leadership. *MIS Quarterly Executive, 15*(2), 141–166.

Schwab, K. (2017). *The fourth industrial revolution*. Crown Business.

Shahi, C., & Sinha, M. (2021). Digital transformation: Challenges faced by organizations and their potential solutions. *International Journal of Innovation Science, 13*(1), 17–33. doi:10.1108/IJIS-09-2020-0157

Sjödin, D. R., Parida, V., Leksell, M., & Petrovic, A. (2018). Smart factory implementation and process innovation. *Research Technology Management, 61*(5), 22–31. doi:10.1080/08956308.2018.1471277

Sousa-Zomer, T. T., Neely, A., & Martinez, V. (2020). Digital transforming capability and performance: A microfoundational perspective. *International Journal of Operations & Production Management, 40*(7/8), 1095–1128. doi:10.1108/IJOPM-06-2019-0444

Stolterman, E., & Fors, A. C. (2004). Information technology and the good life. In Information Systems Research. Springer. doi:10.1007/1-4020-8095-6_45

Tarutė, A., Duobienė, J., Klovienė, L., Vitkauskaitė, E., & Varaniūtė, V. (2018). Identifying factors affecting digital transformation of SMEs. In *Proceedings of the 18th International Conference on Electronic Business* (pp. 373-381). ICEB.

Tekic, Z., & Koroteev, D. (2019). From disruptively digital to proudly analog: A holistic typology of digital transformation strategies. *Business Horizons, 62*(6), 683–693. doi:10.1016/j.bushor.2019.07.002

Ulas, D. (2019). Digital transformation process and SMEs. *Procedia Computer Science, 158*, 662–671. doi:10.1016/j.procs.2019.09.101

Vogelsang, K., Liere-Netheler, K., Packmohr, S., & Hoppe, U. (2019). Success factors for fostering a digital transformation in manufacturing companies. *Journal of Enterprise Transformation, 8*(1-2), 121–142. doi:10.1080/19488289.2019.1578839

Westerman, G., Bonnet, D., & McAfee, A. (2014). *Leading digital: Turning technology into business transformation*. Harvard Business Press.

Westerman, G., Calméjane, C., Bonnet, D., Ferraris, P., & McAfee, A. (2011). Digital Transformation: A Road-Map for Billion-Dollar Organizations (Report). Capgemini Consulting & MIT Center for Digital Business.

Winarsih, I. M., & Fuad, K. (2021). Impact of Covid-19 on Digital Transformation and Sustainability in Small and Medium Enterprises (SMEs): A conceptual framework. In Complex, Intelligent and Software Intensive Systems. CISIS 2020. Advances in Intelligent Systems and Computing (Vol. 1194, pp. 471-476). Springer. doi:10.1007/978-3-030-50454-0_48

Zhai, H., Yang, M., & Chan, K. C. (2022). Does digital transformation enhance a firm's performance? Evidence from China. *Technology in Society*, *68*, 101841. doi:10.1016/j.techsoc.2021.101841

ADDITIONAL READING

Alkaraan, F., Albitar, K., Hussainey, K., & Venkatesh, V. G. (2022). Corporate transformation toward Industry 4.0 and financial performance: The influence of environmental, social, and governance (ESG). *Technological Forecasting and Social Change*, *175*, 121423. doi:10.1016/j.techfore.2021.121423

Busulwa, R., Pickering, M., & Mao, I. (2022). Digital transformation and hospitality management competencies: Toward an integrative framework. *International Journal of Hospitality Management*, *102*, 103132. doi:10.1016/j.ijhm.2021.103132

Fenwick, M., & Vermeulen, E. P. (2020). The end of the corporation: Transformation in corporate governance. In *Challenges and Opportunities of Corporate Governance Transformation in the Digital Era* (pp. 1–17). IGI Global. doi:10.4018/978-1-7998-2011-6.ch001

Hai, T. N., Van, Q. N., & Thi Tuyet, M. N. (2021). Digital transformation: Opportunities and challenges for leaders in the emerging countries in response to COVID-19 pandemic. *Emerging Science Journal*, *5*, 21–36. doi:10.28991/esj-2021-SPER-03

Mikhaylova, A., Sakulyeva, T., Shcherbina, T., Levoshich, N., & Truntsevsky, Y. (2021). Impact of digitalization on the efficiency of supply chain management in the digital economy. *International Journal of Enterprise Information Systems*, *17*(3), 34–46. doi:10.4018/IJEIS.2021070103

Ram-rez, A. M. H., & López-Zapata, E. (2021). Analysis of the factors influencing adoption of 3D design digital technologies in Colombian firms. *Journal of Enterprise Information Management*, *35*(2), 429–454. doi:10.1108/JEIM-10-2020-0416

Scott, S., & Orlikowski, W. (2022). The digital undertow: How the corollary effects of digital transformation affect industry standards. *Information Systems Research*, *33*(1), 311–336. doi:10.1287/isre.2021.1056

Sheu, M., & He, X. X. (2021). Why business digitalization is still so risky: An analysis of 54 cases. *International Journal of Enterprise Information Systems*, *17*(4), 1–15. doi:10.4018/IJEIS.2021100101

Warner, K. S., & Wäger, M. (2019). Building dynamic capabilities for digital transformation: An ongoing process of strategic renewal. *Long Range Planning*, *52*(3), 326–349. doi:10.1016/j.lrp.2018.12.001

Xu, X., Hou, G., & Wang, J. (2022). Research on digital transformation based on complex systems: Visualization of knowledge maps and construction of a theoretical framework. *Sustainability*, *14*(5), 2683. doi:10.3390u14052683

KEY TERMS AND DEFINITIONS

Big Data: Is a diverse, complex, and voluminous sets of data produced at a very high velocity rate used by organizations to help sound, accurate, and fast decision to be made.

Business Model: Is the company's scheme of generating profits from products, or services in the target market the company decided to serve.

Digital Business: Is employing digital technologies throughout the whole business operations to generate revenues, enhance performance, and bring about valuable insights and experience.

Digital Strategy: Is the blueprint that tailors the company's strategy within digital economy.

Disruptive Innovation: Is the innovation that significantly changes the fabric, patterns, and the way companies operates and do business.

E-Wallet (or Digital Wallet): Is sort of software-based system used to conduct online transactions.

Industry 4.0: Is the Fourth Industrial Revolution resulting from automation, industrial internet of things, smart factories, and artificial intelligence.

Chapter 4
COVID-19:
The Pandemic's Outcome on Cryptocurrency-Bitcoin Futures

Sumi K. V.
IMK, India

ABSTRACT

The SARS-CoV-19 coronavirus pandemic has had a huge economic impact around the world. As a result, the behaviour of all financial instruments, including cryptocurrencies, was significantly affected. Following the COVID-19 market crash, cryptocurrency derivative markets have seen a massive increase in popularity as speculators try to profit from the price and trading volume instability. The fluctuations in the virtual currency market during this time span seem to be a reflection of shifts in other capital and commodity markets. During this challenging era, the demand has remained relatively stable. It's yet another example of how cryptocurrencies can be viewed as a fully developed financial tool. Despite mediocre trade volume, the number of markets available increased significantly in the run-up to this case.

INTRODUCTION

At the height of the global financial crisis in 2008, the first cryptocurrency, bitcoin, was launched. Its developers hoped to create a tool that would allow people to conduct transactions over the Internet without the involvement of a central bank. In this light, cryptocurrencies can be viewed as a stand-alone financial tool. Money transfers from one individual to another are currently handled by financial institutions such as banks. The invention of cryptocurrency allowed for direct transactions

DOI: 10.4018/978-1-7998-9117-8.ch004

Figure 1.

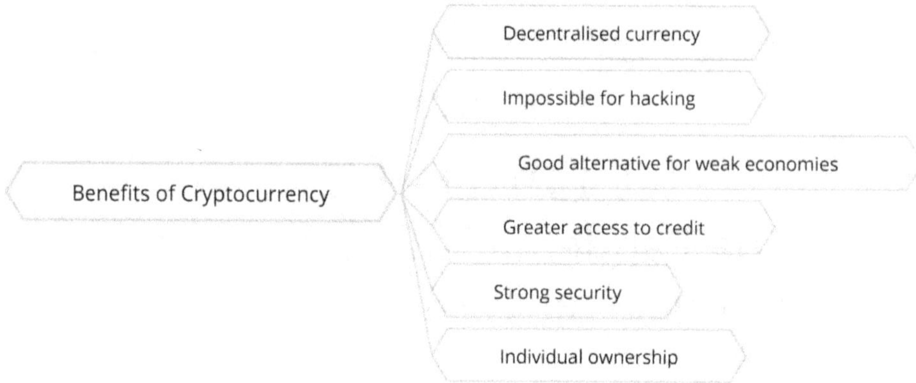

between users without the use of middlemen. Users can transfer money to other users directly using cryptocurrency. In 2009, 'Satoshi Nakamoto' created the first cryptocurrency, Bitcoin. Satoshi Nakamoto's identity is unknown (Serada et al., 2021). Furthermore, this bitcoin is based on blockchain technology. There are only a certain number of coins available. And each bitcoin has its own code. Any coin transaction is saved as a block, and all of the transactions for that coin are linked together in a chain, hence the name blockchain technology. Since bitcoin's code is open source, several related cryptocurrencies such as Etherum and Ripple arose as a result of its development. Anyone can read the code and modify it to create their own version of cryptocurrency.

Types of Cryptocurrency

Cryptocurrencies can behave like real money—in certain ways, they are real money—but they exist in a digital form with no central authority to manage or govern them. Cryptocurrencies are a true product of the digital age, since they work without the intervention of banks, governments, or any other intermediary (Shubhani Aggarwal, Neeraj Kumar, 2021). However, you will almost always need to buy and sell your digital asset via a digital currency exchange.

Cryptocurrency Futures

Bitcoin and other digital currencies are risky investments. Many traders attempt to control their risk by simply purchasing or selling an asset as the price falls or rises. The disadvantage of this strategy is that money is often left on the table when you exit the market. Cryptocurrency futures allow you to optimise your profits by

Figure 2.

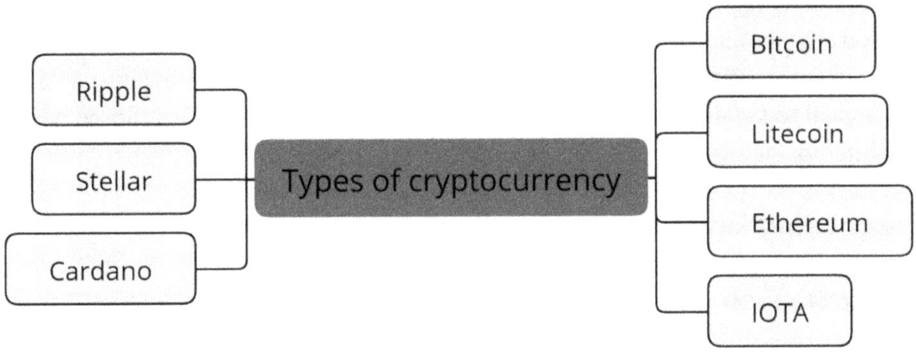

leveraging the power of leverage and employing advanced trading strategies. Use futures to bet on market direction and reduce risk while keeping less cryptocurrency than on a spot exchange.

Futures Trading

Futures, also known as futures contracts, are agreements to purchase or sell an asset at a fixed price at a later date. Traders usually use them to protect other investments or lock in gains while investing in volatile markets. There are a number of benefits to this type of trading.

Figure 3.

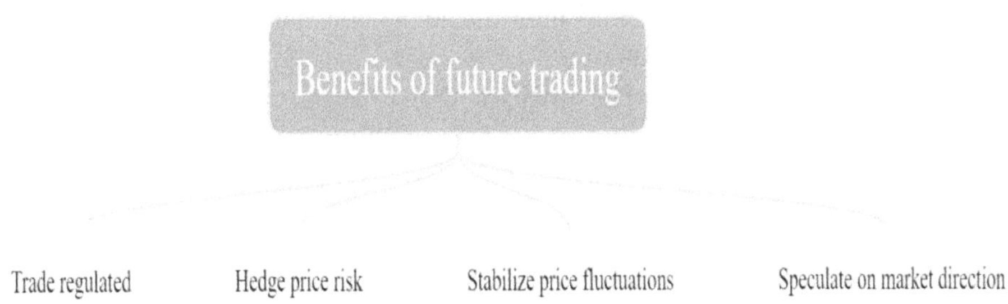

Bitcoin

Bitcoin is a modern digital currency that was developed in 2009 by an anonymous person identified only by the pseudonym Satoshi Nakamoto. No middlemen – that is, no banks – are involved in the transactions. Bitcoin can be used to purchase Xbox games, book hotels on Expedia, and search for furniture on Overstock. Bitcoins can be used to make anonymous purchases. Furthermore, since bitcoins are not bound to any country or controlled, international transfers are simple and inexpensive. They can appeal to small businesses because there are no credit card fees. Some people buy bitcoins purely as a gamble, hoping that their value will rise.

Purchasing Bitcoins

On Exchanges

Many "bitcoin exchanges" enable people to buy and sell bitcoins using a variety of currencies. Coinbase, along with Bitstamp and Bitfinex, is a popular cryptocurrency exchange.

Bitcoin Mining

The passage of time has shifted dramatically. Other ways of earning money are displacing conventional methods. Nowadays, people are looking for ways to make money online. Bitcoin mining is one proven method for making a significant profit on investment. Money can be made by mining Bitcoin, but there is no guarantee of a profit. Mining hardware, energy rates, and Bitcoin's price are all factors to consider. Transactions are broadcasted to the peer-to-peer network through Bitcoin's decentralised design, and once broadcasted, they must be checked, ensuring that the transaction is legitimate, and then registered on the public transaction ledger, known as the Bitcoin blockchain. For mining the things needed is a computer with internet connectivity in order to start mining and become a node in the peer-to-peer network, and to start making Bitcoins.

While mining Bitcoins can be difficult and time-consuming, especially for beginners, the end result will not let you down. Mining Bitcoins necessitates the use of sophisticated machines. To solve mathematical equations in exchange for Bitcoins, such devices consume a lot of electricity. Individually mining Bitcoins could be costly. As a result, it is advised that it is better to enter a mining pool. Working with other miners is a good idea in this case because it will ensure to pool the money and split rewards based on individual results.

The steps involved in bitcoin mining is depicted below:

Figure 4.

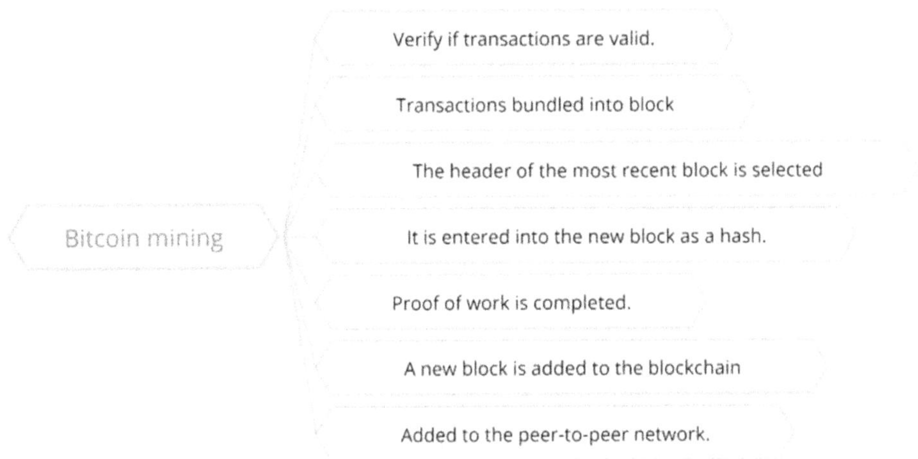

BITCOIN FUTURES

A futures contract is an agreement to buy or sell something at a pre-determined price at a later date. Bitcoin future contracts have become increasingly common in recent years, but managing them can be difficult due to Bitcoin's high volatility. Bitcoin futures, on the other hand, enable investors to bet on the price of Bitcoin in the future. Furthermore, investors can trade Bitcoin effectively even if they do not own the currency at the time (Fiammetta Menchetti, 2021). The aim of Bitcoin trading is for a buyer to lock in a lower price and a seller to lock in a higher price in the future. This ensures that there are no bitcoins involved in the transaction. This is due to the fact that futures are cash-settled contracts, meaning that the buyer pays the value of the bitcoin at the agreed date and the seller collects the value in cash. Bitcoin is a cryptocurrency that does not exchange hands (Corrado, C.J., (1989).).

Bitcoin Futures Exchanges

The Commodity Futures Trading Commission (CFTC) oversees Bitcoin futures trading and clearing. The CFTC is the only regulatory body in charge of Bitcoin futures markets in the United States. However, investors should be aware that regulations vary by region. Bakkt and Intercontinental Exchange are two other exchanges that offer physical delivery of monthly and even regular Bitcoin futures contracts. Physical delivery refers to the requirement that the actual asset be delivered

Figure 5.
Source: Barchart.com

on the agreed date, rather than exchanging it for a different asset, in an options or futures contract (Fostel, A. and Geanakoplos, J., (2012).

Derivative Premiums

Futures' main purpose is to lock in future rates at a reasonable rate by speculating on leverage to produce outsized returns (and losses). This endeavor's success or failure is determined by a variety of internal and external factors. Risk premium is a crucial aspect of contracts that determines outcomes. This is the difference in value between the spot price at a future date and the price of a futures contract of the same maturity date. 4 This premium is typically determined by an asset's cost of carry as well as any depreciation impact.

Benefits and Drawbacks of Trading Bitcoin Futures

Bitcoin futures contracts are now valid for block trading, which means that brokers will exchange massive volumes of them. The one-hour period of inactivity suggests a simple open and close trading time for bitcoin futures, which are exchanged on an exchange. Futures options (having the option to buy or sell at a pre-determined

Figure 6.

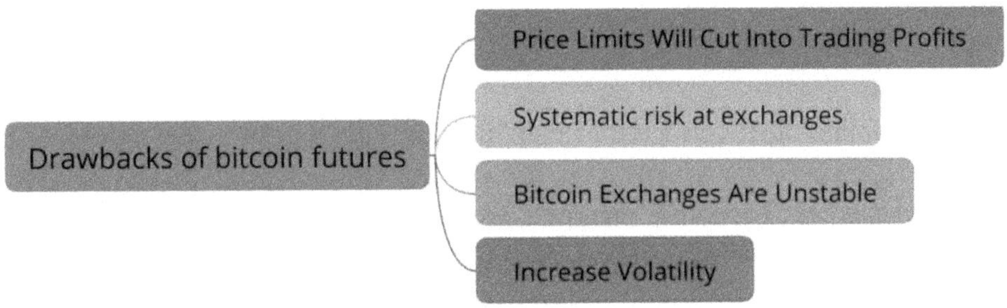

date but not actually obliged to buy or sell) are also open, giving investors another way to control risk or speculate on price.

Drawbacks

Trading futures, in general, necessitates a high level of knowledge. As previously mentioned, the method requires a great deal of speculation, so it might not be suitable for novice investors.(Kaspersky)

1. Price limits will cut the trading profits

The price caps are intended to reduce the negative effects of bitcoin's unpredictable price movements on futures markets. However, they may end up reducing trader profits. This is because the reference price for bitcoin derivatives is derived from uncontrolled market exchanges, where price swings of more than 20% have become commonplace. As a result, futures traders will not gain from a 20% increase in bitcoin prices on the underlying exchanges.

2. Systematic Risk

Bitcoin's limited history is littered with wild price swings and crashes. However, these price movements occurred in short bursts, allowing traders to recoup quickly. The overall impact of such an incident (on bitcoin exchanges) is relatively small.

3. Bitcoin Exchanges are relatively unstable

Bitcoin exchanges, which set the asset's reference price, generally operate in uncontrolled markets. They are vulnerable to manipulation without the watchful eye of a regulator.

4. The Timing of Bitcoin Futures may Increase Volatility

Futures markets, in general, are predecessors to commodity price stability since they attract speculators and traders. However, given the recent price swings in bitcoin, some are questioning the wisdom of bringing in additional players at this time (Bariviera, A.F., 2017)).

Digital Wallet

Since Bitcoin futures trades are settled financially, investors need a digital wallet to exchange them. If traded in Bitcoin, it's better to have a wallet so that the investor don't have all of the coins on an exchange, making less vulnerable to hacking. To use Bitcoin futures, the investor must first open an account with a licenced broker. The broker will keep track of investors account and ensure that trades are completed. Futures commission merchants (FCMs) and launching brokers are two types of futures brokerage firms (IB)

Overall, Bitcoin futures may be a good way to get into Bitcoin without having to purchase and keep tokens. Futures trading, on the other hand, is usually not for beginners and carries a high level of risk. Bitcoin and blockchain in general – may be a volatile commodity in and of itself. Before an investor jump in, make to do a homework so that the investor can find a broker, develop a plan, and even interact with a knowledgeable advisor who can help significantly

Impact of Futures Market on Bitcoin and its Investors

The launch of the bitcoin futures market has little or no effect on price in the long run, as long-term value is determined by core fundamentals (adoption, use-cases etc.). Futures, on the other hand, help to maintain market integrity by reducing uncertainty and increasing liquidity for institutional investors. Investors will be able to better judge consumer sentiment and function as a result of it because it gives them another prism through which to examine the bitcoin market. It also allows for wild speculation to be honed, as seen above, and it aids in market discovery. The addition of derivatives to the bitcoin market was a positive step that helped to solidify the asset's financial structure. The additional access points have encouraged investors to treat BTC holdings like a conventional investment by growing market capitalisation and trade volume. This generates further interest in the space and helps to create bitcoin as a viable investment option (Möser, M. Böhme, R., and Breuker D., 2013).

The Impact of Futures Trading on OTC Firm Yield Generation

Futures trading allows large-holding investors to leverage their current balance sheet and benefit from arbitrage gains and yield from their holdings. This approach is particularly useful for OTC crypto firms, as it allows them to generate interest for their clients by using their custody holdings. Ciaian, P (2016)

Although bitcoin capital gains value is increasing by the day, the real benefit of futures is their ability to protect against black swan events and other big price influencers, or simply reap delta-neutral yield. Firms restrict their downside by protecting their holdings with futures contracts, while greatly increasing the upside for their clients.

Impact of COVID-19 on Crypto-Mining.

Numerous pieces of cryptocurrency mining equipment have been developed over the years, and with prices currently falling, these pieces of equipment are vulnerable to certain inefficiencies. Mining farms became increasingly important for balancing the modern algorithms, as these pieces of equipment became ineffective. Isolation and quarantine are the main causes of this because there is less movement into mining farms, despite the fact that investors consider cryptocurrencies to be "secure assets" throughout these days. Prices continue to depreciate in comparison to initial forecasts (Jamal Bouoiyour, Refk Selmi,2019).

Regulation Still in the Way

Regulation, on the other hand, remains the most significant risk for cryptocurrencies as a whole. Although it is becoming more commonplace, in many countries it is still not generally accepted or supervised. Singapore is one of the most notable exceptions. The Singapore Monetary Authority (MAS) has developed a regulatory structure that will make it easier for individual investors to buy, sell, and keep cryptocurrencies. Given the potential for cryptocurrencies to transform the financial landscape and beyond, countries must act quickly to develop strong regulations. But if the pandemic has taught us something, it's that bitcoin and altcoins have real value in today's world – and it's not just speculation. It's a reality (Mackinlay, C. (1997).

Bitcoin Futures in Post Pandemic Era

There have been several serious financial crises in the past, but the unforeseeable challenges posed by the coronavirus pandemic are unparalleled. One of the most significant distinctions between previous crises, such as the 2008 financial crisis or the Great Depression of the 1930s, is that, unlike the COVID-19 pandemic, they did not place immediate brakes on the economy's wheels. However, with the coronavirus choking economic activity entirely, the global stock market has lost its previous resiliency and is in a severe tailspin. The global financial markets have probably never experienced such a liquidity crisis and faced such an uncertain future in modern history (Cheung, A., Roca, E. and Su, J., (2015)).

The cryptocurrency market could not have remained unaffected by the massive economic challenges that it faces. COVID-19 had a much smaller effect on Bitcoin than it did on global financial markets. To put it another way, global investors were putting their confidence in digital currencies while other asset classes lagged.

Although it is undeniable that Bitcoin and Bitcoin Futures were able to survive the coronavirus outbreak, the issue of their long-term viability in the post-pandemic period remains a source of concern for crypto enthusiasts (Möser, M. Böhme, R., and Breuker D., (2013).

The following are some of the characteristics that distinguish Bitcoin as a specific investment and a contender for being an asset class of choice for investors.

- Bitcoin and other cryptocurrencies are attractive investment opportunities because of their transparency.
- Growing global digitization can also provide a solid base for the potential growth of Bitcoin and Bitcoin futures.
- Unlike gold (which is seen as a good investment in difficult times), Bitcoin is unaffected by supply, logistics, or physical boundary problems.
- Bitcoin's steady evolution over time and increasing adoption, as well as the possibility of investing in Bitcoin futures.
- The post-pandemic era's fiscal instability would hasten the transition from fiat currencies (paper currencies) to digital currencies.

CONCLUSION

The fear of bitcoin halving persists in the minds of investors, who believe that costs will have to be cut in half in order to limit liquidity in the crypto market. In terms of balancing the books, investors and analysts have considered this halving policy to be an intriguing study. These analyses are also expected to materialise in the coming months, which will undoubtedly have an effect on future rates. The only place where we will be able to find the correct answers is in the future. As the coronavirus (COVID-19) pandemic continues to develop, arriving in the future would be the only way to know how things will ultimately turn out. If the twenty-first century was meant to be the era of digital currencies, then the disastrous year of 2020 may be a watershed moment for Bitcoin. It's been said that great things come from hardship, and it's possible that the post-pandemic period will prove to be the ideal time for Bitcoin to usher in a new era of virtual currencies.

REFERENCES

Aggarwal, S., Kumar, N., & Rai, P. (Eds.). (2021). *The Blockchain Technology for Secure and Smart Applications across Industry Verticals* (Vol. 121). Advances in Computers. doi:10.1016/bs.adcom.2020.08.012

Bouoiyour & Selmi. (2019). How do futures contracts affect Bitcoin prices? *Economics Bulletin, 39*(2), 1127-1134.

Cheung, A., Roca, E., & Su, J. (2015). Crypto-currency bubbles: An application of the Phillips Shi-Yu (2013) methodology on Mt. Gox bitcoin prices. *Applied Economics, 47*(23), 2348–2358. doi:10.1080/00036846.2015.1005827

Ciaian, P., Rajcaniova, M., & Kancs, A. (2016). The Economics of Bitcoin Price Formation. *Applied Economics, 48*(19), 1799–1815. doi:10.1080/00036846.2015.1109038

Corrado, C. J. (1989). A non-parametric test for abnormal security price performance in event studies. *Journal of Financial Economics, 23*(2), 385–395. doi:10.1016/0304-405X(89)90064-0

Fostel, A., & Geanakoplos, J. (2012). Tranching, CDS, and Asset Prices: How Financial Innovation Can Cause Bubbles and Crashes. *American Economic Journal. Macroeconomics, 4*(1), 190–225. doi:10.1257/mac.4.1.190

Mackinlay, C. (1997). Event Studies in Finance and Economics. *Journal of Economic Literature, 35*, 13–39.

Menchetti, Cipollini, & Mealli. (2021). *Causal effect of regulated Bitcoin futures on volatility and volume.* Academic Press.

Möser, M., Böhme, R., & Breuker, D. (2013). An inquiry into money laundering tools in the Bitcoin ecosystem. *2013 APWG eCrime Researchers Summit.* https://ieeexplore.ieee.org/document/6805780

Serada, Sihvonen, & Harviainen. (2021). Crypto Kitties and the New Ludic Economy: How Blockchain Introduces Value, Ownership, and Scarcity in Digital Gaming. Academic Press.

What is cryptocurrency and how does it work? (n.d.). https://www.kaspersky.com/resource-center/definitions/what-is-cryptocurrency

ADDITIONAL READING

Bouri, E., Molnár, P., Azzi, G., Roubaud, D., & Hagfors, L. (2017). On the hedge and safe haven properties of Bitcoin: Is it really more than a diversifier? *Finance Research Letters*, *20*, 192–198. doi:10.1016/j.frl.2016.09.025

Cheah, E.-T., & Fry, J. (2015). Speculative bubbles in bitcoin markets? An empirical investigation into the fundamental value of bitcoin. *Economics Letters*, *130*, 32–36. doi:10.1016/j.econlet.2015.02.029

Dwyer, G. P. (2015). The economics of bitcoin and similar private digital currencies. *Journal of Financial Stability*, *17*, 81–91. doi:10.1016/j.jfs.2014.11.006

Foster, F. D., & Viswanathan, S. (1993). Variations in trading volume, return volatility, and trading costs: Evidence on recent price formation models. *The Journal of Finance*, *48*(1), 187–211. doi:10.1111/j.1540-6261.1993.tb04706.x

Hayes, A. S. (2017). Cryptocurrency value formation: An empirical study leading to a cost of production model for valuing bitcoin. *Telematics and Informatics*, *34*(7), 1308–1321. doi:10.1016/j.tele.2016.05.005

Howell, S. T., Niessner, M., & Yermack, D. (2018). *Initial coin offerings: Financing growth with cryptocurrency token sales (No. w24774)*. National Bureau of Economic Research. doi:10.3386/w24774

Raiborn, C., & Sivitanides, M. (2015). Accounting issues related to Bitcoins. *Journal of Corporate Accounting & Finance*, *26*(2), 25–34. doi:10.1002/jcaf.22016

Chapter 5
Examining the Impact of COVID-19 on Cryptocurrency Enforcement in the United States

Leo S. F. Lin
The University of Southern Mississippi, USA

ABSTRACT

This chapter examines how COVID-19 has impacted cryptocurrency enforcement at the state level. This author employs a qualitative single case study method and investigates the cryptocurrency enforcement actions of the United States Securities and Exchange Commission (SEC) in 2020. The data were collected from SEC cryptocurrency press releases and public statements. The US Securities and Exchange Commission (SEC) has brought 28 enforcement actions against companies and individuals in the crypto industry in 2020 regarding the three types of cryptocurrency enforcement actions and trading suspensions (trading suspension, litigation, and administrative proceeding). Among them, litigation is the most common type of cryptocurrency enforcement action taken by the SEC. This author concludes that the law enforcement agencies in the United States faced several challenges before and during the pandemic. Finally, the author suggests some measures that law enforcement agencies can take to address the above challenges.

INTRODUCTION

The Information Age has created a new concept of money–virtual currencies existing

DOI: 10.4018/978-1-7998-9117-8.ch005

solely in cyberspace in the form of intangible computer code (Bal, 2014). Decentralized virtual currencies are a new type of technology that can be used to transfer money, record data, and invest. They are also becoming household words (Hughes, 2017). According to different scholars, virtual currency has its importance and potential in the future economy. For example, virtual currency has the potential to revolutionize "how we transact on the same scale that email did with snail mail" (Brito and Castillo 2013). Virtual currency transactions have very little transactional cost compared to traditional currency transactions. In particular, virtual currencies offer advantages to developing economies and small businesses (Brito and Dourado 2014).

As a new financial technology, the public has a fast-growing interest in cryptocurrency. One continued debate is how heavily or lightly cryptocurrency should be regulated because virtual currency is based on the idea of exchanging value without the approval of an institution (Maftei, 2014). There are three types of schemes in virtual currency that can be identified (Parmar, 2014):

- It is a closed virtual currency scheme, for instance, the type of currency used in an online game.
- It has a unidirectional flow.
- It has bidirectional flows where the virtual currency acts like any other convertible currency, with two exchange rates.

Concerns are raised about the extent to which enforcement actions should be taken to protect the public. Virtual currencies represent a type of unregulated digital money and they provide security risks such as money laundering, financing illegal activities online (Dibrova, 2016). Companies and even criminals are using the gray areas of virtual currencies as they do not always come to the table with clean hands. For example, law enforcement agencies have linked Bitcoin to the deep web black market known as the Silk Road, a notorious source of illegal drugs, firearms, and hitmen. The case of United States v. Ulbricht (2014) shows how virtual currencies have been used as a means of transaction to exchange illicit goods on the dark web site like Silk Road. The regulatory wild-west surrounding virtual currencies and the anonymous nature of the transactions create an environment rife with massive price fluctuations and fraud schemes (Johnson 2016, 637). Lack of legislation and supervision is very beneficial to money launders. Therefore, virtual currencies "doubles the possible negative influence by reducing any possible protection for the society" (Dibrova, 2016).

In this chapter, this author provides an overview of cryptocurrency enforcement in the United States and conducts a qualitative single case-study method to examine the US Securities and Exchange Commission enforcement action as a means to illustrate the importance and risks of cryptocurrency during the pandemic. Secondary data were collected from the US government official websites and other reputed sources.

AN OVERVIEW OF THE DEVELOPMENT OF CRYPTOCURRENCY ENFORCEMENT IN THE UNITED STATES

Even though it is important to define virtual currencies, the definition tends to vary depending on the context, as the digital currency does not comfortably fit any existing classification or legal definition (Dibrova, 2016). Virtual currency is not a foreign currency, a traditional commodity, or a simple payment network (Brito, 2013). Virtual currency is a digital representation of value. It is a medium of exchange that operates like a currency in some environments but does not have all the "real" currency attributes. Virtual currency can be used as a substitute for real currency.

The most prominent agency regarding the regulation of virtual currencies is the Financial Crimes Enforcement Network ("FinCEN"), an enforcement arm of the United States Department of the Treasury. FinCEN's regulations define currency as:

The coin and paper money of the United States or of any other country that is designated as legal tender and that circulates and is customarily used and accepted as a medium of exchange in the country of issuance. (Department of Treasury, n.d.)

In referring to Bitcoin, the IRS states that:

In some environments, it operates like "real" currency—i.e., the coin and paper money of the United States or of any other country that is designated as legal tender circulates, and is customarily used and accepted as a medium of exchange in the country of issuance—but it does not have legal tender status in any jurisdiction. (IRS, 2014)

Legislative acts of the United States explain virtual currency to be a medium of exchange that operates like a currency in some environments but does not have all the attributes of real currency, which points to the absence of legal tender status in any jurisdiction (Dibrova, 2016). FinCEN identified and determined that regulatory treatment of administrators and exchangers are under three categories: "brokers and dealers of e-currencies and e-precious metals," "centralized convertible virtual currencies," and "decentralized convertible virtual currencies." Electronic trading in e-precious metals is the first type of virtual currency activity.

In 2008, FinCEN issued guidance stating that "as long as a broker or dealer in real currency or other commodities accepts and transmits funds solely to effect a *bona fide* purchase or sale of the real currency or other commodities for or with a customer, such person is not acting as a money transmitter under regulations." (U.S. Treasury Financial Crimes Enforcement Network, 2008). The guidance also notes that the definition of money transmitter excludes any person, such as a futures commission merchant, that is "registered with, and regulated or examined by…the Commodity Futures Trading Commission."

The second type is the convertible virtual currency with a centralized administrator or repository. The role is similar to a central bank in a regulated currency system. The administrator of that repository will be a money transmitter to the extent that it allows transferring value between persons or from one location to another. The exchanger's activities may take one of two forms. The first form involves an exchanger that accepts real currency from a user and transmits the value of that real currency to fund the user's convertible virtual currency account. The second form involves a de facto sale of convertible virtual currency that is not entirely transparent. The exchanger accepts currency from a user and privately credits the user with the exchanger's own convertible virtual currency (Stabile, Prior, and Hinkes 2020, 32).

"Decentralized convertible" virtual currency is a final type of convertible virtual currency activity. This type of currency is considered revolutionary because of its use of a distributed ledger. It has "no central repository and no single administrator" and "that persons may obtain it by their computing or manufacturing effort." Decentralized virtual currency distributes a ledger to all users and removes the need for a third-party intermediary. For many users, it is a type of money "without banks." It is difficult for regulatory agencies to monitor Bitcoin activity (Mullan, 2014a).

Bitcoin has emerged as a cryptocurrency because it was created to be superior to centralized currency systems in several respects. Bitcoin is an electronic currency transfer method that removes the costs of current electronic payment systems (Johnson, 2016).

FinCEN published a "Final Rule" on July 21, 2011, which amended definitions and other regulations relating to money services businesses (MSBs). An MSB is defined as,

A person wherever located doing business, whether or not on a regular basis or as an organized or licensed business concern, wholly or in substantial part within the United States, in one or more of the capacities listed in paragraphs (ff)(1) through (ff)(7) of this section. This includes but is not limited to maintenance of any agent, agency, branch, or office within the United States. (Department of Treasury, n.d.)

On July 29, 2011, FinCEN published the "Prepaid Access Rule" in its Final Rule and explained the regulatory treatment under these definitions of persons engaged in virtual currency transactions (Department of the Treasury, 2011).

In 2013, the Financial Crimes Enforcement Network (2013) issued "Guidance on Virtual Currencies and Regulatory Responsibilities" and pointed out that "virtual currencies" are subject to the Bank Secrecy Act (BSA) to persons creating, obtaining, distributing, exchanging, accepting, or transmitting virtual currencies. This guidance clarified that Bitcoin exchanges are considered money transmitters and must obtain all proper licenses to conduct business in the United States. This registration and licensing process include federal registration as a money service business (Mullan, 2014b).

THE REGULATORY CHALLENGE

As virtual currencies continue to enjoy widespread importance in use and growth, stakeholders are seeking more regulatory certainty. However, implementing regulations for cryptocurrency in the United States continues to be an arduous task.

The Supremacy Clause (Article VI, Clause 2) of the Constitution of the United States prescribes that in the case of conflict between federal law and state law, federal law must be applied. With no federal law in place, the oversight responsibility for virtual currencies has largely fallen to the states, resulting in a multiplicity of laws and policy directions on the legality and usage of cryptocurrencies.

One of the biggest challenges to implementing regulation at the federal level is the jurisdictional overlap of regulatory agencies, which will have to be involved if policies are to be put in place. The jurisdictional overlap is further complicated by the multiplicity of classifications and interpretations of what cryptos are by the different government agencies.

While the SEC is seen as the agency that will be the main regulator, Treasury, FinCEN, the Federal Reserve Board, and the CFTC also have roles to play if a robust regulatory policy is to be put in place.

What are Regulators Most Concerned About?

The major concern for regulators revolves around the following: The first concern is money laundering. The anonymity of virtual currencies makes it appealing to people involved in illicit activities. Criminal groups engaged in fraud, terrorism, human trafficking, etc., find cryptocurrencies especially useful for transacting across the globe. Anonymity can make it near-impossible for regulators to detect money laundering and other financial crimes. The threat posed by the ability to transact anonymously has caused government agencies in some quarters to call for global coordination to achieve success in regulating virtual currencies. However, it is very doubtful that total transparency will ever be achieved. As technological developments continue to advance, new methods of increasing anonymity continue to arise. One such method is by employing an algorithmic process called "zero-knowledge proof" to hide the value of the digital currency being transacted. Another method some platforms employ is combining transactions to increase the difficulty of analyzing where the currency was sent.

A second major concern is a fraud and investor protection. The Securities and Exchange Commission (SEC) has designated certain digital currencies as securities, so it treats crimes perpetrated using digital currencies in the same manner as it treats those carried out with fiat currencies. One popular example was the case of Trendon T. Shavers in 2013. He was charged for defrauding investors of what amounted to $4.5 million worth of Bitcoin through Bitcoin Savings and Trust (BTCST), which was deemed as being "an unincorporated online investment scheme" by the SEC. His defense was to argue that Bitcoin isn't money, but the magistrate judge stated, "it is clear that Bitcoin can be used as money. It can be used to purchase goods or services, and as Shaver's stated, it is used to pay for individual living expenses. The only limitation of Bitcoin is that it is limited to those places that accept it as currency. However, it can also be exchanged for conventional currencies, such as the US dollar, Euro, Yen, and Yuan. Therefore, Bitcoin is a currency or form of money, and investors wishing to invest in BTCST provided an investment of money." (Sec. & Exch. Comm'n v. Shavers, 2014)

THE CASE: THE US SECURITIES AND EXCHANGE COMMISSION ENFORCEMENT ACTION

According to Elliptic's analysis of US regulatory enforcement actions since 2009, it shows that $2.5 billion in penalties have been imposed against firms and individuals dealing in crypto. This includes "penalties imposed by the SEC ($1.69 billion), CFTC ($624 million), FinCEN ($183 million), and OFAC ($606k). The majority of these penalties relate to unregistered securities offerings ($1.38 billion), fraud ($928 million), and AML violations ($183 million). The penalties can be categorized as civil penalties ($722 million), disgorgements ($1.62 billion), and restitution ($161 million)." (Robinson, 2021)

The US Securities and Exchange Commission (SEC) started its cryptocurrency enforcement action in 2013. A key purpose of SEC investigations is safeguarding millions of investors and instilling confidence in the integrity of markets (Clayton, 2019). The SEC has a three-part mission to protect investors; maintain fair, orderly, and efficient markets; and facilitate capital formation. SEC investigations and enforcement actions play a critical role in carrying out each of these objectives

(Blackburne et al. 2021). The Enforcement division of the SEC executes the law enforcement function by: (U.S. Securities and Exchange Commission, 2017):

1. recommending the commencement of investigations of securities law violations,
2. recommending that the Commission bring civil actions in federal court or before an administrative law judge, and
3. prosecuting these cases on behalf of the Commission

Violations that may lead to SEC investigations include misrepresentation of important securities information, manipulating market prices, stealing customers' funds, violating broker-dealer's responsibility, insider trading, and selling unregistered securities. The investigations are conducted privately by using various sources, including market surveillance activities, investor tips, and complaints. SEC could take "civil action" and "administrative action." In the civil action, the SEC files a complaint with a US District Court and asks the court for a sanction or remedy; In administrative action, the SEC can seek various sanctions through the administrative proceeding process (U.S. Securities and Exchange Commission, 2017). The federal securities laws also allow the SEC to suspend trading in any stock for up to ten trading days when the SEC determines that a trading suspension is required in the public interest and for the protection of investors.

In response to Covid-19, the Division of Enforcement of SEC took several actions. First, a Coronavirus Steering Committee was formed to oversee the protection of retail investors by coordinating investigations of potential misconduct in the areas of microcap, insider trading, and financial fraud. Second, the Division's Office of Market Intelligence triaged approximately 16,000 tips, complaints, and referrals and opened more than 150 COVID-related inquiries and investigations. More than 700 enforcement cases were brought to attention during 2020 (U.S. Securities and Exchange Commission, 2020). Several cases are highlighted (see Table 1).

Regarding cryptocurrency enforcement, SEC has worked with different agencies, including Commodity Futures Trading Commission (CFTC), Financial Industry Regulatory Authority (FINRA), and FinCEN, for conducting enforcement actions. According to data provided by Cornerstone Research, between 2013 and 2020, there are a total of 75 cryptocurrency enforcement actions and 19 trading suspension orders against digital asset participants. The majority of litigations involved an allegedly fraudulent scheme, unregistered securities offering violation, or allegation of unregistered securities offering combined with a fraud allegation (Cornerstone Research, 2020). During the pandemic in 2020, there were a total of seventeen cryptocurrency litigation actions and nine administrative proceeding actions taken by the SEC. Two trading suspensions were enforced against "Token Communication Ltd" and "Vortex Blockchain Technologies Inc," both were in September (see Figure 1).

Table 1. Important SEC enforcement cases in 2020

Name of the case	Description	Action type	Penalty
Wells Fargo & Co.	Wells Fargo misled investors about the success of its core business strategy at a time when it was opening unauthorized or fraudulent accounts for unknowing customers and selling unnecessary products that went unused.	Settled action	$500 million civil penalty
Telegram Group Inc.	Telegram Group Inc. allegedly operated an unregistered offering of digital tokens called "Grams" in violation of the federal securities laws.	Emergency action	$18.5 million civil penalty
Bausch Health (formerly Valeant Pharmaceuticals)	Valeant improperly recognized revenue and made misleading disclosures in SEC filings and earnings presentations.	Settled action	$45 million civil penalty
BMW AG.	BMW and two of its US subsidiaries disclosed inaccurate and misleading information about BMW's retail sales volume in the US while raising approximately $18 billion from investors in several corporate bond offerings.	Settled action	$18 million (a joint penalty)
J.P. Morgan Securities LLC.	J.P. Morgan fraudulently engaged in manipulative trading of US Treasury securities.	Settled action	$25 million civil penalty

Source: SEC Enforcement Annual Report; Table made by the author

In 2020, there were a total of 15 SEC cryptocurrency press releases and public statements. Many cases involve crimes related to the initial coin offering (ICO) of digital asset securities. One of the key reasons why ICO became popular is that ICO helps raise start-up capital in a short time. Especially for high-tech companies such as the blockchain industry. ICO allows them to attract investors and to walk in a gray area because this field is still "fairly new, non-standardized and poorly regulated" (Lahajnar and Rozanec 2018).

Regulatory Enforcement Challenges Resulting from the Pandemic

According to the SEC Enforcement Report for 2020, "The COVID-19 pandemic has disrupted many of the Division's traditional methods of conducting investigations as it works to promote the safety and well-being of its staff while bringing meaningful cases to protecting investors. For example, the ability to take witness testimony, conduct in-person Wells meetings, and litigate cases in court have all been impacted.

Figure 1. SEC cryptocurrency enforcement actions in 2020

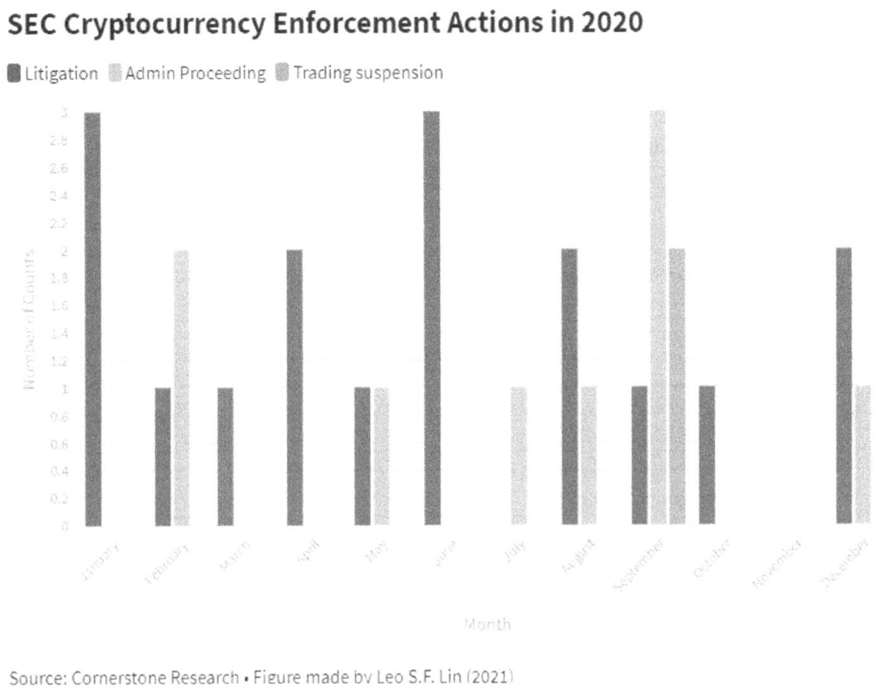

Although these methods cannot be completely replaced, the Division has worked hard to find innovative ways to ensure that investigations continue to move efficiently and quickly."

"While under mandatory telework orders, the Division of Enforcement has conducted numerous remote testimony sessions through internet-based video platforms, which allow staff to share documents with the witness while asking questions. The Division also held Wells meetings by video with multimedia presentations. Even courts have begun conducting remote hearings and bench trials by video, allowing our trial unit to litigate several important cases as a result successfully. As it is uncertain when we will be able to return to our offices and begin live meetings and testimony, we will continue to find ways to improve on our remote capabilities and ways to conduct investigations efficiently remotely." (U.S. Securities and Exchange Commission, 2020)

The fiscal Year 2020 was another successful year for the Division of Enforcement, despite the unprecedented challenges posed by the global COVID-19 pandemic. Since mid-March, the entire Division has been working from home, which has created unique impediments to several important aspects of our work, such as taking testimony from witnesses, gathering evidence, and litigating cases in court. Nevertheless, the

Table 2. SEC cryptocurrency enforcement cases press releases

Date	Title of the press release	Name of main criminal or company
January 17	SEC Charges Convicted Criminal Who Conducted Fraudulent ICO Using a Fake Identity	Boaz Manor
February 11	SEC Charges Orchestrator of Cryptocurrency Scheme Ensnaring Physicians	Michael W. Ackerman
February 19	ICO Issuer Settles SEC Registration Charges, Agrees to Return Funds and Register Tokens As Securities	Enigma MPC
February 27	Actor Steven Seagal Charged With Unlawfully Touting Digital Asset Offering	Steven Seagal
March 20	SEC Emergency Action Stops Digital Asset Scam	Robert Dunlap and Nicole Bowdler
May 28	Unregistered $25.5 Million ICO Issuer to Return Money for Distribution to Investors	BitClave PTE Ltd.
June 19	SEC Emergency Action Halts Brothers' Cryptocurrency Offering Fraud	Sean Hvizdzak and Shane Hvizdzak
June 25	SEC Charges Issuer, CEO, and Lobbyist With Defrauding Investors in AML BitCoin	NAC Foundation
August 13	SEC Charges Issuer and CEO With Misrepresenting Platform Technology in Fraudulent ICO	Boon.Tech
September 11	SEC Charges Film Producer, Rapper, and Others for Participation in Two Fraudulent ICOs	Ryan Felton
September 15	Unregistered ICO Issuer Agrees to Disable Tokens and Pay Penalty for Distribution to Harmed Investors	Unikrn Inc.
October 5	SEC Charges John McAfee With Fraudulently Touting ICOs	John McAfee
October 21	SEC Obtains Final Judgment Against Kik Interactive For Unregistered Offering	Kik Interactive Inc.
December 22	SEC Charges Ripple and Two Executives with Conducting $1.3 Billion Unregistered Securities Offering	Ripple Labs Inc.
December 28	SEC Obtains Emergency Asset Freeze, Charges Crypto Fund Manager with Fraud	Virgil Capital LLC

Source: SEC; Table made by the author

Division found ways to recommend meaningful cases to the Commission and to protect the investing public. In the face of great adversity, the Commission brought 715 enforcement actions in the Fiscal Year 2020. Impressively, the Commission brought 492 of these cases after the instituting mandatory telework in mid-March."

Important Regulatory Enforcement Cases in 2021

Despite the challenges the Commission faced in 2020 due to lockdown measures, the Commission was able to bounce back in 2021. It secured several settlements which include:

SEC vs. BLOTICS (July 14, 2021): The SEC's order discovers that United Kingdom-based Blotics Ltd. violated the anti-touting provisions of the federal securities laws by failing to disclose the compensation it received from issuers of the digital asset securities it profiled (U.S. Securities and Exchange Commission, 2021c).

SEC vs. BLOCKCHAIN Credit Partners and Founders (August 6, 2021): The Securities and Exchange Commission (2021b) … charged two Florida men and their Cayman Islands company for unregistered sales of more than $30 million of securities using smart contracts and so-called "decentralized finance" (DeFi) technology, and for misleading investors concerning the operations and profitability of their business DeFi Money Market.

SEC vs. POLONIEX (August 9, 2021): The Securities and Exchange Commission (2021a) ... announced that Poloniex LLC has agreed to pay more than $10 million to settle charges for operating an unregistered online digital asset exchange in connection with its operation of a trading platform that facilitated buying and selling of digital asset securities.

RECOMMENDATIONS

The SEC and other regulatory agencies are working hard to enhance cryptocurrency enforcement measures, and much success has been recorded since 2020. However, there are still several challenges that US law enforcement agencies are facing.

Nascent Technologies: Policing the technology sector is usually something law enforcement officers are unfamiliar with. For example, blockchain-related technologies are complex and constantly changing. Investigators have to learn and familiarize themselves with initial coin offerings (ICOs) and how criminals use new technology platforms to communicate. The author recommends that the regulatory agencies at the federal and state level collaborate with Crypto Industry experts to set up an ongoing training program for the staff of their agencies, especially those in departments responsible for investigating and recommending which cases the agency should prosecute. Having an in-depth understanding of the technologies and how they can be used will enable investigators to detect criminal activities much more easily. It will also enable investigators to preempt criminal activities and put in place measures that will prevent their occurrence instead of constantly chasing after those who have already perpetrated the crime.

Agility: Regulatory agencies must work with the Legislative and Executive arms of government to ensure resources they require to enforce regulations are available when needed adequately. Criminals who seek to exploit cryptocurrencies to carry out their activities are not resting on their oars. They are constantly deploying their resources towards developing new methods and technologies to facilitate their illicit activities. As new variants of the COVID-19 virus threaten societies worldwide and raise the potential for lockdown measures once again, criminal elements are preparing to capitalize on whatever opportunities they find. Regulatory agencies must, of a necessity, deploy resources in like manner if they are to counteract the activities of criminal elements.

Cross-Border Collaboration: In a digitalized and globalized world, criminals take advantage of the internet and technology for unlawful activities in cyberspace (Lin and Nomikos 2018). Therefore, cryptocurrency is an ideal tool for cybercriminals, as cryptocurrencies are native to the internet, and the internet is a global network that can be accessed from any part of the world. Illicit cryptocurrency activities are occurring on a cross-border basis in multiple jurisdictions. Criminals can carry out fraudulent schemes remotely from the comfort of safe havens across the globe. Many crypto assets are not traceable because they operate outside the United States, and even in cases where they are traceable, if they are out of US jurisdiction, there is very little that regulatory agencies can do if there is no collaboration with the other nation involved. Regulatory agencies across the globe must develop a partnership structure that will enable them to work together to investigate and prosecute cases.

Public-Private Partnerships: Government agencies should engage and work in partnership with private companies operating in the crypto industry to ensure they fully understand the laid-down regulations and how to apply them to their businesses. Government agencies should also develop a means by which private companies, big and small, can share the difficulties they face in meeting regulatory requirements to attain a resolution. The Public-Private partnership could also take the form of an advisory body that gives private businesses a medium through which they can guide regulatory authorities on new developments and help familiarize the government agents with new technologies. Regulatory agencies could also look beyond financial institutions to other non-financial entities within the crypto industry, such as analysts, to develop trusted relationships with them to communicate to their audience the importance of being vigilant and the risks inherent in crypto activities.

Ease of Adoption and Application: Regulators must work with virtual currency companies as they draft policies. While regulators shouldn't allow the companies to dictate what laws will contain, their input is of great importance. Getting licensed to run a virtual currency operation in New York, for example, could cost up to $100,000 when one factor other costs such as legal fees. These fees are too exorbitant, so they triggered a mass emigration of crypto companies, which has been termed "the Mass

Exodus." Pricing licenses out of the majority of businesses not only discourages companies from legalizing their operations but also stifles innovation. Regulators should take steps to ensure all stakeholders are being considered as laws are being formed. Moreover, the final policy presents the industry with an equal playing field for one and all.

CONCLUSION

The illicit use of cryptocurrency is expected to evolve and further expand during the post-pandemic period. With the continuous advancement of cryptocurrency technology and the growing need to use cryptocurrency for transactions, criminals stand to make huge gains. However, in digitized societies, the illicit use of cryptocurrency infringes public safety in cyberspace and across national borders.

Many potential security threats are linked in one way or another to the illicit use of cryptocurrencies, such as terrorist financing and transnational organized crime. Rogue states can also use virtual currencies to avoid international sanctions. These security threats challenge the traditional method of policing companies and whole countries.

US regulatory agencies need to work with state, corporate, and international partners to create a cohesive set of laws that will guide their regulation of cryptocurrencies and enable the smooth conduct of joint international investigations and law enforcement cooperation in the digital age. Even though all countries have the right to write their laws as they deem fit, governments across the globe need to work together under one umbrella to reduce the differences in laws between countries and prioritize public safety and national security in the post-pandemic period.

REFERENCES

Bal, A. M. (2014). *Taxation of virtual currency*. Leiden University.

Blackburne, T., Kepler, J. D., Quinn, P. J., & Taylor, D. (2021). Undisclosed SEC investigations. *Management Science*, *67*(6), 3403–3418. doi:10.1287/mnsc.2020.3805

Brito, J. (2013). *Beyond Silk Road: potential risks, threats, and promises of virtual currencies. In Testimony before the Senate Committee on Homeland Security and Governmental Affairs*. Mercatus Center at George Mason University.

Brito, J., & Castillo, A. (2013). *Bitcoin: A primer for policymakers*. Mercatus Center at George Mason University.

Brito, J., & Dourado, E. (2014). Comments to the New York Department of Financial Services on the proposed virtual currency regulatory framework. Public Interest Comment, Mercatus Center, George Mason University.

Dibrova, A. (2016). Virtual currency: New step in monetary development. *Procedia: Social and Behavioral Sciences*, *229*, 42–49. doi:10.1016/j.sbspro.2016.07.112

Johnson, Z. B. (2016). I Got 988 Problems but Bitcoin Ain't One: The Current Problems Presented by the Internal Revenue Service's Guidance on Virtual Currency. *U. Mem. L. Rev.*, *47*, 633.

Lahajnar & Rozanec. (2018). Initial coin offering (ICO) evaluation model. *Investment Management and Financial Innovations, 15*(4), 169-182.

Lin, L. S., & Nomikos, J. (2018). *Cybercrime in East and Southeast Asia: The Case of Taiwan*. Asia-Pacific Security Challenges.

Giblin, R. (2011). Code Wars: 10 Years of P2P Software Litigation. Edward Elgar Publishing.

Hutchinson, C. A. (2022). *Cryptocurrencies and the Regulatory Challenge*. Routledge.

Hughes, S. D. (2017). Cryptocurrency Regulations and Enforcement in the US. *W. St. UL Rev.*, *45*, 1.

Hofmann, J., Katzenbach, C., & Gollatz, K. (2016). Between Coordination and Regulation: Finding the Governance in Internet Governance. *New Media & Society*.

Maftei, L. (2014). Bitcoin-between legal and informal. *CES Working Papers, 6*(3), 53-59.

Mueller, M. L. (2010). *Networks and States: The Global Politics of Internet Governance*. MIT Press. doi:10.7551/mitpress/9780262014595.001.0001

Mullan, P. C. (2014a). Bitcoin Decentralized Virtual Currency. In The Digital Currency Challenge: Shaping Online Payment Systems through US Financial Regulations (pp. 84-92). Springer.

Nestarcova, D. (2019). *A Critical Appraisal of Initial Coin Offerings: Lifting the "Digital Token's Veil*. Brill. doi:10.1163/9789004416581

Mullan, P. C. (2014b). FIN-2013-G001. In The Digital Currency Challenge: Shaping Online Payment Systems through US Financial Regulations (pp. 118-130). Springer.

Parmar, S. K. M. (2014). *Virtual Currency: A Theoretical Review*. Academic Press.

Stabile, Prior, & Hinkes. (2020). Digital Assets and Blockchain Technology: US Law and Regulation. Edward Elgar Publishing.

Walport, M. (2015). Distributed Ledger Technology: Beyond BlockChain. Academic Press.

United States v. Ulbricht, 31 F. Supp. 3d 540, 547 (S.D.N.Y. 2014).

U.S. Securities and Exchange Commission. (2021a). *SEC Charges Poloniex for Operating Unregistered Digital Asset Exchange*. Retrieved from https://www.sec.gov/news/press-release/2021-147

U.S. Securities and Exchange Commission. (2021b). *SEC Charges Decentralized Finance Lender and Top Executives*. Retrieved from https://www.sec.gov/news/press-release/2021-145

U.S. Securities and Exchange Commission. (2021c). *ICO "Listing" Website Charged With Unlawfully Touting Digital Asset Securities*. Retrieved from https://www.sec.gov/news/press-release/2021-125

U.S. Securities and Exchange Commission. (2020). *Division of Enforcement 2020 Annual Report*. Retrieved from https://www.sec.gov/files/enforcement-annual-report-2020.pdf

Cornerstone Research. (2020). *SEC Cryptocurrency Enforcement Report*. Retrieved from https://www.cornerstone.com/Publications/Reports/SEC-Cryptocurrency-Enforcement-Q3-2013-Q4-2020.pdf

U.S. Securities and Exchange Commission. (2017). *How Investigations Work*. Retrieved from https://www.sec.gov/enforce/how-investigations-work.html

Clayton, J. (2019). *Testimony on "Oversight of the Securities and Exchange Commission" Before the U.S. Senate Committee on Banking, Housing, and Urban Affairs*. U.S. Securities and Exchange Commission. Retrieved from https://www.sec.gov/news/testimony/testimony-clayton-2019-12-10

Robinson, T. (2021). Crypto Enforcement Actions by US Regulators Reach $2.5 Billion. *Elliptic*. Retrieved from https://www.elliptic.co/blog/https/www.elliptic.co/blog/crypto-enforcement-actions-by-us-regulators-reach-2.5-billion

Sec. & Exch. Comm'n v. Shavers, No. 4:13-CV-416, 2014 WL 4652121, at *1 (E.D. Tex. Sept. 18, 2014).

U.S. Treasury Financial Crimes Enforcement Network. (2013). *Application of FinCEN's Regulations to Persons Administering, Exchanging, or Using Virtual Currencies*. Retrieved from https://www.fincen.gov/resources/statutes-regulations/guidance/application-fincens-regulations-persons-administering

Department of the Treasury, Financial Crimes Enforcement Network. (2011, July 29). [Office of the Federal Register, National Archives and Records Administration.]. *Federal Register*, *76*(146), •••.

Department of Treasury, Financial Crimes Enforcement Network. (n.d.). 31 CFR § 1010.100(ff). *Cornell*. Retrieved from https://www.law.cornell.edu/cfr/text/31/1010.100

U.S. Treasury Financial Crimes Enforcement Network. (2008). *Application of the Definition of Money Transmitter to Brokers and Dealers in Currency and Other Commodities*. Retrieved from https://www.fincen.gov/resources/advisories/fincen-guidance-fin-2008-g008

IRS. (2014). *Notice 2014-21*. Retrieved from https://www.irs.gov/pub/irs-drop/n-14-21.pdf

ADDITIONAL READING

Bele, J. L. (2021). Cryptocurrencies as facilitators of cybercrime. In *SHS Web of Conferences* (Vol. 111, p. 01005). EDP Sciences.

Courtois, N. T., Gradon, K. T., & Schmeh, K. (2021). *Crypto Currency Regulation and Law Enforcement Perspectives*. arXiv preprint arXiv:2109.01047.

Hays, D., & Kirilenko, A. (2021). Cryptocurrency regulation and enforcement in the US and Europe. *Fostering FinTech for Financial Transformation*, 26.

Matherson, N. (2021). *The Driving Force of Cryptocurrency and Money Laundering* (Doctoral dissertation). Utica College.

Prytula, A., Lutsyk, V., Sviatoshniuk, A., Tkalia, O., & Kalachenkova, K. (2021). Cryptocurrency in transnational offenses: Criminal and civil legal aspects. *Amazonia Investiga*, *10*(46), 209–216. doi:10.34069/AI/2021.46.10.21

SinghA. (2021). The Regulatory Regime for Cryptocurrency in the Present Global Order. Available at SSRN 3978476. doi:10.2139/ssrn.3978476

Scoular, J. (2021). *Cryptocurrency: Illicit Uses, Legislation, Regulation, and the Burden on Law Enforcement* (Doctoral dissertation). Utica College.

Sonksen, C. (2021). Cryptocurrency Regulations in ASEAN, East Asia, & America: To Regulate or Not to Regulate. *Wash. U. Global Stud. L. Rev.*, *20*, 171.

KEY TERMS AND DEFINITIONS

Cryptocurrency: A type of digital currency in which transactions are done in a decentralized system using encrypted data and technology.

Cryptocurrency Enforcement: Law enforcement's activities in tracing, investigation, and recovering digital assets against unlawful transactions in cryptocurrency done by businesses and individuals.

Cybercrime: The use of a computer, internet, or information technology as a means to further illegal ends.

Digital Asset: Any content that exists in a digital format and is uniquely identifiable with the right to use.

Fraud: A deliberate act or criminal activity aiming to result in financial gains by using deception, false suggestions, or other unethical means, which are trusted by others.

Information Age: A period where information has become a commodity and human civilization features a wider use, access, and control of information technology.

Money Laundering: A financial transaction process for illegally obtained money to avoid government regulations and investigations.

Virtual Currency: A digital currency, issued and controlled by a private issuer, functions as a medium of exchange.

Chapter 6
Principal Components Analysis:
Impact on Alternative Crypto-Currencies

Nabiha Haouas
University of Sousse, Tunisia

Asma Sghaier
https://orcid.org/0000-0002-8651-6459
University of Sousse, Tunisia

ABSTRACT

Today, cryptocurrencies are rapidly gaining popularity and sweeping all the economies of the world, but the bulk of the literature is devoted to a few cryptocurrencies only. The purpose of this chapter is to analyze of the cryptocurrency market. More than 2000 cryptocurrencies are examined, and a set of 70 cryptocurrencies were recovered for a sample spanning 2015-2018. The degree of relationship between the variables was then investigated. The PCA was performed. This analysis allows the initial variables to be replaced by five factors that retain almost all of the information (91.028% of the total information) and have the advantage of being uncorrelated. Therefore, the authors have concluded that the first factor corresponds to the cci30 index used by the crypto funds while the rest of the factors can be distinguished according to some variants.

INTRODUCTION

Nowadays crypto-currencies represent a combined market capitalization of about

DOI: 10.4018/978-1-7998-9117-8.ch006

500 billion dollars, says the portal CoinMarketCap. Moreover, according to the latest report from the US firm "Research and Markets", the global market for crypto-currency and blockchain technology will grow by 35.2% over the 2016-2022 period. Crypto-currencies are a real revolution both technologically and financially. Indeed, crypto-currencies are rapidly gaining popularity in recent years and sweeping all the economies of the world. Now, we have many crypto-currencies, but most are similar and derive from the first full implementation: Bitcoin.

The creation of this crypto-currency corresponds to the financial crisis of 2008, which was a consequence of a loss of investors' confidence in the traditional financial system. Moreover, as any radical innovation, the disruptive nature of the technology that carries the crypto-currency, supported by the new economic logic that generates the expansion of the Internet, appears as a potential threat vis-à-vis the existing monetary order. It should also be emphasized that these crypto-currencies are based on cryptographic mechanisms that have many important properties, such as the transparency of transactions and the absence of a central regulatory authority. Today, they are alternative currencies because they do not have legal tender in any country, even if they are for the moment widely tolerated. It is therefore important to consider crypto-currencies as a means of "democratizing finance" within alternative (transnational) spaces and to restore to individuals this "common good" that is money.

We will start with a small definition of crypto-currency: "A crypto-currency, also called crypto-currency or cryptographic currency, is electronic money usable on a peer-to-peer or decentralized computer network, based on the principles of cryptography, that we can self-issue and settle transactions ". Although the established crypto-currencies have most often a price in euro or dollar (it is easier to reason by saying that 1 Bitcoin worth 11348 USD), a crypto-currency could simply be a means of unencrypted payment. In addition, it is a currency in the primary sense of the term that only allows the measurement of wealth, which will serve as a Gold Exchange Standard. For this reason, these crypto-currencies offer possibilities for expansion and autonomy with respect to the standard system and their current development is a continuation of the upheavals introduced by the deployment of digital techniques in the field of computer software and communication.

At the same time, many innovations have reached maturity. Indeed, these last ten years have seen the maturity of different computer protocols implementing various crypto-currencies. While, regularly quoted in the media, Bitcoin appears as the most popular crypto-currency of the public among the various existing virtual currencies, it is not necessarily the most popular with investors in the market. Internationally, the year 2019 was a decisive year for crypto-currencies with a daily volume of transactions exceeding that of certain stock exchanges. Regardless of all these factors and concerned about the potential cap on the price of equities, investors are increasingly injecting funds into crypto-currencies, a largely untapped market that until recently was still the realm of professional traders. While various laws against fraudulent activity protect traditional financial investments, the crypto-currency markets are totally devoid of this protection. In such a case, any losses due to a stock market crash could be enormous.

The transactions are fast and global, they spread almost instantly on the network and are confirmed in minutes. They are completely indifferent to your physical location, because they occur in a global network of computers. The crypto-currency market is fast and free. Almost every day, new crypto-currencies emerge, old ones disappear, pioneers get richer and investors lose money. To do this, all people ask the same question: what is the best crypto-currency in which to invest? It is therefore essential to examine carefully the crypto-currency in which an investor wants to invest and understand the content of this market.

As already mentioned, everything started with Bitcoin. For some of the players in the market, Litecoin and Ethereum quickly joined and fiercely competed with Bitcoin. Subsequently, several crypto currencies appeared, but none took advantage of the wave experienced by Bitcoin. There is today about 3,000 new crypto-currencies on the market which is experiencing a real boom. This increase and the massive surge in the market capitalization of the crypto-currencies clearly indicate the interest of investors for these new financial assets. In addition, the high price volatility encourages players to try to get into the race for crypto assets. In addition, these crypto assets are among the riskiest in the financial sphere. Indeed, they are at once very volatile and very uncertain, because the market is still not very mature. In contrast, volatility is one of the major features of crypto-currencies. Thus, the value of an encrypted currency can increase or decrease, very quickly and unpredictably. For this reason, investing in crypto-currency is not recommended for conservative profiles with a high-risk aversion.

However, the main players in this sector, including banks and funds, are looking for professional instruments. These instruments are indices similar to those used in the equity and bond markets. Indeed, an equity index is used to describe the performance of the stock market or a part of it, and to compare investment returns. Generally, an index uses a weighted average of the stock price, such as the NASDAQ and the S&P 500.However, despite the enormous growth of the crypto-currency market, scientific research on index funds is rather limited. Recently, a crypto-currency index was launched in October 2017 by a team of specialists led by Igor Rivin CCI30, bringing together the 30 most important crypto-currencies on the market. The calculation of the indicator is quite complex, it involves many stages of calculation. In addition, due to the volatility of this market, it is unreasonable to calculate only the top thirty crypto-currencies.

In the light of the above-mentioned facts, it would be interesting to see if there is a new approach, which allows investors to monitor the crypto market state without the need to study each crypto-currency separately. The rest of this article is structured as follows. Section 2 provides a brief review of the theoretical and empirical literature on crypto-currencies. Section 3 discusses the methodology and data used. Section 4 presents the empirical results and their analysis. Finally, the conclusion summarizes the main observations.

LITERATURE REVIEW

It is worth noting that the literature on Bitcoin and other virtual money systems is very poor, if not virtually non-existent. Indeed, topics related to virtual currencies are extremely new because of their recent appearances, which explains why a doctrine on this subject is not yet really developed. Nevertheless, some specialized webzines and magazines were created such as the Bitcoin Magazine which is the first magazine dedicated to Bitcoin and whose first issue was released in May 2012, the CoinDesk webzine which specializes in digital currencies and other more traditional newspapers devoting several specialized articles to digital currencies such as the Business Insider. Crypto money is gradually emerging from the shadows and is no longer the prerogative elite of computer scientists and geeks (Aglietta, M. (1992, 1998).

The bulk of the scientific literature on the subject dealt with the relationship between Bitcoin and IT or between Bitcoin and its potential economic impact, as well as the commercial revolution it could engender. Most academic articles on the subject of Bitcoin related to the anonymity of this currency, whether it is real or not. Some scientific articles also tackled the encryption methods compared to others. Others covered the history and evolution of encrypted and decentralized currencies. Finally, some scientific articles studied the impact of this new financial trend on the real economy, (Bukovina, J and M Martiček (2016)) the mechanisms that underlie monetary creation, or the role that these types of currencies can have in local economies or in those of developing countries. Indeed, if 8% of US citizens do not have access to the banking system and 20% are under-banked, imagine the effect of this parallel system in other countries of the world where more than half of the population does not have access to the banking services offered today.

The reference to precious metals is crucial in relation to the principles of issuing crypto-currencies. It would be mainly to free the currency from imperfections related to an institutional management, and denounced as being inflationary. In times of quantitative easing that caused an upsurge in the balance sheets of central banks, this type of argument received favourable echoes (Rochard, 2013). Thus, the rhetoric carried by the crypto-currency community is based on the ideology of a healthy currency, pure of any manipulation or human failure, while the identification with the metallic money would contribute to anchoring the currency in a natural order, which alone could preserve its value. Maurer et al. evoke for their part a "Practical materialism" or a «digital metallism22» (Maurer, Nelms and Swartz, 2013). The system design ensures that the total amount of crypto-currencies ($ 21 million at the end of the term sheet for issuance), as well as the annual rate of issue, are determined by the computer program itself. The scarcity of money is therefore inscribed in the so-called infallible code, which serves as an intangible rule of monetary policy. The idea of business rule management, rather than discretionary policy, is part of the long history of a well-known debate by currency theorists (Fischer, 1988). As early as 1936, Simons asserted that "in relation to money, rules of the game which are defined as stable and lawful are of utmost importance for the survival of a system based on freedom and enterprise" (Simons, 1936, p. 339). The rule permits in particular to contain the arbitrariness of a monetary policy related to the judgment of an authority. However, the laws can be changed. Uncertainty about the management of money is therefore not completely eliminated. In the case of Bitcoin, the proponents hope to escape this arbitrariness by freezing the emission in a mathematical rule: 50 BTC are emitted every 10 minutes during the first 4 years of the system. Then, the amount is divided into 2 to go to 25 BTC for the next 4 years and so on until reaching the smallest subdivision and therefore the maximum number of bit coins is around 2140 (Callon, M. (1998), Cartelier, J. (1991), Chaum, D. (1985), Cheung, A, E Roca and JJ Su (2015), Courbis, B., Froment, E., Servet, J.-M. (1990))

The literature on herding emphasized the view that asset markets were driven by the so-called "animal-sprits" (Avery and Zemsky, 1998), where market participants imitated each other's trading behavior or market consensus and ignored their own information. The basic premises of herding stemmed from informational differences, which increased volatility in the market (Bikhchandani and Sharma, 2000). Hwang and Salmon (2004) used another variant of Christie and Huang (1995) by employing cross-sectional dispersion of factor sensitivity of assets within a given market and found lower proclivity to herding during crisis than in normal periods. Blasco and Ferreruela (2008) studied different markets for herding and compared CSSD from each market with an artificially created "herd-free" market, the findings revealed significant herding only in Spanish markets. Chiang and Zheng (2010) examined herding behavior in 25 countries and found evidence of herding in developed markets (except US), and in Asian markets and no evidence of herding in Latin American markets. Further, their results found evidence of asymmetric herding in some markets mainly in Asian markets where it was profound, particularly during rising markets. Yao et al. (2013) studied the Chinese market in a segmented setting and found strong evidence of herding in Chinese B-share markets and further they found herding was more pronounced under declining market conditions. In a recent study, Lee (2017) proposed a new measure of detecting herding based on across-sectional excess co-movement (CSC) of returns. Except in the crisis period, the study found a weak or no evidence of herding during periods of positive price movements and a strong evidence of herding during negative price movements.

All the above reviewed studies focused on equity markets. (Fry, J and ET Cheah (2016), Garcia, D, CJ Tessone, P Mavrodiev and N Perony (2014), Gazé, P. (2003), Godsiff, P (2015), Grinberg, R. (2011), Hayek, F. (1976), Jeong, S. (2013)) To the best of our knowledge, there is no work on herding in crypto-currency markets, which motivates this study. Apart from this, there are two reasons behind exploring the possibility of herding in crypto-currency markets.

First, the crypto-currency market exhibits various common traits to financial markets such as volatility clustering (Bouoiyour and Selmi, 2014; Dwyer, 2015; Dyhrberg, 2016; Bukovina and Martiček, 2016), bubbles (MacDonell, 2014; Cheah and Fry, 2015; Cheung et al., 2015; Fry and Cheah, 2016) and inefficiency (Urquhart, 2016; Nadarajah and Chu, 2017). From the literature, it is clear that these variables are closely interrelated to the herding behavior. Hence, it would interest to see if there is a possibility of herding in the crypto-currency markets. Further, from a theoretical point of view, multi-dimensional uncertainty increases the herding behavior (Avery and Zemsky, 1998), and given the documentary evidences on uncertainties related to crypto-currency markets on aspects such as legal (Moser et al., 2013), technical and regulatory (Vasek and Moore, 2015) and security (Huang et al., 2014; Vasek et al., 2016), the present investigation may be warranted.

METHODOLOGY

This section is devoted to the description of the Principal Component Analysis PCA and a univariate description of the different variables of the study. We also present the results of the correlation analysis, which aims to measure the degree of relationship between the variables.

For some forty years, methods of data analysis have largely proved their effectiveness in the study of large and complex masses of information Karlstrom, H. (2014), Lee, K (2017), Nadarajah, S and J Chu (2017), Nakamoto, S. (2009a), Osterrieder, J and J Lorenz (2017), Pochea, MM, AM Filip and AM Pece (2017), Szczepanski, M. (2014), Taufeeq Ajaz and Anoop S. Kumar (2018), Vasek, M and T Moore (2015), Vasek, M, J Bonneau, R Castellucci, C Keith and T Moore (2016)). These so-called multidimensional methods are in contrast to the conventional descriptive statistics methods, which treat only one or two variables at a time. They thus allow the confrontation of much information and give richer analyzes than their separate examination. These analytical techniques have a common objective: from too numerous interactive data to be directly captured, they extract the most striking trends and prioritize them by eliminating the marginal or one-off effects that disturb the overall perception of the facts. The Principal Component Analysis PCA can be defined as the set of methods for performing linear transformations of a large number of inter-correlated variables to obtain a relatively small number of uncorrelated components. This approach facilitates the analysis by grouping the data into smaller sets. The use of PCA makes it possible to replace the initial variables with principal components that retain almost all the information and have the advantage of being uncorrelated.

Data Collection

The historical data of crypto-currencies is easily available on various platforms and websites. In this work, we use the daily closing price in USD, for 70 crypto-currencies (coinmarketcap.com), over the period from1stJanuary 2015 to 31st December 2018, i.e. 1502 observations. We also checked for the presence of incorrect, incomplete and duplicate data.

Data Description

Table 1 below provides a number of descriptive statistics relating to all the crypto-currencies used in this study, and allows us to make the first assessments of the nature of these series. For each crypto-currency: mean, median, deviation, Skewness, kurtosis, and Jarque-Bera JB statistic are calculated.

Descriptive statistics show that the mean and the standard deviation of BITCOIN are the highest compared to other crypto-currencies, implying that this crypto-currency has a relatively high volatility. It is still the main electronic currency accounting for more than 80% of the total capitalization of virtual currencies.

We can notice that all the Skewness and Kurtosis statistics are respectively different from 0 and from 3. The values of the Skewness coefficients show that there is an asymmetry phenomenon for all the series. Kurtosis, much higher than 3, indicates that the tails of the distributions are thicker than those of the normal distribution. Because of these two parameters, as illustrated by the Jarque-Bera statistics, not all series follow a normal distribution. This result is not the object of this work, but opens a new line of research to study the nature of distribution and the characteristics of crypto-currency series.

Principal Component Analysis

Principal component analysis (PCA) is a widely used tool for dimension reduction. Note that the PCA has been widely applied to the study of financial markets

Table 1. Descriptive statistics

	Mean	Median	Std, Dev,	Skewness	Kurtosis	Jarque-Bera	P.v
BITCOIN	3118,238	928,935	3745,785	1,499439	5,002384	813,7596	0
DASH	147,0274	15,005	233,3434	2,465131	9,989555	4578,682	0
MONERO	61,56853	12,41	91,94036	1,902291	6,272617	1576,153	0
UNOBTANIUM	41,66098	2,985	53,01556	0,971099	2,457302	254,5048	0
LITECOIN	40,36926	4,27	60,64959	2,180147	7,89236	2687,788	0
OMNI	12,89615	3,41	18,40651	2,265755	8,718342	3331,562	0
COUNTERPARTY	6,767604	2,85	10,06596	3,455568	18,68992	18395,59	0
BLOCKNET	6,374586	0,234088	10,54356	1,912523	6,29231	1594,015	0
DIAMOND	2,78829	0,354155	4,780795	2,747248	11,73992	6669,865	0
CLOAKCOIN	2,716586	0,18451	4,683526	2,671351	11,77975	6610,587	0
CLAMS	2,540366	1,58	2,401043	1,786221	5,87051	1314,386	0
NEOSCOIN	1,233985	0,118278	2,253348	3,27203	17,67127	16150,94	0
MONACOIN	1,178596	0,128113	2,341799	3,351834	16,44766	14129,98	0
PEERCOIN	1,070648	0,485598	1,16416	2,523065	11,07477	5674,139	0
NAMECOIN	1,014963	0,504255	0,975826	2,063504	8,69206	3093,603	0
BITUSD	1,014586	1,01	0,081982	1,128991	39,23083	82470,53	0
EMERCOIN	0,874488	0,328926	1,274936	2,436142	10,38202	4896,106	0
VERTCOIN	0,822119	0,072856	1,598066	2,895114	11,7283	6866,012	0
NUBITS	0,805102	0,995168	0,339714	-1,379873	3,155624	478,1631	0
GAMECREDITS	0,721511	0,158927	1,14664	1,981865	6,823196	1898,026	0
I_O_COIN	0,680517	0,237657	1,073652	2,248261	8,326845	3041,173	0
UBIQ	0,665994	0,065792	1,079202	2,491413	10,4976	5071,915	0
VIACOIN	0,625163	0,036893	1,028635	2,538642	10,99598	5614,635	0
CROWN	0,500228	0,017664	0,827478	2,182231	7,922483	2708,567	0
BOOLBERRY	0,439353	0,126775	0,611437	2,091037	8,240792	2813,474	0
NAVCOIN	0,368805	0,046235	0,682459	3,003396	13,43153	9068,223	0
EXCLUSIVECOIN	0,355348	0,006829	0,59846	2,241473	8,670903	3270,351	0
PRIMECOIN	0,334109	0,097231	0,489386	2,900806	13,85815	9485,016	0
GROESTLCOIN	0,235077	0,003442	0,395126	2,11365	7,649332	2471,187	0
RIPPLE	0,224169	0,011203	0,376702	3,422607	20,52887	22161,9	0
VERICOIN	0,19882	0,053547	0,316806	3,303804	18,99916	18752,07	0
MAIDSAFECOIN	0,198783	0,112233	0,201506	1,549096	5,984051	1158,001	0
FAIRCOIN	0,193146	0,029642	0,286051	1,859767	5,851598	1374,74	0
BITCNY	0,155005	0,151864	0,042619	20,80345	500,9109	15623702	0
SOLARCOIN	0,141692	0,065526	0,227458	4,48582	31,76058	56804,48	0
BLACKCOIN	0,118278	0,03794	0,153837	2,619797	11,78396	6546,92	0
CURECOIN	0,117726	0,049025	0,168947	2,737062	12,41591	7423,977	0
SYSCOIN	0,107022	0,010825	0,177707	2,211277	7,594397	2545,106	0
STEALTH	0,101938	0,011046	0,192756	3,892769	21,90373	26157,68	0
EINSTEINIUM	0,090832	0,001484	0,245287	5,514103	40,50469	95641,28	0
STELLAR	0,081117	0,003194	0,134476	1,965887	6,985001	1961,304	0
DNOTES	0,075737	0,012051	0,266866	5,123537	30,72925	54692,43	0
BITSHARES	0,07522	0,008308	0,121429	2,816474	13,44036	8807,427	0
OKCASH	0,070845	0,007337	0,135381	2,591949	9,567531	4381,163	0
NXT	0,070702	0,017697	0,149144	6,228394	55,83894	184440,9	0
FEATHERCOIN	0,056495	0,014259	0,09464	2,677274	10,60733	5416,128	0
E_GULDEN	0,056098	0,01958	0,079219	2,559766	10,4406	5105,054	0
GOLDCOIN	0,052954	0,017661	0,072895	2,246126	9,371786	3803,813	0
POTCOIN	0,046358	0,013385	0,074745	2,513795	10,05122	4693,52	0
MONETARYUNIT	0,045964	0,000869	0,07583	2,474447	10,76654	5307,735	0
GULDEN	0,042582	0,02334	0,057806	2,417871	11,78775	6296,445	0
FLORINCOIN	0,035086	0,004344	0,049841	2,178762	9,690629	3989,846	0
ENERGYCOIN	0,034656	0,004279	0,055387	1,943126	7,318592	2112,387	0
STARTCOIN	0,034425	0,022345	0,044052	4,088858	26,74266	39464,36	0
WHITECOIN	0,031653	0,000437	0,052879	1,940322	6,611456	1758,718	0
HEMPCOIN	0,029182	0,00042	0,08161	4,890311	30,06194	51819,56	0

continued on following page

Table 1. Continued

	Mean	Median	Std, Dev,	Skewness	Kurtosis	Jarque-Bera	P.v
BITBAY	0,018585	0,001374	0,037806	4,189192	25,41616	35840,32	0
CANNABISCOIN	0,018178	0,004381	0,03594	4,905377	33,71002	65046,39	0
VERGE	0,011901	4,70E-05	0,028369	3,904251	21,53619	25318,91	0
DIGIBYTE	0,011071	0,000368	0,017166	2,388495	11,27727	5715,913	0
PINKCOIN	0,007924	0,000689	0,013068	2,699995	13,55742	8800,401	0
BURST	0,007168	0,000795	0,012669	3,382104	18,49937	17897,89	0
GLOBALBOOST_Y	0,00689	0,002593	0,009242	2,917544	14,91708	11018,74	0
FOLDINGCOIN	0,006235	0,001134	0,011419	3,348045	17,96732	16826,06	0
DIGITALNOTE	0,003146	0,000188	0,007598	5,303699	42,05756	102512,1	0
ARTBYTE	0,002994	0,000231	0,005324	3,3072	17,53219	15954,67	0
MYRIAD	0,002408	0,000258	0,004996	4,68723	33,36347	63197,96	0
REDDCOIN	0,001687	4,30E-05	0,003206	3,306486	18,15359	17107,94	0
DOGECOIN	0,001595	0,000264	0,002165	2,206756	9,894768	4194,142	0
BYTECOIN	0,001253	6,05E-05	0,002218	3,751056	29,18435	46430,69	0

(Mbeledogu (2012) and Wang (2014)). Indeed, with an orthogonal transformation, PCA converts a set of observations of possibly correlated variables into a set of linearly uncorrelated components.

Therefore, PCA transforms the data into fewer dimensions, which act as feature summaries. So that, the few first principal components capture the greatest possible variance (i.e. explains as much as possible the variability of the data). The first component has maximum variance, and each subsequent component in turn has the highest possible variance under the constraint of being orthogonal to the preceding components. For more practical aspects see Kritzman (2011) and (Yang et al. 2016).

Note that the Principal Component Analysis PCA is particularly useful when the variables in the dataset are highly correlated. To do this, the first step is to study the correlation matrix. The result indicates that there is a redundancy in the data. We notice that almost all variables are strongly correlated.

The PCA theory ensures that the first factor will correspond to the largest possible proportion of variance presented in the initial variables.

Thus, the principal component analysis puts us in the presence of an equation, which is very similar to the classical regression equation having the following form:

$$F_1 = \hat{a}_1 var_1 + \hat{a}_2 var_2 + \hat{a}_3 var_3 + \cdots + \hat{a}_p var_p$$

With, F1: Factor 1,

$\hat{a}_i$: Weighting of the nth variable,

var_i : n^{th} Variable and $i = 1, \ldots, p$.

This first factor F1 corresponds to the largest proportion. Indeed, it represents 78.317% of the variance present in our initial data. The remaining variance, unexplained by F1, is not ignored in the principal components analysis; but it is in turn subject to the same process of factor extraction. Indeed, it seeks to extract a second factor, independent of the first, which would in turn explain the largest proportion of the possible variance left unexplained by factor F1. Factor F2 will therefore be represented in turn by a new equation where the

Coefficients $\widehat{a}'_1, \hat{a}'_2, \ldots, \widehat{a}'_p$ will correspond to as many new weights of the different initial variables as predictors (independent variables) of F2.

$$F_2 = \hat{a}'_1 \, var_1 + \widehat{a}'_2 var_2 + \hat{a}'_3 \, var_3 + \cdots + \widehat{a}'_p var_p$$

It is obvious that the factors extracted will each explain a less important proportion of variance.

Search for the optimal number of factors

We seek to know the number of factors to consider in this study, by calculating the eigen values of the correlation matrix (Annex XX). Before making this calculation, it is very important to raise the following question: are the data factorizable? Indeed, to answer this question it is necessary:

- First, observe the matrix of correlations; if several variables are correlated (> 0.5), factoring is possible. If not, factoring has no meaning and is not therefore recommended.
- In a second step, we must observe the KMO (Kaiser-Meyer-Olkin) index, which should tend to 1. If this is not the case, factoring is not recommended.
- Finally, we use Bartlett's sphericity test. If the result tends to zero, it is very significant, less than 0.05 significant, between 0.05 and 0.10 acceptable and above 0.10, rejected.

If the Principal Component Analysis PCA meets at least two of these three conditions, we can continue [LE MOEL 2002].

From the correlation matrix, the three conditions are satisfactory. Indeed:

- All variables are strongly correlated (> 0.5).
- The KMO index gives us a value very close to 1.
- Bartlett's sphericity test is very significant (0.000).

Table 2. KMO index and Bartlett test

Kaiser-Meyer-Olkin index for measuring sampling quality.		0,979
Bartlett's sphericity test	Khi-deux approx.	336278,883
	ddl	2415
	Signification	,000

RESULT

The choice of the number of factors is very important. There are different criteria for size selection in Factor Analysis, Besse (1992) and Josse et al. (2012). The criterion we use here is that of Kaiser in order to choose a relevant number of dimensions. It consists in retaining only the axes that carry a greater inertia than the average inertia. We only retain the axes associated with eigenvalues which are greater than 1. This amounts to looking only at components that provide more than the initial variables. We will first look at Table 3, in which each factor explains the crypto-currency series.

Figure 1. Collapsing plot

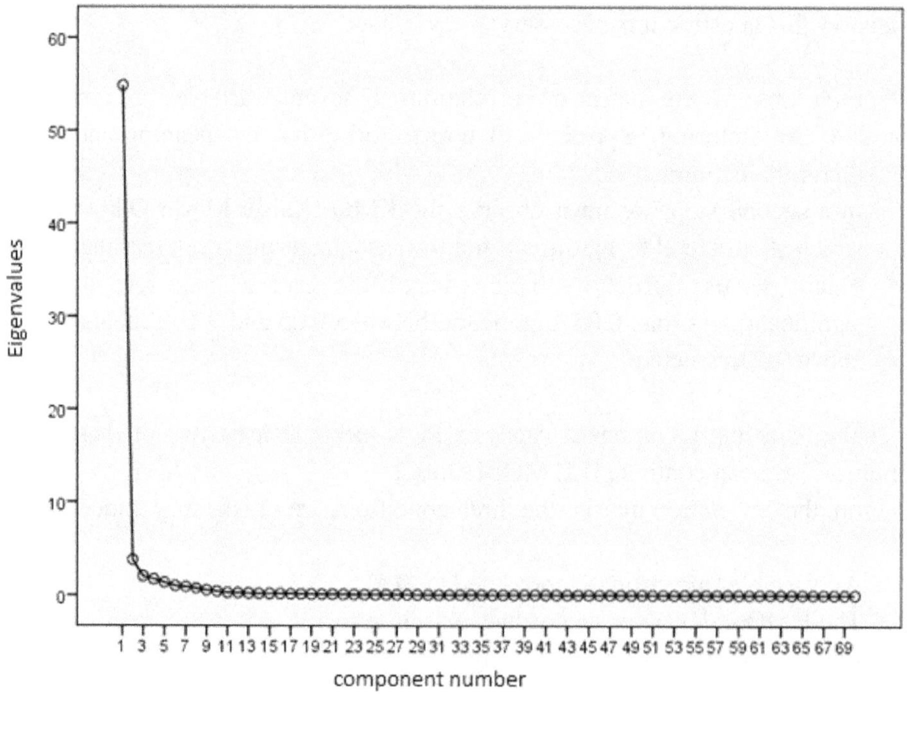

Table 3. Inertia explained by factors

Component	Initial eigenvalues			Extraction sum of squared loadings		
	Total	% of variance	Cumulative %	Total	% of variance	cumulative%
1	54,822	78,317	78,317	54,822	78,317	78,317
2	3,787	5,409	83,726	3,787	5,409	83,726
3	2,030	2,900	86,626	2,030	2,900	86,626
4	1,718	2,454	89,080	1,718	2,454	89,080
5	1,363	1,948	91,028	1,363	1,948	91,028
6	,996	1,423	92,451			
7	,891	1,273	93,724			
8	,728	1,040	94,763			
9	,530	,758	95,521			
10	,408	,582	96,103			
11	,269	,384	96,487			
12	,237	,338	96,825			
13	,202	,288	97,113			
14	,180	,257	97,370			
15	,167	,238	97,608			
16	,154	,220	97,829			
17	,130	,186	98,014			
18	,117	,167	98,181			
19	,099	,142	98,323			
20	,092	,131	98,454			
21	,087	,124	98,577			
22	,081	,115	98,693			
23	,074	,106	98,799			
24	,061	,087	98,886			
25	,058	,082	98,968			
26	,052	,074	99,043			
27	,048	,069	99,112			
28	,043	,061	99,173			
29	,041	,058	99,231			
30	,037	,053	99,284			
31	,033	,047	99,331			
32	,031	,044	99,375			
33	,029	,041	99,416			
34	,028	,040	99,456			
35	,025	,036	99,492			
36	,024	,034	99,526			
37	,022	,032	99,557			
38	,021	,030	99,588			
39	,020	,028	99,616			
40	,018	,026	99,642			
41	,017	,024	99,666			
42	,017	,024	99,689			
43	,016	,023	99,712			
44	,015	,022	99,734			
45	,014	,020	99,755			
46	,013	,018	99,773			
47	,012	,018	99,790			
48	,012	,017	99,807			
49	,011	,016	99,823			
50	,010	,015	99,838			
51	,009	,013	99,851			
52	,009	,013	99,864			
53	,009	,012	99,877			
54	,008	,012	99,888			
55	,008	,011	99,900			

continued on following page

Table 1. Continued

Component	Initial eigenvalues			Extraction sum of squared loadings		
	Total	% of variance	Cumulative %	Total	% of variance	cumulative%
56	,007	,010	99,910			
57	,007	,010	99,920			
58	,006	,009	99,929			
59	,006	,009	99,937			
60	,006	,008	99,945			
61	,005	,008	99,953			
62	,005	,007	99,960			
63	,004	,006	99,967			
64	,004	,006	99,973			
65	,004	,006	99,978			
66	,004	,005	99,984			
67	,003	,005	99,989			
68	,003	,004	99,993			
69	,003	,004	99,997			
70	,002	,003	100,000			

Extraction method: Principal Component Analysis.

The preceding table includes the eigenvalues which are related to the quality of the projection when one passes from N dimensions (N being the number of initial variables, here 70) to a smaller number of dimensions. Indeed, the first eigenvalue is 54,822 and represents 78,317% of the variability. This means that if we represent the data on a single factor, then we will still have 78.317% of the total variability that will be preserved. Each eigenvalue has a factor, which is in fact a linear combination of the starting variables. These factors have the advantage of not being correlated with each other.

To retain the optimal number of factors, we use the Kaiser criterion which is commonly used and consists in retaining only the eigenvalues that are greater than 1. Therefore, we retain only 5 factors to capture 91.028% of the available information, which is a very good result, while recognizing that the variability is almost null starting from the 6thfactor.

The influence of the factors on the various crypto-currencies is observed in Table 4. Indeed, one of the most important steps in the Principal Component Analysis is to identify the extracted factors. To do this, it is common to examine the factors one by one and to determine with which initial variables are more correlated.

The factorial coordinates of the variables, i.e. the coefficients of correlation with the factors, indicate the quality of the representation of each variable. In fact, a factor is a linear combination of the initial variables in which the coefficients are given by the coordinates of the eigenvectors.

To interpret the Principal Component Analysis is to give meaning to these principal components (according to the initial variables). This is done naturally through the calculation of linear correlation coefficients between principal components and initial variables; and we are interested in the strongest coefficients which are in absolute value and close to1.

Table 4. Component matrix

Label of the variable	Component				
	1	2	3	4	5
Bitcoin	,905	-,241	-,309	-,057	-,015
Litecoin	,940	-,165	-,151	-,078	,093
Ripple	,918	-,219	,165	-,116	-,113
Dash	,969	,047	-,187	-,077	,031
Monero	,954	-,178	-,137	-,067	,050
Stellar	,825	-,488	,110	-,093	-,029
Nxt	,793	,098	-,239	-,291	,035
Einsteinium	,757	,093	-,379	-,356	,103
Verge	,884	-,158	,189	-,240	,019
BitShares	,946	-,081	,084	,002	-,050
MonaCoin	,862	-,012	-,348	-,274	,144
Vertcoin	,881	,131	-,333	-,195	,095
Dogecoin	,883	-,302	,099	-,064	-,169
DigiByte	,910	-,277	,152	,051	-,103
Syscoin	,967	-,068	-,004	,022	,098
BitBay	,947	,056	,020	-,206	-,026
DigitalNote	,883	-,086	,385	-,116	-,017
NAVcoin	,975	,069	-,004	-,095	,028
Groestlcoin	,864	-,359	-,187	-,131	,057
OKCash	,883	,263	-,221	,005	,014
PotCoin	,926	,199	-,204	,002	,029
Bytecoin	,856	-,300	,150	,138	,083
GameCredits	,851	,313	,058	,310	-,071
Peercoin	,966	,046	,023	,041	,012
VeriCoin	,955	,076	,105	,025	,021
FoldingCoin	,959	,148	,126	-,013	-,034
Burst	,957	-,112	,213	-,041	-,019
MonetaryUnit	,964	,167	-,081	,069	-,018
Viacoin	,991	-,013	,020	,010	,011
NuBits	-,070	,817	,213	,004	,376
Feathercoin	,943	,001	-,097	-,161	,099
BlackCoin	,942	,171	,068	,112	-,071
Counterparty	,947	,144	,123	,016	,000
ExclusiveCoin	,953	,130	-,124	,058	,017
Namecoin	,933	,041	,010	,116	-,032
FlorinCoin	,959	,009	-,063	,105	-,098
CloakCoin	,959	,001	,007	,032	,028
PinkCoin	,972	,131	,039	,104	-,012
NeosCoin	,936	,221	,106	,091	-,057
ArtByte	,969	,102	,142	,031	-,053
Gulden	,939	,127	,084	,209	-,053
Stealth	,958	,002	,049	-,176	-,046
Blocknet	,942	,060	-,096	,125	,073
I/O Coin	,857	,336	-,113	,221	-,029
Startcoin	,668	,403	,350	-,295	,042
Clams	,859	,280	-,150	,224	-,048
CannabisCoin	,926	,087	,233	-,138	-,039
Myriad	,934	-,050	,271	-,145	-,051
MaidSafeCoin	,907	,077	-,112	,264	-,112
ReddCoin	,908	-,286	,255	-,073	-,003
Unobtanium	,725	-,490	-,230	,232	-,014
Emercoin	,863	-,293	,187	,115	,087
WhiteCoin	,868	-,352	-,135	-,199	-,001
Ubiq	,972	,090	,058	,091	-,020
Boolberry	,887	-,234	-,144	-,024	-,034

continued on following page

Table 1. Continued

Label of the variable	Component				
	1	2	3	4	5
BitCNY	-,038	-,061	,072	-,093	,440
FairCoin	,854	,149	-,369	,114	,009
BitUSD	,021	,003	,160	,035	,810
PrimeCoin	,605	-,620	,044	,305	,183
HempCoin	,893	-,001	,270	-,284	-,047
GlobalBoost-Y	,896	-,007	,067	,032	-,045
GoldCoin	,953	,004	-,016	,166	,005
Diamond	,962	,144	-,071	-,061	,025
Crown	,956	,168	-,027	,086	,020
e-Gulden	,978	,083	-,025	-,024	,050
SolarCoin	,910	,114	,191	-,001	,000
Dnotes	,264	-,510	,013	,397	,341
Energycoin	,925	,218	-,013	,243	-,008
Curecoin	,985	,069	,006	-,014	,015
Omni	,909	,205	,038	,180	-,018

Figure 2. Representation of variables

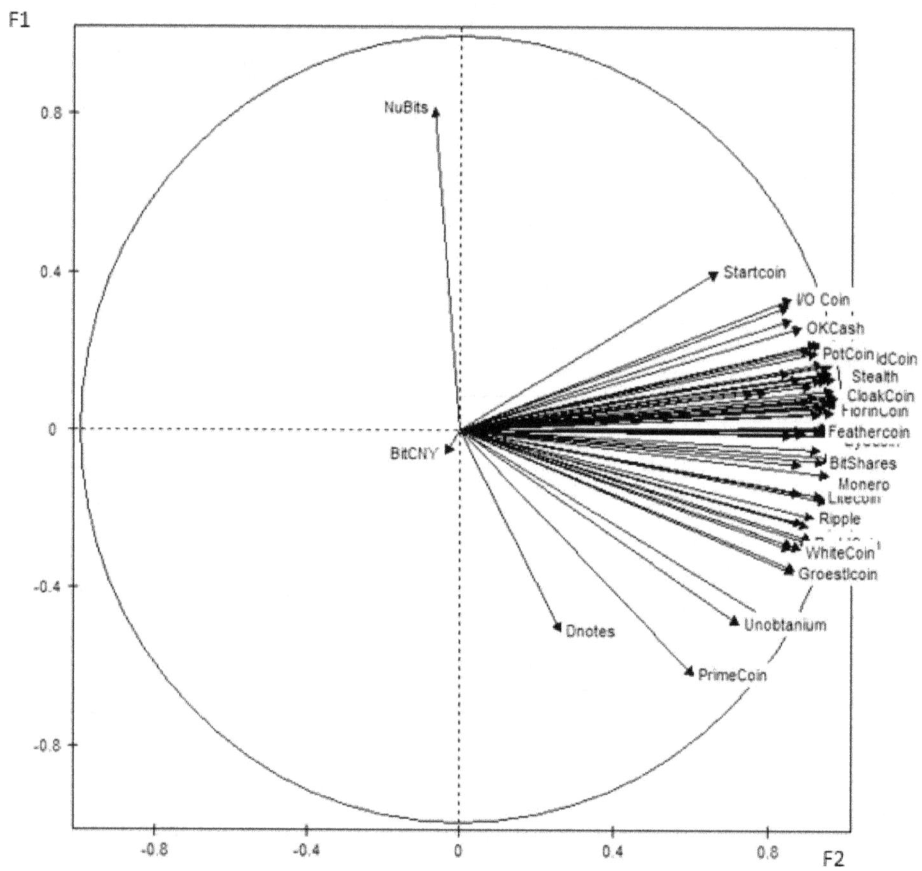

Table 5. Correlation coefficient between CCI30 and F1

Covariance		
Correlation		
Probability	**CCI30**	**F1**
CCI30	12948241	
	1.000000	

F1	3513.554	0.999334
	0.976756	1.000000
	0.0000	-----

The basic result for the variables is the table of variable-factor correlations. These are the linear correlation coefficients between the initial variables and the factors. These correlations will make sense of the factors and interpret them. Indeed, from this table, we can draw some conclusions:

Factor 1 is correlated with all the titles in a quite homogeneous and important way. In addition, this factor is the only one significantly correlated with the Syscoin and CannabisCoin crypto-currencies, as shown in Figure 2.

The following figure shows the cloud variables in the factorial plane 1-2 from the first two columns of Table 4:

This circle of correlations corresponds to a projection of the initial variables on a two-dimensional plane constituted by the first two factors. We see that all the variables are far from the center of the graph, with the exception of the NuBits crypto-currency, and they are close to each other, so they are significantly and positively correlated with this first factor. For the other factors, and when the variables are relatively close to the center of the graph, then any interpretation is risky, and it is necessary to refer to the correlation matrix of other factorial planes to interpret the results. (Besse,P 1992).

In our case, the grouping of all these crypto-currencies leads us to study the Crypto Currencies IndexCCI30. Indeed, this index brings together in its basket the 30 largest crypto-currencies by market capitalization.

The CCI30 index is the first of its kind to follow the evolution of the burgeoning crypto-currency market. It was introduced at the beginning of 2017 by IGOR RIVIN, professor of mathematics, and CARLO SCEVOLA, economist and investor; Rivin et al. (2018). The idea of the index is to have something like the S & P 500 index, but only for the 30 most important crypto-currencies. It is designed to be the benchmark in this sector, and it will be widely adopted by investment funds.

Figure 3. CCI30 and the first factor

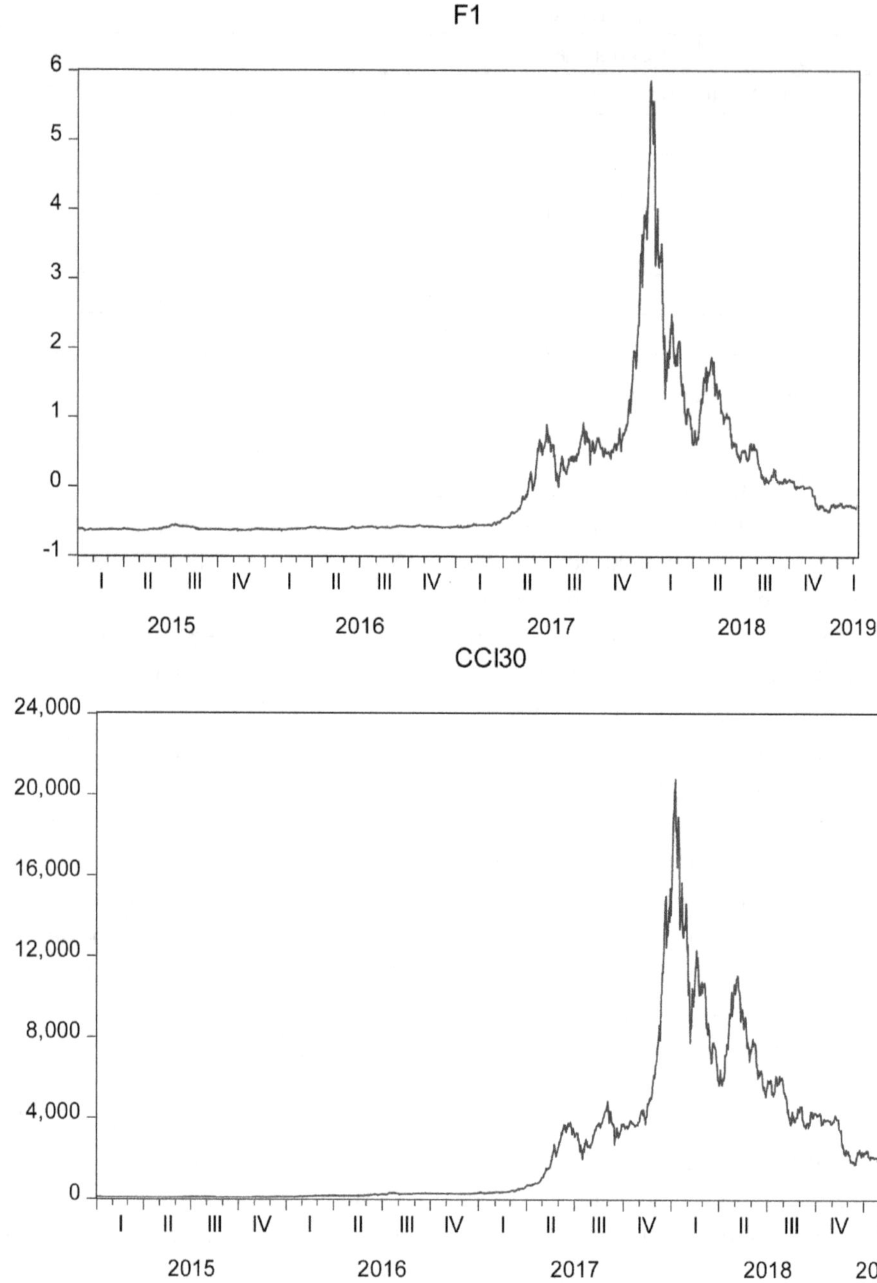

In fact, the strong correlation (Table 6) detected between the CCI30 index and the first factor from our analysis leads us to interpret that this first factor represents the CCI30 index. This is well confirmed by their graphic representation below, which follow the same trajectory of evolution over the period from January 1st, 2015 to the end of December 2018. Indeed, the appearance of this first factor looks very much like the appearance of the CCI30 index. The CCI30 index data is available and updated in real time on the cci30.com website.

As a preliminary, it is necessary to distinguish between different types of crypto-currency.

The first constitutes infrastructure currencies, which are quite particular because they generally encompass an entire ecosystem with them.

The second type includes alternative currencies to Bitcoin, which are usually the simplest crypto-currencies to use and the offer they suggest is usually rather complete. Among these alternatives, you will find for example Litecoin.

The third is the type of anonymous crypto-currency that most certainly looks like cash payment. Among these anonymous coins, you will find for example Monero. Finally, we have the financial instruments currencies, which are currencies that generally do not offer prospects, or offer few of them in the long term.

CONCLUSION

In this work, we presented an analysis of the crypto-currency market. We examined more than 2000 crypto-currencies available on coinmarketcap.com. We chose for our study only 70 crypto-currencies: the oldest on the market and the most volatile, relative to the same period simultaneously. It is about the daily data from January 1st, 2015 to December 31st, 2018. This diversity is our first asset in this research work by offering a diversified exposure to a wide range of crypto-currencies.

It should be noted that despite the increase in the volume of exchange and the massive increase in the market capitalization of crypto-currencies, the bulk of the literature devoted to crypto-currencies focuses on Bitcoin using methods of classical descriptive statistics, which only deal with one or two variables at a time. (Ancel, P. (1988))

In fact, the methods of data analysis allow the confrontation of much more information and give richer analyzes than their separate examination.

The principal component analysis (PCA) applied in this work allowed us to carry out linear transformations of the set of 70 crypto currencies that are highly inter-correlated to obtain only a relatively limited number of uncorrelated components. In addition, the PCA allows the initial variables to be replaced by principal components that retain almost all of the information (91.028% of the total information) and have the advantage of being uncorrelated.

Hence the contribution of this study, which facilitates the analysis by grouping the data (70 variables) into smaller sets (5 components), is allowing investors to monitor the crypto market state without having to study each crypto-currency separately. When identifying these components, we were able to show that the first factor corresponds to the cci30 index used by the Crypto funds for the passive tracking of cryptographic currency quotations, while other factors can be distinguished by the algorithms on which they rely and their operating principles.

PERSPECTIVES

Most articles on crypto-currencies were essentially negative. There was talk of an obscure device, which is at best without great interest, and at worst potentially dangerous. It could also be interesting to explore the profitability of risk management in the crypto-currency markets and study its impact on the existing banking infrastructure and the various issues related to privacy, security, freedom, transparency, etc.

REFERENCES

Aglietta, M. (1992). Genèse des banques centrales et légitimité de la monnaie. *Annales E.S.C.*, *47*(3), 675-698. 10.3406/ahess.1992.279068

Aglietta, M., & Orléan, A. (1998). *La monnaie souveraine*. Odile Jacob.

Ajaz & Kumar. (2018). Herding in crypto-currency markets. *Annals of Financial Economics, 13*(2). DOI: doi:10.1142/S2010495218500069

Ancel, P. (1988). La monnaie électronique: régime juridique. In *Droit et Monnaie, États et espace monétaire transnational* (pp. 302–315). Litec.

Banque de France. (2013, Dec.). Les dangers liés au développement des monnaies virtuelles. *Focus*.

Besse, P. (1992). PCA stability and choice of dimensionality. *Statistics & Probability Letters*, *13*, 405–410.

Bukovina, J., & Martiček, M. (2016). *Sentiment and Bitcoin volatility*. MENDELU Working Papers in Business and Economics 2016–2058, Mendel University in Brno, Faculty of Business and Economics.

Callon, M. (1998). The embeddedness of economic markets in economics. In The Laws of the Markets. Blackwell.

Cartelier, J. (1991). Monnaie et système de paiement: le problème de la formation de l'équilibre. *Revue française d'économie*, *6*(3), 3-37.

Cartelier, J. (1996). *La monnaie*. Flammarion/ Dominos.

Chaum, D. (1985). Security without identification: Transaction systems to make Big Brother obsolete. *Communications of the ACM*, *28*(10).

Cheah, E. T., & Fry, J. (2015). Speculative bubbles in Bitcoin markets? An empirical investigation into the fundamental value of Bitcoin. *Economics Letters*, *130*, 32–36.

Cheung, A., Roca, E., & Su, J. J. (2015). Crypto-currency bubbles: An application of the Phillips–Shi–Yu (2013) methodology on Mt. Gox bitcoin prices. *Applied Economics*, *47*(23), 2348–2358.

Chevalier, M., & Vignolles, B. (2014). *Le bitcoin: défi à la souveraineté monétaire des états et ressource pour le blanchiment d'argent. Regards croisés sur l'économie, 14*. 10.3917/rce.014.0122.

Courbis, B., Froment, E., & Servet, J.-M. (1990). À propos du concept de monnaie. *Cahiers d'Économie Politique*, *18*(18), 5-29. 10.3406/cep.1990.1091

Dowd, K. (2014). *New Private Monies: A Bit-Part Player?* The Institute of Economic Affairs.

Dwyer, G. P. (2015). The economics of Bitcoin and similar private digital currencies. *Journal of Financial Stability*, *17*, 81–91.

Dyhrberg, A. H. (2016). Bitcoin, gold and the dollar— A GARCH volatility analysis. *Finance Research Letters*, *16*, 85–92.

ECB. (2012). *Virtual Currencies Schemes*. http://www.ecb.europa.eu

ECB. (2015). *Virtual Currency Schemes - A Further Analysis*. http://www.ecb.europa.eu.

Fischer, S. (1988). *Rules versus Discretion in monetary policy*. NBER Working Papers 2518. DOI: 10.3386/w2518

Fourcade, M., & Healy, K. (2007). Moral views of market society. *Annual Review of Sociology*, *33*, 287–311.

Fry, J., & Cheah, E. T. (2016). Negative bubbles and shocks in cryptocurrency markets. *International Review of Financial Analysis*, *47*, 343–352.

Garcia, D., Tessone, C. J., Mavrodiev, P., & Perony, N. (2014). The digital traces of bubbles: Feedback cycles between socio-economic signals in the Bitcoin economy. *Journal of the Royal Society, Interface, 11*. Advance online publication. doi:10.1098/?rsif.2014.0623

Gazé, P. (2003). Nouveaux moyens de paiements, nouveaux risques? *Les Cahiers du Numérique, 4*(1), 93–113.

Godsiff, P. (2015). Bitcoin: Bubble or blockchain? In *9th International KES Conference on Agents and Multi-Agent Systems: Technologies and Applications KES-AMSTA-15*. Retrieved from http://epubs.surrey.ac.uk/820645/

Grinberg, R. (2011). Bitcoin: An Innovative Alternative Digital Currency. *Hastings Science & Technology Law Journal, 4*, 159–207.

Hayek, F. (1976). Denationalisation of Money - The Argument Refined. An Analysis of the Theory and Practice of Concurrent Currencies. The Institute of Economic Affairs.

Jeong, S. (2013). *The Bitcoin Protocol as Law, and the Politics of a Stateless Currency*. DOI: 10.2139/ssrn.2294124

Josse, J., & Husson, F. (2012). Selecting the number of components in PCA using cross-validation approximations. *Computational Statistics & Data Analysis, 56*, 1869–1879.

Kaplanov, N. (2012). *Nerdy Money: Bitcoin, the Private Digital Currency, and the Case against its Regulation*. Temple University Legal Studies Research Paper. DOI: 10.2139/ssrn.2115203

Karlstrom, H. (2014). Do Libertarians dream of electronic coins? The material embeddedness of Bitcoin. *Distinktion: Scandinavian Journal of Social Theory, 15*(1), 23–36.

Kritzman, Li, Page, & Rigobon. (2011). Principal Components as a measure of systemic risk. *Journal of Portfolio Management, 37*, 112-126.

Lakomski-Laguerre & Desmedt. (2017). L'alternative monétaire Bitcoin: une perspective institutionnaliste. *Revue de la régulation, 18*. http://journals.openedition.org/regulation/11489

Lee, K. (2017). Herd behavior of the overall market: Evidence based on the cross-sectional comovement of returns. *The North American Journal of Economics and Finance, 42*, 266–284.

MacDonell, A. (2014). *Popping the Bitcoin bubble: An application of log-periodic power law modelling to digital currency.* University of Notre Dame Working Paper.

Maurer, B., Nelms, T. C., & Swartz, L. (2013). When perhaps the real problem is money itself!: The practical materiality of Bitcoin. *Social Semiotics, 23*(2), 261–277.

Mbeledogu, N. N., Odoh, M., & Umeh, M. N. (2012). Stock feature extraction using PrincipleComponent Analysis. In *International Conference on Computer Technology and Science.* IACSIT Press. DOI: 10.7763/IPCSIT.2012.V47.44

Moser, M., Bohme, R., & Breuker, D. (2013). *An inquiry into money laundering tools in the Bitcoin ecosystem. In eCrimeResearchersSummit (eCRS), 2013.* IEEE.

Nadarajah, S., & Chu, J. (2017). On the inefficiency of Bitcoin. *Economics Letters, 150*, 6–9.

Nakamoto, S. (2009a). *Bitcoin: A peer-to-peer electronic cash system.* www.bitcoin.org.

Nakamoto, S. (2009b). *Bitcoin open source implementation of P2P currency.* P2P Foundation.

Orléan, A. (2002). La monnaie, opérateur de totalization. Entretien avec André Orléan réalisé par Françoise Bourdarias. *Journal des anthropologues, 90-91*, 331-352. http://jda.revues.org/2331.

Osterrieder, J., & Lorenz, J. (2017). A statistical risk assessment of Bitcoin and its extreme tail behavior. *Annals of Financial Economics, 12*(1).

Ostroy, J.-M., & Starr, R. M. (1990). The transactions role of Money. In B. Friedman & F. H. Hahn (Eds.), *Handbook of Monetary Economics* (pp. 3–62). North Holland.

Pochea, M. M., Filip, A. M., & Pece, A. M. (2017). Herding behavior in CEE stock markets under asymmetric conditions: A quantile regression analysis. *Journal of Behavioral Finance, 18*(4), 400–416.

Robin, T., Zeynep, Y., & Tomas, L. (2013), Breaking Out of the Bank in Europe – Exploring Collective Emergent Institutional Entrepreneurship through Bitcoin. *15th Annual SNEE Conference.*

Shanghai Stock Exchange 50 Index. (2014). *Discrete Dynamics in Nature and Society Volume 2014.* Author.

Swanson, T. (2014). *The Anatomy of a Money-like Informational Commodity: A Study of Bitcoin.* Creative Commons.

Szczepanski, M. (2014). *Bitcoin: Market, economics and regulation.* European Parliamentary Research Service.

Théret, B. (2007). *La monnaie dévoilée par ses crises.* Éditions de l'EHESS.

Théret, B. (2008). Les trois états de la monnaie. Approche interdisciplinaire du fait monétaire. *Revue Economique, 59*(4), 813–841.

Urquhart, A. (2016). The inefficiency of Bitcoin. *Economics Letters, 148*, 80–82.

Vasek, M., Bonneau, J., Castellucci, R., Keith, C., & Moore, T. (2016). The Bitcoin brain drain: A short paper on the use and abuse of bitcoin brain wallets. In *Financial Cryptography and Data Security*. Lecture Notes in Computer Science. Springer.

Vasek, M., & Moore, T. (2015). There's no free lunch, even using Bitcoin: Tracking the popularity and profits of virtual currency scams. In *International Conference on Financial Cryptography and Data Security* (pp. 44–61). Springer.

World Bank. (2012). *Financial Inclusion Data.* http://datatopics.worldbank.org/financialinclusion/

Wray, L. R. (2014). *From the state theory of money to modern money theory: an alternative to economic orthodoxy.* Levy Economics Institute. 10.2139/ssrn.2407711

Yang, L., Rea, W., & Rea, A. (2016). Stock Selection with Principal Component Analysis. *The Journal of Investment Strategies, 5*, 1–21.

ADDITIONAL READING

MacKenzie, D. (2006). *An Engine, not a Camera: How Financial Models shape Markets.* MIT Press.

KEY TERMS AND DEFINITIONS

Bitcoin: Is the cryptocurrency with the highest valuation. But it is also the name of a blockchain protocol that allows peer-to-peer transactions to be carried out transparently and securely.

CCI30 Index: The CCi30 is a rules-based index designed to objectively measure the overall growth, daily and long-term movement of the blockchain sector. It does so by tracking the 30 largest cryptocurrencies by market capitalization, excluding stablecoins. It serves as a tool for passive investors to participate in this asset class, and as an industry benchmark for investment managers. For achieving its objectives, the CCi30 has been designed with 5 main characteristics: 1. diversified; 2. replicable; 3. transparent; 4. provides in-depth coverage of the entire sector; 5. presents the best risk-adjusted performance profile possible.

CoinDesk: Is a news site specializing in bitcoin and digital currencies. The site was founded by Shakil Khan and was subsequently acquired by Digital Currency Group.

CoinMarketCap: Is the world's most trusted and accurate source for crypto market capitalizations, pricing, and information.

Cryptocurrency: Cryptocurrency, sometimes called crypto-currency or crypto, is any form of currency that exists digitally or virtually and uses cryptography to secure transactions. Cryptocurrencies don't have a central issuing or regulating authority, instead using a decentralized system to record transactions and issue new units.

Ethereum: Is a decentralized exchange protocol allowing users to create smart contracts. These smart contracts are based on a computer protocol to verify or enforce a mutual contract. They are deployed and publicly viewable in a blockchain. Ethereum uses a unit of account called Ether as a means of payment for these contracts. Its corresponding acronym, used by trading platforms, is "ETH". Ethereum is the second largest decentralized cryptocurrency with a capitalization exceeding 448 billion euros in October 2021.

KMO (Kaiser-Meyer-Olkin): Is a statistical measure to determine how suited data is for factor analysis. The test measures sampling adequacy for each variable in the model and the complete model. The statistic is a measure of the proportion of variance among variables that might be common variance. The higher the proportion, the higher the KMO-value, the more suited the data is to factor analysis.

Litecoin: *Litecoin* (LTC) is decentralised money, free from censorship and open to all. Send low cost private, secure, borderless payments to anyone, anytime, anywhere.

Principal Component Analysis (PCA): Or, depending on the field of application, Karhunen–Loève transformation (KLT) or Hotelling transformation, is a method of the family of data analysis and more generally of multivariate statistics, which consists of transforming linked variables between they (known as "correlated" in statistics) into new variables uncorrelated from each other. These new variables are called "principal components" or principal axes. It allows the statistician to summarize information by reducing the number of variables. This is an approach that is both geometric (the variables being represented in a new space, along directions of maximum inertia) and statistical (the search for independent axes best explaining the variability — the variance — of the data). When we want to compress a set of N {\displaystyle N} N random variables, the first n {\displaystyle n} n axes of the principal component analysis are a better choice, from the point of view of inertia or the variance. The mathematical tool is applied in fields other than statistics and is sometimes called orthogonal eigenvalue decomposition or POD.

Chapter 7
Cyber Regulations and Access to Justice During COVID-19

Eltjon Mirashi
University of Salamanca, Spain

ABSTRACT

This chapter aims to study the initiatives to regulate cybersecurity with non-binding norms and the impact of COVID-19 on access to justice. It mentions the principal initiatives to create resilience to cybersecurity and build digital trust. The pandemic situation related to COVID-19 has put in real difficulty the access to justice as a fundamental right. In this chapter, the intention is to expose these initiatives and create an awareness to the related topics, as well to propose possible solutions.

INTRODUCTION

The development of technology urges the development of values and norms to address the impact and challenges that this revolutionary progress presents for the international, regional organization, States, law enforcement agencies, and citizens.

Cybersecurity and cyber regulation need common and global initiatives. We will try to outline in the following pages how these global efforts are implemented. To achieve our goal, we will use as a reference some of the main initiatives to perform the creation of awareness and hygiene related to global cybersecurity.

In this short paper, the intention is to expose some cybersecurity principles, norms, and rules proposed by academia and international organizations that can become binding laws that directly influence our national legislation and criminal codes.

DOI: 10.4018/978-1-7998-9117-8.ch007

Terrorism and the information and communication technology (ICT hereinafter) are not only a local or regional problem urging interventions, but it is also a global challenge that affects States, public-private organizations and civil citizens.

The situation related to Sars - Cov-2 commonly known as Covid-19 is living proof to demonstrate the need for global collaboration to reduce the effects caused by the pandemic, not only on the health of citizens, the economy but even on the access to justice.

GLOBAL CULTURE ON CYBERSECURITY AND DIGITAL TRUST

Initiatives have been taken to face the problems related to ICT and cybersecurity by making valid recommendations for the private sector and the member states of the United Nations (United Nations [UN], 2021). We will see that these interventions are not only laws imposed from international agreements, but some of them come in the form of recommendations, manuals, good practices to have a better and more comprehensive approach to address them and build a culture of cybersecurity.

We will try to expose these initiatives shortly starting from the international level, regional level, and different initiatives taken by the private sector.

The Resolution 57/239 of the General Assembly of the United Nations of the 31 of January 2003, mentions and recognizes that the need for cybersecurity increase as countries increase their participation in the information society. As well invites on being aware since cybersecurity is not merely a matter of government or law enforcement practices, but must be addressed through the prevention, planning, management throughout the society.

The resolution titled 'Creation of global culture of cybersecurity' (International Telecommunication Union [ITU], 2000), addresses the importance that the operators and owners of internet technologies should take measures, being aware of cybersecurity risks, and take interior measurements to create resilience to cyberattacks and to defend their business and their customers. It is clear enough that the customers of the ICT are not just clients but persons and subjects of law.

To create this global culture of cybersecurity it is important to address the following complementary elements: awareness; responsibility; response; ethics; democracy; risk assessments; security design and implementation; security management and reassessment (Resolution 57/239, 2003).

This resolution invites the member states and the principal international and regional organizations to develop and prepare their societies with the culture of cybersecurity. Appeal the Member States and some representative of international organizations to develop and prepare their society with the culture of cybersecurity, differencing clearly with cybercrime.

In the words of Gercke, (2014), "One of the most frequent mistakes is to confuse cybercrime and cybersecurity. By far, not all Cybersecurity incidents are criminal acts" (p.33-40).

This is an affirmation that I personally share and strongly support as shown in previous studies (Mirashi, 2021).

The Resolution 57/239 does not have the characteristics of binding norm-making resolution but is an invitation for global public awareness of the need for adoption of measures and preparation of a global culture on cybersecurity. Besides this, we will need intervention even in the legislation and capacity-building and this in my consideration, brings the resolution to the next level, from advice to real concrete actions.

Is important to mention that this resolution is continuous of precedent initiatives with legal effects evidencing the resolution's (A/RES/55/63, 2001) of 4 of December 2000 on 'Combating the criminal misuse of information technologies' and (A/RES/56/121, 2001) of 19 of December 2001 on establishing the legal basis for combating the criminal misuse of information technologies.

Almost simultaneously with the mentioned resolution at the UN, a regional initiative was approved, The Convention of Cybercrime of Council of Europe (known as the Convention of Budapest) with a regional and global perspective, being the first of the kind in the regulation of cybercrime -broadly international participation on the preparation and implementation of such convention- in different continents and systems of justice.

The criminal and procedural law has been renovated from the entrance into force of this convention (Csonka, 2006; Weber, 2003). Without doubts, this convention has importance for the international perspective and the legal assistance in the cooperation in the investigation to fight cybercrime (Osula, 2015).

In a world so globalized and yet so technological, it is difficult to investigate and prosecute criminals in the best possible way. Therefore, the only way is a joint cooperation between all the factors in order to be able to succeed and put an end to activities that cause harm to people, institutions and society in general. This difficulty in investigating and prosecuting criminals in the technological world depends on different elements such as the legal deficit to investigate, the deficit in human resources and in instrumental resources. For better comprehension, the two principal field of interventions and scopes of this Convention on Cybercrime have been:

Procedural scope. The Convention refers to various investigative measures and specific criminal proceedings, such as the rapid conversation of stored computer data; order of presentation, registration, and confiscation of stored computer data; real-time obtaining of computer data, and interception of data related to the content.

Criminal scope: Scope of substantive criminal law, where the States parties undertake to adopt legislative or other measures that they believe may help to typify four categories of crimes: Title 1- crimes against confidentiality, integrity, and availability of data and computer systems, where to include the criminal precepts of illegal access, illegal interception, attacks on the data integrity, attacks on system integrity and abuse of data devices; Title 2 – Computer-related offences; Title 3 – Content-related offences and Title 4 – Offences related to infringements of copyright and related rights.

The internet governance forum (IGF hereafter), a multistakeholder governance group for policy dialogue on issues of Internet governance, during the 10th main session on cybersecurity named "Enhancing Cybersecurity and Building Digital Trust" in the report of 2015 mentions that the capacity building in cybersecurity is fundamental. During the speech the Minister of IT of Afghanistan Zmriali (Wafa, 2015) related the subject capacity building he correctly expresses:

Having national Cybersecurity strategy will make this job easier. Security trainings are costly. We need strong support from the senior management. We need buy-in. The first step towards the resiliency of the Cybersecurity is then Government should establish a multistakeholder environment, bring the stakeholders together from private sector, academia and operators to address the challenges they face. Critical infrastructure partners must collectively identify priorities, clear goals with clear goals towards their assets. All these threats are shared responsibility. Regular awareness program and training programs are essential in both Government and private sector. In this regard, we need to plan, establish a Centralized Computer Security Incident Management capability which is called national SIRT. To managing CSIRT or SIRTs with a national responsibility, we can provide awareness, manage cyber incidents, support the national Cybersecurity strategy, public/private partnership in Cybersecurity, building a culture of Cybersecurity, national policy framework for Cybersecurity, managing and participating in Cybersecurity exercises, Cybersecurity assessment and evaluation.

This in my opinion is a very accurate call about the concerns we actually have in the world of cybersecurity and especially in the fight against cyber violations making urgent the preparation of all operators to deal with it. We need common rules and regulations, effective ones to fight this enemy and to show that the rule of law, human rights are dominant against disorganization and crime.

As it can be stated the problem is multilevel and needs multilevel action to face it, with a good and effective strategy. Is an added value for this research to put attention with a short mention to the path of the organizations who can create rules, models, norms to be followed or to act as inspiration for the national regulation to build cybersecurity atmosphere and to face the abuse of the law with the use and the help of the technology.

It can be said as an added value in this paper that every international organization and country can create bodies of norms or rules, created just for them to regulate cybersecurity issues, that on a larger scale can be an inspiration for other countries, groups of countries, or regions.

In advance, we believe that having a global problem with transnational characteristics than every contribution on regulations -rules or legal improvement- even if created for local or limited countries or some specific geographic areas for sure can be imported and introduced in other systems of law geographically distant between them. Some interventions can be valid *erga omnes* because the threat is global, dangerous, and challenges all the legal systems and societies. Exportation of norms and the norm making initiatives focused on specific group that can have international or global incidence are not so rare to find in our globalized society.

The Convention against Cybercrime of Council of Europe in 2001, created as an agreement of European Countries with the help of Non-European countries (Japan-USA among others) opened for adhesion for all interested countries. More recently to the current day the EU NIS Directive (Directive EU 2016/1148, 2016) or GDPR (for General Data Protection Regulation) entered into force in 2018 (Regulation (EU) 2016/679, 2016) created for European Union member states that can be exported with regulation and adoption to other systems in other regions or countries are a good illustration of this affirmation as will be explained concerning the territory competences of this regulation.

GDPR has global effects and not just Europeans one by giving more security and protection to the data of the citizens. The global impact and effects of this regulation are included in the body of this legal product, especially the art.3 relating to the 'Territory scope'. Explained the same in simple words, the global organizations' companies who have a physical presence in EU territory or gives services to EU citizens will be subject to the GDPR. To illustrate with a concrete example can be used the case of Facebook related to EU users when Mr. Mark Zuckerberg CEO of this company in May 2018 reported to the EU parliament in issues related to EU citizens and their data protection (European Parliament, 2018). In common sense can be said that GDPR is done for European citizen but the territorial effects of the GDPR are universal but this is still to be proved in practice.

Other groups or organizations can also be active in this discipline and for this we can give other examples, because in the topic that interests for this research there are other actions that deserve to be mentioned that have the purpose of regulation, the promotion of the culture of computer security and the fight against cybercrime.

On the other hand, the intergovernmental military alliance known as the North Atlantic Treaty Organization (NATO hereinafter) had taken initiatives on cybersecurity and the creation of the digital trust. The CCDCOE (for Cooperative Cyber Defense Centre of Excellence) in 2016 reunited a group of legal experts to renovate the Tallinn Manual of 2013 which was concentrated on the interpretation of how the international law should act in the context of cyber operations, by offering guidance on reasonable interpretations of the law and in the development of normative content.

In 2016 the group of experts, nineteen of them, international law experts were covered with the assessment of interpretation of how international laws, treaties, and norms regulate activities in cyberspace and not to create law or norms. In the same idea is one of the authors of the Tallinn 1.0 and 2.0 (Jensen, 2017) when he explains referring to the introduction of the manual:

The intent of the project was never to make law or to produce a manual that would have the force of law. As the introduction makes clear:

Ultimately, Tallinn Manual 2.0 must be understood only as an expression of the opinions of the two International Groups of Experts as to the state of the law... This Manual is meant to be a reflection of the law as it existed at the point of the Manual's adoption by the two International Groups of Experts in June 2016. It is not a 'best practices' guide, does not represent 'progressive development of the law', and is policy and politics-neutral. In other words, Tallinn Manual 2.0 is intended as an objective restatement of the lex lata.

This manual analysis whether exists, the right of States in the self-defense when they are under cyber-attack and the analysis of different cyber-attack cases during the last years by using the interpretation techniques based on the international law principles with soft law perspective.

As the authors have broadly and clearly explained does not pretend to be a representation of the evolution of the international practices related to cyberspace issues. It is an expression of the opinions of the international experts with the mission of improving the research on the related field of cyberspace.

This is done through interpretation based on the principles of international law by experts with a soft law perspective. The aforementioned introduction in my opinion does not prohibit the use of this manual in the future to create rules or to adopt it as law or also to use it as a basis for the formulation of norms.

Even the private sector has done some initiatives for the cybersecurity and the security of cyberspace. An interesting initiative has been launched by Microsoft in 2017 titled 'A Digital Geneva Convention to protect cyberspace' with the mission to create a legally binding framework to govern states' behavior in cyberspace by proposing some behaviors and commitments for the States inspired from the UN and the UNGGE as they claim in different refrains and agreements to do something or to control different sources (Microsoft, 2017).

Generally, these are commitments that have in the center of their existence the citizens, the business, and their economic and safety interest as can be comprehended from the mentioned list. We guess this is influenced by the fact that this proposal comes from a private company and for this, the main focus is human and business safety and security.

Norm making and initiatives in cybersecurity as we saw are an interesting field that catches multiple attention and is an ongoing work. The initiatives are important for the future and indicators of the change that characterize our security and digital approach. These are indicators as well of the need for regulation as we purposely have mentioned by choosing one representant for each category of norm marking: International; Regional; Intergovernmental and private interventions. Beside this what it matters is the present and the present is measured with the approved legislation and regulation.

COVID- 19 AND THE ACCESS TO JUSTICE

Besides the initiatives taken to build this cybersecurity atmosphere with binding and non-binging interventions mentioning the role of the Convention of Budapest in the countries part of this Convention or other regional and private initiatives on building cyber resilience have not been enough in our opinion.

The pandemic situation related to the Covid-19 since March 2020 has shown that the concern on the regulation of the ICT, cybersecurity and clarifying the difference with cybercrime and taking measures for resilience was correct but not enough.

Unfortunately, the situation caused by the Covid-19 showed how weak our system of law was, the access to justice as a fundamental right was/is put in real doubt. In different countries and courts, the service has been suspended or paralyzed due to Covid-19 – some judges get infected or suspected to be affected with Covid-19, due to national or regional lockdowns, difficulty, or impossibility for citizens to reach the courts, the people are more worried about their health than their rights-affecting all areas of our life (European Justice Portal; Yeon Lee; United Nations, 2020).

All the initiatives taken to build digital trust and the culture of cybersecurity have been put in doubt during the pandemic situation related to Covid-19. Some countries are having problems with the hardware infrastructure and IT equipment's, software programs to keep the system of justice functioning, a strong digital gap, lacks in the preparation of judges to deal with cyber and ICT, lacks in the preparation of citizens to use the new technologies and facilities to access to justice existing a digital literacy or *alfabetismo digital*, weak diffusion of the opportunities to access to justice.

United Nations published in April 2020 a report that precise that the 'Human rights are the key to shaping the pandemic response' (United Nations, 2020) and on the publishing of the United Nations Statical Commission precisely on the SDG16 to strengthen equal justice for all, as mentions on the report, it established a new global Sustainable Development Goal, 'Goal 16: Promote just, peaceful and inclusive societies' (United Nations, 2015) and explains that the conflict, insecurity, weak institutions and limited access to justice remain a great threat to sustainable development.

As it is mentioned at the heart of the agenda 2030 for sustainable development lies a vision of a just, equitable, tolerant, open, and socially inclusive world in which the needs of the most vulnerable are met and promises to ensure equal access to justice for all by 2030. To reach this goal it mentions that the tasks to be taken are: Place justice at the heart of sustainable development; put people at the centre of justice systems and move from justice for the few to justice for all (United Nations, 2019).

CONCLUSION

The technological development of the Internet and globalization facilitate the commission of criminal acts. Society, and certainly the Law, must be updated, renewed, and adapted to respond to the increase in cross-border and global crime.

The urgent need for the creation of a deep knowledge about the culture of cybersecurity and cybercrime has been evidenced. We should put the attention for a comprehensive development, even in countries with less economic and technological development.

The Internet and ICTs are not directly regulated in an all-encompassing, immutable and definitive manner in a model code; Which is why interventions are necessary in a reality where the law always lags behind technology and criminal actions. Initiatives must be designed with a view to legislating pro-future and ensuring that technological development does not render legal reforms obsolete in a short time.

In my consideration, only common strategies with different instruments can be effective to facilitate the access to justice with a more active role within international, regional and state-level organization.

As it has been showed in this chapter, we need to enforce our collaboration and efforts in the creation of a global public awareness related the cybersecurity. The pandemic situation, the sanitary situation should not be a justification for violation of human rights, to limit the access to justice, to create more separation between rich and poor societies. We need to bring this from ideas to real actions.

REFERENCES

Csonka, P. (2006). The council of europe's convention on cyber-crime and other European initiatives. *Revue internationale de droit pénal*, *77*, 473-501. . doi:10.3917/ridp.773.0473

European e-Justice Portal. (n.d.). *Impact of Covid-19 on the justice field.* Retrieved 14/04/21 from: https://e-justice.europa.eu/content_impact_of_covid19_on_the_justice_field-37147-en.do

Gercke, M. (2014). Content of a Comprehensive Cybersecurity Legal Framework. *CLRI*, *15*(2), 33–40. doi:10.9785/cri-2014-0202

Jensen, T. E. (2017). The Tallinn Manual 2.0: Highlights and insights. *GJIL*, 735-777.

Mirashi, E. (2021). *Cooperación procesal internacional en la lucha contra la criminalidad transfronteriza: especial referencia al cibercrimen y al terrorismo.* Universidad de Salamanca.

Osula, A. M. (2015). Mutual Legal Assistance & Other Mechanisms for Accessing Extraterritorially Located Data. *MUJLT*, *9*(1), 43–64. doi:10.5817/MUJLT2015-1-4

Pathinfinders. (n.d.). *Justice for all, Report of the task force on justice.* Retrieved 11/04/21 from: https://www.justice.sdg16.plus/report

Policy, M. (2017). *A Digital Geneva Convention to protect cyberspace.* Retrieved from 12/04/21: https://www.microsoft.com/en-us/cybersecurity/content-hub/a-digital-genevaconvention-to-protect-cyberspace.

Task Force on Justice. Justice for All (2019). *Final Report.* New York: Center on International Cooperation. Retrieved 14/04/21 from: https://www.justice.sdg16.plus.

United Nations. (2001a). *Resolution A/RES/55/63, Combating the criminal misuse of information technologies.* Author.

United Nations. (2001b). *Resolution A/RES/56/121, Combating the criminal misuse of information technologies.* Author.

United Nations. (2020a), *UN expert outlines urgent steps to ensure justice systems are not paralysed by COVID-19.* Retrieved 14/04/21 from: https://reliefweb.int/report/world/un-expertoutlines-urgent-steps-ensure-justice-systems-are-not-paralysed-covid-19

United Nations. (2020b). *We are all in this Together: Human Rights and Covid-19 Response and Recovery*. Retrieved 14/04/21 from: https://www.un.org/en/un-coronavirus-communications-team/we-are-all-together-human-rights-and-covid-19-response-and

United Nations. (n.d.). *Goal 16: Promote just, peaceful and inclusive societies*. Retrieved 15/04/21 from: https://www.un.org/sustainabledevelopment/peace-justice/

United Nations. (2003). *UN Resolution 57/239, Creation of a global culture of cybersecurity*. Retrieved 14/04/21 from: https://www.itu.int/ITUD/cyb/cybersecurity/docs/UN_resolution_57_239.pdf

United Nations. (2021). *Peace, dignity and equality on a healthy planet*. Retrieved 14/04/21 from: https://www.un.org/en/

UNODC. (n.d.). *Judicial Suspension and Electronic Access to Justice*. Retrieved 14/04/21 from: https://www.unodc.org/dohadeclaration/en/news/2020/06/judicial-suspension-and-electronic-access-to-justice.html

Wafa, Z. (2015). *Internet Governance Forum*. Retrieved 15/04/21 from: http://www.intgovforum.org/cms/187-igf2015/transcripts-igf-2015/2884-2015-11-12-enhancingcybersecurity-and-building-digital-trust-main-meeting-hall-finished

Weber, M. (2003). The Council of Europe's Convention on Cybercrime. BTLJ, 18(1).

ADDITIONAL READING

Europol. (2020). Internet organized crime threat assessment (IOCTA). Poder Judicial Español. La Comisión Permanente aprueba una guía para la celebración de actuaciones judiciales telemáticas. Retrieved 15/04/2021 from: https://www.poderjudicial.es/

Velasco Nunez, E. (2016). Delitos tecnológicos: Definición, investigación y prueba en el proceso penal. Actualizado a las reformas del Código Penal y de la Ley de Enjuiciamiento Criminal de 2015. *Sepin, Madrid, 2016*, 1–198.

Velasco San Martin, C. (2016). *Jurisdicción y competencia penal en relación al acceso transfronterizo en materia de ciberdelitos*. Tirant lo Blanch.

Vervaele, J. A. E. (2001). Las agencias europeas de cumplimiento de la ley en el espacio de libertad, seguridad y justicia: El binomio Eurojust-Fiscalía Europea. *Nuevo Foro Penal*, *75*(julio-diciembre), 195–228.

KEY TERMS AND DEFINITIONS

Cross-Border Crime: Non lawful acts and criminal acts not limited to a specific geographic area but that includes and are considered as a crime in at least two or more geographic areas.

Culture of Cybersecurity: Events, education, transmission of the know how in the society with the purpose to familiarize them with the concepts of cyber and security.

Cybersecurity Principles: Principles, common decisions that can help define and understand the cybersecurity.

Global Crime: Non lawful acts that influence and can have influence globally.

Global Public Awareness Related to Cybersecurity: Global efforts and initiatives to create an awareness to the risks of cybersecurity. Transmit the idea that we are safer if we are aware, and no one can be safe if one of our friends/countries is not aware of the risks related to cyber.

Globalization: Connection and Interconnection of different geographic areas between them.

Resilience: Initiatives, measurement taken as an answer to an attack or unpleasant situation that changes and challenges our status.

Chapter 8
Coalescing Skills of Gig Players and Fervor of Entrepreneurial Leaders to Provide Resilience Strategies During Global Economic Crises

Manpreet Arora
Central University of Himachal Pradesh, India

Roshan Lal Sharma
Central University of Himachal Pradesh, India

ABSTRACT

The COVID-19 pandemic has caused diverse sorts of disruption across the globe. The pandemic has drastically impacted the economies of almost every country of the world. The international economic scenario is full of despair as the entrepreneurs and business leaders find it hard to come to terms with the extent of damage caused by the pandemic. In view of largely prevalent gloom and despair, it is imperative that certain resilience strategies are worked out so that global economic crisis can be stemmed from further escalation. The gig economy has been viewed as a powerful resilience mechanism to tide over the economic crisis caused the world over by COVID-19. Entrepreneurial leadership can also make significant difference in providing a paddle-push to the pandemic-struck world by reactivating the engines of economic growth. The nature of this chapter is qualitative, and it seeks to theoretically work out certain strategies that can help various economies of the world to stand up and be resilient in the face of complex challenges that the pandemic has thrown before us.

DOI: 10.4018/978-1-7998-9117-8.ch008

INTRODUCTION

When in March 2020, WHO characterized COVID-19 as pandemic, no one had imagined that it might take such a devastating turn affecting all sectors of economy in more than 220 economies across the world. Global economy and financial markets received a powerful blow and disruption could be seen in spheres of production and supply chain, health, tourism, consumer goods, transport, and education leading to high level of loss of livelihoods and employment. Many countries had to impose lockdowns/ curfews/ restrictions to be opened up gradually in a phased manner so that the economic activity could resume. It certainly did gain pace in some countries like USA, Italy, UK, Germany, etc. that were worst hit at one point in time during the first wave of Covid-19 pandemic. On the other hand, developing economies like India and Brazil, saw the largest GDP contraction during 2020-2021. Moreover, India has undergone the second wave of the pandemic which has proved to be deadlier than the first one. It is the second time that the lockdowns/curfews have been imposed here for more than a month. Several South Indian states are now in the grip of the third wave of COVID-19 pandemic. There is a sharp decline in national income as the service sector has totally collapsed. The health system has given in and there is a huge stress on supply chains along with the trade tensions with China that have increased the agony as it had been the largest trading partner of India for a long time. The demand has significantly dropped in almost all nations where lockdowns were imposed.

The COVID-19 pandemic initially did not seem alarming despite the fact that the WHO had declared it as pandemic without any time lapse. But after a point, it spread like wild fire infecting and killing millions of people across the globe. The first world nations at one point were the most adversely affected. The businesses collapsed and economies were hit badly. Out of sheer panic, lockdowns were announced and restrictions were imposed. This pandemic has proven to be unprecedented owing to the life loss as well as the loss of livelihoods and economic damage.

The economic crises faced by the world due to COVID-19 are showing deep and long-lasting effects (Laborde, Martin & Vos, 2021). The interesting fact is the global economic downturn is not caused by economic factors but non-economic ones which have caused such a crisis across the world. Economies are trying hard to revive after the second wave of the pandemic but start-ups and medium-scale organizations which lack liquidity suffered a severe jolt and quite a few of them closed down. On the other hand, many jobs were laid off and only those who were having some technical, digital or specialized skills, could come up with small start ups or ventures and could survive properly. In fact, creativity and skills recued the people in distress during the pandemic. Long-term commitments of the large-scale organizations were shattered due to the disrupted supply chains. Many world renowned experts are of the view that the crises first affected the liquidity of the organizations and now it has started showing negative impacts on the solvency of the firms (Guerini, Nesta, Ragot & Schiavo, 2020). A large number of layoffs, significant fall in income level, disruption in transportation, rise in unemployment and poverty, could be seen in many economies. The income level of households as well as firms including service sector received a severe jolt due to premature deaths, lockdowns, health expenditures, shut down of production facilities, closure of borders, disruptions in global supply chains, workplace absenteeism etc.. The saving, investment and consumption pattern of households changed drastically due to reduced income level (Baker, Farrokhnia, Meyer, Pagel & Yannelis, 2020, Martin, Markhvida, Hallegatte & Walsh, 2020). Tourism, aviation, hospitality sectors were hit badly and thereby many nations where tourism was the backbone of the livelihoods and contributed largely to the income of the country were hit drastically.

By using the secondary data and the existing body of literature, the authors wish to assess the extent of economic crisis being faced by the world economies. The analysis of current news items, reports, and other relevant material can help us to understand the impact of COVID-19 pandemic on world economies. As stated, this pandemic has terribly affected supply chains, production sector and has resulted in lowering of demand by the consumers. In such an abysmal scenario, the entrepreneurs have to come up as leaders and have to take the charge of bringing economies back on the track. As Schumpter (2000) observes that the entrepreneurial spirit of entrepreneurs contributes directly towards creativity and innovation which eventually results in propelling the economic engine and thus brings prosperity. All the technological changes that have been brought in the economy are the result of innovation only which leads to prosperity and welfare of the state (Audretsch, 2007). Otherwise too, entrepreneurs are regarded as the leaders of industrial development (Arora & Sharma, 2017). They are important pillars of any economy. They are basically the employment generators and primarily contribute to the economic growth (Acs, 2006). Therefore, the authors would like to make an attempt to establish a link between the entrepreneurship and leadership by finding theoretically the answers to the following research questions, thereby also analyzing the role of gig economy in coping with existing economic crisis.

METHODOLOGY AND RESEARCH QUESTIONS

The methodology of this chapter is qualitative and it focuses on the perspective building based on literature and emerging concepts in the field of business and economy. The following research questions will be discussed in the discussion that follows to ascertain as to how critically crucial is the role of entrepreneurs, business leaders and gig players in restoring economies to a state of normalcy:

1. Can gig economy serve as a resilience strategy to rebuild economies that have been adversely affected by the pandemic?
2. What are the other resilience strategies to rebuild economies post COVID-19 pandemic?
3. How can entrepreneurial leadership help the pandemic-struck world tide over the worst economic crises ever?
4. How can the problem of loss of employment/livelihoods be dealt with during the post-pandemic era?

AN OVERVIEW OF GLOBAL FINANCIAL CRISES POST-COVID-19

The June 2020 issue of the *Global Economic Prospects* discusses the impact of the pandemic and thereby describing heavy damage caused by to economies and businesses. It reveals that "The baseline forecast envisions a 5.2 percent contraction in global GDP in 2020, using market exchange rate weights—the deepest global recession in decades, despite the extraordinary efforts of governments to counter the downturn with fiscal and monetary policy support. Over the longer horizon, the deep recessions triggered by the pandemic are expected to leave lasting scars through lower investment, an erosion of human capital through lost work and schooling, and fragmentation of global trade and supply linkages." Thus, there has been whole range of crises and urgent action is required to deal with its consequences in health, economic and business sectors. The need of the hour is to strengthen our health facilities and go in for economic recovery measures that are sustainable.

Production in countries like China went down to a great extent and thereby markets of the trade partners like India received a jolt again (Wang & Sun, 2021). In the US, due to quarantine measures, the badly hit sectors were restaurants, hotels, entertainment, food, and airlines. In addition to all these sectors, stock markets and the financial service sector of almost all countries received a shock. Only digital platforms received an increase in customer base. Overall, the saving and investment pattern was hit badly due to reduced incomes in all sectors across the globe (Barua, 2020). Due to badly hit transportation sector the oil demand reduced drastically and it had a great effect on the global financial markets (Ozili & Arun, 2020). Countries like US, Spain, France, Italy, Korea and India were closed for a long time in 2020 then again in 2021 which affected the demand of oil and thereby negatively affected the financial markets. Many researches showed a relationship between number of cases of COVID-19 and stock price volatility (Devpura & Narayan, 2020; Narayan, 2020; Harjoto, Rossi, Lee & Sergi, 2021; Gao, Ren, & Umar, 2021; Shaikh, 2020; Zaremba, Kizys, Aharon & Demir, 2020). A huge fluctuation in oil prices across the globe has laid a significant negative impact on the financial markets and stock prices of the companies (Ebrahim, Inderwildi, & King, 2014; Filis, 2010; Lin & Bai, 2021). The disruptions have impacted not only developing and under-developed nations but the developed nations have also received a severe jolt. The economic crises can be seen in most of the countries in terms of negative or negligible growth rate. The table 1 below shows the GDP growth by country percentage which gives us an idea of how badly the economies got hit in 2020 due to the pandemic:

As evident in the table 1 above, COVID 19 pandemic has drastically affected the GDP growth of several countries negatively. Not only the developing nations but many developed nations were also badly hit. In 2020, many nations were not able to maintain positive growth rate. Small countries like Mongolia, Nauru, Panama, Malta, Dominican Republic, Turkey, Armenia, Cameroon, Zambia, Colombia, Honduras, Costa Rica, Yemen faced negative growth rate ranging from -1 to -3 in the year 2020. The most unfavorably, worst as well as terribly-hit nations were tourist hubs like Zimbabwe (-7.3), Seychelles (-10.8), Mauritius (-6.8), Thailand (-6.6), New Zealand (-7.2), Ecuador (-6.2), Slovak Republic (-6.2), Australia (-6.6), Mexico (-6.6), United Kingdom (-6.5), Switzerland (-5.9), Netherland (-7.4), France (-7.18), Cyprus (-6.4), Croatia (-9.0), Spain (-8), Brazil (-5.3), and Italy (-2.8). Tourist destinations entirely dependent upon international tourists were on the verge of collapse, and some of them are Macao SAR (Special Administrative region of the People's Republic of China, -29.616), Palau (-11.9), Belize (-11.9), Spain (-8). The smallest country of the world, Lebanon which has again a rich traditional and culture suffered a negative growth rate of (-12.01). On the other hand, 16th largest country in the world, Libya shows a shocking picture of COVID-19 hit countries by experiencing a negative growth rate of -58.662. Developed nations like the Unites States (-5.9), Australia (-6.6), and Germany (-6.9) were also badly struck nations. Russia, one of the largest countries in the world which covers 1/8th of Earth's inhabited land area, suffered a negative growth rate of -5.4.The UNCTAD/s report "Impact of the COVID-19 pandemic on trade and development, recovering, but unevenly, 31st March 2021" states that in 2020 approximately "255 million full times jobs was lost due to pandemic", and in 2020 Europe and North America recorded the steepest decline of FDI that is by 42%, the tourism sector suffered 11 times larger losses "experienced during global financial crisis of 2008-09". In such a challenging scenario, how gig players and entrepreneurial leaders can help revive the economy is discussed below:

a) Gig Players: The Paradigm Shift in Labor Market across the Globe

Table 1. GDP Growth by Country (%)

GDP Growth by Country (%)											
Country	2011	2012	2013	2014	2015	2016	2017	2018	2019	2020	Avg Change
Guyana	5.437	5.039	5.018	3.898	3.055	3.356	2.134	4.138	4.663	52.768	8.951
Ethiopia	11.4	8.7	9.9	10.3	10.4	8	10.21	7.703	8.967	3.237	8.882
Nauru	10.778	10.367	30.969	27.229	3.418	3.02	-5.496	5.703	0.959	-1.675	8.527
Turkmenistan	14.72	11.051	10.163	10.346	6.453	6.2	6.47	6.153	6.347	1.845	7.975
Rwanda	7.968	8.639	4.718	6.157	8.873	5.982	6.12	8.606	10.063	3.5	7.063
Mongolia	17.291	12.32	11.649	7.885	2.38	1.168	5.337	7.247	5.099	-1	6.938
China	9.5	7.9	7.8	7.3	6.9	6.849	6.947	6.75	6.11	1.181	6.724
Tajikistan	7.4	7.5	7.4	6.7	6	6.9	7.1	7.3	7.5	1	6.48
Bangladesh	6.494	6.26	6.038	6.314	6.842	7.202	7.584	8.014	7.879	2.019	6.465
Lao P.D.R.	7.986	7.805	8.026	7.621	7.27	7.023	6.832	6.308	4.72	0.723	6.431
Côte d'Ivoire	-4.857	10.864	9.272	8.794	8.843	7.179	7.36	6.793	6.9	2.7	6.384
Cambodia	7.07	7.313	7.357	7.143	7.036	6.863	6.997	7.533	7.045	-1.587	6.277
Myanmar	5.471	6.486	7.899	8.2	7.473	6.408	5.75	6.405	6.5	1.799	6.239
Tanzania	7.905	5.141	6.782	6.732	6.161	6.867	6.773	6.951	6.269	2.014	6.159
India	6.638	5.456	6.386	7.41	7.996	8.256	7.044	6.12	4.228	1.871	6.14
Vietnam	6.413	5.505	5.554	6.422	6.987	6.69	6.94	7.076	7.017	2.7	6.13
Djibouti	7.293	4.842	5.001	7.062	7.696	6.653	5.403	8.408	7.498	1	6.086
Uzbekistan	7.785	7.376	7.585	7.179	7.448	6.094	4.462	5.4	5.6	1.8	6.073
Ghana	14.198	8.504	7.19	2.897	2.178	3.448	8.143	6.263	6.113	1.497	6.042
Guinea	5.615	5.915	3.934	3.708	3.813	10.828	10.338	6.181	5.645	2.92	5.89
Philippines	3.66	6.684	7.064	6.145	6.067	6.884	6.678	6.244	5.905	0.648	5.598
Bhutan	9.866	6.495	3.582	3.968	6.221	7.408	6.322	3.734	5.335	2.671	5.560
Ireland	0.339	0.227	1.352	8.527	25.121	3.678	8.155	8.307	5.543	-6.781	5.447
Panama	11.314	9.779	6.903	5.067	5.733	4.953	5.599	3.692	3.006	-2.05	5.4
Niger	2.365	10.6	5.556	6.564	4.368	5.689	4.998	7.005	5.829	0.953	5.394
Niger	2.365	10.6	5.566	6.564	4.368	5.689	4.998	7.005	5.829	0.953	5.394
Burkina Faso	6.623	6.453	5.793	4.327	3.921	5.959	6.156	6.821	5.689	1.996	5.374
Democratic Republic of the Congo	6.875	7.087	8.482	9.47	6.916	2.4	3.727	5.816	4.381	-2.239	5.291
Togo	6.398	6.544	6.112	5.921	5.743	5.559	4.357	4.91	5.3	1	5.184
Kenya	6.112	4.563	5.879	5.357	5.718	5.879	4.863	6.32	5.626	1.01	5.133
Mozambique	7.404	7.258	6.964	7.399	6.723	3.824	3.741	3.428	2.224	2.2	5.117
Sengal	1.458	5.117	2.822	6.614	6.367	6.356	7.407	6.363	5.287	2.992	5.078
Malta	1.359	2.794	4.839	8.791	10.858	5.83	6.471	7.314	4.384	-2.814	4.983
Benin	2.964	4.811	7.191	6.358	1.778	3.34	5.672	6.697	6.397	4.519	4.973
Indonesia	6.17	6.03	5.557	5.007	4.876	5.033	5.07	5.17	5.025	0.499	4.844
Dominican Republic	3.761	2.869	3.554	7.213	6.509	6.983	4.722	7.015	5.071	-0.965	4.673
Nepal	3.422	4.781	4.129	5.989	3.323	0.589	8.223	6.658	7.051	2.509	4.667
Maldives	8.567	2.517	7.281	7.33	2.885	6.338	6.804	6.889	5.657	-8.074	4.619
Uganda	6.821	2.24	4.714	4.561	5.67	2.323	5.026	6.331	4.92	3.52	4.613
Turkey	11.113	4.79	8.491	5.167	6.086	3.184	7.471	2.827	0.937	-4.998	4.507
Malaysia	5.293	5.474	4.694	6.007	5.007	4.45	5.742	4.741	4.33	-1.7	4.404
Sri Lanka	8.405	9.145	3.396	4.961	5.008	4.487	3.578	3.306	2.283	-0.536	4.403
Iraq	7.546	13.936	7.628	0.738	2.537	15.199	-2.495	-0.563	3.914	-4.723	4.372
Papua New Guinea	1.108	4.657	3.825	13.544	9.484	4.078	3.538	-0.849	5.026	-0.961	4.345
Sierra Leone	6.312	15.178	20.72	4.555	-20.493	6.354	3.771	3.458	5.124	-2.314	4.267
Eritrea	25.71	1.886	-10.456	30.394	-20.621	7.391	-10.015	13.032	3.836	0.109	4.181
Armenia	4.7	7.134	3.412	3.607	3.254	0.195	7.518	5.238	7.597	-1.479	4.118
Cameroon	4.129	4.543	5.404	5.884	5.651	4.648	3.549	4.062	3.747	-1.215	4.04
Mali	2.656	-0.703	2.201	6.775	6.623	5.946	5.037	5.177	5.1	1.532	4.034
Bolivia	5.204	5.122	6.796	5.461	4.857	4.264	4.195	4.224	2.8	-2.9	4.002
Georgia	7.358	6.369	3.621	4.431	3.023	2.906	4.842	4.843	5.148	-3.999	3.854
Tuvala	7.476	-3.885	4.91	1.178	9.23	5.885	4.6	3.662	6	-0.953	3.81
Kyrgyz Republic	5.956	-0.088	10.915	4.024	3.876	4.336	4.74	3.459	4.468	-4.044	3.764

continued on following page

Table 1. Continued

Afghanistan	6.479	13.968	5.683	2.697	0.988	2.161	2.889	2.664	3.037	-3.007	3.756
Pakistan	3.624	3.837	3.683	4.053	4.058	4.563	5.219	5.528	3.294	-1.547	3.631
Egypt	1.765	2.226	3.302	2.916	4.372	4.347	4.077	5.314	5.558	1.952	3.583
Malawi	4.854	1.886	5.2	5.7	2.95	2.27	4	3.17	4.5	1	3.533
Solomon Islands	13.196	4.555	3.018	2.25	2.542	3.221	3.694	3.863	1.24	-2.07	3.551
Zambia	5.565	7.598	5.057	4.698	2.92	3.757	3.524	4.035	1.52	-3.507	3.517
Kazakhstan	7.4	4.8	6	4.2	1.2	1.1	4.1	4.1	4.4	-2.53	3.487
Guinea-Bissau	8.085	-1.713	3.256	0.965	6.134	5.307	5.789	3.8	4.6	-1.5	3.372
Botswana	6.048	4.456	11.344	4.149	-1.698	4.304	2.904	4.479	2.966	-5.379	3.357
Mauritania	4.173	4.47	4.151	4.275	5.376	1.261	3.497	2.115	5.861	-1.986	3.319
Moldova	5.818	-0.59	9.044	5	-0.338	4.409	4.691	4.002	3.58	-3	3.262
Paraguay	4.249	-0.539	8.417	4.861	3.08	4.313	4.954	3.681	0.2	-1	3.222
Peru	6.452	5.951	5.837	2.394	3.274	4.05	2.475	3.969	2.162	-4.534	3.203
Gabon	7.092	5.251	5.517	4.435	3.879	2.091	0.499	0.846	3.402	-1.196	3.182
Qatar	13.375	4.687	4.41	3.979	3.658	2.131	1.58	1.493	0.066	-4.345	3.103
Madagascar	1.578	3.011	2.3	3.132	3.933	3.933	3.933	4.565	4.758	0.39	3.0
Kiribati	1.595	4.713	4.215	-0.698	10.405	5.13	0.897	2.313	2.297	0.001	3.087
Singapore	6.338	4.462	4.837	3.938	2.989	3.243	4.337	3.438	0.733	<strong-3.47 < strong="" ></strong-3.47<>	3.085
Honduras	3.836	4.129	2.792	3.058	3.84	3.893	4.843	3.697	2.651	-2.35	3.039
Colombia	6.948	3.912	5.134	4.499	2.956	2.087	1.359	2.515	3.322	-2.386	3.035
Romania	2.007	2.007	3.515	3.411	3.872	4.801	7.111	4.437	4.078	-5	3.031
Zimbabwe	14.197	16.658	1.975	2.383	1.791	0.742	4.704	3.497	-8.276	-7.383	3.029
Seychelles	5.379	3.68	6.018	4.531	4.911	4.563	4.376	3.754	3.901	-10.835	3.028
Guatemala	4.445	3.148	3.485	4.444	4.092	2.676	3.003	3.056	3.57	-1.963	2.997
São Tomé and Príncipe	4.398	3.142	4.815	6.55	3.798	4.172	3.871	3.028	1.302	-6	2.908
Costa Rica	4.307	4.797	2.269	3.515	3.632	4.246	3.86	2.66	2.084	-3.292	2.808
Poland	5.017	1.608	1.392	3.318	3.839	3.064	4.938	5.148	4.095	-4.579	2.784
Oman	2.565	9.104	5.103	1.423	4.658	4.897	0.346	1.764	0.469	-2.844	2.749
Saudi Arabia	9.997	5.411	2.699	3.652	4.106	1.671	-0.742	2.434	0.331	-2.283	2.728
Comoros	4.144	3.168	4.466	2.107	1.299	3.457	4.177	3.639	1.866	-1.16	2.716
Kosovo	4.377	2.81	3.442	1.222	4.103	4.063	4.226	3.816	4	-5	2.71
Morocco	5.246	3.01	4.535	2.669	4.55	1.047	4.235	2.99	2.203	-3.744	2.674
Estonia	7.444	3.125	1.346	2.987	1.845	2.632	5.749	4.761	4.334	-7.5	2.672
Mauritius	4.077	3.496	3.36	3.745	3.553	3.838	3.814	3.761	3.482	-6.8	2.632
Israel	4.879	2.37	4.269	3.778	2.312	3.982	3.575	3.441	3.503	-6.288	2.582
Bahrain	1.984	3.728	5.416	4.351	2.863	3.473	3.814	1.955	1.819	-3.59	2.581
Fiji	2.7	1.411	4.734	5.604	4.664	2.51	5.425	3.526	0.5	-5.8	2.527
Lithuania	6.025	3.834	3.558	3.508	2.033	2.556	4.248	3.644	3.914	-8.086	2.523
South Korea	3.686	2.403	3.165	3.202	2.809	2.947	3.16	2.665	2.033	-1.178	2.489
The Gambia	-8.13	5.242	2.873	-1.407	4.058	1.943	4.823	6.547	5.975	2.5	2.442
Iceland	1.882	1.296	4.134	2.083	4.749	6.627	4.546	3.814	1.919	-7.206	2.384
Hungary	1.819	-1.472	1.963	4.195	3.846	2.2	4.323	5.094	4.928	-3.1	2.38
Nigeria	4.887	4.279	5.394	6.31	2.653	-1.617	0.806	1.923	2.208	-3.41	2.343
Grenada	0.765	-1.155	2.351	7.342	6.445	3.74	4.439	4.141	3.142	-8.001	2.321
Chile	6.124	5.317	4.048	1.779	2.32	1.714	1.174	3.939	1.124	-4.486	2.305
Liberia	7.7	8.42	8.836	0.695	0.007	-1.63	2.469	1.242	-2.516	-2.501	2.272
Nicaragua	6.317	6.496	4.927	4.785	4.792	4.563	4.631	-3.95	-3.879	-6	2.268
Cabo Verde	3.969	1.082	0.803	0.611	1.007	4.706	3.702	5.078	5.458	-4.04	2.2381
Thailand	0.84	7.243	2.687	0.984	3.134	3.429	4.066	4.151	2.372	-6.662	2.224

continued on following page

Table 1. Continued

Namibia	5.091	5.062	5.615	5.758	4.527	-0.281	-0.062	0.342	-1.395	-2.484	2.217
Taiwan, Province of China	3.674	2.222	2.484	4.719	1.466	2.165	3.311	2.745	2.714	-4.031	2.147
Latvia	6.285	4.134	2.328	1.915	3.261	1.774	3.787	4.285	2.197	-8.608	2.136
Luxembourg	2.539	-0.353	3.654	4.297	4.305	4.575	1.801	3.111	2.298	-4.898	2.133
Timor-Leste	5.807	6.017	2.125	4.451	3.056	3.551	-3.799	-0.78	3.1	-3	2.053
Lesotho	5.716	6.073	3.851	2.824	3.261	3.395	-0.973	0.381	1.196	-5.208	2.052
Chad	0.12	8.807	5.763	6.893	1.77	-5.558	-2.38	2.303	2.96	-0.158	2.051
Eswatini	2.247	5.391	3.862	0.913	2.312	1.268	2.025	2.351	1.037	-0.941	2.047
Uruguay	5.162	3.538	4.638	3.239	0.371	1.69	2.591	1.62	0.222	-3	2.0466
New Zealand	1.904	2.528	2.203	3.17	4.078	4.167	3.774	3.166	2.18	-7.212	1.996
Antigua and Barbuda	-1.959	3.372	-0.601	3.797	3.824	5.498	3.145	7.389	5.264	-9.998	1.973
Bulgaria	2.351	0.361	0.319	1.895	3.99	3.812	3.507	3.084	3.372	-4	1.869
Ecuador	7.868	5.642	4.947	3.789	0.099	-1.226	2.368	1.289	0.054	-6.271	1.856
North Macedonia	2.34	-0.456	2.925	3.629	3.856	2.848	1.082	2.72	3.551	-4	1.85
Slovak Republic	2.865	1.896	0.671	2.753	4.822	2.123	3.041	4.034	2.276	-6.2	1.828
Somalia	n/a	1.2	1.86	2.354	3.46	2.894	1.385	2.8	2.9	-2.5	1.817
Algeria	2.823	3.391	2.8	3.8	3.7	3.2	1.3	1.4	0.7	-5.157	1.796
Vanuata	1.223	1.755	1.969	2.304	0.163	3.472	4.413	2.8	2.91	-3.269	1.774
Jordan	2.782	2.124	2.351	3.395	2.58	2.069	2.116	1.94	2.021	-3.735	1.764
Kuwait	9.628	6.625	1.151	0.499	0.593	2.926	-4.71	1.246	0.734	-1.107	1.756
Hong Kong SAR	4.815	1.7	3.102	2.762	2.388	2.169	3.791	2.862	-1.188	-4.821	1.758
Albania	2.545	1.418	1.002	1.774	2.219	3.315	3.802	4.071	2.214	-5.006	1.735
El Salvador	3.812	2.814	2.239	1.71	2.395	2.542	2.253	2.43	2.385	-5.44	1.714
Australia	2.842	3.8	2.127	2.582	2.306	2.776	2.461	2.73	1.847	-6.665	1.681
Montenegro	3.2	-2.724	3.549	1.784	3.39	2.949	4.716	5.078	3.609	-8.976	1.658

Angola	3.472	8.542	4.955	4.823	0.944	-2.58	-0.15	-1.2	-1.503	-1.374	1.593
Haiti	5.524	2.885	4.241	2.803	1.211	1.453	1.173	1.484	-1.197	-4	1.558
Serbia	2.036	-0.682	2.893	-1.59	1.776	3.34	2.049	4.392	4.187	-3.016	1.539
Mexico	3.663	3.642	1.354	2.804	3.288	2.911	2.118	2.136	-0.146	-6.63	1.514
United States	1.551	2.249	1.842	2.526	2.908	1.638	2.37	2.927	2.334	-5.907	1.444
Bosnia and Herzegovina	0.908	-0.707	2.351	1.15	3.074	3.215	3.114	3.624	2.7	-5	1.443
Czech Republic	1.778	-0.8	-0.484	2.715	5.309	2.451	4.353	2.846	2.566	-6.5	1.423
Republic of Congo	3.393	3.829	3.272	6.843	2.619	-2.829	-1.772	1.59	-0.902	-2.277	1.377
Tonga	1.817	-1.125	-0.627	2.529	3.984	5.103	2.693	0.436	-0.141	-1.245	1.342
Burundi	4.033	4.447	5.944	4.494	-3.868	-0.628	0.544	1.646	1.772	-5.542	1.284
Marshall Islands	-0.756	-2.37	3.718	-0.94	1.591	1.307	4.057	3.625	2.411	-0.24	1.24
Canada	3.146	1.762	2.33	2.868	0.69	1.107	2.979	1.834	1.458	2.1264	1.236
Sweden	3.052	-0.631	1.088	2.747	4.421	2.413	2.412	2.225	1.232	-6.788	1.217
Tunisia	-1.918	4.089	2.822	2.873	1.166	1.249	1.918	2.664	1.043	-4.276	1.163
St. Kitts and Nevis	1.827	-2.228	5.384	6.286	1.032	2.282	-1.978	2.924	2.909	-8.1	1.088
Samoa	4.173	-4.089	-0.419	0.078	4.272	8.054	1.016	-2.168	3.464	-3.668	1.071
Palau	5.828	2.11	-1.304	5.451	8.202	0.019	-3.4	5.158	0.5	-11.949	1.062
United Kingdom	1.54	1.479	2.14	2.608	2.355	1.918	1.892	1.341	1.409	-6.502	1.018
Denmark	1.336	0.229	0.935	1.616	2.343	3.248	2.037	2.389	2.367	-6.5	1
Russia	5.066	3.7	1.8	0.7	-1.955	0.286	1.795	2.535	1.336	-5.466	0.98
Switzerland	1.833	1.006	1.879	2.482	1.266	1.711	1.864	2.744	0.917	-5.966	0.9736
Azerbaijan	-1.573	2.203	5.843	2.798	2.21	3.122	4.833	4.118	2.443	-8.039	0.898

continued on following page

Table 1. Continued

Slovenia	0.861	-2.639	-1.029	2.768	2.21	3.122	4.833	4.118	2.443	-8.039	0.865
Germany	3.913	0.428	0.431	2.218	1.742	2.23	2.465	1.522	0.565	-6.952	0.856
Norway	0.981	2.703	1.034	1.969	1.967	1.072	2.323	1.29	1.151	-6.269	0.822
South Africa	3.284	2.213	2.485	1.847	1.194	0.399	1.415	0.787	0.153	-5.801	0.798
Austria	2.923	0.68	0.026	0.661	1.015	2.083	2.476	2.42	1.585	-6.997	0.687
St. Lucia	4.327	-0.109	-2.005	1.328	0.102	3.428	3.489	2.630	1.729	-8.496	6.432
St. Vincent and the Grenadines	-0.419	1.382	1.833	1.214	1.33	1.897	1	2.163	0.4	-4.547	0.625
Belgium	1.695	0.739	0.459	1.579	2.033	1.511	1.965	1.458	1.365	-6.924	0.588
Netherlands	1.55	-1.031	-0.127	1.424	1.958	2.192	2.911	2.597	1.811	-7.493	0.579
Micronesia	3.189	-1.867	3.68	-2.306	4.622	0.9	2.682	0.212	1.183	-0.384	0.455
Suriname	5.847	2.697	2.931	0.254	-3.414	5.56	1.762	2.662	2.3	-4.9	0.454
Belarus	5.55	1.708	0.999	1.651	-3.83	-2.526	2.532	3.149	1.222	-5.992	0.446
Belize	1.921	2.416	1.301	3.637	2.849	0.085	1.87	2.08	0.297	-11.997	0.446
France	2.193	0.313	0.576	0.956	1.113	1.095	2.26	1.725	1.31	-7.18	0.436
Cyprus	0.402	-3.448	-6.551	-1.865	3.376	6.746	4.362	4.057	3.23	-6.471	0.384
Brunei Darussalam	3.744	0.913	-2.125	-2.508	-0.405	-2.465	1.327	0.053	3.869	1.297	0.37
Japan	-0.115	1.495	2	0.375	1.223	0.522	2.168	0.323	0.654	-5.163	0.348
Finland	2.548	-1.397	-0.902	-0.365	0.544	2.711	3.101	1.63	0.98	-6.031	0.282
Croatia	-0.31	-2.238	-0.548	-0.104	2.437	3.484	3.130	2.695	2.919	-9.024	0.245
Spain	-0.814	-2.958	-1.437	1.382	3.837	3.028	2.895	2.354	1.977	-8	0.226
Jamaica	1.426	-0.501	0.206	0.576	0.871	1.499	0.687	1.886	0.97	-5.605	0.202
Brazil	3.986	1.928	3.008	0.505	-3.551	-3.285	1.314	1.312	1.133	-5.303	0.105
Macao SAR	21.672	9.237	11.2	-1.201	-21.594	-0.719	9.888	5.442	-4.711	-29.616	-0.04
Portugal	-1.696	-4.057	-0.923	0.792	1.792	2.019	3.506	2.637	2.157	-8	-0.177
Dominica	-0.224	-1.059	-0.608	4.389	-2.551	2.522	-9.53	0.533	9.205	-4.677	-0.2
Argentina	6.004	-1.026	2.405	-2.513	2.731	-2.08	2.669	-2.482	-2.163	-5.719	-0.217
The Bahamas	0.613	3.087	-2.952	0.737	0.598	0.446	0.067	1.566	1.801	-8.325	-0.236
Aruba	3.505	-1.368	4.165	0.904	-0.448	0.483	2.342	1.2	0.4	-13.7	-0.252
Barbados	-0.673	-0.45	-1.411	-0.126	2.446	2.485	0.478	-0.583	-0.098	-7.6	-0.553
Central African Republic	4.195	5.054	-36.392	0.08	4.338	4.75	4.528	3.82	2.97	1.044	-0.5613
Iran	3.062	-7.714	-0.325	3.215	-1.586	12.518	3.732	-5.419	-7.586	-5.985	-0.609
Ukraine	5.466	0.239	-0.027	-6.553	-9.773	2.441	2.525	3.277	3.173	-7.731	-0.67
Lebanon	0.867	2.541	3.811	2.461	.0212	1.53	0.851	-1.926	-6.513	-12.019	-0.819
Italy	0.707	-2.981	-1.841	-0.005	0.778	1.293	1.668	0.798	0.301	-9.134	-0.8412
Trinidad and Tobago	-0.192	-0.704	2.229	0.913	1.823	-6.296	-2.312	-0.245	-0.002	-4.54	-1.115
Puerto Rico	-0.359	0.029	-0.307	-1.19	-1.049	-1.263	-2.657	-4.906	2.0	-6.0	-1.57
Libya	-66.657	124.709	-36.829	-53.017	-13.023	-7.389	64.014	17.879	9.89	-58.662	-1.9085
Sudan	-2.825	-17.005	1.963	4.671	1.913	3.468	0.709	-2.294	-2.521	-7.222	-1.914
San Marino	-8.522	-7.207	-0.817	-0.657	2.695	2.344	0.435	1.696	1.1	-12.17	-2.11
Greece	-9.132	-7.3	-3.242	0.74	-0.438	-0.191	1.505	1.934	1.87	-10.04	-2.429
Equatorial Guinea	6.524	8.313	-4.133	0.415	-9.11	-8.817	-5.667	-5.803	-6.096	-5.492	-2.987
South Sudan	n/a	-52.429	29.329	2.918	-0.173	-16.737	-5.491	-1.123	11.283	4.893	-3.059
Yemen	-12.715	2.393	4.824	-0.189	-27.995	-9.375	-5.072	0.752	2.1	-3	-4.827
Venezuela	4.176	5.626	1.343	-3.894	-6.221	-17.04	-15.761	-19.621	-35	-15	-10.130
Syria	n/a	n/a	n/a	n/a	n/a	n/a	n/a	n/a	n/a	n/a	n/a

Source: International Monetary Fund, World Economic Outlook April 2020.

Due to the rapid pace of digitalization, the labor market across the world has undergone a series of a shift. A paradigm shift has taken place in the nature of work, the workplace and the way of work is evident in almost all the sectors. Due to disruptions caused by pandemic, the technology usage increased drastically (Pandey & Pal, 2020; Hassounah, Raheel, & Alhefzi, 2020). The social distancing norms and the contact-free workings have become a norm and it has affected the labor market positively as well as negatively. On one hand, people started working from home, which helped multinational companies save a bulk of amount; on the other, many economies witnessed several layoffs due to disruption in production and supply chain activities (Thun & Hoenig, 2011; McMaster, Nettleton, Tom, Xu, Cao, & Qiao, 2020; Shafi, Liu & Ren, 2020). Technology has played a pivotal role in this paradigm shift and work has no limit of geographical boundaries. Flexibility in working as well as independence in wide variety of activities has become a new normal or norm of disrupted economies across the world. This has reshaped, redefined, repurposed and re-envisioned the works, workplaces and economy as a whole. A clear-cut difference and demarcation have arisen now in the traditional and post- COVID-19 scenario. This paradigm shift has been defined by the way of emergence of Gig Economy. According to Investopedia, "In gig economy, temporary, flexible jobs are commonplace and companies tend to hire independent contractors and freelancers instead of full-time employees. A gig economy undermines the traditional economy of full-time workers who often focus on career development".

Thereby gig economy is an economy which offers a platform for wide variety of workers and connects the client with the customer via online modes. It is quite flexible in nature. The nature of jobs offered is temporary, non-traditional and more of free lancing. It benefits the stakeholders of the economy like workers, businesses at local as well as international level. The important feature of gig economy is that it helps to make work more adaptable according to time and demand. In gig economy, large numbers of people are involved. Gig economy also allows independent contractors of the services to work from home, but the nature of work is often contractual and temporary. During lockdowns, when companies were not in a position to run their operations due to variety of reasons like government restrictions on travel and production, or when they, in the initial phase, were not able to afford the services of people being physically present in the building, then people started offering their services in cheaper and flexible modes from their home (de Jesus, 2021). Most of the time, infrastructural requirements became lesser in this way of operations for organizations and they were able to cut costs.

b) Resilience Strategies to Rebuild Economies post COVID-19 Pandemic

As statedabove, to be able to return to normalcy, the world needs to come to terms with the scenario that has emerged due to COVID-19 pandemic. Several measures need to be taken the world over but each one has to be environmentally friendly as well as sustainable as suggested by OECD Policy response to Coronavirus (COVID-19) in "Building back better: A sustainable, resilient recovery after COVID-19" on June 5, 2020 (www.oecd.org/coronavirus/policy-responses/building-back-better-a-sustainable-resilient-recovery-after-covid-19-52b869f5/).

The same policy response clearly underscores how crucial the awareness about global environment is and how it can cause disasters far more serious than caused by the present pandemic.

First and foremost is the resurrection of the livelihoods the world over followed by nurturing and nourishing of the informal and unorganized sectors particularly in the economies of the developing world. The damage caused by the pandemic has been such that even the first world nations had to give special stimulus packages to help their economically distressed populations. American government was first to release such a financial stimulus package with alacrity within no time. The world governments need to operate in unison to devise strategies and implement them keeping in mind the actual needs of the beneficiaries. Until the capital gets circulated and reaches the poor by way of direct cash transfer through robust and reliable cash-disbursement mechanism, demand cannot be generated, which serves as the biggest driving force behind driving the growth engine of an economy that has touched nadir due to multi-sectoral disruption caused by COVID-19.

Gig players also can play significant role in enlivening the dormant economies across the globe coupled with the precious resource in each country namely entrepreneurs and business leaders. Like gig players, they too have tremendous capacity to adapt in according with the changing times, and thereby operate innovatively while dealing with problems that stare them in the face. Since the organized sectors of most of the global economies got severely hit due to the pandemic, gig players could create opportunities for them to function/ work/ operate in a way that brought them money in fits and starts. With the help of technological advancements and social media platforms, gig players in metropolitan as well as semi-metropolitan cities started clicking successfully. Thus, gig players, entrepreneurs, and business leaders may come together and develop a resilient mechanism to come to terms with the financial crisis the world over, and offer solutions in sustainable ways.

Expeditious response is a must to the situation caused by COVID-19 simply because if governments do not exhibit the same alacrity which was shown while imposing lockdowns, closing educational institutions, and banning all social events, it may delay the process of recovery. Thus, restoring the business activities that were stopped more than year and a half ago in a phased manner seems to be a viable method of coping with the challenges of unemployment and loss of livelihoods due to the pandemic. Acting expeditiously in no way implies acting in haste or irrationally. On the contrary, it is a well thought out resilience strategy that governments across the world need to adopt remaining fully aware of their respective socio-cultural and geo-political contexts. Various stakeholders from business and political arenas have to come together to work out resilience strategies with the governments so that appropriate measures can be taken to overcome the economic and financial crises that the world has been facing for quite some time now. Most important stakeholders to take up the task of economic/ financial recovery can be undertaken by the entrepreneurs and business leaders who have the vision as well as the capital at their disposal.

The Donor Committee for Enterprise Development (DCED) in a note on "COVID-19 and Private Sector Development Synthesis: Emerging economic recovery and resilience strategies" (www.enterprise-development.org/wp-content/uploads/Emerging-economic-recovery-and-resilience-strategies-COVID-19-Synthesis-Note.pdf), observes that despite the devastating effects of COVID-19 pandemic, "rebuilding economies is seen as a window of opportunity to fundamentally re-think the way 'things are done' and to promote businesses and sectors that help address existing global development challenges. Agencies also recognize an urgent need to take more decisive action on SDGs that have been particularly negatively affected by COVID-19." Thus, the emphasis is on sustainable development across the globe. Despite the fact that businesses need to be revived and various economic and financial arenas need to be enlivened and activated, SDGs can be neither ignored nor avoided. Other mechanisms that may alleviate various economies out of the economic distress include ensuring participation of the private sector in the process of recovery. And that is where the entrepreneurs and business leaders play such an important role. Moreover, the enabling environment for resuming the business activities is equally crucial as it directly affects the pace of recovery efforts and the quality of resilience strategies. No resilience mechanism can be efficacious until MSMEs are supported. This is because of the fact that these are critical for supply chains and distribution networks across the globe. Moreover, their financial strengthening implies mobilization of funds and flow of cash at the level of laborers/ workers—an arena that has been hit most severely due to COVID-19 pandemic.

c) Role of Entrepreneurial Leadership in Tiding Over the Worst Economic Crises Ever

Any effort to rebuild the crumbled economies across the globe, the world governments cannot deal with, this scenario/situation that has arisen without roping in entrepreneurial leaders. Whether, the economy is that of an advanced nation or a third world one, intervention of the entrepreneurial leaders seems to be a must. This is owing to the fact that road to recovery from this point is unimaginable without the meaningful intervention of entrepreneurs and entrepreneurial leaders. Still there is a probability that third wave of the pandemic will strike the world sooner or later. This is evident from the latest developments in southern states of India where the third wave has already made its presence felt. It is far from being true that prior to COVID-19 stuck the world, the global economy was in a healthy state. It had its problems then, which were further aggravated by deep recession and then crashing of developing economies along with their already fragile health systems.

Such a scenario discourages us from going in far, short term solutions to the problems that stare us in face today. Any decision to revive an economy would entail large scale participation of various stakeholders in the society. Most important among them being entrepreneurial leaders. This is simply because they have always answers to even the most challenging situations caused by natural calamities and pandemic such as the present one. Entrepreneurs are made of the stuff that is characterized by indomitable will, unswerving commitment and 'never-say-die' approach. The task of rebuilding economies has always been made possible by meaningful contributions extended by entrepreneurial leaders in advanced as well as developing economies. They are the ones who can reliably and sustainably take care of the emerging markets and grievously injured supply chain lifeline. The World Bank Group Vice President for Equitable Growth, Finance and Institutions, rightly observes thus: "Urgent measures are needed to limit the damage, rebuild the economy and make growth more robust, resilient, and sustainable".

Thus, amidst despair, the world requires leaders who besides having positivity have wherewithal to reverse the financial downturn in various economies of the world. Right from restoring basic or essential services to strengthening industrial and marketing sectors entrepreneurs would be required the most. The structural damage that has been done to the infrastructure also needs to be rebuilt in an environmentally friendly manner. Regulatory mechanism need to be relaxed a bit so that the operational ease on the path of business leaders may be insured to strengthen production and facilitate supply chains. It is really heartening that the World Bank group has opened its coffers enormously to fund the developing economies so that they can expedite their progress response to the devastation caused by the pandemic.

The World Bank group has announced that it is going to invest more than 16 billion dollars as financial support over 15 months to extend help to more than hundred countries in order to protect the poor and vulnerable and will also help the private sector so that the economies respond in a better way. Such a substantial support gets reduced to a sheer naught if funds are not managed and utilized meaningfully. And that is precisely where role of visionary entrepreneurial leaders come into being as they have the capability to collaborate successfully with political leaders and other stakeholders in the society. Entrepreneurial effort thus requires to be lent prominence so that their services are availed of as and when the requirements in the developing as well as the developed nations emerge.

Another mode of rebuilding the infrastructural damage is via resorting to measures that are environmentally friendly. This is what has been stipulated emphatically by organisation economic cooperation development (OECD). The idea is that of rebuilding sustainable infrastructure cannot only last longer but also sustain in any abysmal scenario.The most important challenge however remains that of destitute and oppressed people. Their survival remains a problem irrespective of whether the world is free of pandemics or is pandemic struck. Deprivation remains an insurmountable challenge. To this, population of poor and vulnerable people which recently added unemployed and the workless force comprising millions of people across the world, remains a challenge. A thought of it sends shivers down the spine as there seems no solution in the view. It is said that the entrepreneurs and leaders have the capability of moving ahead when the movement becomes absolutely impossible their ilk remain motivated under most of the time circumstances. They know how to utilise the capital at hand and how to generate it despite all odds. All the recovery strategies remain crystal clear in their minds and this enables them to invest money in the form of investing in infrastructure, formal as well as informal sectors, and thereby encouraging greater financial activity. With the help of various technologies available, we can revive the economy at a better pace. There is no doubt that entrepreneurial leaders are important stakeholders. They have short term as well as long term solution to tide over the crisis caused by the one caused by COVID-19 at the present time.

SUMMATIVE REMARKS

Thus, it is evident from the above discussion that gig players and entrepreneurs can play a big role in providing resilience strategies to overcome the global economic crisis caused by COVID-19 pandemic. The outbreak of pandemic evidently leads to the economies of the world in a downturn. A sharp decline in the growth rate of even developed economies could be seen. The economic growth of almost every nation in the world has been hampered badly due to the pandemic. Various governments around the world had to introduce out-of-the-box measures to deal with the pandemic. The financial markets and stock markets also suffered a severe jolt. The shutdown of businesses and disrupted supply chain has hampered the manufacturing sector drastically and increased restrictions on travel and transportation have eroded the financial strength and abilities of the companies. There is a high level of uncertainty and risk in the market and to deal with this, a lot of efforts would be required. Due to a large number of shutdowns, level of output in many economies has drastically fallen, and moreover, reduced income lead to a reduced consumer expenditure, and thereby impacting the production activities negatively.

According to OECD, even the stock markets showed a steep decline over 30% during this pandemic. The reliance of businesses currently on debt financing has increased to a great extent where the risk and uncertainty level has further increased. This heightened turmoil and uncertainty in the global financial markets will have serious bearing on the financial sector. The post-pandemic-crisis era will be a challenging time for economies to recover and an exacted focus on resilience strategies for future is required in order to sustain the markets. Many countries are now debt-ridden. Economies like India had given their citizens opportunities to avail credit facilities to boost the entrepreneurial activities across the country. But the biggest challenge is to save the country as well as the citizens from the debt-trap. The gap between haves and have nots has been broadening at more rapid a pace than ever. The challenge is to survive the crises as well invest in the health sector almost in all economies. Certain innovative solutions are required to deal with the situation.

The gig economy has served the purpose to a great extent, where people have been using various digital platforms to connect with rest of the world to earn livelihoods. The flow of goods and services may bring such a perturbing situation to normal but gradually. Therefore, the sustainable financing and the entrepreneurial qualities of leaders will play an important role in recovery and survival of economies. The onus now lies on the entrepreneurs to take challenges, face risk and help economies survive from the financial setback due to the pandemic. Similarly, gig players have an equally important role to play not only in the service sector but in the manufacturing sector as well. Measures to cut cost, increase operational efficiency and maintain quality will be challenging for businesses; but gig players can come up with wonderful but practicable solutions. To overcome the shocks of the collapse of economies, sustainable financial planning can serve as a key to reduce costs in post-pandemic. Governments will have to analyze the pandemic-caused crises in the past to find certain answers to the challenges posed by the COVID-19 where the entrepreneurial spirits of leaders can show the sagging world economies a new ray of hope and a new phase of development. The question is now is not just how to survive but survive sustainably being mindful of the weal and welfare of our future generations. No ordinary person can lead a way out of such gloom; it requires the zeal of an entrepreneurial leader and ever-renewed skills of gig players who hold the key to pave the way out of such abysmal economic scenario the world over.

REFERENCES

Acs, Z. (2006). How is entrepreneurship good for economic growth? *Innovations: Technology, Governance, Globalization*, *1*(1), 97–107. doi:10.1162/itgg.2006.1.1.97

Arora, M., & Sharma, R. L. (2017). Decoding Diverse Dimensions of Entrepreneurial Leadership with special emphasis on Persuasive Communication. *Management Dynamics, 17*(1).

Audretsch, D. B. (2007). Entrepreneurship capital and economic growth. *Oxford Review of Economic Policy*, *23*(1), 63–78. doi:10.1093/oxrep/grm001

Baker, S. R., Farrokhnia, R. A., Meyer, S., Pagel, M., & Yannelis, C. (2020). How does household spending respond to an epidemic? Consumption during the 2020 COVID-19 pandemic. *The Review of Asset Pricing Studies*, *10*(4), 834–862. doi:10.1093/rapstu/raaa009

Barua, S. (2020). *Understanding Coronanomics: The economic implications of the coronavirus (COVID-19) pandemic*. Available at SSRN 3566477.

de Jesus, D. S. V. (2021). Living on the Edge: Brazilian Creative Workers in the Gig Economy During the COVID-19 Pandemic. *Psychology (Irvine, Calif.)*, *11*(2), 56–62.

Devpura, N., & Narayan, P. K. (2020). Hourly oil price volatility: The role of COVID-19. *Energy Research Letters*, *1*(2), 13683. doi:10.46557/001c.13683

Ebrahim, Z., Inderwildi, O. R., & King, D. A. (2014). Macroeconomic impacts of oil price volatility: Mitigation and resilience. *Frontiers in Energy*, *8*(1), 9–24. doi:10.100711708-014-0303-0

Filis, G. (2010). Macro economy, stock market and oil prices: Do meaningful relationships exist among their cyclical fluctuations? *Energy Economics*, *32*(4), 877–886. doi:10.1016/j.eneco.2010.03.010

Gao, X., Ren, Y., & Umar, M. (2021). To what extent does COVID-19 drive stock market volatility? A comparison between the US and China. *Economic Research-EkonomskaIstraživanja*, 1-21.

Guerini, M., Nesta, L., Ragot, X., & Schiavo, S. (2020). Firm liquidity and solvency under the Covid-19 lockdown in France. *OFCE Policy Brief, 76*, 1-20.

Harjoto, M. A., Rossi, F., Lee, R., & Sergi, B. S. (2021). How do equity markets react to COVID-19? Evidence from emerging and developed countries. *Journal of Economics and Business*, *115*, 105966. doi:10.1016/j.jeconbus.2020.105966 PMID:33518845

Hassounah, M., Raheel, H., & Alhefzi, M. (2020). Digital response during the COVID-19 pandemic in Saudi Arabia. *Journal of Medical Internet Research*, *22*(9), e19338. doi:10.2196/19338 PMID:32790642

Laborde, D., Martin, W., & Vos, R. (2021). Impacts of COVID-19 on global poverty, food security, and diets: Insights from global model scenario analysis. *Agricultural Economics*, *52*(3), 375–390. doi:10.1111/agec.12624 PMID:34230728

Lin, B., & Bai, R. (2021). Oil prices and economic policy uncertainty: Evidence from global, oil importers, and exporters' perspective. *Research in International Business and Finance*, *56*, 101357. doi:10.1016/j.ribaf.2020.101357

Martin, A., Markhvida, M., Hallegatte, S., & Walsh, B. (2020). Socio-economic impacts of COVID-19 on household consumption and poverty. *Economics of Disasters and Climate Change*, *4*(3), 453-479.

McMaster, M., Nettleton, C., Tom, C., Xu, B., Cao, C., & Qiao, P. (2020). Risk management: Rethinking fashion supply chain management for multinational corporations in light of the COVID-19 outbreak. *Journal of Risk and Financial Management*, *13*(8), 173. doi:10.3390/jrfm13080173

Narayan, P. K. (2020). Oil price news and COVID-19—Is there any connection? *Energy Research Letters*, *1*(1), 13176. doi:10.46557/001c.13176

Ozili, P. K., & Arun, T. (2020). *Spillover of COVID-19: impact on the Global Economy*. Available at SSRN 3562570.

Pandey, N., & Pal, A. (2020). Impact of digital surge during Covid-19 pandemic: A viewpoint on research and practice. *International Journal of Information Management*, *55*, 102171. doi:10.1016/j.ijinfomgt.2020.102171 PMID:32836633

Schumpter, J. A. (2000). Entrepreneurship as innovation. *Entrepreneurship: The social science view*, 51-75.

Shafi, M., Liu, J., & Ren, W. (2020). Impact of COVID-19 pandemic on micro, small, and medium-sized Enterprises operating in Pakistan. *Research in Globalization*, *2*, 100018. doi:10.1016/j.resglo.2020.100018

Shaikh, I. (2020). Impact of COVID-19 pandemic disease outbreak on the global equity markets. *Economic Research-EkonomskaIstraživanja*, 1-18.

Thun, J. H., & Hoenig, D. (2011). An empirical analysis of supply chain risk management in the German automotive industry. *International Journal of Production Economics*, *131*(1), 242–249. doi:10.1016/j.ijpe.2009.10.010

Wang, Z., & Sun, Z. (2021). From globalization to regionalization: The United States, China, and the post-Covid-19 world economic order. *Journal of Chinese Political Science*, *26*(1), 69–87. doi:10.100711366-020-09706-3 PMID:33144822

Zaremba, A., Kizys, R., Aharon, D. Y., & Demir, E. (2020). Infected markets: Novel coronavirus, government interventions, and stock return volatility around the globe. *Finance Research Letters*, *35*, 101597. doi:10.1016/j.frl.2020.101597 PMID:32550842

ADDITIONAL READING

Acciarini, C., Boccardelli, P., & Vitale, M. (2021). Resilient companies in the time of Covid-19 pandemic: a case study approach. *Journal of Entrepreneurship and Public Policy*.

Arora, M. (2016). Creative Dimensions of Entrepreneurship: A Key to Business Innovation. *Pacific Business Review International*, *1*(1), 255–259.

Arora, M., & Sharma, R. L. (2021). Neutralizing Maleficent Effects of COVID-19 Through Entrepreneurship: Peeping Through the Lens of Communication. In Effective Strategies for Communicating Insights in Business (pp. 67-86). IGI Global.

Arora, M., & Sharma, R. L. (2021). Repurposing the Role of Entrepreneurs in the Havoc of COVID-19. In Entrepreneurship and Big Data (pp. 229-250). CRC Press. doi:10.1201/9781003097945-16

Ayala, J. C., & Manzano, G. (2014). The resilience of the entrepreneur. Influence on the success of the business. A longitudinal analysis. *Journal of Economic Psychology*, *42*, 126–135. doi:10.1016/j.joep.2014.02.004

Badzaban, F., Rezaei-Moghaddam, K., & Fatemi, M. (2021). Analysing the individual entrepreneurial resilience of rural women. *Journal of Global Entrepreneurship Research*, 1-14.

Bakas, F. E. (2017). Community resilience through entrepreneurship: the role of gender. *Journal of Enterprising Communities: People and Places in the Global Economy*.

Belitski, M., Guenther, C., Kritikos, A. S., & Thurik, R. (2022). Economic effects of the COVID-19 pandemic on entrepreneurship and small businesses. *Small Business Economics*, *58*(2), 593–609. doi:10.100711187-021-00544-y

Beninger, S., & Francis, J. N. (2022). Resources for business resilience in a covid-19 world: A community-centric approach. *Business Horizons*, *65*(2), 227–238. doi:10.1016/j.bushor.2021.02.048

Branicki, L. J., Sullivan-Taylor, B., & Livschitz, S. R. (2017). How entrepreneurial resilience generates resilient SMEs. *International Journal of Entrepreneurial Behavior & Research.*

Broughton, A., Gloster, R., Marvell, R., Green, M., Langley, J., & Martin, A. (2018). *The experiences of individuals in the gig economy*. HM Government.

Bryce, C., Ring, P., Ashby, S., & Wardman, J. K. (2020). Resilience in the face of uncertainty: Early lessons from the COVID-19 pandemic. *Journal of Risk Research, 23*(7-8), 880–887. doi:10.1080/13669877.2020.1756379

Bullough, A., & Renko, M. (2013). Entrepreneurial resilience during challenging times. *Business Horizons, 56*(3), 343–350. doi:10.1016/j.bushor.2013.01.001

Burtch, G., Carnahan, S., & Greenwood, B. N. (2018). Can you gig it? An empirical examination of the gig economy and entrepreneurial activity. *Management Science, 64*(12), 5497–5520. doi:10.1287/mnsc.2017.2916

Castro, M. P., & Zermeño, M. G. G. (2020). Being an entrepreneur post-COVID-19–resilience in times of crisis: a systematic literature review. *Journal of Entrepreneurship in Emerging Economies.*

Crouch, C. (2019). *Will the gig economy prevail?* John Wiley & Sons.

Doern, R. (2017). Strategies for resilience in entrepreneurship: Building resources for small business survival after a crisis. In *Creating Resilient Economies*. Edward Elgar Publishing. doi:10.4337/9781785367649.00008

Fitriasari, F. (2020). How do Small and Medium Enterprise (SME) survive the COVID-19 outbreak? *Jurnal Inovasi Ekonomi, 5*(2).

Graham, M., & Shaw, J. (2017). *Towards a fairer gig economy*. Meatspace Press.

Hadjielias, E., Christofi, M., & Tarba, S. (2022). Contextualizing small business resilience during the COVID-19 pandemic: Evidence from small business owner-managers. *Small Business Economics*, 1–30. doi:10.100711187-021-00588-0

Huang, A., & Farboudi Jahromi, M. (2021). Resilience building in service firms during and post COVID-19. *Service Industries Journal, 41*(1-2), 138–167. doi:10.1080/02642069.2020.1862092

Ignat, R., & Constantin, M. (2020). Multidimensional facets of entrepreneurial resilience during the COVID-19 crisis through the lens of the wealthiest Romanian counties. *Sustainability, 12*(23), 10220. doi:10.3390u122310220

Ingram, C., Morisse, M., & Teigland, R. (2015, March). 'A Bad Apple Went Away': Exploring Resilience among Bitcoin Entrepreneurs. In *Twenty-Third European Conference on Information Systems (ECIS)*, Münster, Germany.

Korber, S., & McNaughton, R. B. (2017). Resilience and entrepreneurship: a systematic literature review. *International Journal of Entrepreneurial Behavior & Research.*

Kuckertz, A., Brändle, L., Gaudig, A., Hinderer, S., Reyes, C. A. M., Prochotta, A., ... Berger, E. S. (2020). Startups in times of crisis–A rapid response to the COVID-19 pandemic. *Journal of Business Venturing Insights*, *13*, e00169. doi:10.1016/j.jbvi.2020.e00169

Kuhn, K. M. (2016). The rise of the "gig economy" and implications for understanding work and workers. *Industrial and Organizational Psychology: Perspectives on Science and Practice*, *9*(1), 157–162. doi:10.1017/iop.2015.129

Lehdonvirta, V. (2018). Flexibility in the gig economy: Managing time on three online piecework platforms. *New Technology, Work and Employment*, *33*(1), 13–29. doi:10.1111/ntwe.12102

Li, B., Zhong, Y., Zhang, T., & Hua, N. (2021). Transcending the COVID-19 crisis: Business resilience and innovation of the restaurant industry in China. *Journal of Hospitality and Tourism Management*, *49*, 44–53. doi:10.1016/j.jhtm.2021.08.024

Liñán, F., & Jaén, I. (2020). The Covid-19 pandemic and entrepreneurship: some reflections. *International Journal of Emerging Markets.*

Linnenluecke, M. K., & McKnight, B. (2017). Community resilience to natural disasters: the role of disaster entrepreneurship. *Journal of Enterprising Communities: People and Places in the Global Economy.*

Liu, Y. (2020). Contextualising risk and building resilience: Returnees versus local entrepreneurs in China. *Applied Psychology*, *69*(2), 415–443. doi:10.1111/apps.12177

Maritz, A., Perenyi, A., De Waal, G., & Buck, C. (2020). Entrepreneurship as the unsung hero during the current COVID-19 economic crisis: Australian perspectives. *Sustainability*, *12*(11), 4612. doi:10.3390u12114612

McNaughton, R. B., & Gray, B. (2017). Entrepreneurship and resilient communities–introduction to the special issue. *Journal of Enterprising Communities: People and Places in the Global Economy.*

Mena, C., Karatzas, A., & Hansen, C. (2022). International trade resilience and the Covid-19 pandemic. *Journal of Business Research*, *138*, 77–91. doi:10.1016/j.jbusres.2021.08.064 PMID:34538982

Nah, F. F. H., & Siau, K. (2020, July). Covid-19 pandemic–role of technology in transforming business to the new normal. In *International Conference on Human-Computer Interaction* (pp. 585-600). Springer. 10.1007/978-3-030-60152-2_43

Ntounis, N., Parker, C., Skinner, H., Steadman, C., & Warnaby, G. (2022). Tourism and Hospitality industry resilience during the Covid-19 pandemic: Evidence from England. *Current Issues in Tourism*, *25*(1), 46–59. doi:10.1080/13683500.2021.1883556

Ozdemir, D., Sharma, M., Dhir, A., & Daim, T. (2022). Supply chain resilience during COVID 19 pandemic. *Technology in Society*, *68*, 101847. doi:10.1016/j.techsoc.2021.101847 PMID:35075312

Păunescu, C., & Mátyus, E. (2020). Resilience measures to dealing with the COVID-19 pandemic. Evidence from Romanian micro and small enterprises. *Management & Marketing, 15.*

Prah, D., & Sibiri, H. (2020). The resilience of African migrant entrepreneurs in China under COVID-19. *Journal of Entrepreneurship in Emerging Economies.*

Prassl, J. (2018). *Humans as a service: The promise and perils of work in the gig economy.* Oxford University Press. doi:10.1093/oso/9780198797012.001.0001

Purnomo, B. R., Adiguna, R., Widodo, W., Suyatna, H., & Nusantoro, B. P. (2021). Entrepreneurial resilience during the Covid-19 pandemic: Navigating survival, continuity and growth. *Journal of Entrepreneurship in Emerging Economies.*

Rahman, S. A., Tuckerman, L., Vorley, T., & Gherhes, C. (2021). Resilient research in the field: Insights and lessons from adapting qualitative research projects during the COVID-19 pandemic. *International Journal of Qualitative Methods*, *20*. doi:10.1177/16094069211016106

Raj, M., Sundararajan, A., & You, C. (2020). COVID-19 and digital resilience: Evidence from Uber Eats. *arXiv preprint arXiv:2006.07204.*

Ramanathan, U., Aluko, O., & Ramanathan, R. (2021). Supply chain resilience and business responses to disruptions of the COVID-19 pandemic. *Benchmarking*. Advance online publication. doi:10.1108/BIJ-01-2021-0023

Sarkar, S., & Clegg, S. R. (2021). Resilience in a time of contagion: Lessons from small businesses during the COVID-19 pandemic. *Journal of Change Management*, *21*(2), 242–267. doi:10.1080/14697017.2021.1917495

Schaltegger, S. (2020). *Sustainability learnings from the COVID-19 crisis. Opportunities for resilient industry and business development.* Sustainability Accounting, Management and Policy Journal.

Sharma, R. L., & Arora, M. (2015). Communication as the mainstay of entrepreneurial leadership: A conceptual framework. *Management Dynamics, 15*(2), 20–28.

Sreenivasan, A., Suresh, M., & Panduro, J. A. T. (2022). Modelling the resilience of start-ups during COVID-19 pandemic. *Benchmarking*. Advance online publication. doi:10.1108/BIJ-09-2021-0530

Sun, J., Buys, N., Wang, X., & McAuley, A. (2011). Using the concept of resilience to explain entrepreneurial success in China. *International Journal of Management and Enterprise Development, 11*(2-4), 182–202. doi:10.1504/IJMED.2011.044637

Vallas, S., & Schor, J. B. (2020). What do platforms do? Understanding the gig economy. *Annual Review of Sociology, 46*(1), 273–294. doi:10.1146/annurev-soc-121919-054857

Williams, N., & Vorley, T. (Eds.). (2017). *Creating resilient economies: Entrepreneurship, growth and development in uncertain times.* Edward Elgar Publishing. doi:10.4337/9781785367649

Woodcock, J., & Graham, M. (2019). *The gig economy. A critical introduction.* Polity.

Zutshi, A., Mendy, J., Sharma, G. D., Thomas, A., & Sarker, T. (2021). From challenges to creativity: Enhancing SMEs' resilience in the context of COVID-19. *Sustainability, 13*(12), 6542. doi:10.3390u13126542

KEY TERMS AND DEFINITIONS

Entrepreneurial Leadership: Entrepreneurial leadership involves organizing and motivating a group of people to achieve a common objective through innovation, risk optimization, taking advantage of opportunities, and managing the dynamic organizational environment.

Entrepreneurship: Entrepreneurship is the process of creation or extraction of value. As per this definition, entrepreneurship is viewed as change, in general parlance it involves risk beyond what is normally encountered in starting a business.

Gig Economy: Gig Economy is that part of labor market which is characterized by the prevalence of short-term contracts or freelance work as opposed to permanent jobs. A large number of people work in part-time or temporary positions or as independent contractors.

Gig Players: The term "gig" is jargon for "temporary job." A large number of people work in part-time or temporary positions or as independent contractors as regarded as gig players.

Global Economic Crisis: The global financial crisis (GFC) refers to the period of extreme stress in global financial markets and banking systems between mid-2007 and early-2009.

Resilience: Psychologists define resilience as the process of adapting well in the face of adversity, trauma, tragedy, threats, or significant sources. In general sense it is bouncing back after adversity.

Chapter 9
The Impact of COVID-19 on Volatility Spillover Between Bitcoin and Turkish Financial Markets

Yakup Ari
https://orcid.org/0000-0002-5666-5365
Alanya Alaaddin Keykubat University, Turkey

Esin Yelgen
Alanya Alaaddin Keykubat University, Turkey

Harun Uçak
https://orcid.org/0000-0001-5290-5846
Alanya Alaaddin Keykubat University, Turkey

ABSTRACT

The aim of this study is to examine the volatility spillover between bitcoin and Turkish financial markets for the pre-COVID-19 and COVID-19 periods. Using GARCH-based volatility spillover indices, the authors find that BTC-USD was a volatility transmitter in the pre-COVID-19 period but has become the main volatility receiver in the COVID-19 period, and its net volatility transmission fell from 0.7% to -10.84%. Moreover, they concluded that the total spillover index increased from 12.49% to 15.25% indicates a low connectedness between the markets in both periods and the error variance in markets is on average 15.25% originated from other markets in the COVID-19 period.

DOI: 10.4018/978-1-7998-9117-8.ch009

INTRODUCTION

Subsequent to the high inflation, sharp drops and volatility in national currency and Istanbul Stock Exchange that are more apparent with the period of pandemic in which economic activities in Turkey has been significantly restricted, search for a safe harbor in the financial markets has directed investors to the cryptocurrencies, especially Bitcoin. The results of Statista Global Consumer Survey indicate that Turkey ranks 4th in the worldwide and first in Europe with the 16 percentages within the world's biggest 74 economies that use mostly cryptocurrencies compared to the population (Buchholz, 2021). However, while Turkey ranks high in the world in the investment of cryptocurrencies, the Central Bank of the Turkish Republic publicly declared a regulation effective stating that direct or indirect use of cryptocurrencies in payments will not be allowed (OG, 2021). In addition to the heavy demand for cryptocurrencies that significantly impact the background of these legal regulations, it is also crucial to investigate the effect of the pandemic process and alternative investment instruments.

In the financial economics literature, there has been a growing interest to analyze the investment benefits of cryptocurrencies. Especially in an unprecedented crisis period such as Covid-19 pandemic, the effect of cryptocurrencies on international financial markets has no longer to be ignored. There are various studies examining the counter return of the cryptocurrency market against other investment instruments before and during the Covid-19 pandemic. We can list these studies briefly as follows.

Baur and Dimpfi (2021) found in their study that the volatility in Bitcoin prices is extreme and almost 10 times higher than the volatility of the main exchange rates (against the US Dollar, Euro and Yen). Goodell and Goutte (2021) found a strong co-movement between Bitcoin prices and Covid-19. Caferra and Vidal-Tomas (2021) pointed out that cryptocurrencies recovered rapidly during the Covid-19 pandemic, but the stock markets failed to show the same recovery. Zhang et al. (2021) pointed out a downside risk spillover that seems to be time dependent between Bitcoin and four assets (stocks, bonds, currencies and commodities). Ghorbel and Jeribi (2021) analyzed the volatility relationships between five cryptocurrencies, American indexes (S&P 500, Nasdaq and VIX), oil, and gold. This study showed that Bitcoin and gold were accepted as hedges for the US investors before the coronavirus crisis. Unlike gold, it was concluded that cryptocurrencies were not a safe haven for the US investors during the coronavirus crisis. Umar et al. (2021) stated that in the case of the first shock experienced in the crypto market from January 2018 to March 2020, the spillover effect was felt by all financial markets. Moreover, they continued to point out that the stock and bond markets created a great persistence in the volatility of cryptocurrencies, showing that mostly cryptocurrencies are the receiver, not the source of the volatility.

The results of Cebrian-Hernandez and Jimenez-Rodriguez's study (2021) examining the relationship between Bitcoin volatility and the variables of basic financial environment (several commodities linked to cryptocurrencies, exchange rates, stock market indexes and company stocks) indicate a certain heterogeneity in the adaptation of different variables and also highlight the lack of correlations with traditional safe harbors such as gold and oil. It has been found out that in each multivariate model they examined, Bitcoin volatility was inversely proportional to USD/EUR. In the commodities taken into account in this study, gold and oil showed an insignificant correlation. The volatility of stocks of companies associated with Blockchain technology- RIOT, NVDA and KBR- and the volatility of payment methods- VISA and MASTERCARD- presented a clear and significant correlation with that of cryptocurrencies.

Chen et al. (2021) came to a conclusion that significant increases in uncertainty for the period between December 31, 2019 and May 20, 2020 result in a higher return on Bitcoin and Bitcoin can be used as a hedge against political uncertainties in China (CEPU index). The results of the study carried out by Corbet et al. (2021) indicated extremely evident and permanent effects of a coronavirus pandemic on Chinese financial markets. Moreover, they found that Covid-19 has a significant impact on the directional spillovers on the Bitcoin market. Next, Fasanya et al. (2021) found evidence in their study that there is a strong risk, information or volatility spillovers among precious metals, with the exception of Bitcoin, which appears to be receiving and transmitting less than precious metals. They pointed out that the connection between Bitcoin and precious metals may not serve as a safe harbor or protection against US economic policy uncertainties, especially during the Covid-19 period.

Iqbal et al. (2021) noted that in the changing levels of pandemic's intensity most of cryptocurrencies absorbed the small shocks of Covid-19 pandemic by registering positive gains. Specifically, Bitcoin, ADA, CRO and Ethereum showed the function of protection by resisting the conditions of extreme market turmoil. Naaem et al. (2021) reported that the Covid-19 pandemic negatively affected the efficiency of four cryptocurrencies (Bitcoin, Ethereum, Litecoin, and Ripple). Although Bitcoin and Ethereum are the hardest affected cryptocurrencies, they recovered faster from their sharp decline to inefficiency at the end of March 2021. Jalan et al. (2021) found that during the Covid-19 pandemic, gold-backed cryptocurrency units were susceptible to the volatility transmitted from gold markets. However, unlike gold, cryptocurrency units cannot rapidly recover from the shock of Covid-19. Mariana et al. (2021) revealed in the results of their study that Ethereum was a better safe haven than Bitcoin during the pandemic period. At the same time, they pointed out that both cryptocurrencies exhibited high volatility.

Shahzad et al. (2021) found much stronger spillovers in all cryptocurrencies in the high volatility regime, consistent with the concept of contagion during the Covid-19 pandemic. Singh (2021) determined that after the Covid-19 market shock, capital began to flow from the stock market to litigation finance and dynamic correlations between litigation finance and Gold (Bitcoin) began to increase (decrease) after this shock.

Focusing on the effect of Covid-19 on the relationships between the gold, oil, Bitcoin prices and risk scales of VIX and EPU indexes, Yaroyava et al. (2021) revealed in the results of their study that the spillover between conventional and Islamic stock exchanges have become stronger during the pandemic while Islamic bonds (Sukuk) show the safe haven feature. Furthermore, they stated in their study that the strongest predictors of the spillovers of traditional Islamic markets are Covid-19, oil and gold, while Bitcoin are not considered as an important determinant of these relationships.

Considering these studies, we designed this study to reveal the relationship between cryptocurrencies and the volatility of Turkish financial markets. Our biggest motivation for creating the study was the increasing interest in cryptocurrencies in Turkey. The contraction in the Turkish economy and financial markets directs investors to alternative assets. Particularly during the Covid-19 period, when uncertainties increased more, interest in the cryptocurrency market increased more in Turkey. In this case, revealing the interaction between cryptocurrency markets and Turkish financial markets has become an important study question. For this purpose, we consider Bitcoin (BTC-USD) and Istanbul Stock Exchange-100 (ISE-100) index, the US Dollar-Turkish Lira (USD-TRY) foreign exchange rate, Gram Gold-Turkish Lira (GAU-TRY) exchange rate, and the Istanbul Stock Exchange overnight repo rate as the interest rate (IR). Then, we investigate the spillovers between return volatilities of financial assets in Turkey and Bitcoin before and during the Covid-19 pandemic. Within the scope of this research, the next sections include methodology and results. The last section ends with the conclusion.

LITERATURE REVIEW OF STUDIES IN PRE-COVID-19 PERIOD

In the introduction, we have included the studies carried out during the Covid-19 period. Thus, we revealed the main motivation of the study. In this section, a summary review has been made that examines the studies on cryptocurrencies and especially Bitcoin volatility in the pre-Covid-19 period. It is argued that cryptocurrencies are an investment tool or a currency over the concept of volatility. Studies involving these discussions are as follows:

Akyıldırım et al (2019) analyze the relationship between the price volatility of a wide range of cryptocurrencies as measured by the VIX and VSTOXX, respectively, and the implied volatility of both the United States and European financial markets. Overall, their results indicate the existence of time-varying positive correlations between the conditional correlations of cryptocurrencies and financial market stress. Furthermore, these correlations were found to increase significantly during periods of high financial market stress, suggesting that the spread of significant financial market fear is affecting these new financial products.

According to Ardia et al. (2019), they test the existence of regime changes in the GARCH volatility dynamics of Bitcoin daily returns using Markov-switched GARCH (MSGARCH) models. They also compare MSGARCH with traditional single regimen GARCH specifications in the next day's Value at Risk (VaR) estimation. The Bayesian approach is used to estimate model parameters and calculate VaR estimates. They find strong evidence for regime changes in the GARCH process and show that MSGARCH models outperform single regime specifications when estimating VaR. Using specifications that can explain structural breaks in GARCH, i.e. Markov-Switching GARCH patterns, we show that Bitcoin daily returns do indeed exhibit regime changes in volatility dynamics. In our sample period, a two-regime MSGARCH model exhibits the best in-sample performance with inverted leverage in both low and high volatility regimes. When estimating the next-day Value at Risk, Markov switching specifications clearly outperform standard single-regime GARCH models.

Kumar and Anandarao (2019) examine the dynamics of ripple propagation between 15-08-2015 and 18-01-2018 in four main cryptocurrencies: Bitcoin, Ethereum, Ripple, and Litecoin. In a first step, an IGARCH (1,1)-DCC (1,1) multivariate GARCH model is estimated to measure the nature of volatility spillovers. From the GARCH results, it seems that there was statistically significant volatility spread from Bitcoin to Ethereum and Litecoin during the analysis period. Conditional correlation measurements point to the possibility of moderate return co-movement among cryptocurrencies. Conditional covariance measures show negligible volatility spread in the early periods and provide evidence for increased volatility spread after 2017. Wavelet coherence measurements show that the correlation between cryptocurrencies is persistent in the short run, while binary wavelet cross-spectral analysis confirms the findings from conditional covariance measurements. Other cryptocurrencies were seen to be affected by fluctuations in Bitcoin prices. Overall, the results point to the possibility of turbulence in the cryptocurrency markets and the possibility of herding behavior in the cryptocurrency markets.

Bitcoin was launched to resolve insecurity and uncertainty in the current financial system. The effect of risk spillover from economic policy uncertainty (EPU) to Bitcoin was investigated using a multivariate quantitative model and the Granger causality risk test. US EPU index, stock market uncertainty index, and VIX are used as a proxy for EPU. The risk spillover effect from EPU to Bitcoin turned out to be negligible in most cases. The study provides useful information on building asset portfolios for investors with investment strategies in Bitcoin, as Bitcoin can be used as a safe haven or diversifier under EPU shocks (Wang et al., 2019).

Baur et al (2018) analyze the relationship between Bitcoin, gold, and the US dollar and states that Bitcoin can be classified as something between gold and the US dollar. The paper uses the same sample and econometric models to replicate the findings, showing that exact replication is not possible and alternative statistical methods provide more reliable but very different results. The findings, based on the original sample and an extended sample period, show that Bitcoin exhibits distinctly different returns, volatility, and correlation characteristics compared to other assets, including gold and the US dollar.

Byström and Krygier (2018) looked at the link between Bitcoin market volatility and volatility in other related traditional markets, namely gold, currency, and the stock market. They also sought to answer whether the volatility in the Bitcoin market could be explained by retail investor-driven internet search volumes, or perhaps by the overall level of risk in the financial system as measured by two market-wide risk indicators. They used daily, weekly and monthly data covering the period 2011-2017. The correlations and retracements reveal a weak but positive concurrent link between changes in Bitcoin volatility and changes in the volatility of the trade-weighted USD currency index. The significant relation found between Google search volumes and points of market volatility by retail investors rather than large institutions is the most important driver of Bitcoin volatility.

Gajardo et al (2018) applied MF-ADCCA to analyze the existence and asymmetry of cross-correlations between major exchange rates, Bitcoin and the Dow Jones Industrial Average (DJIA), gold price and crude oil market. They concluded that in each cross-correlation studied, there is multi-fractalism and there is asymmetry in the cross-correlation exponents under the different bias of WTI, Gold and DJIA. Bitcoin shows a larger multifractal spectrum than other currencies in its cross-correlation with WTI, Gold and DJIA. Bitcoin clearly shows a different relationship with commodities and stock market indices to consider when investing.

Klein *et al.* (2018) Cryptocurrencies like Bitcoin present themselves as an investment asset. In their work, they tried to reveal the conditional variance properties of Bitcoin and gold. They also applied a BEKK-GARCH model to predict time-varying conditional correlations and found that gold plays an important role in emerging financial markets during market downturns. Besides, the results of the study show that Bitcoin behaves like the opposite and is positively correlated with downside markets.

Baur and Dimpfi (2017) suggest that if a currency fluctuates excessively, its use as a currency is limited. Through an in-depth analysis of Bitcoin's volatility, they showed that Bitcoin's volatility is extreme (30 times greater) compared to the major currencies US dollar, Euro, and Japanese Yen. The findings imply that Bitcoin cannot function as a currency. Kasper (2017) stated in his study that Bitcoin volatility is high compared to several currencies and financial assets such as stocks and gold. The study found that Bitcoin volatility is still significantly higher than that of least developed countries' currencies. Only five more currencies were volatile for more than 10% of the analyzed timeframe.

Dyhrberg (2016) explores Bitcoin's financial asset capabilities using GARCH models. The first model showed several similarities with gold and the dollar, demonstrating the capabilities and advantages of hedging as a medium of exchange. Asymmetric GARCH showed that Bitcoin can be useful in risk management and ideal for risk-averse investors in anticipation of negative shocks to the market. Overall, Bitcoin has a place in financial markets and portfolio management as it can be classified as something between gold and the US dollar on a scale from exchange advantages to store of value advantages

METHODOLOGY

GARCH-Type Volatility Models

We apply the following GARCH model extensions under the assumption that innovations have different probability distributions. We define these models except Exponential GARCH using Hentschel's (1995) GARCH-family which is

$$\sigma_t^{\lambda} = \omega + \sum_{i=1}^{p} \alpha_i \sigma_{t-i}^{\lambda} \left[\left| \varepsilon_{t-i} - \eta_{2i} \right| - \eta_{1i} \left(\varepsilon_{t-i} - \eta_{2i} \right) \right]^{\delta} + \sum_{i=1}^{q} \beta_i \sigma_{t-i}^{\lambda}$$

with σ_t denoting the conditional standard deviation, ω the intercept and ε_t the residuals from the mean filtration process. The shape of the conditional standard is determined by λ, and the parameter δ transforms the absolute value function which it subject to rotations and shifts through the η_{1i} and η_{2i} parameters respectively

1. Standard GARCH if $\lambda = \delta = 2$ and $\eta_{1i} = \eta_{2i} = 0$.
2. Glosten-Jagannathan-Runkle GARCH (GJR-GARCH) if $\lambda = \delta = 2$ and $\eta_{2i} = 0$.
3. Asymmetric Power ARCH (APARCH) if $\lambda = \delta$, $\eta_{2i} = 0$ and $\left|\eta_{1i}\right| \leq 1$.
4. ALLGARCH if $\lambda = \delta$.
5. Absolute Value GARCH (AVGARCH) if $\lambda = \delta = 1$ and $\left|\eta_{1i}\right| \leq 1$.

6. Threshold GARCH (TGARCH) if $\lambda = \delta = 1$, $\eta_{2i} = 0$ and $\left|\eta_{1i}\right| \leq 1$.
7. Nonlinear GARCH (NGARCH) if $\lambda = \delta$ and $\eta_{1i} = \eta_{2i} = 0$.
8. Nonlinear Asymmetric GARCH (NAGARCH) if $\lambda = \delta = 2$ and $\eta_{1i} = 0$.
9. Integrated GARCH (IGARCH) if $\lambda = \delta = 2$, $\eta_{1i} = \eta_{2i} = 0$ and the sum of the ARCH and GARCH parameters is 1.
10. Exponential GARCH (EGARCH) is $\ln\left(\sigma_t^2\right) = \omega + \sum_{i=1}^{p}\left[\alpha_i \varepsilon_{t-i} + \left(\gamma_i \left|\varepsilon_{t-i}\right| - E\left[\left|\varepsilon_{t-i}\right|\right]\right)\right] + \sum_{i=1}^{q}\beta_i \ln\left(\sigma_{t-i}^2\right)$ where the coefficient α_i captures the sign effect and γ_i the size effect.

The conditional distributions for the innovations are

1. Normal (norm),
2. Skewed-Normal (snorm),
3. Student-t (std),
4. Skew Student-t (sstd),
5. Generalized Error Distribution (ged),
6. Skewed-GED (sged),
7. Normal Inverse Gaussian (nig) and
8. Johnson's SU (jsu) distributions.

GARCH-type models are compared according to several information criteria, and likelihood values. One can see the studies of Ghalanos (2020a, 2020b) and Chu et al (2017) for details on GARCH-type models.

Diebolod-Yilmaz Approach for Volatility Spillover Effect

Diebold and Yilmaz (2009) describe the return and volatility spillover on the basis of the Vector Autoregressive (VAR) model. The total spillover index is measured based on the Cholesky decomposition. But, in the later study of Diebold and Yilmaz (2012), they developed a methodology to evaluate directional spillover in a generalized VAR framework. Thus, h-step-forecast error-variance decompositions from the VAR framework are defined as follows:

$$\theta_{ij}^{g} = \frac{\sigma_{ij}^{-1} \sum_{h=0}^{H-1} \left(\blacklozenge_i^T A_h \pounds \blacklozenge_j \right)^2}{\sum_{h=0}^{H-1} \left(\blacklozenge_i^T A_h \pounds A_h^T \blacklozenge_i \right)} \tag{1}$$

where σ_{ij} represents the standard deviation of the error term, £ is variance-covariance matrix, A_i are NxN coefficient matrix of moving average representation of VAR model and �$_i$ is the selection vector of which i[th] element is equal to 1 and the other elements are 0. The spillover effects can be computed as follows.

$$\tilde{\theta}_{ij}^{g}\left(H\right)=\frac{\theta_{ij}^{g}\left(H\right)}{\sum_{j=1}^{N}\theta_{ij}^{g}\left(H\right)} \tag{2}$$

with $\sum_{j=1}^{N}\tilde{\theta}_{ij}^{g}\left(H\right)=1$ and $\sum_{i,j=1}^{N}\tilde{\theta}_{ij}^{g}\left(H\right)=N$.

In the light of the above definitions and equations, Diebold and Yilmaz (2012) defined total, directional and net spillovers as follows.

The total volatility spillovers index based on h-step-ahead forecasts with the following equation:

$$TS^{g}\left(H\right)=\frac{\sum_{\substack{i,j=1\\ i\neq j}}^{N}\tilde{\theta}_{ij}^{g}\left(H\right)}{\sum_{i,j=1}^{N}\tilde{\theta}_{ij}^{g}\left(H\right)}x100=\frac{\sum_{\substack{i,j=1\\ i\neq j}}^{N}\tilde{\theta}_{ij}^{g}\left(H\right)}{N}x100 \tag{3}$$

Directional volatility spillovers to i market from other j markets:

$$DS_{j\rightarrow i}^{g}\left(H\right)=\frac{\sum_{\substack{j=1\\ i\neq j}}^{N}\tilde{\theta}_{ij}^{g}\left(H\right)}{N}x100 \tag{4}$$

Directional volatility spillovers from market i to other j markets:

$$DS_{i\rightarrow j}^{g}\left(H\right)=\frac{\sum_{\substack{j=1\\ i\neq j}}^{N}\tilde{\theta}_{ji}^{g}\left(H\right)}{N}x100 \tag{5}$$

The net spillover index is obtained using Equations 4 and 5 as follow

Figure 1. The time-series plot of the log-returns

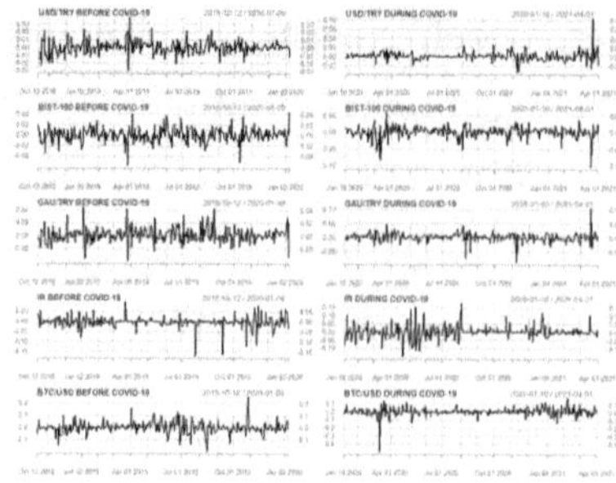

$$NS_i^g\left(H\right) = DS_{i\to j}^g\left(H\right) - DS_{j\to i}^g\left(H\right) \tag{6}$$

DATA

The log-returns of the ISE-100 index, the USD-TRY, GAU-TRY, and the ISE overnight repo rate as the interest rate (IR) are used in the analysis to reveal the volatility spillover between BTC-USD and Turkish financial markets. The date of establishment of the Coronavirus Scientific Board of the Ministry of Health that is 2020-01-10 is accepted to determine the epidemic period. Although the effects of the Covid-19 pandemic began to appear in the countries where the epidemic started before January 10, 2020, it was thought that the epidemic would remain in a limited region in Turkey. In other words, the epidemic was ignored and not discussed in the Turkish public. Therefore, the effect of the epidemic on the markets began to be seen towards March 2020. As a result of these, considering the maturation of the effects of the epidemic period, January 10, 2020, was chosen as the beginning of the epidemic period. In order for the pre-pandemic and pandemic period observation numbers to be equal, the data period was started from 2018-10-12. The full period of data is between the dates 2018-10-12 and 2021-04-01. The time-series plot of the log-return data set is given in Figure 1.

EMPIRICAL RESULTS

Empirical Results for GARCH-Type Models

We applied the GARCH-type models mentioned in Section 2.1 and the different probability distributions mentioned in the same section to model the conditional volatility of the ISE-100 index, the USD-TRY, GAU-TRY, and IR log-returns in the pre-Covid-19 and Covid-19 period. We estimate the parameters of GARCH (1,1)-type models. Thus, we fit 80 different GARCH-type models for each log-returns of the variables. We selected the most adequate model according to the information criteria and likelihood values. The most convenient GARCH-type models with different probability distributions for each variable are given in Table 3 in Appendix A. This table contains only the best 5 models among 80 models that are estimated for both periods and are evaluated based on the information criteria and likelihood values. The parameter estimation of the GARCH-type models and the diagnostics test results are given in Table 4 and Table 5 in Appendix B for both periods. The results obtained from diagnostic tests are as follows:

According to Ljung-Box on Standardized Residuals (LB) test results, there is no autocorrelation between residuals in any model. Moreover, Ljung-Box on Squared Standardized Residuals (LB^2) and ARCH Lagrange Multiplier (ARCH LM) tests show that there is no serial dependence between the squared residuals. In other words, all models are successful to capture heteroscedasticity. The Sign Bias Tests (SBT) indicate that there is no misspecification of models. The adjusted Pearson goodness-of-fit test results show that the assumed empirical and theoretical distributions of innovations are identical for all models except for interest rate volatility models of both periods.

One of the inferences that can be made from GARCH-type models is the persistence and the half-life. Since the estimated volatility model for USD-TRY in the pre-Covid-19 period is IGARCH, the half-life is infinite. While volatility persistence of USD-TRY and ISE-100 decreased, those of other variables increased in the Covid-19 period. It is concluded that although the persistence of the BTC-USD volatility has increased slightly, the half-life of the persistence has increased more than twice.

Empirical Results for Diebold-Yilmaz Spillover Index

We revealed the results of volatility spillovers, in other words, variance decomposition, between BTC-USD and Turkish financial markets using the Diebold-Yilmaz Spillover connectedness approach to volatility data obtained from best fit GARCH-type models for the period before and during Covid-19.

The correlations between the volatility series of variables are given in Table 6 in Appendix B. What stands out in the correlation table is that there was a low negative insignificant correlation between USD-TRY and BTC-USD before Covid-19, while a relatively higher positive significant correlation emerged in the Covid-19 period. The second important result is the high positive correlation values between GAU-TRY and USD-TRY in both periods. It is seen that gold prices decrease in the world but

Table 1. Volatility spillovers

SPILLOVERS BEFORE COVID-19							SPILLOVERS DURING COVID-19					
	USD	BIST	GAU	BTC	IR	CfO		USD	BIST	GAU	BTC	IR	CfO
USD	73.06	6.86	17.63	2.01	0.45	26.94	USD	73.44	11.92	13.19	1.11	0.33	26.56
BIST	0.47	97.94	0.20	0.53	0.86	2.06	BIST	1.12	90.85	4.05	3.69	0.29	9.15
GAU	17.02	3.55	79.18	0.05	0.20	20.82	GAU	5.29	6.12	87.09	0.83	0.67	12.91
BTC	0.10	0.57	0.05	97.24	2.03	2.76	BTC	0.08	16.47	0.11	82.52	0.82	17.48
IR	1.45	5.03	2.42	0.96	90.14	9.86	IR	4.92	0.64	3.60	1.00	89.84	10.16
CtO	19.04	16.02	20.31	3.54	3.53	12.49	CtO	11.40	35.15	20.96	6.64	2.12	15.25
CtOO	92.09	113.96	99.49	100.79	93.67	500.00	CtOO	84.84	126.00	108.04	89.16	91.95	500.00
NS	-7.91	13.96	-0.51	0.79	-6.33		NS	-15.16	26.00	8.04	-10.84	-8.05	
TSI	12.49						TSI	15.25					

CfO: Contribution from others, CtO: Contribution to others (spillover),
CtOO: Contribution to others including own, NS: Net Spillover, TSI: Total Spillover Index

rise due to the increase in the exchange rate in Turkey. Therefore, a high correlation between exchange rates and gold prices is an expected situation. The last important conclusion to be inferred from the correlation analysis is that there is no significant correlation between BTC-USD and IR. The Diebold-Yilmaz spillover index shows the contribution of the volatility in price indices to the forecasting error variance. Thus, the results of the total volatility spillovers index are based on a 10-step-ahead.

Based on the results of the volatility spillover index given in Table 1, it is understood that the variable that transmitted the most volatility to other indices is the ISE-100 index for both periods. In the pre-Covid-19 period, only 2.6% of the forecasting error variance of the ISE-100 index was due to the variances of other variables. In the same period, the net ISE-100 index increases the risk of other returns with its volatility spillover of 13.96% to the variances of other variables. In the Covid-19 period, the net volatility transmission of the stock market index almost doubled from the previous period to 26%. ISE-100 index has become an investment tool that poses more risk. From the results of the spillover index, it is inferred that during the Covid-19 period, Bitcoin caused 16.3% of the total spillover effect of the ISE-100 index.

It is understood that the USD-TRY is the volatility receiver in both periods. The net risk it received the Covid-19 period almost doubled, and 15.16% of the error variance was due to other indices. In both periods, through which the USD-TRY exchange rate transferred the most volatility was the GAU-TRY rate. Interest rates were subjected to the same rate of volatility transmission in both periods. In the Covid-19 period, while the effect of USD-TRY on the forecasting error variance of IR increased, there was no significant change in the effect of BTC-USD. Another

Table 2. Net pairwise spillovers

BEFORE COVID-19					DURING COVID-19			
USD-BIST	**USD-GAU**	**USD-BTC**	**USD-IR**		**USD-BIST**	**USD-GAU**	**USD-BTC**	**USD-IR**
-6.39	-0.61	-2.11	1.00		-10.8	-7.9	-1.19	4.59
	BIST-GAU	**BIST-BTC**	**BIST-IR**			**BIST-GAU**	**BIST-BTC**	**BIST-IR**
	3.35	0.04	4.17			2.07	12.78	0.35
		GAU-BTC	**GAU-IR**				**GAU-BTC**	**GAU-IR**
		0.00	2.22				-0.72	2.93
			BTC-IR					**BTC-IR**
			-1.07					0.18

striking situation is that gold prices became volatility transmitter in the Covid-19 period and contributed to the volatility of other variables by 8.4%.

BTC-USD, which was volatility transmitter in the pre-Covid-19 period, became a serious volatility receiver in the following period, and its net volatility transmission fell from 0.79% to -10.84%. If a portfolio containing the Turkish financial market instruments mentioned with Bitcoin is created, 10.84% of the forecasting error variance of BTC-USD will be caused by the others. The pairwise spillovers are given in Table 2.

The fact that total spillover index increased from 12.49% to 15.25% indicates a low connectedness between the markets in both periods and the error variance in markets is on average 15.25% originated from other markets in the Covid-19 period.

Average spillover effects over the full sampling period are obtained by generalized spillover analysis. Diebold and Yilmaz (2009, 2012, 2014) stated that full sample spillover measurements cannot clearly reflect the important sustained and cyclical movement in spillovers. A rolling window framework was created that allows time-varying spillover indices to overcome its current shortcomings in the spillover index, using a 20-day subsample. The estimation of the dynamic net and total spillover indexes is given in the following figures. These rolling windows were obtained using 10-step-ahead forecasting spillovers. In the period of October - November 2020, that is, the period when the rapid upward trend in BTC-USD started, BTC-USD is a risk transmitter. For example, the net spillover from BTC-USD was 44.75% on 09-04-20 and 29.66% on 11-06-20.

Figure 2. Rolling net spillover and total spillover before COVID-19

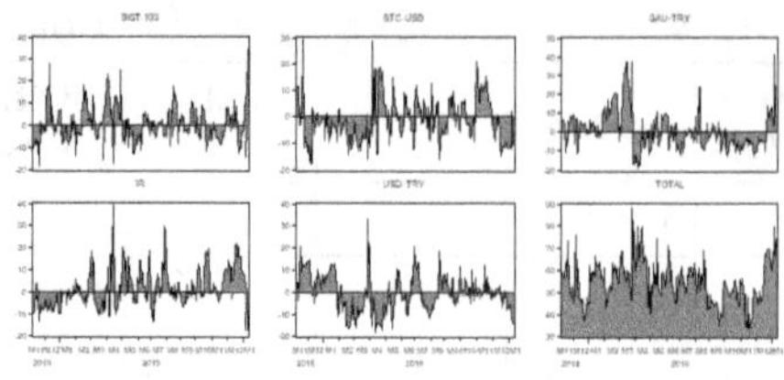

Figure 3. Rolling net spillover and total spillover during COVID-19

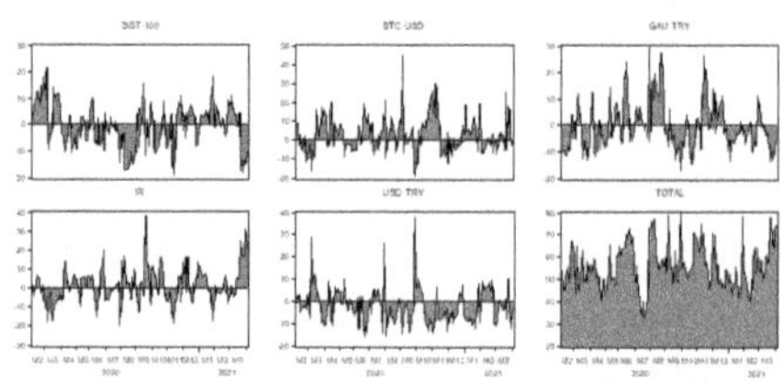

CONCLUSION

In this study, first, we estimated best-fit volatility models for the ISE-100 index, USD-TRY, GAU-TRY, and IR log-returns using GARCH-type models. We then applied the Diebold-Yilmaz approach using GARCH-based volatilities to reveal the spillover between these volatilities. We found that the variable that transmitted the most volatility to other indices is the ISE-100 index for both periods. In the pre-Covid-19 period, only 2.6% of the forecasting error variance of the ISE-100 index was due to the variances of other variables. In the same period, the net ISE-100 index increases the risk of other returns with its volatility spillover of 13.96% to the variances of other variables. Also, we inferred that 16.3% of the total spillover effect of the ISE-100 index was caused by Bitcoin during the Covid-19 period. In the Covid-19 period, while the effect of USD-TRY on the forecasting error variance of IR increased, there was no significant change in the effect of BTC-USD. Another striking situation is that gold prices became volatility transmitters in the Covid-19 period and contributed to the volatility of other variables by 8.4%. BTC-USD, which was a volatility transmitter in the pre-Covid-19 period, became a serious volatility receiver in the following period, and its net volatility transmission fell from 0.7% to -10.84%. Another significant result is that if a portfolio containing the mentioned Turkish financial market instruments with Bitcoin is created, 10.84% of the forecasting error variance of BTC-USD is caused by the others.

Although the spillover effect of interest rates increased at the end of the Covid-19 period, interest rates do not have a wide spillover effect in both periods. This can be understood as a result of the low-interest rate policy despite the high exchange rate. The high exchange rate and the resulting fluctuation in gold prices increased the spillover effect of the GAU-TRY exchange rate during the Covid-19 period. In addition, ISE-100 index is a volatility transmitter in both periods. It is understood that Bitcoin is an important resource in the total spillover effect of the ISE-100 index, especially in the Covid-19 period. In particular, the high risk and high spillover effect created by the Istanbul stock exchange directs investors to alternative investment instruments.

Although the results point to a low connectedness between Bitcoin and Turkish financial markets, in the Covid-19 period, Bitcoin has been a volatility receiver investment tool rather than a volatility transmitter. The state of uncertainty and increased risk in the domestic financial markets during the Covid-19 supports Bitcoin and other cryptocurrencies to be a preferred investment asset in Turkey. In conclusion, there is a low level of financial connectedness between Bitcoin and key assets in the Turkish financial market, this financial connectedness appears to have increased during the Covid-19 period. For this reason, investors who make a portfolio diversification decision based on these financial instruments and determine a risk management strategy should also consider the risk transmission between these indexes.

REFERENCES

Akyıldırım, E., Corbet, S., Lucey, B., Sensoy, A., & Yarovaya, L. (2019). The relationship between implied volatility and cryptocurrency returns. *Finance Research Letters*. Advance online publication. doi:10.1016/j.frl.2019.06.010

Albulescu, C. T. (2021). COVID-19 and the United States financial markets' volatility. *Finance Research Letters*, *38*, 1–5. doi:10.1016/j.frl.2020.101699 PMID:32837380

Ardia, D., Bluteau, K., & Rüede, M. (2019). Regime changes in Bitcoin GARCH volatility Dynamics. *Finance Research Letters*, *29*, 266–271. doi:10.1016/j.frl.2018.08.009

BaurD. G.DimpfiT. (2017). Realized Bitcoin Volatility. doi:10.2139/ssrn.2949754

Baur, D. G., & Dimpfi, T. (2021). The volatility of Bitcoin and its role as a medium of exchange and a store of value. *Empirical Economics*, *61*(5), 2663–2683. Advance online publication. doi:10.100700181-020-01990-5 PMID:33424101

Baur, D. G., Dimpfi, T., & Kuck, K. (2018). Bitcoin, gold and the US dollar – A replication and extension. *Finance Research Letters*, *25*, 103–110. doi:10.1016/j.frl.2017.10.012

Buchholz, K. (2021). *How common is crypto?* Available at: https://www.statista.com/chart/18345/crypto-currency-adoption/

Byström, H., & Krygier, D. (2018). What Drives Bitcoin Volatility? *Knut Wicksell Working Paper*, (3), 1-46.

Chen, T., Lau, C.K.M., Cheema, S., & Koo, C.K. (2021). *Economic Policy Uncertainty in China and Bitcoin Returns: Evidence From the COVID-19 Period.* . doi:10.3389/fpubh.2021.651051

Corbet, S., Hou, Y., Hu, Y., Oxley, L., & Xu, D. (2021). Pandemic-related financial market volatility spillovers: Evidence from the Chinese COVID-19 epicentre. *International Review of Economics & Finance*, *71*, 56–81. doi:10.1016/j.iref.2020.06.022

Diebold, F. X., & Yilmaz, K. (2009). Measuring financial asset return and volatility spillovers, with application to global equity markets. *Economic Journal (London)*, *119*(534), 158–171. doi:10.1111/j.1468-0297.2008.02208.x

Diebold, F. X., & Yilmaz, K. (2012). Better to give than to receive: Predictive directional measurement of volatility spillovers. *International Journal of Forecasting*, *28*(1), 57–66. doi:10.1016/j.ijforecast.2011.02.006

Diebold, F. X., & Yilmaz, K. (2014). On the network topology of variance decompositions: Measuring the connectedness of financial firms. *Journal of Economics*, *182*(1), 119–134. doi:10.1016/j.jeconom.2014.04.012

Dyhrberg, A. H. (2016). Bitcoin, gold and the dollar –A GARCH volatility analysis. *Finance Research Letters*, *16*, 85–92. doi:10.1016/j.frl.2015.10.008

Fasanya, I. O., Oliyide, J. A., Adekoya, O. B., & Agbatogun, T. (2021). How does economic policy uncertainty connect with the dynamic spillovers between precious metals and bitcoin markets? *Resources Policy*, *72*, 1–17. doi:10.1016/j.resourpol.2021.102077

Gajardo, G., Kristjanpoller, W. D., & Minutolo, M. (2018). Does Bitcoin exhibit the same asymmetric multifractal cross-correlations with crude oil, gold and DJIA as the Euro, Great British Pound and Yen? *Chaos, Solitons, and Fractals*, *109*, 195–205. doi:10.1016/j.chaos.2018.02.029

Ghalanos, A. (2020a). *rugarch: Univariate GARCH models*. R package version 1.4-2. Available at: https://cran.r-project.org/web/packages/rugarch/rugarch.pdf

Ghalanos, A. (2020b). *Introduction to the rugarch package*. Technical Report Available at: https://cran.r-project.org/web/packages/rugarch/vignettes/Introduction_to_the_rugarch_package.pdf

Ghorbel, A., & Jeribi, A. (2021). *Investigating the relationship between volatilities of cryptocurrencies and other financial assets*. Decisions in Economics and Finance. doi:10.100710203-020-00312-9

Goodell, J. W., & Goutte, S. (2021). Co-movement of COVID-19 and Bitcoin: Evidence from wavelet coherence analysis. *Finance Research Letters*, *38*, 1–6. doi:10.1016/j.frl.2020.101625

Hentschel, L. (1995). All in The Family Nesting Symmetric and Asymmetric GARCH Models. *Journal of Financial Economics*, *39*(1), 71–104. doi:10.1016/0304-405X(94)00821-H

Iqbal, N., Fareed, Z., Wan, G., & Shahzad, F. (2021). Asymmetric nexus between COVID-19 outbreak in the world and cryptocurrency market. *International Review of Financial Analysis*, *73*, 1–16. doi:10.1016/j.irfa.2020.101613

JalanA.MatkovskyyR.YarovayaL. (2021). “Shiny” crypto assets: A systemic look at gold-backed cryptocurrencies during the COVID-19 pandemic. doi:10.2139/ssrn.3796837

Kasper, J. (2017). Evolution of bitcoin: Volatility comparisons with least developed countries’ currencies. *Journal of Internet Banking and Commerce*, *22*(3), 1–18.

Klein, T., Thu, H. P., & Walther, T. (2018). Bitcoin is not the New Gold – A comparison of volatility, correlation, and portfolio performance. *International Review of Financial Analysis*, *59*, 105–116. doi:10.1016/j.irfa.2018.07.010

Kumar, A. S., & Anandarao, S. (2019). Volatility spillover in crypto-currency markets: Some evidences from GARCH and wavelet analysis. *Physica A*, *524*, 448–458. doi:10.1016/j.physa.2019.04.154

Mariana, C. D., Ekaputra, I. A., & Husodo, Z. A. (2021). Are Bitcoin and Ethereum safe-havens for stocks during the COVID-19 pandemic? *Finance Research Letters*, (38), 1–7. PMID:33100925

OG. (n.d.). *Ödemelerde kripto varlıkların kullanılmamasına dair yönetmelik.* Available at: https://www.resmigazete.gov.tr/eskiler/2021/04/20210416-4.htm

Singh, A. (2021). Investigating the dynamic relationship between litigation funding, gold, bitcoin and the stock market: The case of Australia. *Economic Modelling*, *97*, 45–57. doi:10.1016/j.econmod.2021.01.007

Umar, M., Rizvi, S. K. A., & Naqvi, B. (2021). Dance with the devil? The nexus of fourth industrial revolution, technological financial products and volatility spillovers in global financial system. *Technological Forecasting and Social Change*, *163*, 1–11. doi:10.1016/j.techfore.2020.120450

Urbina, J. (2020). *Spillover Index Based on VAR Modelling*. R package version 0.1. Available at: https://cran.r-project.org/web/packages/Spillover/Spillover.pdf

Wang, G. J., Xie, C., Wen, D., & Zhao, L. (2019). When Bitcoin meets economic policy uncertainty (EPU): Measuring risk spillover effect from EPU to Bitcoin. *Finance Research Letters*, *31*, 489–497. doi:10.1016/j.frl.2018.12.028

Yarovaya, L., Elsayed, A. H., & Hammoudeh, S. (2021). Determinants of spillovers between islamic and conventional financial markets: Exploring the safe haven assets during the COVID-19 pandemic. *Finance Research Letters*, *43*, 101979. Advance online publication. doi:10.1016/j.frl.2021.101979

Zhang, Y.-J., Bouri, E., Gupta, R., & Ma, S.-J. (2021). Risk spillover between Bitcoin and conventional financial markets: An expectile-based approach. *The North American Journal of Economics and Finance*, *55*, 1–10. doi:10.1016/j.najef.2020.101296

ADDITIONAL READING

Antonakakis, N., Chatziantoniou, I., & Gabauer, D. (2020). Refined Measures of Dynamic Connectedness based on Time-Varying Parameter Vector Autoregressions. *Journal of Risk and Financial Management, 13*(4), 84. doi:10.3390/jrfm13040084

Arı, Y. (2021). Volatility spillovers effect analysis during Covid-19 period using EWMA model: The case of health sector stocks in ISE. *Ömer Halisdemir Üniversitesi İktisadi ve İdari Bilimler Fakültesi Dergisi*, *14*(4), 1453-1467. doi:10.25287/ohuiibf.917674

Arı, Y. (2021). Engle-Granger Cointegration Analysis Between GARCH-Type Volatilities of Gold and Silver Returns. *Alanya Akademik Bakış*, *5*(2), 589–618. doi:10.29023/alanyaakademik.838284

Bollerslev, T. (2010). Glossary to ARCH (GARCH*). In T. Bollerslev, J. Russell, & M. Watson (Eds.), *Volatility and Time Series Econometrics: Essays in Honor of Robert Engle*. doi:10.1093/acprof:oso/9780199549498.001.0001

Diebold, F. X., & Yilmaz, K. (2015). *Financial and Macroeconomic Connectedness: A Network Approach to Measurement and Monitoring*. Oxford University Press. doi:10.1093/acprof:oso/9780199338290.001.0001

Diebold, F. X., & Yilmaz, K. (2016). Trans-Atlantic Equity Volatility Connectedness: U.S. and European Financial Institutions, 2004-2014. *Journal of Financial Econometrics*, *14*, 81–127.

Tsay, R. S. (2012). *An Introduction to Analysis of Financial Data with R*. Wiley.

Tsay, R. S. (2013). *Multivariate Time Series Analysis: With R and Financial Applications*. Wiley.

Yilmaz, K. (2014). *Book, Articles and Working Papers on Financial and Macroeconomic Connectedness*. Available at: http://financialconnectedness.org/research.html

KEY TERMS AND DEFINITIONS

Conditional Volatility: The conditional volatility can be defined as a measure of risk or a statistical measure of the change in the values of a financial asset over time. In other words, it is an estimated standard deviation of financial time series under the specified probability distribution.

Connectedness: Connectedness is a statistical measure of the relationship between variables that allows asymmetries in bilateral connections between markets, instead of inherently symmetrical (hence non-directional) measures such as correlation. Hence, the connectedness index estimates the directional measure of volatility spillover.

Correlation: Correlation measures the direction and strength of linear dependence between two variables. The correlation function is symmetric and undirected, so it is only a bilateral measure of the relationship.

Leverage Effects: The leverage effect which is defined as a measure of the effect of negative shocks on volatility helps to describe those unexpected negative shocks have a greater influence on volatility than positive shocks.

Volatility Clusters: The volatility clusters which are the characteristic of financial returns mirror the leptokurtic shape (fat tails) of the return of the financial assets. The source of the volatility clusters is the direction and magnitude of the price changes. Volatility clustering takes place to large/small price changes being followed by large/small changes in either direction.

Volatility Persistence: Volatility persistence is the strength of the volatility feedback effect High persistence means that volatility shocks will be felt further in the future, albeit to a lesser extent. The persistence of volatility affects the predictability of future economic variables and the predictability of changes in the risk-return balance over business cycles.

Volatility Spillover: Volatility spillover is a transmission of instability or a contagion of risk from market to market.

APPENDIX 1

Table 3. GARCH model evaluation

GARCH-TYPE MODEL EVALUATION FOR THE PERIOD BEFORE COVID-19							GARCH-TYPE MODEL EVALUATION FOR THE PERIOD COVID-19					
Model	**AIC**	**BIC**	**SIC**	**HQIC**	**LH**	**Variable**	**Model**	**AIC**	**BIC**	**SIC**	**HQIC**	**LH**
						USD-TRY						
std igarch11	-6.9230934	-6.8868474	-6.9232796	-6.9086022	1072.6179		std egarch11	-7.2452623	-7.1848522	-7.2457749	-7.2211102	1124.393
std nagarch11	-6.9230438	-6.8626337	-6.9235564	-6.8988917	1074.6103		jsu egarch11	-7.2374696	-7.1649775	-7.2382047	-7.2084871	1124.189
nig igarch11	-6.9212591	-6.872931	-6.9215886	-6.9019374	1073.3345		nig egarch11	-7.2317977	-7.1593057	-7.2325328	-7.2028153	1123.3127
std avgarch11	-6.9201806	-6.8476886	-6.9209157	-6.8911981	1075.1679		std avgarch11	-7.2310786	-7.1585865	-7.2318137	-7.2020961	1123.2016
jsu igarch11	-6.9198465	-6.8715185	-6.920176	-6.9005249	1073.1163		jsu avgarch11	-7.2245962	-7.1400221	-7.2255926	-7.1907833	1123.2001
						BIST-100						
sged egarch11	-5.907887	-5.835395	-5.9086221	-5.8789046	918.76855		nig nagarch11	-5.7106891	-5.638197	-5.7114242	-5.6817066	888.30146
jsu egarch11	-5.9056063	-5.8331142	-5.9063414	-5.8766238	918.41617		nig tgarch11	-5.7087537	-5.6362617	-5.7094888	-5.6797713	888.00245
std egarch11	-5.9039866	-5.8435765	-5.9044992	-5.8798345	917.16593		jsu nagarch11	-5.707855	-5.6353629	-5.7085901	-5.6788725	887.86359
ged egarch11	-5.9001879	-5.8397778	-5.9007005	-5.8760358	916.57902		nig allgarch11	-5.7072723	-5.6106162	-5.7085683	-5.668629	889.77356
norm egarch11	-5.8979208	-5.8495928	-5.8982503	-5.8785992	915.22877		jsu tgarch11	-5.7052476	-5.6327555	-5.7059827	-5.6762651	887.46075
						GAU-TRY						
std GARCH11	-6.2539989	-6.2056709	-6.2543284	-6.2346773	970.24283		jsu ngarch11	-5.8594044	-5.7869123	-5.8601395	-5.8304219	911.27797
nig GARCH11	-6.2530011	-6.1925911	-6.2535137	-6.2288491	971.08867		jsu tgarch11	-5.8551192	-5.7826272	-5.8558543	-5.8261368	910.61592
jsu GARCH11	-6.2528076	-6.1923976	-6.2533203	-6.2286556	971.05878		nig ngarch11	-5.8517034	-5.7792113	-5.8524385	-5.8227209	910.08817
std igarch11	-6.2513359	-6.2150899	-6.2515221	-6.2368447	968.8314		jsu allgarch11	-5.8513046	-5.7546485	-5.8526006	-5.8126613	912.02656
std nagarch11	-6.2495266	-6.1891166	-6.2500393	-6.2253746	970.55187		jsu egarch11	-5.8511461	-5.7786541	-5.8518812	-5.8221637	910.00208
						BTC-USD						
jsu ngarch11	-3.7702254	-3.6977333	-3.7709605	-3.7412429	588.49983		std egarch11	-3.5458766	-3.4854666	-3.5463893	-3.5217246	552.83794
nig ngarch11	-3.7698101	-3.697318	-3.7705452	-3.7408276	588.43565		std nagarch11	-3.5435346	-3.4831245	-3.5440472	-3.5193825	552.47609
std ngarch11	-3.7668045	-3.7063945	-3.7673171	-3.7426525	586.9713		jsu egarch11	-3.5433596	-3.4708675	-3.5440947	-3.5143771	553.44905
sstd ngarch11	-3.7668045	-3.7063945	-3.7673171	-3.7426525	586.9713		std gjrgarch11	-3.5430212	-3.4826112	-3.5435339	-3.5188692	552.39678
jsu aparch11	-3.7659639	-3.6813898	-3.7669603	-3.732151	588.84142		std tgarch11	-3.5425203	-3.4821102	-3.5430329	-3.5183682	552.31939
						IR						
std aparch11	-5.2034472	-5.1309552	-5.2041823	-5.1744647	809.93259		ged tgarch11	-4.512492	-4.4520819	-4.5130046	-4.4883399	702.18001
std ngarch11	-5.1756625	-5.1152524	-5.1761751	-5.1515104	804.63985		ged avgarch11	-4.5060546	-4.4335626	-4.5067897	-4.4770721	702.18544
ged egarch11	-5.0739308	-5.0135208	-5.0744435	-5.0497788	788.92231		sged tgarch11	-4.5059376	-4.4334456	-4.5066727	-4.4769552	702.16736
ged nagarch11	-5.066105	-5.005695	-5.0666177	-5.041953	787.71323		ged egarch11	-4.4933208	-4.4329107	-4.4938334	-4.4691687	699.21806
ged gjrgarch11	-5.064058	-5.0036479	-5.0645706	-5.0399059	787.39695		sged egarch11	-4.4836514	-4.4111593	-4.4843865	-4.4546689	698.72414

APPENDIX 2

Table 4. The parameter estimation of GARCH models and diagnostics test results for the period before COVID-19

	GARCH-TYPE VOLATILITY MODELS FOR THE PERIOD BEFORE COVID-19																			
	std-IGARCH(1,1) for USD				std-EGARCH(1,1) for BIST				std-GARCH(1,1) for GAU				jsu-NGARCH(1,1) for BTC				std-NAGARCH(1,1) for IR			
Param	**est**	**Std.Err**	**t-stat**	**sig**	**est**	**Std.Err**	**t-stat**	**sig**	**est**	**Std.Err**	**t-stat**	**sig**	**est**	**Std.Err**	**t-stat**	**sig**	**est**	**Std.Err**	**t-stat**	**sig**
omega	0.00	0.00	0.37	0.71	-0.35	0.00	-12238.04	0.00	0.00	0.00	1.48	0.14	0.02	0.02	0.83	0.41	0.13	0.04	2.93	0.00
alpha1	0.21	0.13	1.68	0.09	-0.11	0.00	-633.68	0.00	0.18	0.09	2.02	0.04	0.13	0.06	2.19	0.03	0.41	0.06	7.10	0.00
beta1	0.79	NA	NA	NA	0.96	0.00	14816.57	0.00	0.65	0.16	4.08	0.00	0.86	0.04	21.50	0.00	0.48	0.07	6.84	0.00
eta11																	0.50	0.14	3.58	0.00
gamma1					-0.14	0.00	-8550.99	0.00					0.35	0.32	1.11	0.27				
lambda													0.07	0.06	1.09	0.28	0.09	0.04	2.36	0.02
skew													0.93	0.09	9.82	0.00				
shape	4.26	0.85	5.04	0.00	6.37	0.00	2042.21	0.00	4.47	1.17	3.83	0.00					2.11	0.05	43.74	0.00
		stat	**sig**			**stat**	**sig**			**stat**	**sig**			**stat**	**sig**			**stat**	**sig**	
LB		4.10	0.24			1.51	0.74			3.14	0.38			5.72	0.10			0.00	1.00	
LB²		1.43	0.76			8.32	0.11			2.39	0.85			3.43	0.69			0.02	1.00	
ARCH LM		1.38	0.62			6.39	0.12			0.86	0.94			3.87	0.37			0.01	1.00	
SBT Joint		0.39	0.94			3.86	0.28			7.54	0.16			2.05	0.56			2.13	0.55	
Perason GoF		9.12	0.97			18.18	0.51			17.67	0.54			12.36	0.87			34.11	0.02	
Persistence	1.00				0.96				0.84				0.96				0.82			
Half-life	inf				16.62				3.88				15.76				3.59			

Table 5. The parameter estimation of GARCH models and diagnostics test results for during COVID-19 period

	GARCH-TYPE VOLATILITY MODELS FOR DURING THE COVID-19 PERIOD																			
	std-EGARCH(1,1) for USD				nig-NAGARCH(1,1) for BIST				jsu-NGARCH(1,1) for GAU				std-EGARCH(1,1) for BTC				nig-EGARCH(1,1) for IR			
Param	**est**	**Std.Err**	**t-stat**	**sig**	**est**	**Std.Err**	**t-stat**	**sig**	**est**	**Std.Err**	**t-stat**	**sig**	**est**	**Std.Err**	**t-stat**	**sig**	**est**	**Std.Err**	**t-stat**	**sig**
omega	-0.23	0.18	-1.29	0.19	0.00	0.00	2.05	0.04	0.04	0.07	0.60	0.55	-0.12	0.06	-1.94	0.05	0.00	0.00	2.25	0.02
alpha1	-0.13	0.08	-1.67	0.09	0.11	0.06	1.64	0.10	0.11	0.08	1.34	0.18	0.06	0.04	1.46	0.14	0.90	0.33	2.72	0.01
beta1	0.97	0.02	54.26	0	0.37	0.32	1.16	0.25	0.81	0.07	10.97	0.00	0.98	0.01	96.51	0.00	0.52	0.09	5.83	0.00
eta11																	0.23	0.18	1.26	0.21
eta21					1.81	0.90	2.00	0.05												
gamma1	0.91	0.23	3.88	0									0.20	0.06	3.45	0.00				
lambda									0.18	0.44	0.40	0.69								
skew					-0.39	0.08	-4.58	0.00	-0.44	0.14	-3.11	0.00								
shape	2.74	0.55	5.02	0	0.81	0.32	2.56	0.01	1.27	0.16	8.08	0.00	3.03	0.57	5.32	0.00	0.47	0.08	5.71	0.00
		stat	**sig**			**stat**	**sig**			**stat**	**sig**			**stat**	**sig**			**stat**	**sig**	
LB		4.44	0.20			4.17	0.23			3.03	0.40			5.15	0.14			6.15	0.08	
LB^2		0.37	0.98			0.53	1.00			2.42	0.85			0.51	1.00			2.53	0.83	
ARCH LM		0.47	0.90			0.09	1.00			0.88	0.93			0.59	0.97			1.45	0.83	
SBT Joint		2.28	0.50			1.16	0.76			1.51	0.68			2.47	0.48			3.49	0.32	
Perason GoF		27.5	0.09			8.61	0.98			15.85	0.67			61.39	0.11			49.90	0.00	
Persistence	0.98				0.82				0.91				0.98				0.99			
Half-life	24.59				3.51				7.33				37.05				692.74			

Table 6. Pearson correlations between GARCH-type volatilities

	CORRELATIONS OF VOLATILITIES- BEFORE COVID-19						CORRELATIONS OF VOLATILITIES- AFTER COVID-19				
Variables	**USD**	**BIST**	**GAU**	**BTC**	**INT**		**USD**	**BIST**	**GAU**	**BTC**	**INT**
USD	1.000						1.000				
BIST	0.268***	1.000					0.197***	1.000			
GAU	0.604***	0.249***	1.000				0.482***	0.278***	1.000		
BTC	-0.058	0.170***	0.119**	1.000			0.229***	0.130**	0.152***	1.000	
INTEREST	-0.257***	-0.309***	-0.208***	0.014	1.000		-0.193***	0.049	-0.130**	0.079	1.000

Note. * p <0.10, ** p <0.05, *** p < 0.01

Chapter 10
The Importance of Partnership for the Public and Private Sectors in the Renewable Energy Technology Industry in Algeria

Hadda Rebbouh
Independent Researcher, Algeria

Mekhelfi Amina
Technologic Institut, Algeria

ABSTRACT

The aim of this study is to show the importance of partnership in developing renewable energy technology in Algeria by focusing on Algeria's renewable resources and addressing the incentive mechanisms adopted by Algeria in the field of encouraging partnership with renewable energy and diagnosing the most important projects resulting from the partnership between the public and private sectors (domestic and foreign). The study concluded that there is a cooperation as many institutions and renewable energy production stations appeared in the Algerian market resulting from the partnership, but this cooperation is insufficient and is limited by many obstacles, the most important of which are monopoly and lack of experience in the field.

DOI: 10.4018/978-1-7998-9117-8.ch010

INTRODUCTION

The development of renewable energies has been marked in the world in recent years. Investments in the field of renewable energy have witnessed a considerable increase since 2004 (Christopher Kaminker, 2012). It reached 280 billion $ in 2018, mainly from the private sector (90%) (Amin Z Adnan, 2018). The generation capacity also increased in 2019 as 176 GW have been added. This transition aims to achieve a set of goals, including reducing dependence on fossil resources, ensuring energy security, limiting climate change, especially that energy is responsible for 80% of carbon emissions, which are increasing clearly, it has arrived at 1.3% during the period (2014-2019). In comparison, they decreased exceptionally in 2020 (Francesco la camera, 2021).

Algeria, like other countries, is seeking to reduce carbon emissions, especially as it is a strategic party in the production of fossil energy, whether gas or petroleum (Mourad Zaid, 2017). It has produced an LN capacity of 56 million m^3/ year (World Energy Council, 2020) as fossil resources are the main component of the Algerian economy. Algeria has witnessed an economic crisis since 2014 due to the decrease in oil price when the budget deficit reached 20% of the GDP. On the other hand, the average need for electricity increased to 6% compared to previous years in 2015 (Saliha Haddoum, 2018). Thus, the trend towards renewable energies became a strategic option, especially since Algeria has one of the largest solar fields in the world. Yet, it is not exploited as renewable electricity is less than 1% of the energy mix (H. Lohoues, 2016). Still, the transition of renewable energy resources is determined by many problems; the most important is financing.

Therefore, Algeria has resorted to opening the way for partnership. It is considered one of the assisting factors in the energy industry, whether fossil energy or renewable energy projects. It has several forms, such as contractual and cooperative projects (GRANT, 2012) . Algeria witnessed a decline in partnership contracts in the field of energy between 1993 and 2000. It introduced many legal amendments to open the way for investors. During the period (2001-2006), Algeria witnessed a noticeable increase due to the 07/05 law that allows opening up to foreign companies. With regard to renewable energy, the openness of the partnership began to become evident since the 2011 program. To understand the contribution of the partnership in developing renewable energy, we show the following problem (Manal Malizi, 2021):

To what extent does the partnership contribute to developing renewable energy technology in Algeria?

And in the main question, we include the following sub-questions:

What are the capabilities of Algeria in renewable energy resources?

What are the incentive mechanisms adopted by Algeria in renewable energy development?

What is the status of the partnership in the renewable energy technology market in Algeria?

METHODOLOGY

This paper relied on the descriptive-analytical method. It diagnoses the reality and actual data of the importance of partnership in developing renewable energy technology in Algeria. It was based on a selection of international articles such as (Bindzi Zogo Emmanuel Cedrick, 2017). It considers the partnership a mechanism for developing renewable energy, while (Sophie Jablonski, 2013) has discussed the importance of partnership in spreading renewable energies and the obstacles governments face in the Mediterranean countries. On the other hand, (Amal Rahmane, 2019) has called attention to the experience of the partnership between Algeria and Germany in the field of renewable energy and presented a group of studies, including (Boudghene, 2011) and (Mohammed Bouznit, 2020), which demonstrated the Algerian experience in the field of renewable energy.

Furthermore, the paper depended on different international and national reports such as IRENA, CDER, CEREFE, and the Ministry of energy Algerian. The official websites of many institutions such as CONDOR, ENIE, SONATRACH, SONALGAZ and other institutions have also been taken into consideration.

DISCUSSION AND RESULT

Renewable Energy in Algeria

The Potential of Renewable Energy in Algeria

1. **Solar potential**

The use of Solar energy in Algeria goes back to 1954 by France for the purpose of ceramics fabrication (Boudghene, 2011) . It is one of the best regions in the world (Figure 1) to the characteristics of the Algerian desert region and its availability on the production conditions for solar power: abundant sunshine, low humidity, and precipitation. The potential for power generation is enormous compared to regional and global energy demand. Roughly, 10% of the Algerian Sahara desert could meet the EU demand. The insulation time over the quasi-totality of the national territory exceeds 2000 h annually and may reach 3900 h (high plains and Sahara). The daily obtained energy on a horizontal surface of 1 m^2 is of 5 kWh over the major part of the national territory, or about 1700 kWh/m^2/year for the North and 2263 kWh/m^2/year for the South of the country (A. BoudgheneStambouli, 2012).

Figure 1. Potential sites for solar electricity supply from North Africa (in kWh/m^2/year) and example of the overall daily exposure received (in kWh/m^2/day) in Algeria

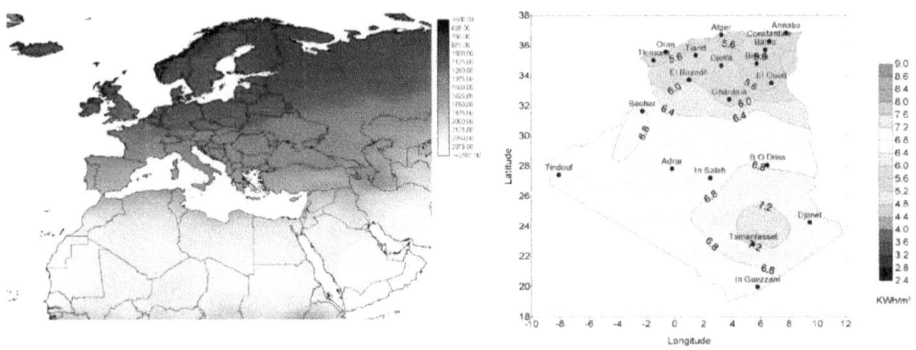

2. Wind energy potential

The first experiment to connect wind turbines was in 1957 (Ouahiba GUERRI, 2021). The distribution of winds varies according to the region's geographical location. In Algeria, the northern winds are less rapid than the southern winds, and the southwest region is considered the best location for Algeria in the Adrar region (Khenfri Khaider, 2018). The distribution of the average speed (m / s) of the wind over Algerian territory at the height of 80 m reaches (7 to 8 m / s). For an optimal assessment of the wind resource available (Noureddine YASSAA, 2020), note the fig2:

3. Geothermal energy potential

There are more than 240 springs in Algeria. The temperature of the hot water ranges between 22 °C and 98 °C. The highest temperature was recorded in the north-eastern region with 98 °C, while it reached 80 °C in the central region and 68 °C in the northwestern part. In addition, the average of the springs in the South is 50 °C (fig3((Abdelkader HARROUZ).

Figure 2. Wind speed in Algeria

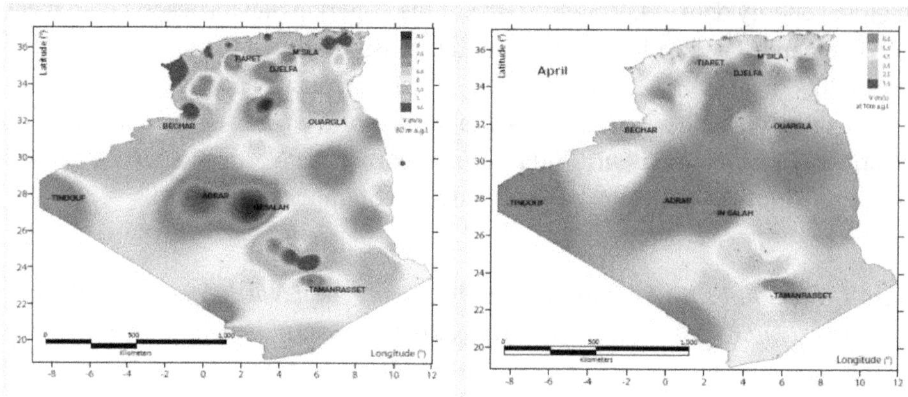

Figure 3. Geothermal in Algeria

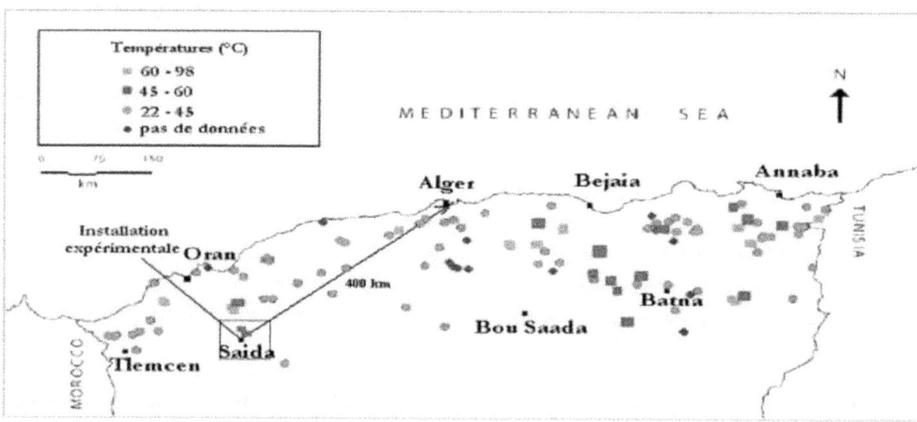

4. **Biomass energy potential**

There are two ways to generate energy from biomass: thermochemical conversion by combustion and conversion by anaerobic digestion (Amine Akbi, 2017). In Algeria, the forest areas cover about 250 million hectares of the country's total surface. This potential is estimated at 37 mtep of which about 10% could be recovered. According to the Center for the Development of Renewable Energy, it is possible for the power generation from a vital source to reach more than 1900 MW / hour (table1) electrical energy given that the average per capita consumption is about 1236 kw / hour (Abdelahak Razagui, 2019).

Table 1. The potential of bioenergy in Algeria

Sources	Annual vital capacities (million / m3)	Power generation power (gigawatts)
Urban waste Household waste Sewage	- 974 22.91	- 1646 38.72
Waste from olive farms Olive kernel Vegetable water Dairy products powder	- 10.5 2.35	215.5 17.74 3.97
Total	**1009.76**	**1921.93**

5. Hydroelectricity energy potential

It is the energy produced from the water resources in dams and the waters of the oceans and seas. A large reservoir is built in which the water is collected and then left flowing at a constant rate, moving the turbines which generate electrical energy flows. In Algeria, they are estimated at 65 billion cubic meters, but they are of little benefit: precipitation days are few and are concentrated in specific areas which decrease in the South. The Renewable Energies Development Center recorded 130 dams, and only 50 are operating status. The share of these small-sized production parks is about 5%, the total capacity of 13 of them is 269.208 MW, as shown in table2 (Amine BoudgheneStambouli, 2011).

The Legal Framework for Renewable Energy in Algeria

The Algerian government has issued many laws and decrees to improve the investment climate and develop renewable energy. Table 3 shows the most important laws regulating the renewable energy market regarding enhancing the work environment for the companies that are active in the Algerian market (Amina Mekhelfi, 2018)

Governmental Mechanisms for Developing Renewable Energy Technology in Algeria

1 Programs

Algeria adopted the renewable energy strategy by launching the National Program for Renewable Energy and Energy Efficiency in 2011 to generate 40% of renewable electricity by 2030. 22,000 MW of which 100 MW are meant for export to the European Union (Zhour Abada, 2018), but the program failed, and the government

Table 2. Hydroelectric production park in Algeria

Plant	Plant Installed power (MW)
Darguina	71.5
Ighil Emda	24
Mansouria	100
Erraguene	16
Djemaa	8.085
Souk El Tizi Meden	4.458
Ghrib	7.000
Ighzerncheb	2.712
Gouriet	6.425
Bouhanifia	5.700
Oued Fodda	15.600
Beni Behde	3.500
Tessala	4.224
Total	269.208

Table 3. Algerian legal text of RE

Year issued	Law N°	Subject & content
July, 28, 1999	**N°99-99**	Control of energy
February, 05, 2002	**N°11-02**	Ecotricity and Distribution public gas channels
August, 14, 2004	**N° 09- 04**	Promotion of capacities in the context of sustainable development
December, 30, 2009	**N° 09- 04**	Bearing of finance law for 2010 including its article 64 establishing the national fund for renewable energies and cogeneration (FNER)
July, 18, 2011	**N°09-09**	Including the Supplementary Finance Act 2011 noted the level of tax revenues that finances the National RE Fund and the expansion of the National Fund and the expansion of the field applied to cogeneration plants.
December, 20, 2014	**N° 14- 10**	Bearing the Finance Act of 2015, Article 108 provides for the merger of the tow special funds "the National Fund for the Control of Energy (FNCE /FNME) and the National Fund for RE and Cogeneration (FNER).
2017	-	Introduction of the energy efficiency tax which contributes to the improvement of the National Fund for the Control of RE and Energy Cogeneration

Figure 4. The national program for renewable energy and energy efficiency

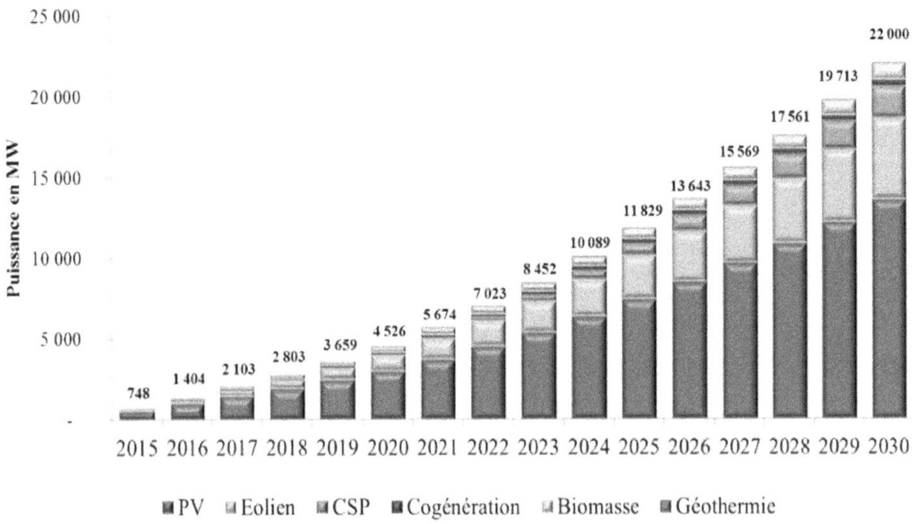

reviewed it with new goals in 2015. Reaching 27% of the renewable electricity by 2030 and the projects for the national market will be implemented in two stages:

The first stage 2015 -2020: This phase will achieve a power of 4010 MW between photovoltaic and wind power and 515 MW between biomass, cogeneration, and geothermal energy.

The second stage 2021- 2030: The development of the electrical interconnection between the North and the Sahara will allow the installation of large renewable energy plants in the regions of In Salah, Adrar, Timimoune, and Bechar. This also means their integration in the national energy system (Ministère de l'Énergie, 2021)) Fig 4(.

2. Financing:

The Finance Bill of 2015 created the National Fund for Energy Management (NFREC), which aims to promote and finance electricity generation from RE and cogeneration systems. It derives its inputs from oil revenue taxes (1%) and taxes on energy users. The government has also provided aid to implement projects that are involved in the renewable energy technology industry, finance training, research, and development (R&D) by Executive Decree No. 17-168 (22 May 2017). It amends and supplements Executive Decree No. 15-319 (13 December 2015). Renewable energy activities benefit from the concessions in the framework of legislation and regulation related to investment promotion. The government has also introduced incentives to produce electricity from renewable energy stations, including feed-in

Table 4. Financial aid granted to producers of solar thermal energy with the solar-hybrid system

Granted Bonus (% of price per kWh)	Contribution of Solar Energies
200%	**25% and more**
180%	**20 –25%**
16%	**15–20%**
14%	**10–15%**
100%	**5–10%**
0%	**0 –5%**

tariffs as Law No 25/14 dated in 2004. It includes the purchase price of renewable energies by the investor who produced them according to the type of technology used and the percentage of the contribution of the renewable resource (table 4) (Mohammed Bouznit, 2020).

3. Tender and Auctions

Algeria has issued several legal decrees to encourage competition by submitting bids and tenders to local and foreign investors. In November 2015, the Electricity and Gas Control Committee published the Power Purchase Agreement (PPA) Conditions for renewable energy projects. The contract for energy projects between producers and private investors was set to 20 years from the date of operation of the factory, and the specified period can be reduced by means of three decrees: (Executive Decree 428-06 of November 26, 2006, which is the recipient of the Power Purchase Agreement), (Executive Decree 06-429 of November 26, 2006 regarding the rules for grant recipients), and (Decree 13-228 of July 18, 2013) (serdouk, 2017) . On 26 February 2017, Algeria issued a basis for submitting a tender in renewable energy (the Executive Decree No 17-98). The decree specifies two types of requests: requests for proposals to investors and requests for proposals by auction. The first one, requests for proposals to investors (RPI), includes two components related to energy and activities such as (supply of equipment, design, marketing of produced electricity). It is divided into three batches of 1350 MW that can be developed and financed by a particular purpose vehicle held by private investors (49%) and state-owned companies and/or private Algerian companies (51%). The second component is the industrial one. It includes industrial projects that are concerned with manufacturing equipment or supplying renewable equipment. The Algerian government launched the first solar tender in 2018. This tender aims to install electric power of 150 MW, which will be located in the south-east regions with a capacity of 10 MW with annual energy of 20 GW/H for each station as follows: (Ghardaia 5), (Biskra 5), (Ouargla 3), (Eloued 02).

Status of the Partnership in the Renewable Energy Technology Market in Algeria

1. Analysis of the contribution of cooperation (PPP) in the development of renewable energy technology in Algeria:

With regard to the institutions that make up the renewable energy market in Algeria, we mention two types: the public company Sonatrach or one of its branches, the most important of which is the Electricity and Renewable Energy Company, which is responsible for marketing renewable energy. It was assigned to the experimental phase of the national program as it started producing 343 M in 2004, which is distributed in the high plateaus. Not to mention the realization of 21 solar power stations and a wind farm (10.2 MW) in Adrar as part of this phase with a total capacity of 354.2 (Mohamed M.Alichikouche, 2021). We also find private institutions that are active in the field of installation such as (SOLAR TECHNO and SIGMA). Most of these institutions represent a foreign partnership with mixed investments such as (TOTAL ENERGIE, PHOTOWATT) (S. Labed, 2003) or a local private company such as the Mila project 2020 with a capacity of 100 M. Also, the ZERGOUN GREEN ENERGY company project was launched in 2020 in Ouargla with a capacity of 100 megawatts, and therefore the production capacity of solar photovoltaic panels will be 450M. Other institutions also produce accessories and equipment such as metal structures (Noureddine YASSAA, 2020).

Result of the National Public-Private Partnership in the Production of RE the beginning of the Activity in the Field of Renewable Energy

The law that was issued on 14 April 1990 on loans is the basis for engaging the private sector in economic activity in Algeria. The partnership between the public and private sectors in Algeria is linked by many contracts such as concession contracts and investment according to BOT contracts. Algeria signed a partnership agreement, which aims at a policy of economic diversification, and made many amendments to the partnership laws, which opened the way for companies to engage in renewable energy activities, especially in 2017 (Karima Shayb baba, 2019) . The Algerian market also witnessed a remarkable increase in the national institutions in renewable energy. The most important company is Condor, which has established a partnership with (ENKI Technologie) Corporation of America and produced

Table 5. Private sector partnership for renewable energy in the Algerian market

Company name	Date	Field of activity
ENIE (Mariyana Yaneva, 2021)	**2013**	ENIE has invested DZD 2 billion (USD 20.1 m / EUR 18 m) to equip the factory with an automated line supplied by US firm Spire Semiconductor. The plant, located at ENIE's site at Sidi Bel Abbes, western Algeria, with a production capacity of 25 MW per year.
(EDIELEC) (Slimani, 2021)	**2012**	The company's concept is to provide streetlights equipped with a small wind turbine at low wind (2 meter / second), equipped with a wind generator that transforms the energy of the wind into electricity stored in batteries. The company also manufactures panels. It can produce 150 photovoltaic panels per day, with a national integration rate of 95%. different sizes (80W,160 W, and 260 W).
Condor (Condor, 2021)	**2012**	An Algerian private group, a leader in household appliances and consumer electronics, started on renewable energies and produced photovoltaic panels for a total annual capacity of 50 megawatts at Bordj Bou Arreridj invested nearly 938 million dinars (9 million euros) for the construction of this factory. The company markets photovoltaic solar panels with a power range between 70 W and 380 W per panel.
NEAL (Noureddine YASSAA, 2020)	**28th of July 2002**	It is owned by Sonelgaz, Sonatrach, and SIM (Le Groupe Semoulerie Industrielle de la Mitidja), respectively at 45%, 45%, and 10%. His missions included a wide range of actions in its sphere of activity, including the promotion and development of renewable energies and the realization of projects related to the field.

(modules photovoltaïque) as these panels fit the region's characteristics. The market has witnessed the birth of new institutions resulting from partnerships between the private and public sectors such as NEAL. A summary of the most important institutions is located in table 5:

The Result of a Foreign Partnership (Public and Private) in the Field of Renewable Energy Technology in Algeria

Partenaire Algéro-Espagnol in the Field of Renewable Energy

1. **The hybrid power plant of Hassi R'mel**

The station started in January 2011 between the Algerian company NIALL and the Spanish company OBENER in the Hassi R'Mel area (South of Algeria) to produce electricity, gas and solar energy with an investment of around 350 million euros. It is considered the largest gas field in Africa, with a production of 150 MW, of which 120 MW is produced by gas and 30 MW by solar energy. It is connected to the national electricity grid. The station covers an area of 64 hectares as there are 224 solar panels each panel is 150 m long (Ali Smai, 2016).

This factory comprises two parts: the solar field and the combined cycle. The solar field is made up of cylindrical-parabolic collectors distributed over two surfaces. Each surface contains 28 loops of four modules divided into two rows. The module is formed of 12 segments, each comprising several mirrors. The direct component of the incident solar radiation is concentrated by the mirrors on a receiver located at the focal point of the dish. A heat transfer fluid HTF (Heat Transfer Fluid) circulates inside the receiver. The heated fluid, which can reach a temperature of 393 °C, passes through a series of heat exchangers to transfer its heat to the water and thus produce water vapor (solar steam generator). The combined cycle comprises two gas turbines (running on natural gas). The latter operates a steam turbine with a nominal power of 80.08 MW (Najla, 2021).

2. Algerian-Spanish Partnership (The High Commissioner for the Development of the Steppe (HCDS)

Within the complementary growth project framework, the program supports the electrification of 16 villages in southern Algeria and one for the development of the highlands, which concerns localities in the steppe areas.

Projects led by the High Commissioner for Development of Steppe (HCDS), a public institution, the mission is to develop steppe and pastoral areas. It has also allowed the electrification of more than 3000 homes with a capacity of 550 KWC, the provision of 160 solar pups for a power of 240 WC, and 80 wind pumps equivalent to a power of 120 KWC. In the North, it cites a 10 KWC photovoltaic plant connected to the national grid (A.Ghezloun, 2011).

The Algerian - France Partnership in the Field of Renewable Energy

The Algerian company Condor Electronics is based in Bordj Bou Arreridj, an industrial city located 200 km east of Algiers. On October 29 2014, the company announced that it had acquired 50% of the shares of the company Aurès Solaire. It is an Algerian-French joint venture that manufactures new-generation photovoltaic solar panels. With a capacity of 25 MW, the company aims to increase its production capacity to 50 MW rapidly. Inaugurated in 2014 in Batna (400 km south-east of Algiers in the Aurès mountain range), the group's factory had been 49% owned by the French company Vincent Industrie and 51% by an Algerian industrialist, Houcine Nouacer, who was the CEO of the group. The factory also manufactures solar panels using another technology. This partnership aims to expand the manufacturing process for photovoltaic glass modules and solar cell encapsulation (Belkessam, 2021).

The Italian-Algerian Partnership in the Field of Renewable Energy

ENI has been present in Algeria since 1981 and currently operates 32 mining permits in the country with an equity production of 90 000 barrels of oil equivalent per day, making the company a leading international player in Algeria (ENI, 2021).

The station was launched in November 2018 in Bir Rebaa Nord BRN(Ouargla) in southern Algeria. Covering an area of 20 hectares with a capacity of 1 MW, the plant's annual production is estimated at 18 GW/ hour. The cost of the project is 16 million $. The project uses 31 320 solar panels. The contracting works have been delivered for firm Sino hydro CO.LTD (Chinese company). Algeria suggested the areas of cooperation wishes to deepen with the Italian side concerning geothermal energy, solar energy, scientific research, green hydrogen, as well as support for standardization through the mutual sharing of expertise and experience, know-how, capacity building, in particular, training through support for the creation of institutes such as the Institute for Energy Transition and Renewable Energies (ITEER) (Sonatrach, 2019).

German-Algerian Partnership in the Field of Renewable Energy

Partnership negotiations with Germany began in 2010 about the DESERTEC project, which aims to generate renewable electricity for Europe (Trek, 2020). An Energy partnership was signed in Berlin on March 26, 2015. It aimed to strengthen bilateral energy relations by establishing dialogue on various energy policy topics, such as diversifying the energy mix, developing renewable energies, improving energy efficiency (EE), and environmental protection. As part of the implementation of this declaration, a steering committee and two objective working groups (RES and EE), represented by the governments and economic sectors of both countries, has been formed. The first session of the steering committee was held in Berlin on May 20, 2015, during which priority topics were discussed to be implemented. The second session of the Algerian-German Energy Partnership steering committee was held on the sidelines of the Fourth Berlin Energy Transfer Dialogue (BETD), which took place from 17 to 18 April 2018. The first Algerian-German planning workshop was held in Algiers on 25 May 2016. Nevertheless, the second meeting of the working groups "Renewable Energy" and "Energy Efficiency" took place on April 25, 2018, in Algiers, on the sidelines of the Algerian-German Day held on April 24, 2018 in Algiers. To implement this partnership, the parties jointly developed an action plan for 2017/2018 with a timetable for implementation, focusing on four objective priorities in the areas of renewable energies and energy efficiency (Amal Rahmane, 2019).

OBSTACLES TO PARTNERSHIP AND RENEWABLE ENERGY TECHNOLOGY DEVELOPMENT IN ALGERIA

The development of renewable energy partnerships in Algeria faces many problems, the most important of which are as follows (Tewfik Hasni, 2021):

1. Renewable energy projects require an increase in capital, which is impossible for some private investors, especially since the large part of financing by investments is for fossil energy projects (15 billion $ per year compared to 1% for financing renewable energy).
2. Energy policy in Algeria is centered in Sonatrach. It controls electricity projects with some unattractive conditions for foreign investors, such as the inability to realize any investment in renewable energy without local manufacturing.
3. Lack of clarity in the economic policy, despite the existence of many laws and legislations concerned with the incorporation of renewable energy, but the actual implementation is late in many projects. In addition to the inaccurate feasibility study, this led to mistakes and incorrect estimates, such as correcting the 2011 renewable energy program and replacing it with a program in 2015.
4. Bureaucracy and the presence of some administrative problems related to competition conditions and contracts have caused the delay in many projects with foreign and national companies and the cancellation of some others.
5. Long-term investment returns in renewable energy projects require financial arrangements to ensure more competitiveness.
6. Lack of specialized human resources and infrastructure that contribute to the entire renewable energy industry.

CONCLUSION AND RECOMMENDATIONS

The research explained the importance of partnership for the public and private sectors in Algeria's renewable energy technology industry. It has meant to answer the main question, **to what extent does the partnership contribute to developing renewable energy technology in Algeria?**

The research data showed Algeria's great potential in the field of renewable energy and its conscious choice and determination for energy transition and the development of renewable energy technology in the Algerian market, especially solar energy. This was evident in many laws, decrees, and legislations.

This was also evident through the incentive mechanisms provided to private investors and foreigners, such as opening tenders, allocating 1% of oil revenue taxes, and establishing the National Fund for Energy Management. The latter contributes to financing many projects and launching the National Renewable Energies Program in 2011. This climate allowed the opening of a partnership, whether private or public, local or foreign. The European Union (Spain, France, Germany, Italy) has opened many projects, the most important of which is the **Hassi Rmel** station with the Spanish partner. It is one of the most important projects in the African continent. The provision of 16 villages in the steppe development project is a good example. The partnership also gave birth to many institutions specialized in installing and producing renewable energy equipment such as **(EDIELEC, NEAL)**. More importantly, it increased competitiveness among many private enterprises (**Condor and others**). Cooperation and partnership need further attention to develop renewable energy technologies because many problems still hinder the required progress. More importantly, monopoly and lack of experience, inaccurate feasibility studies, and the lack of actual implementation of projects make renewable energy in a very weak rank, representing (less than 1%) in the energy mix

We offer some recommendations such as:

- Providing more facilities in terms of administrative procedures and applying digitization and data to eliminate bureaucratic obstacles.
- Real implementation of projects, activation of dialogue and partnership, and more facilities, especially for private investors should be guaranteed.
- Establishing clear financial support and providing the infrastructure to create an attractive industrial climate for foreign investors.
- Promoting trans-national partnership to benefit from foreign expertise.
- The technical and management capacities of institutions in this area should be supported and strengthened.

REFERENCES

Francesco la camera. (2021). *World Energy Transitions outlook.* Abu Dhabi: International Renewable Energy Agency.

Boudghene, A., & Stambouli, N. Z. (2012). A review on the renewable energy development in Algeria: Current perspective,energy scenario and sustainability issues. *Renewable & Sustainable Energy Reviews*, •••, 4449.

A. Ghezloun, S. E. (2011). Algerian energy strategy in the context of sustainable development. Energy Procedia, 322. Advance online publication. 10.1016/j.egypro.2011.05.036

Abdelahak Razagui, A. O. (2019). *Renewable energy resource Atlas 1. Alger.* Renewable Energy Development Center.

Abdelkader, H. (n.d.). Smart Grid and Renewable Energy in Algeria. *International conference on Renwable Energy Research and Application*, 1167.

Ali Smai, M. L. (2016). Les Potentialites De L'algerie En Energies Renouvelables. *Recherches économiques et managériale, 39.*

Amal Rahmane, A. B. (2019). Exploitation of solar energy between the German leadership and the reality of the Algerian experience: Analytical study during the period (2000-2017). *International Journal of Sustainable Energy and Environmental Research*, *8*(2), 117. doi:10.18488/journal.13.2019.82.108.120

Amin Z. A. (2018). *Corporate sourcing of renewables: Market and industry trends.* International Renewable Energy Agency.

Amina Mekhelfi, F. Z. (2018). Electricity generation from renewable sources: Algeria cases (Situation and Prospects). In *The European Conference on Sustainability, Energy & the Environment 2018* (p. 6). The International Academic Forum. http://25qt511nswfi49iayd31ch80-wpengine.netdna-ssl.com/wp-content/uploads/papers/ecsee2018/ECSEE2018_41539.pdf

Amine Akbi, M. S. (2017). An overview of sustainable bioenergy potential in Algeria. *Renewable & Sustainable Energy Reviews*, *241*. Advance online publication. doi:10.1016/j.rser.2017.01.072

Amine Boudghene Stambouli. (2011). Algerian renewable energy as sessment: The challenge of sustainability. *Energy Policy*, 4513-4514. doi:10.1016/j.enpol.2010.10.005

BelkessamA. (2021, March 18). www.econostrum.info

Bindzi Zogo Emmanuel Cedrick, P. W. (2017). Investment motivation in renewable energy:APP Approach. *Energy Procedia*, 115.

Boudghene, S. A. (2011). Promotion of renewable energies in Algeria: Strategies and perspectives. *Renewable & Sustainable Energy Reviews*, *15*, 1171. doi:10.1016/j.rser.2010.11.017

Christopher Kaminker, F. S. (2012). *The Role of institutional investors in Financing Clean Energy*. Organization for Economic Cooperation and Development. https://www.oecd.org/pensions/WP_23_TheRoleOfInstitutionalInvestorsInFinancingCleanEnergy.pdf

Condor. (2021, Mars 28). http://www.condor.dz/ar/condor-electronics-ar/photovoltaique-ar

ENI. (2021, Mars 26). https://www.eni.com/assets/documents/press-release/migrated/2018/11/PR_Eni_BRN.pdf

Grant, B. (2012). Joint ventures in the Canadian energy industry. *Alberta Law Review, 375.*

Lohoues, H. A. O. (2016). *People's Democratic Republic of Algeria interim country strategy paper 2016-2018.* African Development Bank. https://www.afdb.org/fileadmin/uploads/afdb/Documents/Project-and-Operations/Algeria_interim-_CSP_2016-2018.pdf

Karima Shayb Baba, I. M. (2019). Public-private partnership methods in the framework of the completion of public projects. *The Professor Researcher of Legal Political Studies, 4*(2), 14-15.

Khenfri Khaider, G. M. (2018). Renewable energy in Algeria reality and perspective. *Journal of Information Systems and Technology Management, 3*(10), 8.

Malizi, M. (2021). *Evaluating the performance of joint ventures in the petroleum institutions - case study of the joint venture HESP* (PhD thesis). Université kasidi Merbah.

Yaneva, M. (2021, March 29). Récupéré sur Renwables Now: https://renewablesnow.com/news/algerian-enie-to-open-25-mw-solar-panel-factory-486383/

de l'ÉnergieM. (2021, March 29). https://www.energy.gov.dz/?rubrique=energies-nouvelles--et-maitrise-de-lrenergie#

Alichikouche. (2021, March 2). https://www.sktm.dz/?page=article&ida=101&id=10

Mohammed Bouznit, M. R.-B. (2020). Measures to Promote Renewable Energy for. *Sustainability, 6-7.* Advance online publication. doi:10.3390u12041468

Mourad Zaid, S. K. (2017). Strategy of the renewable energy in Algeria, as an inevitable drift to diversification of the economy. *Algerian Business Performance Review, 6*, 62.

NajlaE. G. (2021, March 24). https://www.cder.dz/vlib/bulletin/pdf/bulletin_021_11.pdf

Noureddine, Y. (2020). *Transition energétique en Algérie: Leçons, Etat des Lieux et Perspectives pour un Développement Accéléré des Energies Renouvelables.* Alger: Le Commissariat aux Energies Renouvelables et à l'Efficacité Energétique. https://www.cerefe.gov.dz/fr/2020/11/29/transition-energetique-en-algerie/

OuahibaG. (2021, March 25). https://www.cder.dz/vlib/bulletin/pdf/ber37_6_7.pdf

Labed, S., E. L. (2003). Evaluation of the Algerian photovoltaic market potential. *Progress in Photovoltaics: Research and Applications, 67.* Advance online publication. doi:10.1002/pip.461

Saliha Haddoum, H. B. (2018). Algerian energy policy: Perspectives, barriers, and missed. *Global Challenges (Hoboken, NJ), 1.* Advance online publication. doi:10.1002/gch2.201700134

Serdouk, F. (2017). *A legal framework of renewable energies and climate change in Algeria. Environmental protection mechanisms.* Center for the Generation of Scientific Research.

SlimaniS. (2021, March 22). https://www.webmanagercenter.com/2009/05/14/75224/algerie-edielec-l-eclairage-public-revolutionne/

Sonatrach. (2019, March 20). http://us-algeria.org/attachments/article/280/solar.pdf

Sophie Jablonski, M. T. (2013). Assessment of selected energy efficiency and renewable energy. *Energy Strategy Reviews*, (2). Advance online publication. doi:10.1016/j.esr.2013.02.009

Tewfik Hasni, R. M. (2021). *L'Algérie 100% Énergies Renouvelables.* Friedrich-Ebert-Stiftung. http://library.fes.de/pdf-files/bueros/algerien/17412.pdf

Trek, F. (2020). Solar energy in Algeria between exploitation policies and export potential. *Journal of the New Economy, 12*(2), 285.

World Energy Council. (2020). *World Energy.* London: World Energy Council. https://www.worldenergy.org/assets/downloads/World_Energy_Issues_Monitor_2020_-_Full_Report.pdf

Zhour Abada, M. B. (2018). Study of management strategy of energy resources in Algeria. *Energy Reports, 3.* Advance online publication. doi:10.1016/j.egyr.2017.09.004

ADDITIONAL READING

Awuku, S. A., Bennadji, A., Muhammad-Sukki, F., & Sellami, N. (2022). Public-Private Partnership in Ghana's Solar Energy Industry: The History, Current State, Challenges, Prospects and Theoretical Perspective. *Energy Nexus, 100058.*

Awuku, S. A., Bennadji, A., Muhammad-Sukki, F., & Sellami, N. (2021). Promoting the Solar Industry in Ghana through Effective Public-Private Partnership (PPP): Some Lessons from South Africa and Morocco. *Energies*, *15*(1), 17.

Eitan, A., Herman, L., Fischhendler, I., & Rosen, G. (2019). Community–private sector partnerships in renewable energy. *Renewable & Sustainable Energy Reviews*, *105*, 95–104.

Kruckenberg, L. J. (2015). North–South partnerships for sustainable energy: Knowledge–power relations in development assistance for renewable energy. *Energy for Sustainable Development*, *29*, 91–99.

KEY TERMS AND DEFINITIONS

Auction: Is a custom procedure. It is based on an evaluation standard defined by the sellers and is based on a publicly available set of rules designed to allocate the reward items and outcomes.

Energy Efficiency: Use less energy to produce the same effect or perform the same function.

Renewable Energy: Is a natural and permanent inexhaustible resources that exist in nature. It has several sources, including the solar, the wind, water, and bioenergy.

Renewable Energy Contracts: An agreement between the government or one of its agencies and private sector companies to license them. Exploitation of natural resources to produce energy over a period of time. Against a set of obligations.

Renewable Energy Technology: Is the integration of renewable energy sources into modern technology.

Tender: Is the process through which the official authorities and companies invite to submit bids for large projects that are specified in a period of time.

Glossary

Auction: Is a custom procedure. It is based on an evaluation standard defined by the sellers and is based on a publicly available set of rules designed to allocate the reward items and outcomes.

Big Data: Is a diverse, complex, and voluminous sets of data produced at a very high velocity rate used by organizations to help sound, accurate, and fast decision to be made.

Bitcoin: It's a type of digital currency in which a record of transactions is maintained, and new units of currency are generated by the computational solution of mathematical problems, and which operates independently of a central bank.

Blockchain: A blockchain is a distributed database that is shared among the nodes of a computer network. As a database, a blockchain stores information electronically in digital format. Blockchains are best known for their crucial role in cryptocurrency systems, such as bitcoin, for maintaining a secure and decentralized record of transactions. The innovation with a blockchain is that it guarantees the fidelity and security of a record of data and generates trust without the need for a trusted third party. One key difference between a typical database and a blockchain is how the data is structured. A blockchain collects information together in groups, known as blocks, that hold sets of information. Blocks have certain storage capacities and, when filled, are closed and linked to the previously filled block, forming a chain of data known as the blockchain. All new information that follows that freshly added block is compiled into a newly formed block that will then also be added to the chain once filled. A database usually structures its data into tables, whereas a blockchain, like its name implies, structures its data into chunks (blocks) that are strung together. This data structure inherently makes an irreversible timeline of data when implemented in a decentralized nature. When a block is filled, it is set in stone and becomes a part of this timeline. Each block in the chain is given an exact time stamp when it is added to the chain.

Business Model: Is the company's scheme of generating profits from products, or services in the target market the company decided to serve.

CCI30 Index: The CCi30 is a rules-based index designed to objectively measure the overall growth, daily and long-term movement of the blockchain sector. It does so by tracking the 30 largest cryptocurrencies by market capitalization, excluding stablecoins. It serves as a tool for passive investors to participate in this asset class, and as an industry benchmark for investment managers. For achieving its objectives, the CCi30 has been designed with 5 main characteristics: 1. diversified; 2. replicable; 3. transparent; 4. provides in-depth coverage of the entire sector; 5. presents the best risk-adjusted performance profile possible.

CoinDesk: Is a news site specializing in bitcoin and digital currencies. The site was founded by Shakil Khan and was subsequently acquired by Digital Currency Group.

CoinMarketCap: Is the world's most trusted and accurate source for crypto market capitalizations, pricing, and information.

Conditional Volatility: The conditional volatility can be defined as a measure of risk or a statistical measure of the change in the values of a financial asset over time. In other words, it is an estimated standard deviation of financial time series under the specified probability distribution.

Connectedness: Connectedness is a statistical measure of the relationship between variables that allows asymmetries in bilateral connections between markets, instead of inherently symmetrical (hence non-directional) measures such as correlation. Hence, the connectedness index estimates the directional measure of volatility spillover.

Correlation: Correlation measures the direction and strength of linear dependence between two variables. The correlation function is symmetric and undirected, so it is only a bilateral measure of the relationship.

Cross-Border Crime: Non lawful acts and criminal acts not limited to a specific geographic area but that includes and are considered as a crime in at least two or more geographic areas.

Cryptocurrency: Sometimes called crypto-currency or crypto, is any form of currency that exists digitally or virtually and uses cryptography to secure transactions.

Cryptocurrencies don't have a central issuing or regulating authority, instead using a decentralized system to record transactions and issue new units. Cryptocurrency is a digital payment system that doesn't rely on banks to verify transactions. It's a peer-to-peer system that can enable anyone anywhere to send and receive payments. Instead of being physical money carried around and exchanged in the real world, cryptocurrency payments exist purely as digital entries to an online database describing specific transactions. When you transfer cryptocurrency funds, the transactions are recorded in a public ledger. Cryptocurrency is stored in digital wallets. Cryptocurrency received its name because it uses encryption to verify transactions. This means advanced coding is involved in storing and transmitting cryptocurrency data between wallets and to public ledgers. The aim of encryption is to provide security and safety. The first cryptocurrency was bitcoin, which was founded in 2009 and remains the best known today. Much of the interest in cryptocurrencies is to trade for profit, with speculators at times driving prices skyward.

Cryptocurrency Enforcement: Law enforcement's activities in tracing, investigation, and recovering digital assets against unlawful transactions in cryptocurrency done by businesses and individuals.

Culture of Cybersecurity: Events, education, transmission of the know how in the society with the purpose to familiarize them with the concepts of cyber and security.

Cybercrime: The use of a computer, internet, or information technology as a means to further illegal ends.

Cybersecurity Principles: Principles, common decisions that can help define and understand the cybersecurity.

Digital Asset: Any content that exists in a digital format and is uniquely identifiable with the right to use.

Digital Business: Is employing digital technologies throughout the whole business operations to generate revenues, enhance performance, and bring about valuable insights and experience.

Digital Currency: Digital currency is a form of currency that is available only in digital or electronic form. It is also called digital money, electronic money, electronic currency, or cybercash. Digital currencies are currencies that are only accessible with computers or mobile phones because they only exist in electronic form.

Digital Strategy: Is the blueprint that tailors the company's strategy within digital economy.

Digital Transformation: Is the process of using digital technologies to create new—or modify existing—business processes, culture, and customer experiences to meet changing business and market requirements. This reimagining of business in the digital age is digital transformation.

Disruptive Innovation: Is the innovation that significantly changes the fabric, patterns, and the way companies operates and do business.

Energy Efficiency: Use less energy to produce the same effect or perform the same function.

Entrepreneurial Leadership: Entrepreneurial leadership involves organizing and motivating a group of people to achieve a common objective through innovation, risk optimization, taking advantage of opportunities, and managing the dynamic organizational environment.

Entrepreneurship: Entrepreneurship is the process of creation or extraction of value. As per this definition, entrepreneurship is viewed as change, in general parlance it involves risk beyond what is normally encountered in starting a business.

Ethereum: Is a decentralized exchange protocol allowing users to create smart contracts. These smart contracts are based on a computer protocol to verify or enforce a mutual contract. They are deployed and publicly viewable in a blockchain. Ethereum uses a unit of account called Ether as a means of payment for these contracts. Its corresponding acronym, used by trading platforms, is "ETH". Ethereum is the second largest decentralized cryptocurrency with a capitalization exceeding 448 billion euros in October 2021.

E-Wallet (or Digital Wallet): Is sort of software-based system used to conduct online transactions.

Fraud: A deliberate act or criminal activity aiming to result in financial gains by using deception, false suggestions, or other unethical means, which are trusted by others.

Gig Economy: Gig Economy is that part of labor market which is characterized by the prevalence of short-term contracts or freelance work as opposed to permanent jobs. A large number of people work in part-time or temporary positions or as independent contractors.

Gig Players: The term "gig" is jargon for "temporary job." A large number of people work in part-time or temporary positions or as independent contractors as regarded as gig players.

Global Crime: Non lawful acts that influence and can have influence globally.

Global Economic Crisis: The global financial crisis (GFC) refers to the period of extreme stress in global financial markets and banking systems between mid-2007 and early-2009.

Global Public Awareness Related to Cybersecurity: Global efforts and initiatives to create an awareness to the risks of cybersecurity. Transmit the idea that we are safer if we are aware, and no one can be safe if one of our friends/countries is not aware of the risks related to cyber.

Globalization: Connection and Interconnection of different geographic areas between them.

Industry 4.0: Is the Fourth Industrial Revolution resulting from automation, industrial internet of things, smart factories, and artificial intelligence.

Information Age: A period where information has become a commodity and human civilization features a wider use, access, and control of information technology.

KMO (Kaiser-Meyer-Olkin): Is a statistical measure to determine how suited data is for factor analysis. The test measures sampling adequacy for each variable in the model and the complete model. The statistic is a measure of the proportion of variance among variables that might be common variance. The higher the proportion, the higher the KMO-value, the more suited the data is to factor analysis.

Leverage Effects: The leverage effect which is defined as a measure of the effect of negative shocks on volatility helps to describe those unexpected negative shocks have a greater influence on volatility than positive shocks.

Litecoin: Litecoin (LTC) is decentralised money, free from censorship and open to all. Send low cost private, secure, borderless payments to anyone, anytime, anywhere.

Money Laundering: A financial transaction process for illegally obtained money to avoid government regulations and investigations.

Principal Component Analysis (PCA): Or, depending on the field of application, Karhunen–Loève transformation (KLT) or Hotelling transformation, is a method of the family of data analysis and more generally of multivariate statistics, which consists of transforming linked variables between they (known as "correlated" in statistics) into new variables uncorrelated from each other. These new variables are called "principal components" or principal axes. It allows the statistician to summarize information by reducing the number of variables. This is an approach that is both geometric (the variables being represented in a new space, along directions of maximum inertia) and statistical (the search for independent axes best explaining the variability — the variance — of the data). When we want to compress a set of N {\displaystyle N} N random variables, the first n {\displaystyle n} n axes of the principal component analysis are a better choice, from the point of view of inertia or the variance. The mathematical tool is applied in fields other than statistics and is sometimes called orthogonal eigenvalue decomposition or POD.

Renewable Energy: Is a natural and permanent inexhaustible resources that exist in nature. It has several sources, including the solar, the wind, water, and bioenergy.

Renewable Energy Contracts: An agreement between the government or one of its agencies and private sector companies to license them. Exploitation of natural resources to produce energy over a period of time. Against a set of obligations.

Renewable Energy Technology: Is the integration of renewable energy sources into modern technology.

Resilience: Initiatives, measurement taken as an answer to an attack or unpleasant situation that changes and challenges our status.

Tender: Is the process through which the official authorities and companies invite to submit bids for large projects that are specified in a period of time.

Typical Digital Currencies: Do not require intermediaries and are often the cheapest method for trading currencies. All cryptocurrencies are digital currencies, but not all digital currencies are cryptocurrencies.

Virtual Currency: A digital currency, issued and controlled by a private issuer, functions as a medium of exchange.

Volatility Clusters: The volatility clusters which are the characteristic of financial returns mirror the leptokurtic shape (fat tails) of the return of the financial assets. The source of the volatility clusters is the direction and magnitude of the price changes. Volatility clustering takes place to large/small price changes being followed by large/small changes in either direction.

Volatility Persistence: Volatility persistence is the strength of the volatility feedback effect High persistence means that volatility shocks will be felt further in the future, albeit to a lesser extent. The persistence of volatility affects the predictability of future economic variables and the predictability of changes in the risk-return balance over business cycles.

Volatility Spillover: Volatility spillover is a transmission of instability or a contagion of risk from market to market.

Compilation of References

A. Ghezloun, S. E. (2011). Algerian energy strategy in the context of sustainable development. Energy Procedia, 322. Advance online publication. 10.1016/j.egypro.2011.05.036

Abdelahak Razagui, A. O. (2019). *Renewable energy resource Atlas 1. Alger*. Renewable Energy Development Center.

Abdelkader, H . (n.d.). Smart Grid and Renewable Energy in Algeria. *International conference on Renwable Energy Research and Application*, 1167.

Abdo & Zeadally. (2020). Multi-utility framework: blockchain exchange platform for sustainable development. *International Journal of Pervasive Computing*.

Abou-Foul, M., Ruiz-Alba, J. L., & Soares, A. (2021). The impact of digitalization and servitization on the financial performance of a firm: An empirical analysis. *Production Planning and Control, 32*(12), 975–989. doi:10.1080/09537287.2020.1780508

Acs, Z. (2006). How is entrepreneurship good for economic growth? *Innovations: Technology, Governance, Globalization, 1*(1), 97–107. doi:10.1162/itgg.2006.1.1.97

Aggarwal, S., Kumar, N., & Rai, P. (Eds.). (2021). *The Blockchain Technology for Secure and Smart Applications across Industry Verticals* (Vol. 121). Advances in Computers. doi:10.1016/bs.adcom.2020.08.012

Aglietta, M. (1992). Genèse des banques centrales et légitimité de la monnaie. *Annales E.S.C., 47*(3), 675-698. 10.3406/ahess.1992.279068

Aglietta, M., & Orléan, A. (1998). *La monnaie souveraine*. Odile Jacob.

Ahmad, A., Alshurideh, M., Al Kurdi, B., Aburayya, A., & Hamadneh, S. (2021). Digital transformation metrics: A conceptual view. *Journal of management Information and Decision Sciences, 24*(7), 1-18.

Ajaz & Kumar. (2018). Herding in crypto-currency markets. *Annals of Financial Economics, 13*(2). Doi:10.1142/S2010495218500069

Akyıldırım, E., Corbet, S., Lucey, B., Sensoy, A., & Yarovaya, L. (2019). The relationship between implied volatility and cryptocurrency returns. *Finance Research Letters*. Advance online publication. doi:10.1016/j.frl.2019.06.010

Alain B. (2018). Transforming the bank. In *Banking strategy in the digital age*. Dunod.

Alarabiat, A., Hujran, O., Soares, D., & Tarhini, A. (2021). Examining students' continuous use of online learning in the post-COVID-19 era: an application of the process virtualization theory. Information Technology & People. doi:10.1108/ITP-02-2021-0142

Albayati, H., Kim, S. K., & Rho, J. J. (2020). Accepting financial transactions using blockchain technology and cryptocurrency: A customer perspective approach. *Technology in Society*.

Albulescu, C. T. (2021). COVID-19 and the United States financial markets' volatility. *Finance Research Letters*, *38*, 1–5. doi:10.1016/j.frl.2020.101699 PMID:32837380

Ali Smai, M. L. (2016). Les Potentialites De L'algerie En Energies Renouvelables. *Recherches économiques et managériale, 39.*

Ali, T., Clarke, D., & McCorry, P. (2015). Bitcoin: Perils of an unregulated global p2p currency. Newcastle University, Technical Report Series, no 1470.

Alichikouche. (2021, March 2). https://www.sktm.dz/?page=article&ida=101&id=10

Allmendinger, G., & Lombreglia, R. (2005). Four strategies for the age of smart services. *Harvard Business Review*, *83*(10), 131–145.

Amal Rahmane, A. B. (2019). Exploitation of solar energy between the German leadership and the reality of the Algerian experience: Analytical study during the period (2000-2017). *International Journal of Sustainable Energy and Environmental Research*, *8*(2), 117. doi:10.18488/journal.13.2019.82.108.120

Amin Z. A. (2018). *Corporate sourcing of renewables: Market and industry trends*. International Renewable Energy Agency.

Amina Mekhelfi, F. Z. (2018). Electricity generation from renewable sources: Algeria cases (Situation and Prospects). In *The European Conference on Sustainability, Energy & the Environment 2018* (p. 6). The International Academic Forum. http://25qt511nswfi49iayd31ch80-wpengine.netdna-ssl.com/wp-content/uploads/papers/ecsee2018/ECSEE2018_41539.pdf

Amine Akbi, M. S. (2017). An overview of sustainable bioenergy potential in Algeria. *Renewable & Sustainable Energy Reviews*, *241*. Advance online publication. doi:10.1016/j.rser.2017.01.072

Amine Boudghene Stambouli. (2011). Algerian renewable energy as sessment: The challenge of sustainability. *Energy Policy*, 4513-4514. doi:10.1016/j.enpol.2010.10.005

Ancel, P. (1988). La monnaie électronique: régime juridique. In *Droit et Monnaie, États et espace monétaire transnational* (pp. 302–315). Litec.

Aral, S., & Weill, P. D. (2007). IT assets, organizational capabilities, and firm performance: How resource allocations and organizational differences explain performance variation. *Organization Science*, *18*(5), 763–780. doi:10.1287/orsc.1070.0306

Ardia, D., Bluteau, K., & Rüede, M. (2019). Regime changes in Bitcoin GARCH volatility Dynamics. *Finance Research Letters*, *29*, 266–271. doi:10.1016/j.frl.2018.08.009

Arora, M., & Sharma, R. L. (2017). Decoding Diverse Dimensions of Entrepreneurial Leadership with special emphasis on Persuasive Communication. *Management Dynamics*, *17*(1).

Audretsch, D. B. (2007). Entrepreneurship capital and economic growth. *Oxford Review of Economic Policy*, *23*(1), 63–78. doi:10.1093/oxrep/grm001

Baker, S. R., Farrokhnia, R. A., Meyer, S., Pagel, M., & Yannelis, C. (2020). How does household spending respond to an epidemic? Consumption during the 2020 COVID-19 pandemic. *The Review of Asset Pricing Studies*, *10*(4), 834–862. doi:10.1093/rapstu/raaa009

Bal, A. M. (2014). *Taxation of virtual currency*. Leiden University.

Banque de France. (2013, Dec.). Les dangers liés au développement des monnaies virtuelles. *Focus*.

Barua, S. (2020). *Understanding Coronanomics: The economic implications of the coronavirus (COVID-19) pandemic*. Available at SSRN 3566477.

BaurD. G.DimpfiT. (2017). Realized Bitcoin Volatility. doi:10.2139/ssrn.2949754

Baur, D. G., & Dimpfi, T. (2021). The volatility of Bitcoin and its role as a medium of exchange and a store of value. *Empirical Economics*, *61*(5), 2663–2683. Advance online publication. doi:10.100700181-020-01990-5 PMID:33424101

Baur, D. G., Dimpfi, T., & Kuck, K. (2018). Bitcoin, gold and the US dollar – A replication and extension. *Finance Research Letters*, *25*, 103–110. doi:10.1016/j.frl.2017.10.012

BelkessamA. (2021, March 18). www.econostrum.info

Berdi & Sebbar. (2018). Contribution to the study of the strategic nature of information and communication technologies (ICT) for the organization: case of the Moroccan banking sector. *Moroccan Review of Research in Management and Marketing, 18*.

Berman, S. J. (2012). Digital transformation: Opportunities to create new business models. *Strategy and Leadership*, *40*(2), 16–24. doi:10.1108/10878571211209314

Besse, P. (1992). PCA stability and choice of dimensionality. *Statistics & Probability Letters*, *13*, 405–410.

Bharadwaj, A., El Sawy, O., Pavlou, P., & Venkatraman, N. (2013). Digital business strategy: Toward a next generation of insights. *Management Information Systems Quarterly*, *37*(2), 471–482. doi:10.25300/MISQ/2013/37:2.3

Bindzi Zogo Emmanuel Cedrick, P. W. (2017). Investment motivation in renewable energy:APP Approach. *Energy Procedia*, 115.

Blackburne, T., Kepler, J. D., Quinn, P. J., & Taylor, D. (2021). Undisclosed SEC investigations. *Management Science*, *67*(6), 3403–3418. doi:10.1287/mnsc.2020.3805

Böhme, R., Christin, N., Edelman, B., & Moore, T. (2015). Bitcoin: Economics, technology and governance. *Journal of Economic Perspectives, 29*(2), 213-238.

Bos. (2018). Digital transformation, towards increased strategic management? Céline Bos, Ea Conseil & formation, DIF 2018.

Bouarar, A. C., Mouloudj, S., & Mouloudj, K. (2021). Extending the theory of planned behavior to explain intention to use online food delivery services in the context of COVID -19 pandemic. In C. Cobanoglu & V. Della Corte (Eds.), *Advances in global services and retail management* (pp. 1–16). USF M3 Publishing. https://www.doi.org/10.5038/9781955833035

Boudghene, A., & Stambouli, N. Z. (2012). A review on the renewable energy development in Algeria: Current perspective,energy scenario and sustainability issues. *Renewable & Sustainable Energy Reviews*, •••, 4449.

Boudghene, S. A. (2011). Promotion of renewable energies in Algeria: Strategies and perspectives. *Renewable & Sustainable Energy Reviews*, *15*, 1171. doi:10.1016/j.rser.2010.11.017

Bouoiyour & Selmi. (2019). How do futures contracts affect Bitcoin prices? *Economics Bulletin, 39*(2), 1127-1134.

Boyton, A. C., & Zmud, R. W. (1984). An assessment of critical success factors. *Sloan Management Review*, *25*, 17–27.

Brito, J., & Dourado, E. (2014). Comments to the New York Department of Financial Services on the proposed virtual currency regulatory framework. Public Interest Comment, Mercatus Center, George Mason University.

Brito, J. (2013). *Beyond Silk Road: potential risks, threats, and promises of virtual currencies. In Testimony before the Senate Committee on Homeland Security and Governmental Affairs*. Mercatus Center at George Mason University.

Brito, J., & Castillo, A. (2013). *Bitcoin: A primer for policymakers*. Mercatus Center at George Mason University.

Buchholz, K. (2021). *How common is crypto?* Available at: https://www.statista.com/chart/18345/crypto-currency-adoption/

Bukovina, J., & Martiček, M. (2016). *Sentiment and Bitcoin volatility*. MENDELU Working Papers in Business and Economics 2016–2058, Mendel University in Brno, Faculty of Business and Economics.

Buterin, V. (2015). *On public and private blockchains*. Blog Ethereum. https://blog.ethereum.org/ 2015/08/07/on-public-and-private-blockchains/

Butt, J. (2020). A conceptual framework to support digital transformation in manufacturing using an integrated business process management approach. *Designs*, *4*(3), 1–39. doi:10.3390/designs4030017

Byström, H., & Krygier, D. (2018). What Drives Bitcoin Volatility? *Knut Wicksell Working Paper*, (3), 1-46.

Callon, M. (1998). The embeddedness of economic markets in economics. In The Laws of the Markets. Blackwell.

Cao, M., & Zhang, Q. (2011). Supply chain collaboration: Impact on collaborative advantage and firm performance. *Journal of Operations Management*, *29*(3), 163–180. doi:10.1016/j.jom.2010.12.008

Ca, P. (2021, April). Surfing blockchain wave, or drowning? Shaping the future of distributed ledgers and decentralized technologies. *Technological Forecasting and Social ChangeVolume*, *165*, 120463.

Carstens, A. (2021). *Digital currencies and the future of the monetary system*. Working Paper. Bank for International Settlements.

Cartelier, J. (1991). Monnaie et système de paiement: le problème de la formation de l'équilibre. *Revue française d'économie*, *6*(3), 3-37.

Cartelier, J. (1996). *La monnaie*. Flammarion/ Dominos.

Chanias, S., Myers, M. D., & Hess, T. (2019). Digital transformation strategy making in pre-digital organizations: The case of a financial services provider. *The Journal of Strategic Information Systems*, *28*(1), 17–33. doi:10.1016/j.jsis.2018.11.003

Chaum, D. (1985). Security without identification: Transaction systems to make Big Brother obsolete. *Communications of the ACM*, *28*(10).

Cheah, E. T., & Fry, J. (2015). Speculative bubbles in Bitcoin markets? An empirical investigation into the fundamental value of Bitcoin. *Economics Letters*, *130*, 32–36.

Chen, T., Lau, C.K.M., Cheema, S., & Koo, C.K. (2021). *Economic Policy Uncertainty in China and Bitcoin Returns: Evidence From the COVID-19 Period*. . doi:10.3389/fpubh.2021.651051

Chen, Y.-Y. K., Jaw, Y.-L., & Wu, B.-L. (2016). Effect of digital transformation on organisational performance of SMEs: Evidence from the Taiwanese textile industry's web portal. *Internet Research*, *26*(1), 186–212. doi:10.1108/IntR-12-2013-0265

Cheung, A., Roca, E., & Su, J. (2015). Crypto-currency bubbles: An application of the Phillips Shi-Yu (2013) methodology on Mt. Gox bitcoin prices. *Applied Economics*, *47*(23), 2348–2358. doi:10.1080/00036846.2015.1005827

Cheung, A., Roca, E., & Su, J. J. (2015). Crypto-currency bubbles: An application of the Phillips–Shi–Yu (2013) methodology on Mt. Gox bitcoin prices. *Applied Economics*, *47*(23), 2348–2358.

Chevalier, M., & Vignolles, B. (2014). *Le bitcoin: défi à la souveraineté monétaire des états et ressource pour le blanchiment d'argent. Regards croisés sur l'économie, 14*. 10.3917/rce.014.0122.

Christin, N., & Moore, T. (2013). Beware the middleman: empirical analysis of bitcoin-exchange risk. In *Financial cryptography and data security*. Springer.

Christopher Kaminker, F. S. (2012). *The Role of institutional investors in Financing Clean Energy*. Organization for Economic Cooperation and Development. https://www.oecd.org/pensions/WP_23_TheRoleOfInstitutionalInvestorsInFinancingCleanEnergy.pdf

Ciaian, P., Rajcaniova, M., & Kancs, A. (2016). The Economics of Bitcoin Price Formation. *Applied Economics*, *48*(19), 1799–1815. doi:10.1080/00036846.2015.1109038

Cioroianu, I., Corbet, S., & Larkin, C. (2021). The differential impact of corporate blockchain-development as conditioned by sentiment and financial desperation. *Journal of Corporate Finance*.

Clayton, J. (2019). *Testimony on "Oversight of the Securities and Exchange Commission" Before the U.S. Senate Committee on Banking, Housing, and Urban Affairs*. U.S. Securities and Exchange Commission. Retrieved from https://www.sec.gov/news/testimony/testimony-clayton-2019-12-10

CMF (2019) Contrôle Monétaire et Financier article L552-2 du Création LOI n°2019-486 du 22 mai 2019 - art. 85,

CMF (2021) Contrôle Monétaire et Financier en France L'article L54-10-1(2021) https://www.legifrance.gouv.fr/codes/article_lc/LEGIARTI000038509570/

Condor. (2021, Mars 28). http://www.condor.dz/ar/condor-electronics-ar/photovoltaique-ar

Corbet. (2020). Evaluating a decade of cryptocurrency development: Navigating financial progress through technological and regulatory ambiguity. *Cryptocurrency and Blockchain Technology*.

Corbet, S., Hou, Y., Hu, Y., Oxley, L., & Xu, D. (2021). Pandemic-related financial market volatility spillovers: Evidence from the Chinese COVID-19 epicentre. *International Review of Economics & Finance*, *71*, 56–81. doi:10.1016/j.iref.2020.06.022

Cornerstone Research. (2020). *SEC Cryptocurrency Enforcement Report*. Retrieved from https://www.cornerstone.com/Publications/Reports/SEC-Cryptocurrency-Enforcement-Q3-2013-Q4-2020.pdf

Corrado, C. J. (1989). A non-parametric test for abnormal security price performance in event studies. *Journal of Financial Economics*, *23*(2), 385–395. doi:10.1016/0304-405X(89)90064-0

Courbis, B., Froment, E., & Servet, J.-M. (1990). À propos du concept de monnaie. *Cahiers d'Économie Politique*, *18*(18), 5-29. 10.3406/cep.1990.1091

CoxJ. (2021). https://www.cnbc.com/2021/09/22/the-fed-is-evaluating-whether-to-launch-a-digital-currency-and-in-what-form-powell-says.htm

CPMI. (2015). *Digital currencies*. Committee on Payments and Market Infrastructures, Bank of International Settlement.

Csonka, P. (2006). The council of europe's convention on cyber-crime and other European initiatives. *Revue internationale de droit pénal, 77*, 473-501. . doi:10.3917/ridp.773.0473

Dalenogare, L. S., Benitez, G. B., Ayala, N. F., & Frank, A. G. (2018). The expected contribution of Industry 4.0 technologies for industrial performance. *International Journal of Production Economics*, *204*, 383–394. doi:10.1016/j.ijpe.2018.08.019

Daley, N. (2003). ICTs and retail banking: Prospects and challenges. Digital Notebooks, 4.

Daley, N., & Dyhrberg, A. H. (2016). Hedging capabilities of Bitcoin. Is it the virtual gold? *Finance Research Letters*, *16*, 139–144.

de Jesus, D. S. V. (2021). Living on the Edge: Brazilian Creative Workers in the Gig Economy During the COVID-19 Pandemic. *Psychology (Irvine, Calif.)*, *11*(2), 56–62.

de l'ÉnergieM. (2021, March 29). https://www.energy.gov.dz/?rubrique=energies-nouvelles--et-maitrise-de-lrenergie#

Deloitte. (2020). *Digital financial services: Weapon in the fight against the progression of COVID 19 and for the resilience of African economies*. Author.

Department of the Treasury, Financial Crimes Enforcement Network. (2011, July 29). [Office of the Federal Register, National Archives and Records Administration.]. *Federal Register*, *76*(146), •••.

Department of Treasury, Financial Crimes Enforcement Network. (n.d.). 31 CFR § 1010.100(ff). *Cornell*. Retrieved from https://www.law.cornell.edu/cfr/text/31/1010.100

Devpura, N., & Narayan, P. K. (2020). Hourly oil price volatility: The role of COVID-19. *Energy Research Letters*, *1*(2), 13683. doi:10.46557/001c.13683

Dibrova, A. (2016). Virtual currency: New step in monetary development. *Procedia: Social and Behavioral Sciences*, *229*, 42–49. doi:10.1016/j.sbspro.2016.07.112

Didenko, N., Skripnuk, D., Kikkas, K., Kalinina, O., & Kosinski, E. (2021). The impact of digital transformation on the micrologistic system, and the open innovation in logistics. *Journal of Open Innovation*, *7*(2), 115. doi:10.3390/joitmc7020115

Diebold, F. X., & Yilmaz, K. (2009). Measuring financial asset return and volatility spillovers, with application to global equity markets. *Economic Journal (London)*, *119*(534), 158–171. doi:10.1111/j.1468-0297.2008.02208.x

Diebold, F. X., & Yilmaz, K. (2012). Better to give than to receive: Predictive directional measurement of volatility spillovers. *International Journal of Forecasting*, *28*(1), 57–66. doi:10.1016/j.ijforecast.2011.02.006

Diebold, F. X., & Yilmaz, K. (2014). On the network topology of variance decompositions: Measuring the connectedness of financial firms. *Journal of Economics*, *182*(1), 119–134. doi:10.1016/j.jeconom.2014.04.012

Dowd, K. (2014). *New Private Monies: A Bit-Part Player?* The Institute of Economic Affairs.

Dupré, D., Ponsot, J-F., & Servet, J-M. (2015). *Le bitcoin contre la révolution des communs* (5th ed.). Congrès de l'Afep.

Dwyer, G. (2014). *The economics of bitcoin and similar private digital currencies.* MPRA Paper, No 57360.

Dwyer, G. P. (2015). The economics of Bitcoin and similar private digital currencies. *Journal of Financial Stability*, *17*, 81–91.

Dyhrberg, A. H. (2016). Bitcoin, gold and the dollar— A GARCH volatility analysis. *Finance Research Letters*, *16*, 85–92.

Dyhrberg, A. H. (2016). Bitcoin, gold and the dollar –A GARCH volatility analysis. *Finance Research Letters*, *16*, 85–92. doi:10.1016/j.frl.2015.10.008

Ebrahim, Z., Inderwildi, O. R., & King, D. A. (2014). Macroeconomic impacts of oil price volatility: Mitigation and resilience. *Frontiers in Energy*, *8*(1), 9–24. doi:10.100711708-014-0303-0

ECB. (2012). *Virtual Currencies Schemes*. http://www.ecb.europa.eu

ECB. (2015). *Virtual Currency Schemes - A Further Analysis*. http://www.ecb.europa.eu.

ENI. (2021, Mars 26). https://www.eni.com/assets/documents/press-release/migrated/2018/11/PR_Eni_BRN.pdf

European e-Justice Portal. (n.d.). *Impact of Covid-19 on the justice field.* Retrieved 14/04/21 from: https://e-justice.europa.eu/content_impact_of_covid19_on_the_justice_field-37147-en.do

Fasanya, I. O., Oliyide, J. A., Adekoya, O. B., & Agbatogun, T. (2021). How does economic policy uncertainty connect with the dynamic spillovers between precious metals and bitcoin markets? *Resources Policy*, *72*, 1–17. doi:10.1016/j.resourpol.2021.102077

FE (Federal Reserve). (2015). *Strategies for improving the US payment system.* Author.

Ferrari. (2020). *The regulation of crypto-assets in the EU–investment and payment tokens under the radar.* Academic Press.

FerrariV. (2020). Maastricht Journal of European and Comparative. journals.sagepub.com

Filis, G. (2010). Macro economy, stock market and oil prices: Do meaningful relationships exist among their cyclical fluctuations? *Energy Economics*, *32*(4), 877–886. doi:10.1016/j.eneco.2010.03.010

Fischer, S. (1988). *Rules versus Discretion in monetary policy.* NBER Working Papers 2518. DOI: 10.3386/w2518

Fitzgerald, M., Kruschwitz, N., Bonnet, D., & Welch, M. (2014). Embracing digital technology: A new strategic imperative. *MIT Sloan Management Review*, *55*(2), 1–12.

FMI (Fonds Monétaire International). (2016). *Virtual currencies and beyond: initial considerations*. Staff Discussion Note, No 3.

Fostel, A., & Geanakoplos, J. (2012). Tranching, CDS, and Asset Prices: How Financial Innovation Can Cause Bubbles and Crashes. *American Economic Journal. Macroeconomics*, *4*(1), 190–225. doi:10.1257/mac.4.1.190

Fourcade, M., & Healy, K. (2007). Moral views of market society. *Annual Review of Sociology*, *33*, 287–311.

Francesco la camera. (2021). *World Energy Transitions outlook*. Abu Dhabi: International Renewable Energy Agency.

Fry, J., & Cheah, E. T. (2016). Negative bubbles and shocks in cryptocurrency markets. *International Review of Financial Analysis*, *47*, 343–352.

Gajardo, G., Kristjanpoller, W. D., & Minutolo, M. (2018). Does Bitcoin exhibit the same asymmetric multifractal cross-correlations with crude oil, gold and DJIA as the Euro, Great British Pound and Yen? *Chaos, Solitons, and Fractals*, *109*, 195–205. doi:10.1016/j.chaos.2018.02.029

Gao, X., Ren, Y., & Umar, M. (2021). To what extent does COVID-19 drive stock market volatility? A comparison between the US and China. *Economic Research-EkonomskaIstraživanja*, 1-21.

Garcia, D., Tessone, C. J., Mavrodiev, P., & Perony, N. (2014). The digital traces of bubbles: Feedback cycles between socio-economic signals in the Bitcoin economy. *Journal of the Royal Society, Interface*, *11*. Advance online publication. doi:10.1098/?rsif.2014.0623

Gazé, P. (2003). Nouveaux moyens de paiements, nouveaux risques? *Les Cahiers du Numérique*, *4*(1), 93–113.

Gebayew, C., Hardini, I. R., Panjaitan, G. H. A., & Kurniawan, N. B., & Suhardi, (2018). A systematic literature review on digital transformation. In *International Conference on Information Technology Systems and Innovation* (pp. 260-265). 10.1109/ICITSI.2018.8695912

Geoffrion, A. M., & Krishnan, R. (2003). E-business and management science: Mutual impacts (Part 1 of 2). *Management Science*, *49*(10), 1275–1286. doi:10.1287/mnsc.49.10.1275.17311

Gercke, M. (2014). Content of a Comprehensive Cybersecurity Legal Framework. *CLRI*, *15*(2), 33–40. doi:10.9785/cri-2014-0202

Ghalanos, A. (2020a). *rugarch: Univariate GARCH models*. R package version 1.4-2. Available at: https://cran.r-project.org/web/packages/rugarch/rugarch.pdf

Ghalanos, A. (2020b). *Introduction to the rugarch package*. Technical Report Available at: https://cran.r-project.org/web/packages/rugarch/vignettes/Introduction_to_the_rugarch_package.pdf

Ghorbel, A., & Jeribi, A. (2021). *Investigating the relationship between volatilities of cryptocurrencies and other financial assets*. Decisions in Economics and Finance. doi:10.100710203-020-00312-9

Giblin, R. (2011). Code Wars: 10 Years of P2P Software Litigation. Edward Elgar Publishing.

Godsiff, P. (2015). Bitcoin: Bubble or blockchain? In *9th International KES Conference on Agents and Multi-Agent Systems: Technologies and Applications KES-AMSTA-15*. Retrieved from http://epubs.surrey.ac.uk/820645/

Goodell, J. W., & Goutte, S. (2021). Co-movement of COVID-19 and Bitcoin: Evidence from wavelet coherence analysis. *Finance Research Letters*, *38*, 1–6. doi:10.1016/j.frl.2020.101625

Grant, B. (2012). Joint ventures in the Canadian energy industry. *Alberta Law Review, 375*.

Grinberg, R. (2011). Bitcoin: An Innovative Alternative Digital Currency. *Hastings Science & Technology Law Journal*, *4*, 159–207.

Guerini, M., Nesta, L., Ragot, X., & Schiavo, S. (2020). Firm liquidity and solvency under the Covid-19 lockdown in France. *OFCE Policy Brief, 76*, 1-20.

Guesmi, K., Saadi, S., Abid, I., & Ftiti, Z. (2019). Portfolio diversification with virtual currency: Evidence from bitcoin. *International Review of Financial Analysis*, *63*, 431–437.

Guo, L., & Xu, L. (2021). The Effects of Digital Transformation on Firm Performance: Evidence from China's Manufacturing Sector. *Sustainability*, *13*(22), 12844. doi:10.3390u132212844

Gupta, S. (2018). *Organizational barriers to digital transformation. KTH Royal Institute of Technology*. School of Industrial Engineering and Management.

Hanelt, A., Firk, S., Hildebrandt, B., & Kolbe, L. M. (2021). Digital M&A, digital innovation, and firm performance: An empirical investigation. *European Journal of Information Systems*, *30*(1), 3–26. doi:10.1080/0960085X.2020.1747365

Harjoto, M. A., Rossi, F., Lee, R., & Sergi, B. S. (2021). How do equity markets react to COVID-19? Evidence from emerging and developed countries. *Journal of Economics and Business*, *115*, 105966. doi:10.1016/j.jeconbus.2020.105966 PMID:33518845

Hassounah, M., Raheel, H., & Alhefzi, M. (2020). Digital response during the COVID-19 pandemic in Saudi Arabia. *Journal of Medical Internet Research*, *22*(9), e19338. doi:10.2196/19338 PMID:32790642

Hayek, F. (1976). Denationalisation of Money - The Argument Refined. An Analysis of the Theory and Practice of Concurrent Currencies. The Institute of Economic Affairs.

Heavin, C., & Power, D. J. (2018). Challenges for digital transformation – towards a conceptual decision support guide for managers. *Journal of Decision Systems*, *27*(1), 38–45. doi:10.1080/12460125.2018.1468697

Henriette, E., Feki, M., & Boughzala, I. (2016). Digital transformation challenges. In *Proceedings of the 10th Mediterranean Conference on Information Systems* (pp. 1-8). Academic Press.

Hentschel, L. (1995). All in The Family Nesting Symmetric and Asymmetric GARCH Models. *Journal of Financial Economics*, *39*(1), 71–104. doi:10.1016/0304-405X(94)00821-H

Hess, T., Benlian, A., Matt, C., & Wiesböck, F. (2016). Options for formulating a digital transformation strategy. *MIS Quarterly Executive*, *15*(2), 123–139. doi:10.7892/boris.105447

Hofmann, J., Katzenbach, C., & Gollatz, K. (2016). Between Coordination and Regulation: Finding the Governance in Internet Governance. *New Media & Society*.

Hu, Hou, Oxley, & Corbet. (2021). Does blockchain patent-development influence Bitcoin risk? *Journal of International Financial*.

Hughes, S. D. (2017). Cryptocurrency Regulations and Enforcement in the US. *W. St. UL Rev.*, *45*, 1.

Hutchinson, C. A. (2022). *Cryptocurrencies and the Regulatory Challenge*. Routledge.

Hu, Y., Hou, Y. G., Oxley, L., & Corbet, S. (2021). Does blockchain patent-development influence Bitcoin risk? *Journal of International Financial Markets, Institutions and Money*.

Iqbal, N., Fareed, Z., Wan, G., & Shahzad, F. (2021). Asymmetric nexus between COVID-19 outbreak in the world and cryptocurrency market. *International Review of Financial Analysis*, *73*, 1–16. doi:10.1016/j.irfa.2020.101613

IRS. (2014). *Notice 2014-21*. Retrieved from https://www.irs.gov/pub/irs-drop/n-14-21.pdf

Jafari-Sadeghi, V., Garcia-Perez, A., Candelo, E., & Couturier, J. (2021). Exploring the impact of digital transformation on technology entrepreneurship and technological market expansion: The role of technology readiness, exploration and exploitation. *Journal of Business Research*, *124*, 100–111. doi:10.1016/j.jbusres.2020.11.020

JalanA.MatkovskyyR.YarovayaL. (2021). "Shiny" crypto assets: A systemic look at gold-backed cryptocurrencies during the COVID-19 pandemic. doi:10.2139/ssrn.3796837

Jensen, T. E. (2017). The Tallinn Manual 2.0: Highlights and insights. *GJIL*, 735-777.

Jeong, S. (2013). *The Bitcoin Protocol as Law, and the Politics of a Stateless Currency*. DOI: 10.2139/ssrn.2294124

Johnson, Z. B. (2016). I Got 988 Problems but Bitcoin Ain't One: The Current Problems Presented by the Internal Revenue Service's Guidance on Virtual Currency. *U. Mem. L. Rev.*, *47*, 633.

Jonathan, G. M. (2020). Digital transformation in the public sector: Identifying critical success factors. In M. Themistocleous & M. Papadaki (Eds.), *Information Systems. EMCIS 2019. Lecture Notes in Business Information Processing* (Vol. 381). Springer. doi:10.1007/978-3-030-44322-1_17

Josse, J., & Husson, F. (2012). Selecting the number of components in PCA using cross-validation approximations. *Computational Statistics & Data Analysis*, *56*, 1869–1879.

Kaplanov, N. (2012). *Nerdy Money: Bitcoin, the Private Digital Currency, and the Case against its Regulation.* Temple University Legal Studies Research Paper. DOI: 10.2139/ssrn.2115203

Karima Shayb Baba, I. M. (2019). Public-private partnership methods in the framework of the completion of public projects. *The Professor Researcher of Legal Political Studies, 4*(2), 14-15.

Karlstrom, H. (2014). Do Libertarians dream of electronic coins? The material embeddedness of Bitcoin. *Distinktion: Scandinavian Journal of Social Theory*, *15*(1), 23–36.

Kasper, J. (2017). Evolution of bitcoin: Volatility comparisons with least developed countries' currencies. *Journal of Internet Banking and Commerce*, *22*(3), 1–18.

Khenfri Khaider, G. M. (2018). Renewable energy in Algeria reality and perspective. *Journal of Information Systems and Technology Management*, *3*(10), 8.

Kher, R., Terjesen, S., & Liu, C. (2020). Blockchain, Bitcoin, and ICOs: A review and research agenda. *Small Business Economics*.

Kim, H. M., Laskowski, M., Zargham, M., & Turesson, H. (2021). *Token Economics in Real Life: Cryptocurrency and Incentives Design for Insolar's Blockchain Network.* IEEE Computer Society. ieeexplore.ieee.org

Klein, T., Thu, H. P., & Walther, T. (2018). Bitcoin is not the New Gold – A comparison of volatility, correlation, and portfolio performance. *International Review of Financial Analysis*, *59*, 105–116. doi:10.1016/j.irfa.2018.07.010

Koski, H. (2010). *Firm growth and profitability: The role of mobile IT and organizational practices.* Discussion Paper No. 1222. Available at: https://www.etla.fi/wp-content/uploads/2012/09/dp1222.pdf

Kraus, S., Jones, P., Kailer, N., Weinmann, A., Chaparro-Banegas, N., & Roig-Tierno, N. (2021). Digital transformation: An overview of the current state of the art of research. *SAGE Open*, *11*(3). doi:10.1177/21582440211047576

Kritzman, Li, Page, & Rigobon. (2011). Principal Components as a measure of systemic risk. *Journal of Portfolio Management, 37*, 112-126.

Kumar, A. S., & Anandarao, S. (2019). Volatility spillover in crypto-currency markets: Some evidences from GARCH and wavelet analysis. *Physica A*, *524*, 448–458. doi:10.1016/j.physa.2019.04.154

Labed, S., E. L. (2003). Evaluation of the Algerian photovoltaic market potential. *Progress in Photovoltaics: Research and Applications*, *67*. Advance online publication. doi:10.1002/pip.461

Laborde, D., Martin, W., & Vos, R. (2021). Impacts of COVID-19 on global poverty, food security, and diets: Insights from global model scenario analysis. *Agricultural Economics*, *52*(3), 375–390. doi:10.1111/agec.12624 PMID:34230728

Lahajnar & Rozanec. (2018). Initial coin offering (ICO) evaluation model. *Investment Management and Financial Innovations, 15*(4), 169-182.

Lakomski-Laguerre & Desmedt. (2017). L'alternative monétaire Bitcoin: une perspective institutionnaliste. *Revue de la régulation, 18*. http://journals.openedition.org/regulation/11489

Latifi, M. A., Nikou, S., & Bouwman, H. (2021). Business model innovation and firm performance: Exploring causal mechanisms in SMEs. *Technovation*, *107*, 102274. doi:10.1016/j.technovation.2021.102274

Lee, K. (2017). Herd behavior of the overall market: Evidence based on the cross-sectional comovement of returns. *The North American Journal of Economics and Finance*, *42*, 266–284.

Lin & Xue. (2020). Research on the Development of Digital Currencies under the COVID-19 Epidemic. *Procedia Computer Science, 187*, 89–96.

Lin, B., & Bai, R. (2021). Oil prices and economic policy uncertainty: Evidence from global, oil importers, and exporters' perspective. *Research in International Business and Finance*, *56*, 101357. doi:10.1016/j.ribaf.2020.101357

Lin, L. S., & Nomikos, J. (2018). *Cybercrime in East and Southeast Asia: The Case of Taiwan*. Asia-Pacific Security Challenges.

Llopis-Albert, C., Rubio, F., & Valero, F. (2021). Impact of digital transformation on the automotive industry. *Technological Forecasting and Social Change*, *162*, 120343. doi:10.1016/j.techfore.2020.120343 PMID:33052150

Lohoues, H. A. O. (2016). *People's Democratic Republic of Algeria interim country strategy paper 2016-2018.* African Development Bank. https://www.afdb.org/fileadmin/uploads/afdb/Documents/Project-and-Operations/Algeria_interim-_CSP_2016-2018.pdf

MacDonell, A. (2014). *Popping the Bitcoin bubble: An application of log-periodic power law modelling to digital currency.* University of Notre Dame Working Paper.

Machado, C. G., Winroth, M., Carlsson, D., Almström, P., Centerholt, V., & Hallin, M. (2019). Industry 4.0 readiness in manufacturing companies: Challenges and enablers towards increased digitalization. *Procedia CIRP*, *81*, 1113–1118. doi:10.1016/j.procir.2019.03.262

Mackinlay, C. (1997). Event Studies in Finance and Economics. *Journal of Economic Literature*, *35*, 13–39.

Maftei, L. (2014). Bitcoin-between legal and informal. *CES Working Papers, 6*(3), 53-59.

Malizi, M. (2021). *Evaluating the performance of joint ventures in the petroleum institutions - case study of the joint venture HESP* (PhD thesis). Université kasidi Merbah.

Mariana, C. D., Ekaputra, I. A., & Husodo, Z. A. (2021). Are Bitcoin and Ethereum safe-havens for stocks during the COVID-19 pandemic? *Finance Research Letters*, (38), 1–7. PMID:33100925

Martin, A., Markhvida, M., Hallegatte, S., & Walsh, B. (2020). Socio-economic impacts of COVID-19 on household consumption and poverty. *Economics of Disasters and Climate Change, 4*(3), 453-479.

Martin, J. F. (2018). *Unlocking success in digital transformations*. McKinsey & Company.

Martino, Wang, & Bellavitis. (2019). *New Frontiers in Entrepreneurial Finance Research*. World Scientific.

Martino, Wang, & Bellavitis. (2020). *An introduction to blockchain, cryptocurrency and initial coin offerings*. Academic Press.

Matt, C., Hess, T., & Benlian, A. (2015). Digital transformation strategies. *Business & Information Systems Engineering, 57*(5), 339–343. doi:10.100712599-015-0401-5

Maurer, B., Nelms, T. C., & Swartz, L. (2013). When perhaps the real problem is money itself!: The practical materiality of Bitcoin. *Social Semiotics, 23*(2), 261–277.

Mbeledogu, N. N., Odoh, M., & Umeh, M. N. (2012). Stock feature extraction using PrincipleComponent Analysis. In *International Conference on Computer Technology and Science*. IACSIT Press. DOI: 10.7763/IPCSIT.2012.V47.44

McMaster, M., Nettleton, C., Tom, C., Xu, B., Cao, C., & Qiao, P. (2020). Risk management: Rethinking fashion supply chain management for multinational corporations in light of the COVID-19 outbreak. *Journal of Risk and Financial Management, 13*(8), 173. doi:10.3390/jrfm13080173

Menchetti, Cipollini, & Mealli. (2021). *Causal effect of regulated Bitcoin futures on volatility and volume*. Academic Press.

Mirashi, E. (2021). *Cooperación procesal internacional en la lucha contra la criminalidad transfronteriza: especial referencia al cibercrimen y al terrorismo*. Universidad de Salamanca.

Mohammed Bouznit, M. R.-B. (2020). Measures to Promote Renewable Energy for. *Sustainability, 6-7*. Advance online publication. doi:10.3390u12041468

Morakanyane, R., Grace, A., & O'Reilly, P. (2017). Conceptualizing digital transformation in business organizations: A systematic review of literature. In *Proceedings of the 30th Bled EConference on Digital Transformation – From Connecting Things to Transforming Our Lives* (pp. 427–443). 10.18690/978-961-286-043-1.30

Möser, M., Böhme, R., & Breuker, D. (2013). An inquiry into money laundering tools in the Bitcoin ecosystem. *2013 APWG eCrime Researchers Summit*. https://ieeexplore.ieee.org/document/6805780

Moser, M., Bohme, R., & Breuker, D. (2013). *An inquiry into money laundering tools in the Bitcoin ecosystem. In eCrimeResearchersSummit (eCRS), 2013*. IEEE.

Mouloudj, K., Bouarar, A. C., & Stojczew, K. (2021). Analyzing the students' intention to use online learning system in the context of COVID-19 pandemic: A theory of planned behavior approach. In W. B. James, C. Cobanoglu, & M. Cavusoglu (Eds.), *Advances in global education and research* (Vol. 4, pp. 1–17). USF M3 Publishing. https://www.doi.org/10.5038/9781955833042

Mourad Zaid, S. K. (2017). Strategy of the renewable energy in Algeria, as an inevitable drift to diversification of the economy. *Algerian Business Performance Review*, *6*, 62.

Mubarak, M. F., Shaikh, F. A., Mubarik, M., Samo, K. A., & Mastoi, S. (2019). The impact of digital transformation on business performance: A study of Pakistani SMEs. *Engineering, Technology &. Applied Scientific Research*, *9*(6), 5056–5061. doi:10.48084/etasr.3201

Mueller, M. L. (2010). *Networks and States: The Global Politics of Internet Governance*. MIT Press. doi:10.7551/mitpress/9780262014595.001.0001

Mullan, P. C. (2014a). Bitcoin Decentralized Virtual Currency. In The Digital Currency Challenge: Shaping Online Payment Systems through US Financial Regulations (pp. 84-92). Springer.

Mullan, P. C. (2014b). FIN-2013-G001. In The Digital Currency Challenge: Shaping Online Payment Systems through US Financial Regulations (pp. 118-130). Springer.

Nadarajah, S., & Chu, J. (2017). On the inefficiency of Bitcoin. *Economics Letters*, *150*, 6–9.

NajlaE. G. (2021, March 24). https://www.cder.dz/vlib/bulletin/pdf/bulletin_021_11.pdf

Nakamoto, S. (2008). Bitcoin: A peer-to-peer electronic cash system. *Consulted*, *1*, 28.

Nakamoto, S. (2009a). *Bitcoin: A peer-to-peer electronic cash system*. www.bitcoin.org.

Nakamoto, S. (2009b). *Bitcoin open source implementation of P2P currency*. P2P Foundation.

Narayanan, A., Bonneau, J., Felten, E., Miller, A., & Goldfeder, S. (2016). *Bitcoin and Cryptocurrency Technologies*. Princeton University Press.

Narayan, P. K. (2020). Oil price news and COVID-19—Is there any connection? *Energy Research Letters*, *1*(1), 13176. doi:10.46557/001c.13176

Nestarcova, D. (2019). *A Critical Appraisal of Initial Coin Offerings: Lifting the "Digital Token's Veil*. Brill. doi:10.1163/9789004416581

Noureddine, Y. (2020). *Transition energétique en Algérie: Leçons, Etat des Lieux et Perspectives pour un Développement Accéléré des Energies Renouvelables*. Alger: Le Commissariat aux Energies Renouvelables et à l'Efficacité Energétique. https://www.cerefe.gov.dz/fr/2020/11/29/transition-energetique-en-algerie/

Nwankpa, J. K., & Roumani, Y. (2016). IT capability and digital transformation: A firm performance perspective. In *Proceedings of the 37th International Conference on Information Systems* (vol. 5, pp. 3839-3854). Academic Press.

OG. (n.d.). *Ödemelerde kripto varlıkların kullanılmamasına dair yönetmelik*. Available at: https://www.resmigazete.gov.tr/eskiler/2021/04/20210416-4.htm

Orléan, A. (2002). La monnaie, opérateur de totalization. Entretien avec André Orléan réalisé par Françoise Bourdarias. *Journal des anthropologues*, *90-91*, 331-352. http://jda.revues.org/2331.

Osterrieder, J., & Lorenz, J. (2017). A statistical risk assessment of Bitcoin and its extreme tail behavior. *Annals of Financial Economics*, *12*(1).

Ostroy, J.-M., & Starr, R. M. (1990). The transactions role of Money. In B. Friedman & F. H. Hahn (Eds.), *Handbook of Monetary Economics* (pp. 3–62). North Holland.

Osula, A. M. (2015). Mutual Legal Assistance & Other Mechanisms for Accessing Extraterritorially Located Data. *MUJLT*, *9*(1), 43–64. doi:10.5817/MUJLT2015-1-4

OuahibaG. (2021, March 25). https://www.cder.dz/vlib/bulletin/pdf/ber37_6_7.pdf

Ozili, P. K., & Arun, T. (2020). *Spillover of COVID-19: impact on the Global Economy*. Available at SSRN 3562570.

Pandey, N., & Pal, A. (2020). Impact of digital surge during Covid-19 pandemic: A viewpoint on research and practice. *International Journal of Information Management*, *55*, 102171. doi:10.1016/j.ijinfomgt.2020.102171 PMID:32836633

Parmar, S. K. M. (2014). *Virtual Currency: A Theoretical Review*. Academic Press.

Parviainen, P., Tihinen, M., Kääriäinen, J., & Teppola, S. (2017). Tackling the digitalisation challenge: How to benefit from digitalisation in practice. *International Journal of Information Systems and Project Management*, *5*(1), 63–77. doi:10.12821/ijispm050104

Pathinfinders. (n.d.). *Justice for all, Report of the task force on justice*. Retrieved 11/04/21 from: https://www.justice.sdg16.plus/report

Pereira, C. S., Durão, N., Fonseca, D., Ferreira, M. J., & Moreira, F. (2020). An educational approach for present and future of digital transformation in Portuguese organizations. *Applied Sciences (Basel, Switzerland)*, *10*(3), 1–22. doi:10.3390/app10030757

Pochea, M. M., Filip, A. M., & Pece, A. M. (2017). Herding behavior in CEE stock markets under asymmetric conditions: A quantile regression analysis. *Journal of Behavioral Finance*, *18*(4), 400–416.

Policy, M. (2017). *A Digital Geneva Convention to protect cyberspace*. Retrieved from 12/04/21: https://www.microsoft.com/en-us/cybersecurity/content-hub/a-digital-genevaconvention-to-protect-cyberspace.

Popović-Pantić, S., Semenčenko, D., & Vasilić, N. (2019). The influence of digital transformation on business performance: Evidence of the women-owned companies. *Ekonomika Preduzeća*, *67*(7-8), 397–414. doi:10.5937/EKOPRE1908397P

Popović-Pantić, S., Semenčenko, D., & Vasilić, N. (2020). Digital technologies and the financial performance of female SMES in Serbia: The mediating role of innovation. *Economic Annals*, *65*(224), 53–81. doi:10.2298/EKA2024053P

Reis, J., Amorim, M., Melão, N., & Matos, P. (2018). Digital transformation: A literature review and guidelines for future research. In Trends and Advances in Information Systems and Technologies. Springer International Publishing. doi:10.1007/978-3-319-77703-0_41

Rennick, E. (2015). *The Fintech 2.0 Paper: rebooting financial services*. Santander InnoVentures.

Revue de l'ACPR. (2014). https://acpr.banque-france.fr/publications/revue-de-lacpr/revue-de-lacpr-2014

Robinson, T. (2021). Crypto Enforcement Actions by US Regulators Reach $2.5 Billion. *Elliptic*. Retrieved from https://www.elliptic.co/blog/https/www.elliptic.co/blog/crypto-enforcement-actions-by-us-regulators-reach-2.5-billion

Robin, T., Zeynep, Y., & Tomas, L. (2013), Breaking Out of the Bank in Europe – Exploring Collective Emergent Institutional Entrepreneurship through Bitcoin. *15th Annual SNEE Conference*.

Sajić, M., Bundalo, D., Bundalo, Z., & Pašalić, D. (2018). Digital technologies in transformation of classical retail bank into digital bank. *2017 25th Telecommun. Forum, TELFOR 2017- Proc.*, 1–4. doi:10.1109/TELFOR.2017.8249404

Saliha Haddoum, H. B. (2018). Algerian energy policy: Perspectives, barriers, and missed. *Global Challenges (Hoboken, NJ)*, *1*. Advance online publication. doi:10.1002/gch2.201700134

Sari, T., Güleş, H. K., & Yiğitol, B. (2020). Awareness and readiness of industry 4.0: The case of Turkish manufacturing industry. *Advances in Production Engineering & Management*, *15*(1), 57–68. doi:10.14743/apem2020.1.349

Sawy, O. A. E., Amsinck, H., Kræmmergaard, P., & Vinther, A. L. (2016). How LEGO built the foundations and enterprise capabilities for digital leadership. *MIS Quarterly Executive*, *15*(2), 141–166.

Schumpter, J. A. (2000). Entrepreneurship as innovation. *Entrepreneurship: The social science view*, 51-75.

Schwab, K. (2017). *The fourth industrial revolution*. Crown Business.

Sec. & Exch. Comm'n v. Shavers, No. 4:13-CV-416, 2014 WL 4652121, at *1 (E.D. Tex. Sept. 18, 2014).

Selgin, G. (2013). *Synthetic Commodity Money*. University of Georgia, Working Paper.

Selmi, R., Mensi, W., Hammoudeh, S., & Bouoiyour, J. (2018). Is Bitcoin a hedge, a safe haven or a diversifier for oil price movements? A comparison with gold. *Energy Econ.*, *74*, 787–801.

Serada, Sihvonen, & Harviainen. (2021). Crypto Kitties and the New Ludic Economy: How Blockchain Introduces Value, Ownership, and Scarcity in Digital Gaming. Academic Press.

Serdouk, F. (2017). *A legal framework of renewable energies and climate change in Algeria. Environmental protection mechanisms*. Center for the Generation of Scientific Research.

Shafi, M., Liu, J., & Ren, W. (2020). Impact of COVID-19 pandemic on micro, small, and medium-sized Enterprises operating in Pakistan. *Research in Globalization*, *2*, 100018. doi:10.1016/j.resglo.2020.100018

Shahi, C., & Sinha, M. (2021). Digital transformation: Challenges faced by organizations and their potential solutions. *International Journal of Innovation Science*, *13*(1), 17–33. doi:10.1108/IJIS-09-2020-0157

Shaikh, I. (2020). Impact of COVID-19 pandemic disease outbreak on the global equity markets. *Economic Research-EkonomskaIstraživanja*, 1-18.

Shaker, M., Aliee, F. S., & Fotohi, R. (2021). Online rating system development using blockchain-based distributed ledger technology. *Wireless Networks*.

Shanaev, S., Sharma, S., & Ghimire, B. (2020). Taming the blockchain beast? Regulatory implications for the cryptocurrency market. *Research in International Business and Finance*.

Shanghai Stock Exchange 50 Index. (2014). *Discrete Dynamics in Nature and Society Volume 2014*. Author.

Shao, Nib, Wanga, & Wang. (2020). Research on venture capital based on information entropy. *Procedia Computer Science, 187*, 278-283.

Sharma, A. M. (2021). *Cryptocurrency and Financial Risks*. digitalcommons.liberty.edu

Singh, A. (2021). Investigating the dynamic relationship between litigation funding, gold, bitcoin and the stock market: The case of Australia. *Economic Modelling*, *97*, 45–57. doi:10.1016/j.econmod.2021.01.007

Siu, T. K. (2021). The risks of cryptocurrencies with long memory in volatility, non-normality and behavioural insights. *Applied Economics*.

Sjödin, D. R., Parida, V., Leksell, M., & Petrovic, A. (2018). Smart factory implementation and process innovation. *Research Technology Management*, *61*(5), 22–31. doi:10.1080/08956308.2018.1471277

SlimaniS. (2021, March 22). https://www.webmanagercenter.com/2009/05/14/75224/algerie-edielec-l-eclairage-public-revolutionne/

Sonatrach. (2019, March 20). http://us-algeria.org/attachments/article/280/solar.pdf

Sophie Jablonski, M. T. (2013). Assessment of selected energy efficiency and renewable energy. *Energy Strategy Reviews*, (2). Advance online publication. doi:10.1016/j.esr.2013.02.009

Sousa-Zomer, T. T., Neely, A., & Martinez, V. (2020). Digital transforming capability and performance: A microfoundational perspective. *International Journal of Operations & Production Management*, *40*(7/8), 1095–1128. doi:10.1108/IJOPM-06-2019-0444

Stabile, Prior, & Hinkes. (2020). Digital Assets and Blockchain Technology: US Law and Regulation. Edward Elgar Publishing.

Stolterman, E., & Fors, A. C. (2004). Information technology and the good life. In Information Systems Research. Springer. doi:10.1007/1-4020-8095-6_45

Swanson, T. (2014). *The Anatomy of a Money-like Informational Commodity: A Study of Bitcoin*. Creative Commons.

Symitsi, E., & Chalvatzis, K. J. (2019). The economic value of Bitcoin: A portfolio analysis of currencies, gold, oil and stocks. *Research in International Business and Finance*, *48*, 97–110.

Szczepanski, M. (2014). *Bitcoin: Market, economics and regulation.* European Parliamentary Research Service.

Tarutė, A., Duobienė, J., Klovienė, L., Vitkauskaitė, E., & Varaniūtė, V. (2018). Identifying factors affecting digital transformation of SMEs. In *Proceedings of the 18th International Conference on Electronic Business* (pp. 373-381). ICEB.

Task Force on Justice. Justice for All (2019). *Final Report.* New York: Center on International Cooperation. Retrieved 14/04/21 from: https://www.justice.sdg16.plus.

Tekic, Z., & Koroteev, D. (2019). From disruptively digital to proudly analog: A holistic typology of digital transformation strategies. *Business Horizons*, *62*(6), 683–693. doi:10.1016/j.bushor.2019.07.002

Tewfik Hasni, R. M. (2021). *L'Algérie 100% Énergies Renouvelables*. Friedrich-Ebert-Stiftung. http://library.fes.de/pdf-files/bueros/algerien/17412.pdf

Théret, B. (2007). *La monnaie dévoilée par ses crises*. Éditions de l'EHESS.

Théret, B. (2008). Les trois états de la monnaie. Approche interdisciplinaire du fait monétaire. *Revue Economique*, *59*(4), 813–841.

Thun, J. H., & Hoenig, D. (2011). An empirical analysis of supply chain risk management in the German automotive industry. *International Journal of Production Economics*, *131*(1), 242–249. doi:10.1016/j.ijpe.2009.10.010

Trek, F. (2020). Solar energy in Algeria between exploitation policies and export potential. *Journal of the New Economy, 12*(2), 285.

U.S. Securities and Exchange Commission. (2017). *How Investigations Work.* Retrieved from https://www.sec.gov/enforce/how-investigations-work.html

U.S. Securities and Exchange Commission. (2020). *Division of Enforcement 2020 Annual Report*. Retrieved from https://www.sec.gov/files/enforcement-annual-report-2020.pdf

U.S. Securities and Exchange Commission. (2021a). *SEC Charges Poloniex for Operating Unregistered Digital Asset Exchange*. Retrieved from https://www.sec.gov/news/press-release/2021-147

U.S. Securities and Exchange Commission. (2021b). *SEC Charges Decentralized Finance Lender and Top Executives*. Retrieved from https://www.sec.gov/news/press-release/2021-145

U.S. Securities and Exchange Commission. (2021c). *ICO "Listing" Website Charged With Unlawfully Touting Digital Asset Securities*. Retrieved from https://www.sec.gov/news/press-release/2021-125

U.S. Treasury Financial Crimes Enforcement Network. (2008). *Application of the Definition of Money Transmitter to Brokers and Dealers in Currency and Other Commodities*. Retrieved from https://www.fincen.gov/resources/advisories/fincen-guidance-fin-2008-g008

U.S. Treasury Financial Crimes Enforcement Network. (2013). *Application of FinCEN's Regulations to Persons Administering, Exchanging, or Using Virtual Currencies*. Retrieved from https://www.fincen.gov/resources/statutes-regulations/guidance/application-fincens-regulations-persons-administering

Ulas, D. (2019). Digital transformation process and SMEs. *Procedia Computer Science*, *158*, 662–671. doi:10.1016/j.procs.2019.09.101

Umar, M., Rizvi, S. K. A., & Naqvi, B. (2021). Dance with the devil? The nexus of fourth industrial revolution, technological financial products and volatility spillovers in global financial system. *Technological Forecasting and Social Change*, *163*, 1–11. doi:10.1016/j.techfore.2020.120450

United Nations. (2001a). *Resolution A/RES/55/63, Combating the criminal misuse of information technologies*. Author.

United Nations. (2001b). *Resolution A/RES/56/121, Combating the criminal misuse of information technologies*. Author.

United Nations. (2003). *UN Resolution 57/239, Creation of a global culture of cybersecurity*. Retrieved 14/04/21 from: https://www.itu.int/ITUD/cyb/cybersecurity/docs/UN_resolution_57_239.pdf

United Nations. (2020a), *UN expert outlines urgent steps to ensure justice systems are not paralysed by COVID-19*. Retrieved 14/04/21 from: https://reliefweb.int/report/world/un-expertoutlines-urgent-steps-ensure-justice-systems-are-not-paralysed-covid-19

United Nations. (2020b). *We are all in this Together: Human Rights and Covid-19 Response and Recovery*. Retrieved 14/04/21 from: https://www.un.org/en/un-coronavirus-communications-team/we-are-all-together-human-rights-and-covid-19-response-and

United Nations. (2021). *Peace, dignity and equality on a healthy planet.* Retrieved 14/04/21 from: https://www.un.org/en/

United Nations. (n.d.). *Goal 16: Promote just, peaceful and inclusive societies.* Retrieved 15/04/21 from: https://www.un.org/sustainabledevelopment/peace-justice/

United States v. Ulbricht, 31 F. Supp. 3d 540, 547 (S.D.N.Y. 2014).

UNODC. (n.d.). *Judicial Suspension and Electronic Access to Justice.* Retrieved 14/04/21 from: https://www.unodc.org/dohadeclaration/en/news/2020/06/judicial-suspension-and-electronic-access-to-justice.html

Urbina, J. (2020). *Spillover Index Based on VAR Modelling.* R package version 0.1. Available at: https://cran.r-project.org/web/packages/Spillover/Spillover.pdf

Urquhart, A. (2016). The inefficiency of Bitcoin. *Economics Letters, 148*, 80–82.

Vasek, M., Bonneau, J., Castellucci, R., Keith, C., & Moore, T. (2016). The Bitcoin brain drain: A short paper on the use and abuse of bitcoin brain wallets. In *Financial Cryptography and Data Security.* Lecture Notes in Computer Science. Springer.

Vasek, M., & Moore, T. (2015). There's no free lunch, even using Bitcoin: Tracking the popularity and profits of virtual currency scams. In *International Conference on Financial Cryptography and Data Security* (pp. 44–61). Springer.

Vogelsang, K., Liere-Netheler, K., Packmohr, S., & Hoppe, U. (2019). Success factors for fostering a digital transformation in manufacturing companies. *Journal of Enterprise Transformation, 8*(1-2), 121–142. doi:10.1080/19488289.2019.1578839

Wafa, Z. (2015). *Internet Governance Forum.* Retrieved 15/04/21 from: http://www.intgovforum.org/cms/187-igf2015/transcripts-igf-2015/2884-2015-11-12-enhancingcybersecurity-and-building-digital-trust-main-meeting-hall-finished

Walport, M. (2015). Distributed Ledger Technology: Beyond BlockChain. Academic Press.

Wang, G. J., Xie, C., Wen, D., & Zhao, L. (2019). When Bitcoin meets economic policy uncertainty (EPU): Measuring risk spillover effect from EPU to Bitcoin. *Finance Research Letters, 31*, 489–497. doi:10.1016/j.frl.2018.12.028

Wang, Z., & Sun, Z. (2021). From globalization to regionalization: The United States, China, and the post-Covid-19 world economic order. *Journal of Chinese Political Science, 26*(1), 69–87. doi:10.100711366-020-09706-3 PMID:33144822

Weber, M. (2003). The Council of Europe's Convention on Cybercrime. BTLJ, 18(1).

Wen, S., Xiong, W., Tan, J., Chen, S., & Li, Q. (2021). Blockchain enhanced price incentive demand response for building user energy network in sustainable society. *Sustainable Cities and Society.*

Westerman, G., Calméjane, C., Bonnet, D., Ferraris, P., & McAfee, A. (2011). Digital Transformation: A Road-Map for Billion-Dollar Organizations (Report). Capgemini Consulting & MIT Center for Digital Business.

Westerman, G., Bonnet, D., & McAfee, A. (2014). *Leading digital: Turning technology into business transformation*. Harvard Business Press.

What is cryptocurrency and how does it work? (n.d.). https://www.kaspersky.com/resource-center/definitions/what-is-cryptocurrency

Winarsih, I. M., & Fuad, K. (2021). Impact of Covid-19 on Digital Transformation and Sustainability in Small and Medium Enterprises (SMEs): A conceptual framework. In Complex, Intelligent and Software Intensive Systems. CISIS 2020. Advances in Intelligent Systems and Computing (Vol. 1194, pp. 471-476). Springer. doi:10.1007/978-3-030-50454-0_48

Wood. (2019). Tunisia issues central bank digital currency. *Ledger Insights*.

World Bank. (2012). *Financial Inclusion Data*. http://datatopics.worldbank.org/financialinclusion/

World Energy Council. (2020). *World Energy*. London: World Energy Council. https://www.worldenergy.org/assets/downloads/World_Energy_Issues_Monitor_2020_-_Full_Report.pdf

Wray, L. R. (2014). *From the state theory of money to modern money theory: an alternative to economic orthodoxy*. Levy Economics Institute. 10.2139/ssrn.2407711

Yadav, S. P., Agrawal, K. K., Bhati, B. S., & Al-Turjman, F. (2020). *Blockchain-Based Cryptocurrency Regulation: An Overview. In Computational Economics*. Springer.

Yaneva, M. (2021, March 29). Récupéré sur Renwables Now: https://renewablesnow.com/news/algerian-enie-to-open-25-mw-solar-panel-factory-486383/

Yang, L., Rea, W., & Rea, A. (2016). Stock Selection with Principal Component Analysis. *The Journal of Investment Strategies*, *5*, 1–21.

Yarovaya, L., Elsayed, A. H., & Hammoudeh, S. (2021). Determinants of spillovers between islamic and conventional financial markets: Exploring the safe haven assets during the COVID-19 pandemic. *Finance Research Letters*, *43*, 101979. Advance online publication. doi:10.1016/j.frl.2021.101979

Zaremba, A., Kizys, R., Aharon, D. Y., & Demir, E. (2020). Infected markets: Novel coronavirus, government interventions, and stock return volatility around the globe. *Finance Research Letters*, *35*, 101597. doi:10.1016/j.frl.2020.101597 PMID:32550842

Zhai, H., Yang, M., & Chan, K. C. (2022). Does digital transformation enhance a firm's performance? Evidence from China. *Technology in Society*, *68*, 101841. doi:10.1016/j.techsoc.2021.101841

Zhang, Y.-J., Bouri, E., Gupta, R., & Ma, S.-J. (2021). Risk spillover between Bitcoin and conventional financial markets: An expectile-based approach. *The North American Journal of Economics and Finance*, *55*, 1–10. doi:10.1016/j.najef.2020.101296

Zhour Abada, M. B. (2018). Study of management strategy of energy resources in Algeria. *Energy Reports*, *3*. Advance online publication. doi:10.1016/j.egyr.2017.09.004

Related References

To continue our tradition of advancing information science and technology research, we have compiled a list of recommended IGI Global readings. These references will provide additional information and guidance to further enrich your knowledge and assist you with your own research and future publications.

Abdul Razak, R., & Mansor, N. A. (2021). Instagram Influencers in Social Media-Induced Tourism: Rethinking Tourist Trust Towards Tourism Destination. In M. Dinis, L. Bonixe, S. Lamy, & Z. Breda (Eds.), *Impact of New Media in Tourism* (pp. 135-144). IGI Global. https://doi.org/10.4018/978-1-7998-7095-1.ch009

Abir, T., & Khan, M. Y. (2022). Importance of ICT Advancement and Culture of Adaptation in the Tourism and Hospitality Industry for Developing Countries. In C. Ramos, S. Quinteiro, & A. Gonçalves (Eds.), *ICT as Innovator Between Tourism and Culture* (pp. 30–41). IGI Global. https://doi.org/10.4018/978-1-7998-8165-0.ch003

Abir, T., & Khan, M. Y. (2022). Importance of ICT Advancement and Culture of Adaptation in the Tourism and Hospitality Industry for Developing Countries. In C. Ramos, S. Quinteiro, & A. Gonçalves (Eds.), *ICT as Innovator Between Tourism and Culture* (pp. 30–41). IGI Global. https://doi.org/10.4018/978-1-7998-8165-0.ch003

Abtahi, M. S., Behboudi, L., & Hasanabad, H. M. (2017). Factors Affecting Internet Advertising Adoption in Ad Agencies. *International Journal of Innovation in the Digital Economy*, *8*(4), 18–29. doi:10.4018/IJIDE.2017100102

Afenyo-Agbe, E., & Mensah, I. (2022). Principles, Benefits, and Barriers to Community-Based Tourism: Implications for Management. In I. Mensah & E. Afenyo-Agbe (Eds.), *Prospects and Challenges of Community-Based Tourism and Changing Demographics* (pp. 1–29). IGI Global. doi:10.4018/978-1-7998-7335-8.ch001

Agbo, V. M. (2022). Distributive Justice Issues in Community-Based Tourism. In I. Mensah & E. Afenyo-Agbe (Eds.), *Prospects and Challenges of Community-Based Tourism and Changing Demographics* (pp. 107–129). IGI Global. https://doi.org/10.4018/978-1-7998-7335-8.ch005

Agrawal, S. (2017). The Impact of Emerging Technologies and Social Media on Different Business(es): Marketing and Management. In O. Rishi & A. Sharma (Eds.), *Maximizing Business Performance and Efficiency Through Intelligent Systems* (pp. 37–49). Hershey, PA: IGI Global. doi:10.4018/978-1-5225-2234-8.ch002

Ahmad, A., & Johari, S. (2022). Georgetown as a Gastronomy Tourism Destination: Visitor Awareness Towards Revisit Intention of Nasi Kandar Restaurant. In M. Valeri (Ed.), *New Governance and Management in Touristic Destinations* (pp. 71–83). IGI Global. https://doi.org/10.4018/978-1-6684-3889-3.ch005

Alkhatib, G., & Bayouq, S. T. (2021). A TAM-Based Model of Technological Factors Affecting Use of E-Tourism. *International Journal of Tourism and Hospitality Management in the Digital Age*, *5*(2), 50–67. https://doi.org/10.4018/IJTHMDA.20210701.oa1

Altinay Ozdemir, M. (2021). Virtual Reality (VR) and Augmented Reality (AR) Technologies for Accessibility and Marketing in the Tourism Industry. In C. Eusébio, L. Teixeira, & M. Carneiro (Eds.), *ICT Tools and Applications for Accessible Tourism* (pp. 277-301). IGI Global. https://doi.org/10.4018/978-1-7998-6428-8.ch013

Anantharaman, R. N., Rajeswari, K. S., Angusamy, A., & Kuppusamy, J. (2017). Role of Self-Efficacy and Collective Efficacy as Moderators of Occupational Stress Among Software Development Professionals. *International Journal of Human Capital and Information Technology Professionals*, *8*(2), 45–58. doi:10.4018/IJHCITP.2017040103

Aninze, F., El-Gohary, H., & Hussain, J. (2018). The Role of Microfinance to Empower Women: The Case of Developing Countries. *International Journal of Customer Relationship Marketing and Management*, *9*(1), 54–78. doi:10.4018/IJCRMM.2018010104

Antosova, G., Sabogal-Salamanca, M., & Krizova, E. (2021). Human Capital in Tourism: A Practical Model of Endogenous and Exogenous Territorial Tourism Planning in Bahía Solano, Colombia. In V. Costa, A. Moura, & M. Mira (Eds.), *Handbook of Research on Human Capital and People Management in the Tourism Industry* (pp. 282–302). IGI Global. https://doi.org/10.4018/978-1-7998-4318-4.ch014

Arsenijević, O. M., Orčić, D., & Kastratović, E. (2017). Development of an Optimization Tool for Intangibles in SMEs: A Case Study from Serbia with a Pilot Research in the Prestige by Milka Company. In M. Vemić (Ed.), *Optimal Management Strategies in Small and Medium Enterprises* (pp. 320–347). Hershey, PA: IGI Global. doi:10.4018/978-1-5225-1949-2.ch015

Aryanto, V. D., Wismantoro, Y., & Widyatmoko, K. (2018). Implementing Eco-Innovation by Utilizing the Internet to Enhance Firm's Marketing Performance: Study of Green Batik Small and Medium Enterprises in Indonesia. *International Journal of E-Business Research, 14*(1), 21–36. doi:10.4018/IJEBR.2018010102

Asero, V., & Billi, S. (2022). New Perspective of Networking in the DMO Model. In M. Valeri (Ed.), *New Governance and Management in Touristic Destinations* (pp. 105–118). IGI Global. https://doi.org/10.4018/978-1-6684-3889-3.ch007

Atiku, S. O., & Fields, Z. (2017). Multicultural Orientations for 21st Century Global Leadership. In N. Baporikar (Ed.), *Management Education for Global Leadership* (pp. 28–51). Hershey, PA: IGI Global. doi:10.4018/978-1-5225-1013-0.ch002

Atiku, S. O., & Fields, Z. (2018). Organisational Learning Dimensions and Talent Retention Strategies for the Service Industries. In N. Baporikar (Ed.), *Global Practices in Knowledge Management for Societal and Organizational Development* (pp. 358–381). Hershey, PA: IGI Global. doi:10.4018/978-1-5225-3009-1.ch017

Atsa'am, D. D., & Kuset Bodur, E. (2021). Pattern Mining on How Organizational Tenure Affects the Psychological Capital of Employees Within the Hospitality and Tourism Industry: Linking Employees' Organizational Tenure With PsyCap. *International Journal of Tourism and Hospitality Management in the Digital Age, 5*(2), 17–28. https://doi.org/10.4018/IJTHMDA.2021070102

Ávila, L., & Teixeira, L. (2018). The Main Concepts Behind the Dematerialization of Business Processes. In M. Khosrow-Pour, D.B.A. (Ed.), Encyclopedia of Information Science and Technology, Fourth Edition (pp. 888-898). Hershey, PA: IGI Global. https://doi.org/ doi:10.4018/978-1-5225-2255-3.ch076

Ayorekire, J., Mugizi, F., Obua, J., & Ampaire, G. (2022). Community-Based Tourism and Local People's Perceptions Towards Conservation: The Case of Queen Elizabeth Conservation Area, Uganda. In I. Mensah & E. Afenyo-Agbe (Eds.), *Prospects and Challenges of Community-Based Tourism and Changing Demographics* (pp. 56–82). IGI Global. https://doi.org/10.4018/978-1-7998-7335-8.ch003

Baleiro, R. (2022). Tourist Literature and the Architecture of Travel in Olga Tokarczuk and Patti Smith. In R. Baleiro & R. Pereira (Eds.), *Global Perspectives on Literary Tourism and Film-Induced Tourism* (pp. 202-216). IGI Global. https://doi.org/10.4018/978-1-7998-8262-6.ch011

Barat, S. (2021). Looking at the Future of Medical Tourism in Asia. *International Journal of Tourism and Hospitality Management in the Digital Age*, *5*(1), 19–33. https://doi.org/10.4018/IJTHMDA.2021010102

Barbosa, C. A., Magalhães, M., & Nunes, M. R. (2021). Travel Instagramability: A Way of Choosing a Destination? In M. Dinis, L. Bonixe, S. Lamy, & Z. Breda (Eds.), *Impact of New Media in Tourism* (pp. 173-190). IGI Global. https://doi.org/10.4018/978-1-7998-7095-1.ch011

Bari, M. W., & Khan, Q. (2021). Pakistan as a Destination of Religious Tourism. In E. Alaverdov & M. Bari (Eds.), *Global Development of Religious Tourism* (pp. 1-10). IGI Global. https://doi.org/10.4018/978-1-7998-5792-1.ch001

Bartens, Y., Chunpir, H. I., Schulte, F., & Voß, S. (2017). Business/IT Alignment in Two-Sided Markets: A COBIT 5 Analysis for Media Streaming Business Models. In S. De Haes & W. Van Grembergen (Eds.), *Strategic IT Governance and Alignment in Business Settings* (pp. 82–111). Hershey, PA: IGI Global. doi:10.4018/978-1-5225-0861-8.ch004

Bashayreh, A. M. (2018). Organizational Culture and Organizational Performance. In W. Lee & F. Sabetzadeh (Eds.), *Contemporary Knowledge and Systems Science* (pp. 50–69). Hershey, PA: IGI Global. doi:10.4018/978-1-5225-5655-8.ch003

Bechthold, L., Lude, M., & Prügl, R. (2021). Crisis Favors the Prepared Firm: How Organizational Ambidexterity Relates to Perceptions of Organizational Resilience. In A. Zehrer, G. Glowka, K. Schwaiger, & V. Ranacher-Lackner (Eds.), *Resiliency Models and Addressing Future Risks for Family Firms in the Tourism Industry* (pp. 178–205). IGI Global. https://doi.org/10.4018/978-1-7998-7352-5.ch008

Bedford, D. A. (2018). Sustainable Knowledge Management Strategies: Aligning Business Capabilities and Knowledge Management Goals. In N. Baporikar (Ed.), *Global Practices in Knowledge Management for Societal and Organizational Development* (pp. 46–73). Hershey, PA: IGI Global. doi:10.4018/978-1-5225-3009-1.ch003

Bekjanov, D., & Matyusupov, B. (2021). Influence of Innovative Processes in the Competitiveness of Tourist Destination. In J. Soares (Ed.), *Innovation and Entrepreneurial Opportunities in Community Tourism* (pp. 243–263). IGI Global. https://doi.org/10.4018/978-1-7998-4855-4.ch014

Bharwani, S., & Musunuri, D. (2018). Reflection as a Process From Theory to Practice. In M. Khosrow-Pour, D.B.A. (Ed.), Encyclopedia of Information Science and Technology, Fourth Edition (pp. 1529-1539). Hershey, PA: IGI Global. doi:10.4018/978-1-5225-2255-3.ch132

Bhatt, G. D., Wang, Z., & Rodger, J. A. (2017). Information Systems Capabilities and Their Effects on Competitive Advantages: A Study of Chinese Companies. *Information Resources Management Journal*, *30*(3), 41–57. doi:10.4018/IRMJ.2017070103

Bhushan, M., & Yadav, A. (2017). Concept of Cloud Computing in ESB. In R. Bhadoria, N. Chaudhari, G. Tomar, & S. Singh (Eds.), *Exploring Enterprise Service Bus in the Service-Oriented Architecture Paradigm* (pp. 116–127). Hershey, PA: IGI Global. doi:10.4018/978-1-5225-2157-0.ch008

Bhushan, S. (2017). System Dynamics Base-Model of Humanitarian Supply Chain (HSCM) in Disaster Prone Eco-Communities of India: A Discussion on Simulation and Scenario Results. *International Journal of System Dynamics Applications*, *6*(3), 20–37. doi:10.4018/IJSDA.2017070102

Binder, D., & Miller, J. W. (2021). A Generations' Perspective on Employer Branding in Tourism. In V. Costa, A. Moura, & M. Mira (Eds.), *Handbook of Research on Human Capital and People Management in the Tourism Industry* (pp. 152–174). IGI Global. https://doi.org/10.4018/978-1-7998-4318-4.ch008

Birch Freeman, A. A., Mensah, I., & Antwi, K. B. (2022). Smiling vs. Frowning Faces: Community Participation for Sustainable Tourism in Ghanaian Communities. In I. Mensah & E. Afenyo-Agbe (Eds.), *Prospects and Challenges of Community-Based Tourism and Changing Demographics* (pp. 83–106). IGI Global. https://doi.org/10.4018/978-1-7998-7335-8.ch004

Biswas, A., & De, A. K. (2017). On Development of a Fuzzy Stochastic Programming Model with Its Application to Business Management. In S. Trivedi, S. Dey, A. Kumar, & T. Panda (Eds.), *Handbook of Research on Advanced Data Mining Techniques and Applications for Business Intelligence* (pp. 353–378). Hershey, PA: IGI Global. doi:10.4018/978-1-5225-2031-3.ch021

Boragnio, A., & Faracce Macia, C. (2021). "Taking Care of Yourself at Home": Use of E-Commerce About Food and Care During the COVID-19 Pandemic in the City of Buenos Aires. In M. Korstanje (Ed.), *Socio-Economic Effects and Recovery Efforts for the Rental Industry: Post-COVID-19 Strategies* (pp. 45–71). IGI Global. https://doi.org/10.4018/978-1-7998-7287-0.ch003

Borges, V. D. (2021). Happiness: The Basis for Public Policy in Tourism. In A. Perinotto, V. Mayer, & J. Soares (Eds.), *Rebuilding and Restructuring the Tourism Industry: Infusion of Happiness and Quality of Life* (pp. 1–25). IGI Global. https://doi.org/10.4018/978-1-7998-7239-9.ch001

Bücker, J., & Ernste, K. (2018). Use of Brand Heroes in Strategic Reputation Management: The Case of Bacardi, Adidas, and Daimler. In A. Erdemir (Ed.), *Reputation Management Techniques in Public Relations* (pp. 126–150). Hershey, PA: IGI Global. doi:10.4018/978-1-5225-3619-2.ch007

Buluk Eşitti, B. (2021). COVID-19 and Alternative Tourism: New Destinations and New Tourism Products. In M. Demir, A. Dalgıç, & F. Ergen (Eds.), *Handbook of Research on the Impacts and Implications of COVID-19 on the Tourism Industry* (pp. 786–805). IGI Global. https://doi.org/10.4018/978-1-7998-8231-2.ch038

Bureš, V. (2018). Industry 4.0 From the Systems Engineering Perspective: Alternative Holistic Framework Development. In R. Brunet-Thornton & F. Martinez (Eds.), *Analyzing the Impacts of Industry 4.0 in Modern Business Environments* (pp. 199–223). Hershey, PA: IGI Global. doi:10.4018/978-1-5225-3468-6.ch011

Buzady, Z. (2017). Resolving the Magic Cube of Effective Case Teaching: Benchmarking Case Teaching Practices in Emerging Markets – Insights from the Central European University Business School, Hungary. In D. Latusek (Ed.), *Case Studies as a Teaching Tool in Management Education* (pp. 79–103). Hershey, PA: IGI Global. doi:10.4018/978-1-5225-0770-3.ch005

Camillo, A. (2021). *Legal Matters, Risk Management, and Risk Prevention: From Forming a Business to Legal Representation*. IGI Global. doi:10.4018/978-1-7998-4342-9.ch004

Căpusneanu, S., & Topor, D. I. (2018). Business Ethics and Cost Management in SMEs: Theories of Business Ethics and Cost Management Ethos. In I. Oncioiu (Ed.), *Ethics and Decision-Making for Sustainable Business Practices* (pp. 109–127). Hershey, PA: IGI Global. doi:10.4018/978-1-5225-3773-1.ch007

Chan, R. L., Mo, P. L., & Moon, K. K. (2018). Strategic and Tactical Measures in Managing Enterprise Risks: A Study of the Textile and Apparel Industry. In K. Strang, M. Korstanje, & N. Vajjhala (Eds.), *Research, Practices, and Innovations in Global Risk and Contingency Management* (pp. 1–19). Hershey, PA: IGI Global. doi:10.4018/978-1-5225-4754-9.ch001

Charlier, S. D., Burke-Smalley, L. A., & Fisher, S. L. (2018). Undergraduate Programs in the U.S: A Contextual and Content-Based Analysis. In J. Mendy (Ed.), *Teaching Human Resources and Organizational Behavior at the College Level* (pp. 26–57). Hershey, PA: IGI Global. doi:10.4018/978-1-5225-2820-3.ch002

Chumillas, J., Güell, M., & Quer, P. (2022). The Use of ICT in Tourist and Educational Literary Routes: The Role of the Guide. In C. Ramos, S. Quinteiro, & A. Gonçalves (Eds.), *ICT as Innovator Between Tourism and Culture* (pp. 15–29). IGI Global. https://doi.org/10.4018/978-1-7998-8165-0.ch002

Dahlberg, T., Kivijärvi, H., & Saarinen, T. (2017). IT Investment Consistency and Other Factors Influencing the Success of IT Performance. In S. De Haes & W. Van Grembergen (Eds.), *Strategic IT Governance and Alignment in Business Settings* (pp. 176–208). Hershey, PA: IGI Global. doi:10.4018/978-1-5225-0861-8.ch007

Damnjanović, A. M. (2017). Knowledge Management Optimization through IT and E-Business Utilization: A Qualitative Study on Serbian SMEs. In M. Vemić (Ed.), *Optimal Management Strategies in Small and Medium Enterprises* (pp. 249–267). Hershey, PA: IGI Global. doi:10.4018/978-1-5225-1949-2.ch012

Daneshpour, H. (2017). Integrating Sustainable Development into Project Portfolio Management through Application of Open Innovation. In M. Vemić (Ed.), *Optimal Management Strategies in Small and Medium Enterprises* (pp. 370–387). Hershey, PA: IGI Global. doi:10.4018/978-1-5225-1949-2.ch017

Daniel, A. D., & Reis de Castro, V. (2018). Entrepreneurship Education: How to Measure the Impact on Nascent Entrepreneurs. In A. Carrizo Moreira, J. Guilherme Leitão Dantas, & F. Manuel Valente (Eds.), *Nascent Entrepreneurship and Successful New Venture Creation* (pp. 85–110). Hershey, PA: IGI Global. doi:10.4018/978-1-5225-2936-1.ch004

David, R., Swami, B. N., & Tangirala, S. (2018). Ethics Impact on Knowledge Management in Organizational Development: A Case Study. In N. Baporikar (Ed.), *Global Practices in Knowledge Management for Societal and Organizational Development* (pp. 19–45). Hershey, PA: IGI Global. doi:10.4018/978-1-5225-3009-1.ch002

De Uña-Álvarez, E., & Villarino-Pérez, M. (2022). Fostering Ecocultural Resources, Identity, and Tourism in Inland Territories (Galicia, NW Spain). In G. Fernandes (Ed.), *Challenges and New Opportunities for Tourism in Inland Territories: Ecocultural Resources and Sustainable Initiatives* (pp. 1-16). IGI Global. https://doi.org/10.4018/978-1-7998-7339-6.ch001

Delias, P., & Lakiotaki, K. (2018). Discovering Process Horizontal Boundaries to Facilitate Process Comprehension. *International Journal of Operations Research and Information Systems*, *9*(2), 1–31. doi:10.4018/IJORIS.2018040101

Denholm, J., & Lee-Davies, L. (2018). Success Factors for Games in Business and Project Management. In *Enhancing Education and Training Initiatives Through Serious Games* (pp. 34–68). Hershey, PA: IGI Global. doi:10.4018/978-1-5225-3689-5.ch002

Deshpande, M. (2017). Best Practices in Management Institutions for Global Leadership: Policy Aspects. In N. Baporikar (Ed.), *Management Education for Global Leadership* (pp. 1–27). Hershey, PA: IGI Global. doi:10.4018/978-1-5225-1013-0.ch001

Deshpande, M. (2018). Policy Perspectives for SMEs Knowledge Management. In N. Baporikar (Ed.), *Knowledge Integration Strategies for Entrepreneurship and Sustainability* (pp. 23–46). Hershey, PA: IGI Global. doi:10.4018/978-1-5225-5115-7.ch002

Dezdar, S. (2017). ERP Implementation Projects in Asian Countries: A Comparative Study on Iran and China. *International Journal of Information Technology Project Management*, *8*(3), 52–68. doi:10.4018/IJITPM.2017070104

Domingos, D., Respício, A., & Martinho, R. (2017). Reliability of IoT-Aware BPMN Healthcare Processes. In C. Reis & M. Maximiano (Eds.), *Internet of Things and Advanced Application in Healthcare* (pp. 214–248). Hershey, PA: IGI Global. doi:10.4018/978-1-5225-1820-4.ch008

Dosumu, O., Hussain, J., & El-Gohary, H. (2017). An Exploratory Study of the Impact of Government Policies on the Development of Small and Medium Enterprises in Developing Countries: The Case of Nigeria. *International Journal of Customer Relationship Marketing and Management*, *8*(4), 51–62. doi:10.4018/IJCRMM.2017100104

Durst, S., Bruns, G., & Edvardsson, I. R. (2017). Retaining Knowledge in Smaller Building and Construction Firms. *International Journal of Knowledge and Systems Science*, *8*(3), 1–12. doi:10.4018/IJKSS.2017070101

Edvardsson, I. R., & Durst, S. (2017). Outsourcing, Knowledge, and Learning: A Critical Review. *International Journal of Knowledge-Based Organizations*, *7*(2), 13–26. doi:10.4018/IJKBO.2017040102

Edwards, J. S. (2018). Integrating Knowledge Management and Business Processes. In M. Khosrow-Pour, D.B.A. (Ed.), Encyclopedia of Information Science and Technology, Fourth Edition (pp. 5046-5055). Hershey, PA: IGI Global. doi:10.4018/978-1-5225-2255-3.ch437

Eichelberger, S., & Peters, M. (2021). Family Firm Management in Turbulent Times: Opportunities for Responsible Tourism. In A. Zehrer, G. Glowka, K. Schwaiger, & V. Ranacher-Lackner (Eds.), *Resiliency Models and Addressing Future Risks for Family Firms in the Tourism Industry* (pp. 103–124). IGI Global. https://doi.org/10.4018/978-1-7998-7352-5.ch005

Eide, D., Hjalager, A., & Hansen, M. (2022). Innovative Certifications in Adventure Tourism: Attributes and Diffusion. In R. Augusto Costa, F. Brandão, Z. Breda, & C. Costa (Eds.), *Planning and Managing the Experience Economy in Tourism* (pp. 161-175). IGI Global. https://doi.org/10.4018/978-1-7998-8775-1.ch009

Ejiogu, A. O. (2018). Economics of Farm Management. In *Agricultural Finance and Opportunities for Investment and Expansion* (pp. 56–72). Hershey, PA: IGI Global. doi:10.4018/978-1-5225-3059-6.ch003

Ekanem, I., & Abiade, G. E. (2018). Factors Influencing the Use of E-Commerce by Small Enterprises in Nigeria. *International Journal of ICT Research in Africa and the Middle East, 7*(1), 37–53. doi:10.4018/IJICTRAME.2018010103

Ekanem, I., & Alrossais, L. A. (2017). Succession Challenges Facing Family Businesses in Saudi Arabia. In P. Zgheib (Ed.), *Entrepreneurship and Business Innovation in the Middle East* (pp. 122–146). Hershey, PA: IGI Global. doi:10.4018/978-1-5225-2066-5.ch007

El Faquih, L., & Fredj, M. (2017). Ontology-Based Framework for Quality in Configurable Process Models. *Journal of Electronic Commerce in Organizations, 15*(2), 48–60. doi:10.4018/JECO.2017040104

Faisal, M. N., & Talib, F. (2017). Building Ambidextrous Supply Chains in SMEs: How to Tackle the Barriers? *International Journal of Information Systems and Supply Chain Management, 10*(4), 80–100. doi:10.4018/IJISSCM.2017100105

Fernandes, T. M., Gomes, J., & Romão, M. (2017). Investments in E-Government: A Benefit Management Case Study. *International Journal of Electronic Government Research, 13*(3), 1–17. doi:10.4018/IJEGR.2017070101

Figueira, L. M., Honrado, G. R., & Dionísio, M. S. (2021). Human Capital Management in the Tourism Industry in Portugal. In V. Costa, A. Moura, & M. Mira (Eds.), *Handbook of Research on Human Capital and People Management in the Tourism Industry* (pp. 1–19). IGI Global. doi:10.4018/978-1-7998-4318-4.ch001

Gao, S. S., Oreal, S., & Zhang, J. (2018). Contemporary Financial Risk Management Perceptions and Practices of Small-Sized Chinese Businesses. In I. Management Association (Ed.), Global Business Expansion: Concepts, Methodologies, Tools, and Applications (pp. 917-931). Hershey, PA: IGI Global. doi:10.4018/978-1-5225-5481-3.ch041

Garg, R., & Berning, S. C. (2017). Indigenous Chinese Management Philosophies: Key Concepts and Relevance for Modern Chinese Firms. In B. Christiansen & G. Koc (Eds.), *Transcontinental Strategies for Industrial Development and Economic Growth* (pp. 43–57). Hershey, PA: IGI Global. doi:10.4018/978-1-5225-2160-0.ch003

Gencer, Y. G. (2017). Supply Chain Management in Retailing Business. In U. Akkucuk (Ed.), *Ethics and Sustainability in Global Supply Chain Management* (pp. 197–210). Hershey, PA: IGI Global. doi:10.4018/978-1-5225-2036-8.ch011

Gera, R., Arora, S., & Malik, S. (2021). Emotional Labor in the Tourism Industry: Strategies, Antecedents, and Outcomes. In V. Costa, A. Moura, & M. Mira (Eds.), *Handbook of Research on Human Capital and People Management in the Tourism Industry* (pp. 73–91). IGI Global. https://doi.org/10.4018/978-1-7998-4318-4.ch004

Giacosa, E. (2018). The Increasing of the Regional Development Thanks to the Luxury Business Innovation. In L. Carvalho (Ed.), *Handbook of Research on Entrepreneurial Ecosystems and Social Dynamics in a Globalized World* (pp. 260–273). Hershey, PA: IGI Global. doi:10.4018/978-1-5225-3525-6.ch011

Glowka, G., Tusch, M., & Zehrer, A. (2021). The Risk Perception of Family Business Owner-Manager in the Tourism Industry: A Qualitative Comparison of the Intra-Firm Senior and Junior Generation. In A. Zehrer, G. Glowka, K. Schwaiger, & V. Ranacher-Lackner (Eds.), *Resiliency Models and Addressing Future Risks for Family Firms in the Tourism Industry* (pp. 126–153). IGI Global. https://doi.org/10.4018/978-1-7998-7352-5.ch006

Glykas, M., & George, J. (2017). Quality and Process Management Systems in the UAE Maritime Industry. *International Journal of Productivity Management and Assessment Technologies*, *5*(1), 20–39. doi:10.4018/IJPMAT.2017010102

Glykas, M., Valiris, G., Kokkinaki, A., & Koutsoukou, Z. (2018). Banking Business Process Management Implementation. *International Journal of Productivity Management and Assessment Technologies*, *6*(1), 50–69. doi:10.4018/IJPMAT.2018010104

Gomes, J., & Romão, M. (2017). The Balanced Scorecard: Keeping Updated and Aligned with Today's Business Trends. *International Journal of Productivity Management and Assessment Technologies*, *5*(2), 1–15. doi:10.4018/IJPMAT.2017070101

Gomes, J., & Romão, M. (2017). Aligning Information Systems and Technology with Benefit Management and Balanced Scorecard. In S. De Haes & W. Van Grembergen (Eds.), *Strategic IT Governance and Alignment in Business Settings* (pp. 112–131). Hershey, PA: IGI Global. doi:10.4018/978-1-5225-0861-8.ch005

Goyal, A. (2021). Communicating and Building Destination Brands With New Media. In M. Dinis, L. Bonixe, S. Lamy, & Z. Breda (Eds.), *Impact of New Media in Tourism* (pp. 1-20). IGI Global. https://doi.org/10.4018/978-1-7998-7095-1.ch001

Grefen, P., & Turetken, O. (2017). Advanced Business Process Management in Networked E-Business Scenarios. *International Journal of E-Business Research*, *13*(4), 70–104. doi:10.4018/IJEBR.2017100105

Guasca, M., Van Broeck, A. M., & Vanneste, D. (2021). Tourism and the Social Reintegration of Colombian Ex-Combatants. In J. da Silva, Z. Breda, & F. Carbone (Eds.), *Role and Impact of Tourism in Peacebuilding and Conflict Transformation* (pp. 66-86). IGI Global. https://doi.org/10.4018/978-1-7998-5053-3.ch005

Haider, A., & Saetang, S. (2017). Strategic IT Alignment in Service Sector. In S. Rozenes & Y. Cohen (Eds.), *Handbook of Research on Strategic Alliances and Value Co-Creation in the Service Industry* (pp. 231–258). Hershey, PA: IGI Global. doi:10.4018/978-1-5225-2084-9.ch012

Hajilari, A. B., Ghadaksaz, M., & Fasghandis, G. S. (2017). Assessing Organizational Readiness for Implementing ERP System Using Fuzzy Expert System Approach. *International Journal of Enterprise Information Systems*, *13*(1), 67–85. doi:10.4018/IJEIS.2017010105

Haldorai, A., Ramu, A., & Murugan, S. (2018). Social Aware Cognitive Radio Networks: Effectiveness of Social Networks as a Strategic Tool for Organizational Business Management. In H. Bansal, G. Shrivastava, G. Nguyen, & L. Stanciu (Eds.), *Social Network Analytics for Contemporary Business Organizations* (pp. 188–202). Hershey, PA: IGI Global. doi:10.4018/978-1-5225-5097-6.ch010

Hall, O. P. Jr. (2017). Social Media Driven Management Education. *International Journal of Knowledge-Based Organizations*, *7*(2), 43–59. doi:10.4018/IJKBO.2017040104

Hanifah, H., Halim, H. A., Ahmad, N. H., & Vafaei-Zadeh, A. (2017). Innovation Culture as a Mediator Between Specific Human Capital and Innovation Performance Among Bumiputera SMEs in Malaysia. In N. Ahmad, T. Ramayah, H. Halim, & S. Rahman (Eds.), *Handbook of Research on Small and Medium Enterprises in Developing Countries* (pp. 261–279). Hershey, PA: IGI Global. doi:10.4018/978-1-5225-2165-5.ch012

Hartlieb, S., & Silvius, G. (2017). Handling Uncertainty in Project Management and Business Development: Similarities and Differences. In Y. Raydugin (Ed.), *Handbook of Research on Leveraging Risk and Uncertainties for Effective Project Management* (pp. 337–362). Hershey, PA: IGI Global. doi:10.4018/978-1-5225-1790-0.ch016

Hass, K. B. (2017). Living on the Edge: Managing Project Complexity. In Y. Raydugin (Ed.), *Handbook of Research on Leveraging Risk and Uncertainties for Effective Project Management* (pp. 177–201). Hershey, PA: IGI Global. doi:10.4018/978-1-5225-1790-0.ch009

Hawking, P., & Carmine Sellitto, C. (2017). Developing an Effective Strategy for Organizational Business Intelligence. In M. Tavana (Ed.), *Enterprise Information Systems and the Digitalization of Business Functions* (pp. 222–237). Hershey, PA: IGI Global. doi:10.4018/978-1-5225-2382-6.ch010

Hawking, P., & Sellitto, C. (2017). A Fast-Moving Consumer Goods Company and Business Intelligence Strategy Development. *International Journal of Enterprise Information Systems*, *13*(2), 22–33. doi:10.4018/IJEIS.2017040102

Hawking, P., & Sellitto, C. (2017). Business Intelligence Strategy: Two Case Studies. *International Journal of Business Intelligence Research*, *8*(2), 17–30. doi:10.4018/IJBIR.2017070102

Hee, W. J., Jalleh, G., Lai, H., & Lin, C. (2017). E-Commerce and IT Projects: Evaluation and Management Issues in Australian and Taiwanese Hospitals. *International Journal of Public Health Management and Ethics*, *2*(1), 69–90. doi:10.4018/IJPHME.2017010104

Hernandez, A. A. (2018). Exploring the Factors to Green IT Adoption of SMEs in the Philippines. *Journal of Cases on Information Technology*, *20*(2), 49–66. doi:10.4018/JCIT.2018040104

Hollman, A., Bickford, S., & Hollman, T. (2017). Cyber InSecurity: A Post-Mortem Attempt to Assess Cyber Problems from IT and Business Management Perspectives. *Journal of Cases on Information Technology*, *19*(3), 42–70. doi:10.4018/JCIT.2017070104

Ibrahim, F., & Zainin, N. M. (2021). Exploring the Technological Impacts: The Case of Museums in Brunei Darussalam. *International Journal of Tourism and Hospitality Management in the Digital Age*, *5*(1), 1–18. https://doi.org/10.4018/IJTHMDA.2021010101

Igbinakhase, I. (2017). Responsible and Sustainable Management Practices in Developing and Developed Business Environments. In Z. Fields (Ed.), *Collective Creativity for Responsible and Sustainable Business Practice* (pp. 180–207). Hershey, PA: IGI Global. doi:10.4018/978-1-5225-1823-5.ch010

Iwata, J. J., & Hoskins, R. G. (2017). Managing Indigenous Knowledge in Tanzania: A Business Perspective. In P. Jain & N. Mnjama (Eds.), *Managing Knowledge Resources and Records in Modern Organizations* (pp. 198–214). Hershey, PA: IGI Global. doi:10.4018/978-1-5225-1965-2.ch012

Jain, P. (2017). Ethical and Legal Issues in Knowledge Management Life-Cycle in Business. In P. Jain & N. Mnjama (Eds.), *Managing Knowledge Resources and Records in Modern Organizations* (pp. 82–101). Hershey, PA: IGI Global. doi:10.4018/978-1-5225-1965-2.ch006

James, S., & Hauli, E. (2017). Holistic Management Education at Tanzanian Rural Development Planning Institute. In N. Baporikar (Ed.), *Management Education for Global Leadership* (pp. 112–136). Hershey, PA: IGI Global. doi:10.4018/978-1-5225-1013-0.ch006

Janošková, M., Csikósová, A., & Čulková, K. (2018). Measurement of Company Performance as Part of Its Strategic Management. In R. Leon (Ed.), *Managerial Strategies for Business Sustainability During Turbulent Times* (pp. 309–335). Hershey, PA: IGI Global. doi:10.4018/978-1-5225-2716-9.ch017

Jean-Vasile, A., & Alecu, A. (2017). Theoretical and Practical Approaches in Understanding the Influences of Cost-Productivity-Profit Trinomial in Contemporary Enterprises. In A. Jean Vasile & D. Nicolò (Eds.), *Sustainable Entrepreneurship and Investments in the Green Economy* (pp. 28–62). Hershey, PA: IGI Global. doi:10.4018/978-1-5225-2075-7.ch002

Joia, L. A., & Correia, J. C. (2018). CIO Competencies From the IT Professional Perspective: Insights From Brazil. *Journal of Global Information Management*, *26*(2), 74–103. doi:10.4018/JGIM.2018040104

Juma, A., & Mzera, N. (2017). Knowledge Management and Records Management and Competitive Advantage in Business. In P. Jain & N. Mnjama (Eds.), *Managing Knowledge Resources and Records in Modern Organizations* (pp. 15–28). Hershey, PA: IGI Global. doi:10.4018/978-1-5225-1965-2.ch002

K., I., & A, V. (2018). Monitoring and Auditing in the Cloud. In K. Munir (Ed.), *Cloud Computing Technologies for Green Enterprises* (pp. 318-350). Hershey, PA: IGI Global. https://doi.org/ doi:10.4018/978-1-5225-3038-1.ch013

Kabra, G., Ghosh, V., & Ramesh, A. (2018). Enterprise Integrated Business Process Management and Business Intelligence Framework for Business Process Sustainability. In A. Paul, D. Bhattacharyya, & S. Anand (Eds.), *Green Initiatives for Business Sustainability and Value Creation* (pp. 228–238). Hershey, PA: IGI Global. doi:10.4018/978-1-5225-2662-9.ch010

Kaoud, M. (2017). Investigation of Customer Knowledge Management: A Case Study Research. *International Journal of Service Science, Management, Engineering, and Technology*, *8*(2), 12–22. doi:10.4018/IJSSMET.2017040102

Katuu, S. (2018). A Comparative Assessment of Enterprise Content Management Maturity Models. In N. Gwangwava & M. Mutingi (Eds.), *E-Manufacturing and E-Service Strategies in Contemporary Organizations* (pp. 93–118). Hershey, PA: IGI Global. doi:10.4018/978-1-5225-3628-4.ch005

Khan, M. Y., & Abir, T. (2022). The Role of Social Media Marketing in the Tourism and Hospitality Industry: A Conceptual Study on Bangladesh. In C. Ramos, S. Quinteiro, & A. Gonçalves (Eds.), *ICT as Innovator Between Tourism and Culture* (pp. 213–229). IGI Global. https://doi.org/10.4018/978-1-7998-8165-0.ch013

Kinnunen, S., Ylä-Kujala, A., Marttonen-Arola, S., Kärri, T., & Baglee, D. (2018). Internet of Things in Asset Management: Insights from Industrial Professionals and Academia. *International Journal of Service Science, Management, Engineering, and Technology*, *9*(2), 104–119. doi:10.4018/IJSSMET.2018040105

Klein, A. Z., Sabino de Freitas, A., Machado, L., Freitas, J. C. Jr, Graziola, P. G. Jr, & Schlemmer, E. (2017). Virtual Worlds Applications for Management Education. In L. Tomei (Ed.), *Exploring the New Era of Technology-Infused Education* (pp. 279–299). Hershey, PA: IGI Global. doi:10.4018/978-1-5225-1709-2.ch017

Kővári, E., Saleh, M., & Steinbachné Hajmásy, G. (2022). The Impact of Corporate Digital Responsibility (CDR) on Internal Stakeholders' Satisfaction in Hungarian Upscale Hotels. In M. Valeri (Ed.), *New Governance and Management in Touristic Destinations* (pp. 35–51). IGI Global. https://doi.org/10.4018/978-1-6684-3889-3.ch003

Kożuch, B., & Jabłoński, A. (2017). Adopting the Concept of Business Models in Public Management. In M. Lewandowski & B. Kożuch (Eds.), *Public Sector Entrepreneurship and the Integration of Innovative Business Models* (pp. 10–46). Hershey, PA: IGI Global. doi:10.4018/978-1-5225-2215-7.ch002

Kumar, J., Adhikary, A., & Jha, A. (2017). Small Active Investors' Perceptions and Preferences Towards Tax Saving Mutual Fund Schemes in Eastern India: An Empirical Note. *International Journal of Asian Business and Information Management, 8*(2), 35–45. doi:10.4018/IJABIM.2017040103

Latusi, S., & Fissore, M. (2021). Pilgrimage Routes to Happiness: Comparing the Camino de Santiago and Via Francigena. In A. Perinotto, V. Mayer, & J. Soares (Eds.), *Rebuilding and Restructuring the Tourism Industry: Infusion of Happiness and Quality of Life* (pp. 157–182). IGI Global. https://doi.org/10.4018/978-1-7998-7239-9.ch008

Lavassani, K. M., & Movahedi, B. (2017). Applications Driven Information Systems: Beyond Networks toward Business Ecosystems. *International Journal of Innovation in the Digital Economy, 8*(1), 61–75. doi:10.4018/IJIDE.2017010104

Lazzareschi, V. H., & Brito, M. S. (2017). Strategic Information Management: Proposal of Business Project Model. In G. Jamil, A. Soares, & C. Pessoa (Eds.), *Handbook of Research on Information Management for Effective Logistics and Supply Chains* (pp. 59–88). Hershey, PA: IGI Global. doi:10.4018/978-1-5225-0973-8.ch004

Lechuga Sancho, M. P., & Martín Navarro, A. (2022). Evolution of the Literature on Social Responsibility in the Tourism Sector: A Systematic Literature Review. In G. Fernandes (Ed.), *Challenges and New Opportunities for Tourism in Inland Territories: Ecocultural Resources and Sustainable Initiatives* (pp. 169–186). IGI Global. https://doi.org/10.4018/978-1-7998-7339-6.ch010

Lederer, M., Kurz, M., & Lazarov, P. (2017). Usage and Suitability of Methods for Strategic Business Process Initiatives: A Multi Case Study Research. *International Journal of Productivity Management and Assessment Technologies, 5*(1), 40–51. doi:10.4018/IJPMAT.2017010103

Lee, I. (2017). A Social Enterprise Business Model and a Case Study of Pacific Community Ventures (PCV). In V. Potocan, M. Ünğan, & Z. Nedelko (Eds.), *Handbook of Research on Managerial Solutions in Non-Profit Organizations* (pp. 182–204). Hershey, PA: IGI Global. doi:10.4018/978-1-5225-0731-4.ch009

Leon, L. A., Seal, K. C., Przasnyski, Z. H., & Wiedenman, I. (2017). Skills and Competencies Required for Jobs in Business Analytics: A Content Analysis of Job Advertisements Using Text Mining. *International Journal of Business Intelligence Research*, *8*(1), 1–25. doi:10.4018/IJBIR.2017010101

Levy, C. L., & Elias, N. I. (2017). SOHO Users' Perceptions of Reliability and Continuity of Cloud-Based Services. In M. Moore (Ed.), *Cybersecurity Breaches and Issues Surrounding Online Threat Protection* (pp. 248–287). Hershey, PA: IGI Global. doi:10.4018/978-1-5225-1941-6.ch011

Levy, M. (2018). Change Management Serving Knowledge Management and Organizational Development: Reflections and Review. In N. Baporikar (Ed.), *Global Practices in Knowledge Management for Societal and Organizational Development* (pp. 256–270). Hershey, PA: IGI Global. doi:10.4018/978-1-5225-3009-1.ch012

Lewandowski, M. (2017). Public Organizations and Business Model Innovation: The Role of Public Service Design. In M. Lewandowski & B. Kożuch (Eds.), *Public Sector Entrepreneurship and the Integration of Innovative Business Models* (pp. 47–72). Hershey, PA: IGI Global. doi:10.4018/978-1-5225-2215-7.ch003

Lhannaoui, H., Kabbaj, M. I., & Bakkoury, Z. (2017). A Survey of Risk-Aware Business Process Modelling. *International Journal of Risk and Contingency Management*, *6*(3), 14–26. doi:10.4018/IJRCM.2017070102

Li, J., Sun, W., Jiang, W., Yang, H., & Zhang, L. (2017). How the Nature of Exogenous Shocks and Crises Impact Company Performance?: The Effects of Industry Characteristics. *International Journal of Risk and Contingency Management*, *6*(4), 40–55. doi:10.4018/IJRCM.2017100103

Lopez-Fernandez, M., Perez-Perez, M., Serrano-Bedia, A., & Cobo-Gonzalez, A. (2021). Small and Medium Tourism Enterprise Survival in Times of Crisis: "El Capricho de Gaudí. In D. Toubes & N. Araújo-Vila (Eds.), *Risk, Crisis, and Disaster Management in Small and Medium-Sized Tourism Enterprises* (pp. 103–129). IGI Global. doi:10.4018/978-1-7998-6996-2.ch005

Mahajan, A., Maidullah, S., & Hossain, M. R. (2022). Experience Toward Smart Tour Guide Apps in Travelling: An Analysis of Users' Reviews on Audio Odigos and Trip My Way. In R. Augusto Costa, F. Brandão, Z. Breda, & C. Costa (Eds.), *Planning and Managing the Experience Economy in Tourism* (pp. 255-273). IGI Global. https://doi.org/10.4018/978-1-7998-8775-1.ch014

Malega, P. (2017). Small and Medium Enterprises in the Slovak Republic: Status and Competitiveness of SMEs in the Global Markets and Possibilities of Optimization. In M. Vemić (Ed.), *Optimal Management Strategies in Small and Medium Enterprises* (pp. 102–124). Hershey, PA: IGI Global. doi:10.4018/978-1-5225-1949-2.ch006

Malewska, K. M. (2017). Intuition in Decision-Making on the Example of a Non-Profit Organization. In V. Potocan, M. Üngan, & Z. Nedelko (Eds.), *Handbook of Research on Managerial Solutions in Non-Profit Organizations* (pp. 378–399). Hershey, PA: IGI Global. doi:10.4018/978-1-5225-0731-4.ch018

Maroofi, F. (2017). Entrepreneurial Orientation and Organizational Learning Ability Analysis for Innovation and Firm Performance. In N. Baporikar (Ed.), *Innovation and Shifting Perspectives in Management Education* (pp. 144–165). Hershey, PA: IGI Global. doi:10.4018/978-1-5225-1019-2.ch007

Marques, M., Moleiro, D., Brito, T. M., & Marques, T. (2021). Customer Relationship Management as an Important Relationship Marketing Tool: The Case of the Hospitality Industry in Estoril Coast. In M. Dinis, L. Bonixe, S. Lamy, & Z. Breda (Eds.), Impact of New Media in Tourism (pp. 39-56). IGI Global. https://doi.org/doi:10.4018/978-1-7998-7095-1.ch003

Martins, P. V., & Zacarias, M. (2017). A Web-based Tool for Business Process Improvement. *International Journal of Web Portals*, *9*(2), 68–84. doi:10.4018/IJWP.2017070104

Matthies, B., & Coners, A. (2017). Exploring the Conceptual Nature of e-Business Projects. *Journal of Electronic Commerce in Organizations*, *15*(3), 33–63. doi:10.4018/JECO.2017070103

Mayer, V. F., Fraga, C. C., & Silva, L. C. (2021). Contributions of Neurosciences to Studies of Well-Being in Tourism. In A. Perinotto, V. Mayer, & J. Soares (Eds.), *Rebuilding and Restructuring the Tourism Industry: Infusion of Happiness and Quality of Life* (pp. 108–128). IGI Global. https://doi.org/10.4018/978-1-7998-7239-9.ch006

McKee, J. (2018). Architecture as a Tool to Solve Business Planning Problems. In M. Khosrow-Pour, D.B.A. (Ed.), Encyclopedia of Information Science and Technology, Fourth Edition (pp. 573-586). Hershey, PA: IGI Global. doi:10.4018/978-1-5225-2255-3.ch050

McMurray, A. J., Cross, J., & Caponecchia, C. (2018). The Risk Management Profession in Australia: Business Continuity Plan Practices. In N. Bajgoric (Ed.), *Always-On Enterprise Information Systems for Modern Organizations* (pp. 112–129). Hershey, PA: IGI Global. doi:10.4018/978-1-5225-3704-5.ch006

Meddah, I. H., & Belkadi, K. (2018). Mining Patterns Using Business Process Management. In R. Hamou (Ed.), *Handbook of Research on Biomimicry in Information Retrieval and Knowledge Management* (pp. 78–89). Hershey, PA: IGI Global. doi:10.4018/978-1-5225-3004-6.ch005

Melian, A. G., & Camprubí, R. (2021). The Accessibility of Museum Websites: The Case of Barcelona. In C. Eusébio, L. Teixeira, & M. Carneiro (Eds.), *ICT Tools and Applications for Accessible Tourism* (pp. 234–255). IGI Global. https://doi.org/10.4018/978-1-7998-6428-8.ch011

Mendes, L. (2017). TQM and Knowledge Management: An Integrated Approach Towards Tacit Knowledge Management. In D. Jaziri-Bouagina & G. Jamil (Eds.), *Handbook of Research on Tacit Knowledge Management for Organizational Success* (pp. 236–263). Hershey, PA: IGI Global. doi:10.4018/978-1-5225-2394-9.ch009

Menezes, V. D., & Cavagnaro, E. (2021). Communicating Sustainable Initiatives in the Hotel Industry: The Case of the Hotel Jakarta Amsterdam. In F. Brandão, Z. Breda, R. Costa, & C. Costa (Eds.), *Handbook of Research on the Role of Tourism in Achieving Sustainable Development Goals* (pp. 224-234). IGI Global. https://doi.org/10.4018/978-1-7998-5691-7.ch013

Menezes, V. D., & Cavagnaro, E. (2021). Communicating Sustainable Initiatives in the Hotel Industry: The Case of the Hotel Jakarta Amsterdam. In F. Brandão, Z. Breda, R. Costa, & C. Costa (Eds.), *Handbook of Research on the Role of Tourism in Achieving Sustainable Development Goals* (pp. 224-234). IGI Global. https://doi.org/10.4018/978-1-7998-5691-7.ch013

Mitas, O., Bastiaansen, M., & Boode, W. (2022). If You're Happy, I'm Happy: Emotion Contagion at a Tourist Information Center. In R. Augusto Costa, F. Brandão, Z. Breda, & C. Costa (Eds.), *Planning and Managing the Experience Economy in Tourism* (pp. 122-140). IGI Global. https://doi.org/10.4018/978-1-7998-8775-1.ch007

Mnjama, N. M. (2017). Preservation of Recorded Information in Public and Private Sector Organizations. In P. Jain & N. Mnjama (Eds.), *Managing Knowledge Resources and Records in Modern Organizations* (pp. 149–167). Hershey, PA: IGI Global. doi:10.4018/978-1-5225-1965-2.ch009

Mokoqama, M., & Fields, Z. (2017). Principles of Responsible Management Education (PRME): Call for Responsible Management Education. In Z. Fields (Ed.), *Collective Creativity for Responsible and Sustainable Business Practice* (pp. 229–241). Hershey, PA: IGI Global. doi:10.4018/978-1-5225-1823-5.ch012

Monteiro, A., Lopes, S., & Carbone, F. (2021). Academic Mobility: Bridging Tourism and Peace Education. In J. da Silva, Z. Breda, & F. Carbone (Eds.), *Role and Impact of Tourism in Peacebuilding and Conflict Transformation* (pp. 275-301). IGI Global. https://doi.org/10.4018/978-1-7998-5053-3.ch016

Muniapan, B. (2017). Philosophy and Management: The Relevance of Vedanta in Management. In P. Ordóñez de Pablos (Ed.), *Managerial Strategies and Solutions for Business Success in Asia* (pp. 124–139). Hershey, PA: IGI Global. doi:10.4018/978-1-5225-1886-0.ch007

Murad, S. E., & Dowaji, S. (2017). Using Value-Based Approach for Managing Cloud-Based Services. In A. Turuk, B. Sahoo, & S. Addya (Eds.), *Resource Management and Efficiency in Cloud Computing Environments* (pp. 33–60). Hershey, PA: IGI Global. doi:10.4018/978-1-5225-1721-4.ch002

Mutahar, A. M., Daud, N. M., Thurasamy, R., Isaac, O., & Abdulsalam, R. (2018). The Mediating of Perceived Usefulness and Perceived Ease of Use: The Case of Mobile Banking in Yemen. *International Journal of Technology Diffusion*, *9*(2), 21–40. doi:10.4018/IJTD.2018040102

Naidoo, V. (2017). E-Learning and Management Education at African Universities. In N. Baporikar (Ed.), *Management Education for Global Leadership* (pp. 181–201). Hershey, PA: IGI Global. doi:10.4018/978-1-5225-1013-0.ch009

Naidoo, V., & Igbinakhase, I. (2018). Opportunities and Challenges of Knowledge Retention in SMEs. In N. Baporikar (Ed.), *Knowledge Integration Strategies for Entrepreneurship and Sustainability* (pp. 70–94). Hershey, PA: IGI Global. doi:10.4018/978-1-5225-5115-7.ch004

Naumov, N., & Costandachi, G. (2021). Creativity and Entrepreneurship: Gastronomic Tourism in Mexico. In J. Soares (Ed.), *Innovation and Entrepreneurial Opportunities in Community Tourism* (pp. 90–108). IGI Global. https://doi.org/10.4018/978-1-7998-4855-4.ch006

Nayak, S., & Prabhu, N. (2017). Paradigm Shift in Management Education: Need for a Cross Functional Perspective. In N. Baporikar (Ed.), *Management Education for Global Leadership* (pp. 241–255). Hershey, PA: IGI Global. doi:10.4018/978-1-5225-1013-0.ch012

Nedelko, Z., & Potocan, V. (2017). Management Solutions in Non-Profit Organizations: Case of Slovenia. In V. Potocan, M. Ünğan, & Z. Nedelko (Eds.), *Handbook of Research on Managerial Solutions in Non-Profit Organizations* (pp. 1–22). Hershey, PA: IGI Global. doi:10.4018/978-1-5225-0731-4.ch001

Nedelko, Z., & Potocan, V. (2017). Priority of Management Tools Utilization among Managers: International Comparison. In V. Wang (Ed.), *Encyclopedia of Strategic Leadership and Management* (pp. 1083–1094). Hershey, PA: IGI Global. doi:10.4018/978-1-5225-1049-9.ch075

Nedelko, Z., Raudeliūnienė, J., & Črešnar, R. (2018). Knowledge Dynamics in Supply Chain Management. In N. Baporikar (Ed.), *Knowledge Integration Strategies for Entrepreneurship and Sustainability* (pp. 150–166). Hershey, PA: IGI Global. doi:10.4018/978-1-5225-5115-7.ch008

Nguyen, H. T., & Hipsher, S. A. (2018). Innovation and Creativity Used by Private Sector Firms in a Resources-Constrained Environment. In S. Hipsher (Ed.), *Examining the Private Sector's Role in Wealth Creation and Poverty Reduction* (pp. 219–238). Hershey, PA: IGI Global. doi:10.4018/978-1-5225-3117-3.ch010

Obicci, P. A. (2017). Risk Sharing in a Partnership. In *Risk Management Strategies in Public-Private Partnerships* (pp. 115–152). Hershey, PA: IGI Global. doi:10.4018/978-1-5225-2503-5.ch004

Obidallah, W. J., & Raahemi, B. (2017). Managing Changes in Service Oriented Virtual Organizations: A Structural and Procedural Framework to Facilitate the Process of Change. *Journal of Electronic Commerce in Organizations, 15*(1), 59–83. doi:10.4018/JECO.2017010104

Ojo, O. (2017). Impact of Innovation on the Entrepreneurial Success in Selected Business Enterprises in South-West Nigeria. *International Journal of Innovation in the Digital Economy, 8*(2), 29–38. doi:10.4018/IJIDE.2017040103

Okdinawati, L., Simatupang, T. M., & Sunitiyoso, Y. (2017). Multi-Agent Reinforcement Learning for Value Co-Creation of Collaborative Transportation Management (CTM). *International Journal of Information Systems and Supply Chain Management, 10*(3), 84–95. doi:10.4018/IJISSCM.2017070105

Olivera, V. A., & Carrillo, I. M. (2021). Organizational Culture: A Key Element for the Development of Mexican Micro and Small Tourist Companies. In J. Soares (Ed.), *Innovation and Entrepreneurial Opportunities in Community Tourism* (pp. 227–242). IGI Global. doi:10.4018/978-1-7998-4855-4.ch013

Ossorio, M. (2022). Corporate Museum Experiences in Enogastronomic Tourism. In R. Augusto Costa, F. Brandão, Z. Breda, & C. Costa (Eds.), Planning and Managing the Experience Economy in Tourism (pp. 107-121). IGI Global. https://doi.org/doi:10.4018/978-1-7998-8775-1.ch006

Ossorio, M. (2022). Enogastronomic Tourism in Times of Pandemic. In G. Fernandes (Ed.), *Challenges and New Opportunities for Tourism in Inland Territories: Ecocultural Resources and Sustainable Initiatives* (pp. 241–255). IGI Global. https://doi.org/10.4018/978-1-7998-7339-6.ch014

Özekici, Y. K. (2022). ICT as an Acculturative Agent and Its Role in the Tourism Context: Introduction, Acculturation Theory, Progress of the Acculturation Theory in Extant Literature. In C. Ramos, S. Quinteiro, & A. Gonçalves (Eds.), *ICT as Innovator Between Tourism and Culture* (pp. 42–66). IGI Global. https://doi.org/10.4018/978-1-7998-8165-0.ch004

Pal, K. (2018). Building High Quality Big Data-Based Applications in Supply Chains. In A. Kumar & S. Saurav (Eds.), *Supply Chain Management Strategies and Risk Assessment in Retail Environments* (pp. 1–24). Hershey, PA: IGI Global. doi:10.4018/978-1-5225-3056-5.ch001

Palos-Sanchez, P. R., & Correia, M. B. (2018). Perspectives of the Adoption of Cloud Computing in the Tourism Sector. In J. Rodrigues, C. Ramos, P. Cardoso, & C. Henriques (Eds.), *Handbook of Research on Technological Developments for Cultural Heritage and eTourism Applications* (pp. 377–400). Hershey, PA: IGI Global. doi:10.4018/978-1-5225-2927-9.ch018

Papadopoulou, G. (2021). Promoting Gender Equality and Women Empowerment in the Tourism Sector. In F. Brandão, Z. Breda, R. Costa, & C. Costa (Eds.), Handbook of Research on the Role of Tourism in Achieving Sustainable Development Goals (pp. 152-174). IGI Global. https://doi.org/ doi:10.4018/978-1-7998-5691-7.ch009

Papp-Váry, Á. F., & Tóth, T. Z. (2022). Analysis of Budapest as a Film Tourism Destination. In R. Baleiro & R. Pereira (Eds.), *Global Perspectives on Literary Tourism and Film-Induced Tourism* (pp. 257-279). IGI Global. https://doi.org/10.4018/978-1-7998-8262-6.ch014

Patiño, B. E. (2017). New Generation Management by Convergence and Individual Identity: A Systemic and Human-Oriented Approach. In N. Baporikar (Ed.), *Innovation and Shifting Perspectives in Management Education* (pp. 119–143). Hershey, PA: IGI Global. doi:10.4018/978-1-5225-1019-2.ch006

Patro, C. S. (2021). Digital Tourism: Influence of E-Marketing Technology. In M. Dinis, L. Bonixe, S. Lamy, & Z. Breda (Eds.), *Impact of New Media in Tourism* (pp. 234-254). IGI Global. https://doi.org/10.4018/978-1-7998-7095-1.ch014

Pawliczek, A., & Rössler, M. (2017). Knowledge of Management Tools and Systems in SMEs: Knowledge Transfer in Management. In A. Bencsik (Ed.), *Knowledge Management Initiatives and Strategies in Small and Medium Enterprises* (pp. 180–203). Hershey, PA: IGI Global. doi:10.4018/978-1-5225-1642-2.ch009

Pejic-Bach, M., Omazic, M. A., Aleksic, A., & Zoroja, J. (2018). Knowledge-Based Decision Making: A Multi-Case Analysis. In R. Leon (Ed.), *Managerial Strategies for Business Sustainability During Turbulent Times* (pp. 160–184). Hershey, PA: IGI Global. doi:10.4018/978-1-5225-2716-9.ch009

Perano, M., Hysa, X., & Calabrese, M. (2018). Strategic Planning, Cultural Context, and Business Continuity Management: Business Cases in the City of Shkoder. In A. Presenza & L. Sheehan (Eds.), *Geopolitics and Strategic Management in the Global Economy* (pp. 57–77). Hershey, PA: IGI Global. doi:10.4018/978-1-5225-2673-5.ch004

Pereira, R., Mira da Silva, M., & Lapão, L. V. (2017). IT Governance Maturity Patterns in Portuguese Healthcare. In S. De Haes & W. Van Grembergen (Eds.), *Strategic IT Governance and Alignment in Business Settings* (pp. 24–52). Hershey, PA: IGI Global. doi:10.4018/978-1-5225-0861-8.ch002

Pérez-Uribe, R. I., Torres, D. A., Jurado, S. P., & Prada, D. M. (2018). Cloud Tools for the Development of Project Management in SMEs. In R. Perez-Uribe, C. Salcedo-Perez, & D. Ocampo-Guzman (Eds.), *Handbook of Research on Intrapreneurship and Organizational Sustainability in SMEs* (pp. 95–120). Hershey, PA: IGI Global. doi:10.4018/978-1-5225-3543-0.ch005

Petrisor, I., & Cozmiuc, D. (2017). Global Supply Chain Management Organization at Siemens in the Advent of Industry 4.0. In L. Saglietto & C. Cezanne (Eds.), *Global Intermediation and Logistics Service Providers* (pp. 123–142). Hershey, PA: IGI Global. doi:10.4018/978-1-5225-2133-4.ch007

Pierce, J. M., Velliaris, D. M., & Edwards, J. (2017). A Living Case Study: A Journey Not a Destination. In N. Silton (Ed.), *Exploring the Benefits of Creativity in Education, Media, and the Arts* (pp. 158–178). Hershey, PA: IGI Global. doi:10.4018/978-1-5225-0504-4.ch008

Pipia, S., & Pipia, S. (2021). Challenges of Religious Tourism in the Conflict Region: An Example of Jerusalem. In E. Alaverdov & M. Bari (Eds.), *Global Development of Religious Tourism* (pp. 135-148). IGI Global. https://doi.org/10.4018/978-1-7998-5792-1.ch009

Poulaki, P., Kritikos, A., Vasilakis, N., & Valeri, M. (2022). The Contribution of Female Creativity to the Development of Gastronomic Tourism in Greece: The Case of the Island of Naxos in the South Aegean Region. In M. Valeri (Ed.), *New Governance and Management in Touristic Destinations* (pp. 246–258). IGI Global. https://doi.org/10.4018/978-1-6684-3889-3.ch015

Radosavljevic, M., & Andjelkovic, A. (2017). Multi-Criteria Decision Making Approach for Choosing Business Process for the Improvement: Upgrading of the Six Sigma Methodology. In J. Stanković, P. Delias, S. Marinković, & S. Rochhia (Eds.), *Tools and Techniques for Economic Decision Analysis* (pp. 225–247). Hershey, PA: IGI Global. doi:10.4018/978-1-5225-0959-2.ch011

Radovic, V. M. (2017). Corporate Sustainability and Responsibility and Disaster Risk Reduction: A Serbian Overview. In M. Camilleri (Ed.), *CSR 2.0 and the New Era of Corporate Citizenship* (pp. 147–164). Hershey, PA: IGI Global. doi:10.4018/978-1-5225-1842-6.ch008

Raghunath, K. M., Devi, S. L., & Patro, C. S. (2018). Impact of Risk Assessment Models on Risk Factors: A Holistic Outlook. In K. Strang, M. Korstanje, & N. Vajjhala (Eds.), *Research, Practices, and Innovations in Global Risk and Contingency Management* (pp. 134–153). Hershey, PA: IGI Global. doi:10.4018/978-1-5225-4754-9.ch008

Raman, A., & Goyal, D. P. (2017). Extending IMPLEMENT Framework for Enterprise Information Systems Implementation to Information System Innovation. In M. Tavana (Ed.), *Enterprise Information Systems and the Digitalization of Business Functions* (pp. 137–177). Hershey, PA: IGI Global. doi:10.4018/978-1-5225-2382-6.ch007

Rao, Y., & Zhang, Y. (2017). The Construction and Development of Academic Library Digital Special Subject Databases. In L. Ruan, Q. Zhu, & Y. Ye (Eds.), *Academic Library Development and Administration in China* (pp. 163–183). Hershey, PA: IGI Global. doi:10.4018/978-1-5225-0550-1.ch010

Ravasan, A. Z., Mohammadi, M. M., & Hamidi, H. (2018). An Investigation Into the Critical Success Factors of Implementing Information Technology Service Management Frameworks. In K. Jakobs (Ed.), *Corporate and Global Standardization Initiatives in Contemporary Society* (pp. 200–218). Hershey, PA: IGI Global. doi:10.4018/978-1-5225-5320-5.ch009

Rezaie, S., Mirabedini, S. J., & Abtahi, A. (2018). Designing a Model for Implementation of Business Intelligence in the Banking Industry. *International Journal of Enterprise Information Systems*, *14*(1), 77–103. doi:10.4018/IJEIS.2018010105

Richards, V., Matthews, N., Williams, O. J., & Khan, Z. (2021). The Challenges of Accessible Tourism Information Systems for Tourists With Vision Impairment: Sensory Communications Beyond the Screen. In C. Eusébio, L. Teixeira, & M. Carneiro (Eds.), *ICT Tools and Applications for Accessible Tourism* (pp. 26–54). IGI Global. https://doi.org/10.4018/978-1-7998-6428-8.ch002

Rodrigues de Souza Neto, V., & Marques, O. (2021). Rural Tourism Fostering Welfare Through Sustainable Development: A Conceptual Approach. In A. Perinotto, V. Mayer, & J. Soares (Eds.), *Rebuilding and Restructuring the Tourism Industry: Infusion of Happiness and Quality of Life* (pp. 38–57). IGI Global. https://doi.org/10.4018/978-1-7998-7239-9.ch003

Romano, L., Grimaldi, R., & Colasuonno, F. S. (2017). Demand Management as a Success Factor in Project Portfolio Management. In L. Romano (Ed.), *Project Portfolio Management Strategies for Effective Organizational Operations* (pp. 202–219). Hershey, PA: IGI Global. doi:10.4018/978-1-5225-2151-8.ch008

Rubio-Escuderos, L., & García-Andreu, H. (2021). Competitiveness Factors of Accessible Tourism E-Travel Agencies. In C. Eusébio, L. Teixeira, & M. Carneiro (Eds.), *ICT Tools and Applications for Accessible Tourism* (pp. 196–217). IGI Global. https://doi.org/10.4018/978-1-7998-6428-8.ch009

Rucci, A. C., Porto, N., Darcy, S., & Becka, L. (2021). Smart and Accessible Cities?: Not Always – The Case for Accessible Tourism Initiatives in Buenos Aries and Sydney. In C. Eusébio, L. Teixeira, & M. Carneiro (Eds.), *ICT Tools and Applications for Accessible Tourism* (pp. 115–145). IGI Global. https://doi.org/10.4018/978-1-7998-6428-8.ch006

Ruhi, U. (2018). Towards an Interdisciplinary Socio-Technical Definition of Virtual Communities. In M. Khosrow-Pour, D.B.A. (Ed.), Encyclopedia of Information Science and Technology, Fourth Edition (pp. 4278-4295). Hershey, PA: IGI Global. doi:10.4018/978-1-5225-2255-3.ch371

Ryan, L., Catena, M., Ros, P., & Stephens, S. (2021). Designing Entrepreneurial Ecosystems to Support Resource Management in the Tourism Industry. In V. Costa, A. Moura, & M. Mira (Eds.), *Handbook of Research on Human Capital and People Management in the Tourism Industry* (pp. 265–281). IGI Global. https://doi.org/10.4018/978-1-7998-4318-4.ch013

Sabuncu, I. (2021). Understanding Tourist Perceptions and Expectations During Pandemic Through Social Media Big Data. In M. Demir, A. Dalgıç, & F. Ergen (Eds.), *Handbook of Research on the Impacts and Implications of COVID-19 on the Tourism Industry* (pp. 330–350). IGI Global. https://doi.org/10.4018/978-1-7998-8231-2.ch016

Safari, M. R., & Jiang, Q. (2018). The Theory and Practice of IT Governance Maturity and Strategies Alignment: Evidence From Banking Industry. *Journal of Global Information Management*, *26*(2), 127–146. doi:10.4018/JGIM.2018040106

Sahoo, J., Pati, B., & Mohanty, B. (2017). Knowledge Management as an Academic Discipline: An Assessment. In B. Gunjal (Ed.), *Managing Knowledge and Scholarly Assets in Academic Libraries* (pp. 99–126). Hershey, PA: IGI Global. doi:10.4018/978-1-5225-1741-2.ch005

Saini, D. (2017). Relevance of Teaching Values and Ethics in Management Education. In N. Baporikar (Ed.), *Management Education for Global Leadership* (pp. 90–111). Hershey, PA: IGI Global. doi:10.4018/978-1-5225-1013-0.ch005

Sambhanthan, A. (2017). Assessing and Benchmarking Sustainability in Organisations: An Integrated Conceptual Model. *International Journal of Systems and Service-Oriented Engineering*, *7*(4), 22–43. doi:10.4018/IJSSOE.2017100102

Sambhanthan, A., & Potdar, V. (2017). A Study of the Parameters Impacting Sustainability in Information Technology Organizations. *International Journal of Knowledge-Based Organizations*, *7*(3), 27–39. doi:10.4018/IJKBO.2017070103

Sánchez-Fernández, M. D., & Manríquez, M. R. (2018). The Entrepreneurial Spirit Based on Social Values: The Digital Generation. In P. Isaias & L. Carvalho (Eds.), *User Innovation and the Entrepreneurship Phenomenon in the Digital Economy* (pp. 173–193). Hershey, PA: IGI Global. doi:10.4018/978-1-5225-2826-5.ch009

Sanchez-Ruiz, L., & Blanco, B. (2017). Process Management for SMEs: Barriers, Enablers, and Benefits. In M. Vemić (Ed.), *Optimal Management Strategies in Small and Medium Enterprises* (pp. 293–319). Hershey, PA: IGI Global. doi:10.4018/978-1-5225-1949-2.ch014

Sanz, L. F., Gómez-Pérez, J., & Castillo-Martinez, A. (2018). Analysis of the European ICT Competence Frameworks. In V. Ahuja & S. Rathore (Eds.), *Multidisciplinary Perspectives on Human Capital and Information Technology Professionals* (pp. 225–245). Hershey, PA: IGI Global. doi:10.4018/978-1-5225-5297-0.ch012

Sarvepalli, A., & Godin, J. (2017). Business Process Management in the Classroom. *Journal of Cases on Information Technology, 19*(2), 17–28. doi:10.4018/JCIT.2017040102

Saxena, G. G., & Saxena, A. (2021). Host Community Role in Medical Tourism Development. In M. Singh & S. Kumaran (Eds.), *Growth of the Medical Tourism Industry and Its Impact on Society: Emerging Research and Opportunities* (pp. 105–127). IGI Global. https://doi.org/10.4018/978-1-7998-3427-4.ch006

Saygili, E. E., Ozturkoglu, Y., & Kocakulah, M. C. (2017). End Users' Perceptions of Critical Success Factors in ERP Applications. *International Journal of Enterprise Information Systems, 13*(4), 58–75. doi:10.4018/IJEIS.2017100104

Saygili, E. E., & Saygili, A. T. (2017). Contemporary Issues in Enterprise Information Systems: A Critical Review of CSFs in ERP Implementations. In M. Tavana (Ed.), *Enterprise Information Systems and the Digitalization of Business Functions* (pp. 120–136). Hershey, PA: IGI Global. doi:10.4018/978-1-5225-2382-6.ch006

Schwaiger, K. M., & Zehrer, A. (2021). The COVID-19 Pandemic and Organizational Resilience in Hospitality Family Firms: A Qualitative Approach. In A. Zehrer, G. Glowka, K. Schwaiger, & V. Ranacher-Lackner (Eds.), *Resiliency Models and Addressing Future Risks for Family Firms in the Tourism Industry* (pp. 32–49). IGI Global. https://doi.org/10.4018/978-1-7998-7352-5.ch002

Scott, N., & Campos, A. C. (2022). Cognitive Science of Tourism Experiences. In R. Augusto Costa, F. Brandão, Z. Breda, & C. Costa (Eds.), Planning and Managing the Experience Economy in Tourism (pp. 1-21). IGI Global. https://doi.org/ doi:10.4018/978-1-7998-8775-1.ch001

Seidenstricker, S., & Antonino, A. (2018). Business Model Innovation-Oriented Technology Management for Emergent Technologies. In M. Khosrow-Pour, D.B.A. (Ed.), Encyclopedia of Information Science and Technology, Fourth Edition (pp. 4560-4569). Hershey, PA: IGI Global. doi:10.4018/978-1-5225-2255-3.ch396

Selvi, M. S. (2021). Changes in Tourism Sales and Marketing Post COVID-19. In M. Demir, A. Dalgıç, & F. Ergen (Eds.), *Handbook of Research on the Impacts and Implications of COVID-19 on the Tourism Industry* (pp. 437–460). IGI Global. doi:10.4018/978-1-7998-8231-2.ch021

Senaratne, S., & Gunarathne, A. D. (2017). Excellence Perspective for Management Education from a Global Accountants' Hub in Asia. In N. Baporikar (Ed.), *Management Education for Global Leadership* (pp. 158–180). Hershey, PA: IGI Global. doi:10.4018/978-1-5225-1013-0.ch008

Sensuse, D. I., & Cahyaningsih, E. (2018). Knowledge Management Models: A Summative Review. *International Journal of Information Systems in the Service Sector, 10*(1), 71–100. doi:10.4018/IJISSS.2018010105

Seth, M., Goyal, D., & Kiran, R. (2017). Diminution of Impediments in Implementation of Supply Chain Management Information System for Enhancing its Effectiveness in Indian Automobile Industry. *Journal of Global Information Management, 25*(3), 1–20. doi:10.4018/JGIM.2017070101

Seyal, A. H., & Rahman, M. N. (2017). Investigating Impact of Inter-Organizational Factors in Measuring ERP Systems Success: Bruneian Perspectives. In M. Tavana (Ed.), *Enterprise Information Systems and the Digitalization of Business Functions* (pp. 178–204). Hershey, PA: IGI Global. doi:10.4018/978-1-5225-2382-6.ch008

Shaqrah, A. A. (2018). Analyzing Business Intelligence Systems Based on 7s Model of McKinsey. *International Journal of Business Intelligence Research, 9*(1), 53–63. doi:10.4018/IJBIR.2018010104

Sharma, A. J. (2017). Enhancing Sustainability through Experiential Learning in Management Education. In N. Baporikar (Ed.), *Management Education for Global Leadership* (pp. 256–274). Hershey, PA: IGI Global. doi:10.4018/978-1-5225-1013-0.ch013

Shetty, K. P. (2017). Responsible Global Leadership: Ethical Challenges in Management Education. In N. Baporikar (Ed.), *Innovation and Shifting Perspectives in Management Education* (pp. 194–223). Hershey, PA: IGI Global. doi:10.4018/978-1-5225-1019-2.ch009

Sinthupundaja, J., & Kohda, Y. (2017). Effects of Corporate Social Responsibility and Creating Shared Value on Sustainability. *International Journal of Sustainable Entrepreneurship and Corporate Social Responsibility, 2*(1), 27–38. doi:10.4018/IJSECSR.2017010103

Škarica, I., & Hrgović, A. V. (2018). Implementation of Total Quality Management Principles in Public Health Institutes in the Republic of Croatia. *International Journal of Productivity Management and Assessment Technologies, 6*(1), 1–16. doi:10.4018/IJPMAT.2018010101

Skokic, V. (2021). How Small Hotel Owners Practice Resilience: Longitudinal Study Among Small Family Hotels in Croatia. In A. Zehrer, G. Glowka, K. Schwaiger, & V. Ranacher-Lackner (Eds.), *Resiliency Models and Addressing Future Risks for Family Firms in the Tourism Industry* (pp. 50–73). IGI Global. doi:10.4018/978-1-7998-7352-5.ch003

Smuts, H., Kotzé, P., Van der Merwe, A., & Loock, M. (2017). Framework for Managing Shared Knowledge in an Information Systems Outsourcing Context. *International Journal of Knowledge Management, 13*(4), 1–30. doi:10.4018/IJKM.2017100101

Sousa, M. J., Cruz, R., Dias, I., & Caracol, C. (2017). Information Management Systems in the Supply Chain. In G. Jamil, A. Soares, & C. Pessoa (Eds.), *Handbook of Research on Information Management for Effective Logistics and Supply Chains* (pp. 469–485). Hershey, PA: IGI Global. doi:10.4018/978-1-5225-0973-8.ch025

Spremic, M., Turulja, L., & Bajgoric, N. (2018). Two Approaches in Assessing Business Continuity Management Attitudes in the Organizational Context. In N. Bajgoric (Ed.), *Always-On Enterprise Information Systems for Modern Organizations* (pp. 159–183). Hershey, PA: IGI Global. doi:10.4018/978-1-5225-3704-5.ch008

Steenkamp, A. L. (2018). Some Insights in Computer Science and Information Technology. In *Examining the Changing Role of Supervision in Doctoral Research Projects: Emerging Research and Opportunities* (pp. 113–133). Hershey, PA: IGI Global. doi:10.4018/978-1-5225-2610-0.ch005

Stipanović, C., Rudan, E., & Zubović, V. (2022). Reaching the New Tourist Through Creativity: Sustainable Development Challenges in Croatian Coastal Towns. In M. Valeri (Ed.), *New Governance and Management in Touristic Destinations* (pp. 231–245). IGI Global. https://doi.org/10.4018/978-1-6684-3889-3.ch014

Tabach, A., & Croteau, A. (2017). Configurations of Information Technology Governance Practices and Business Unit Performance. *International Journal of IT/Business Alignment and Governance, 8*(2), 1–27. doi:10.4018/IJITBAG.2017070101

Talaue, G. M., & Iqbal, T. (2017). Assessment of e-Business Mode of Selected Private Universities in the Philippines and Pakistan. *International Journal of Online Marketing, 7*(4), 63–77. doi:10.4018/IJOM.2017100105

Tam, G. C. (2017). Project Manager Sustainability Competence. In *Managerial Strategies and Green Solutions for Project Sustainability* (pp. 178–207). Hershey, PA: IGI Global. doi:10.4018/978-1-5225-2371-0.ch008

Tambo, T. (2018). Fashion Retail Innovation: About Context, Antecedents, and Outcome in Technological Change Projects. In I. Management Association (Ed.), Fashion and Textiles: Breakthroughs in Research and Practice (pp. 233-260). Hershey, PA: IGI Global. https://doi.org/ doi:10.4018/978-1-5225-3432-7.ch010

Tantau, A. D., & Frăţilă, L. C. (2018). Information and Management System for Renewable Energy Business. In *Entrepreneurship and Business Development in the Renewable Energy Sector* (pp. 200–244). Hershey, PA: IGI Global. doi:10.4018/978-1-5225-3625-3.ch006

Teixeira, N., Pardal, P. N., & Rafael, B. G. (2018). Internationalization, Financial Performance, and Organizational Challenges: A Success Case in Portugal. In L. Carvalho (Ed.), *Handbook of Research on Entrepreneurial Ecosystems and Social Dynamics in a Globalized World* (pp. 379–423). Hershey, PA: IGI Global. doi:10.4018/978-1-5225-3525-6.ch017

Teixeira, P., Teixeira, L., Eusébio, C., Silva, S., & Teixeira, A. (2021). The Impact of ICTs on Accessible Tourism: Evidence Based on a Systematic Literature Review. In C. Eusébio, L. Teixeira, & M. Carneiro (Eds.), *ICT Tools and Applications for Accessible Tourism* (pp. 1–25). IGI Global. doi:10.4018/978-1-7998-6428-8.ch001

Trad, A., & Kalpić, D. (2018). The Business Transformation Framework, Agile Project and Change Management. In M. Khosrow-Pour, D.B.A. (Ed.), Encyclopedia of Information Science and Technology, Fourth Edition (pp. 620-635). Hershey, PA: IGI Global. https://doi.org/ doi:10.4018/978-1-5225-2255-3.ch054

Trad, A., & Kalpić, D. (2018). The Business Transformation and Enterprise Architecture Framework: The Financial Engineering E-Risk Management and E-Law Integration. In B. Sergi, F. Fidanoski, M. Ziolo, & V. Naumovski (Eds.), *Regaining Global Stability After the Financial Crisis* (pp. 46–65). Hershey, PA: IGI Global. doi:10.4018/978-1-5225-4026-7.ch003

Trengereid, V. (2022). Conditions of Network Engagement: The Quest for a Common Good. In R. Augusto Costa, F. Brandão, Z. Breda, & C. Costa (Eds.), *Planning and Managing the Experience Economy in Tourism* (pp. 69-84). IGI Global. https://doi.org/10.4018/978-1-7998-8775-1.ch004

Turulja, L., & Bajgoric, N. (2018). Business Continuity and Information Systems: A Systematic Literature Review. In N. Bajgoric (Ed.), *Always-On Enterprise Information Systems for Modern Organizations* (pp. 60–87). Hershey, PA: IGI Global. doi:10.4018/978-1-5225-3704-5.ch004

Vargas-Hernández, J. G. (2017). Professional Integrity in Business Management Education. In N. Baporikar (Ed.), *Management Education for Global Leadership* (pp. 70–89). Hershey, PA: IGI Global. doi:10.4018/978-1-5225-1013-0.ch004

Varnacı Uzun, F. (2021). The Destination Preferences of Foreign Tourists During the COVID-19 Pandemic and Attitudes Towards: Marmaris, Turkey. In M. Demir, A. Dalgıç, & F. Ergen (Eds.), *Handbook of Research on the Impacts and Implications of COVID-19 on the Tourism Industry* (pp. 285–306). IGI Global. https://doi.org/10.4018/978-1-7998-8231-2.ch014

Vasista, T. G., & AlAbdullatif, A. M. (2017). Role of Electronic Customer Relationship Management in Demand Chain Management: A Predictive Analytic Approach. *International Journal of Information Systems and Supply Chain Management, 10*(1), 53–67. doi:10.4018/IJISSCM.2017010104

Vieru, D., & Bourdeau, S. (2017). Survival in the Digital Era: A Digital Competence-Based Multi-Case Study in the Canadian SME Clothing Industry. *International Journal of Social and Organizational Dynamics in IT, 6*(1), 17–34. doi:10.4018/IJSODIT.2017010102

Vijayan, G., & Kamarulzaman, N. H. (2017). An Introduction to Sustainable Supply Chain Management and Business Implications. In M. Khan, M. Hussain, & M. Ajmal (Eds.), *Green Supply Chain Management for Sustainable Business Practice* (pp. 27–50). Hershey, PA: IGI Global. doi:10.4018/978-1-5225-0635-5.ch002

Vlachvei, A., & Notta, O. (2017). Firm Competitiveness: Theories, Evidence, and Measurement. In A. Vlachvei, O. Notta, K. Karantininis, & N. Tsounis (Eds.), *Factors Affecting Firm Competitiveness and Performance in the Modern Business World* (pp. 1–42). Hershey, PA: IGI Global. doi:10.4018/978-1-5225-0843-4.ch001

Wang, C., Schofield, M., Li, X., & Ou, X. (2017). Do Chinese Students in Public and Private Higher Education Institutes Perform at Different Level in One of the Leadership Skills: Critical Thinking?: An Exploratory Comparison. In V. Wang (Ed.), *Encyclopedia of Strategic Leadership and Management* (pp. 160–181). Hershey, PA: IGI Global. doi:10.4018/978-1-5225-1049-9.ch013

Wang, J. (2017). Multi-Agent based Production Management Decision System Modelling for the Textile Enterprise. *Journal of Global Information Management, 25*(4), 1–15. doi:10.4018/JGIM.2017100101

Wiedemann, A., & Gewald, H. (2017). Examining Cross-Domain Alignment: The Correlation of Business Strategy, IT Management, and IT Business Value. *International Journal of IT/Business Alignment and Governance, 8*(1), 17–31. doi:10.4018/IJITBAG.2017010102

Wolf, R., & Thiel, M. (2018). Advancing Global Business Ethics in China: Reducing Poverty Through Human and Social Welfare. In S. Hipsher (Ed.), *Examining the Private Sector's Role in Wealth Creation and Poverty Reduction* (pp. 67–84). Hershey, PA: IGI Global. doi:10.4018/978-1-5225-3117-3.ch004

Yablonsky, S. (2018). Innovation Platforms: Data and Analytics Platforms. In *Multi-Sided Platforms (MSPs) and Sharing Strategies in the Digital Economy: Emerging Research and Opportunities* (pp. 72–95). Hershey, PA: IGI Global. doi:10.4018/978-1-5225-5457-8.ch003

Yaşar, B. (2021). The Impact of COVID-19 on Volatility of Tourism Stocks: Evidence From BIST Tourism Index. In M. Demir, A. Dalgıç, & F. Ergen (Eds.), *Handbook of Research on the Impacts and Implications of COVID-19 on the Tourism Industry* (pp. 23–44). IGI Global. https://doi.org/10.4018/978-1-7998-8231-2.ch002

Yusoff, A., Ahmad, N. H., & Halim, H. A. (2017). Agropreneurship among Gen Y in Malaysia: The Role of Academic Institutions. In N. Ahmad, T. Ramayah, H. Halim, & S. Rahman (Eds.), *Handbook of Research on Small and Medium Enterprises in Developing Countries* (pp. 23–47). Hershey, PA: IGI Global. doi:10.4018/978-1-5225-2165-5.ch002

Zacher, D., & Pechlaner, H. (2021). Resilience as an Opportunity Approach: Challenges and Perspectives for Private Sector Participation on a Community Level. In A. Zehrer, G. Glowka, K. Schwaiger, & V. Ranacher-Lackner (Eds.), *Resiliency Models and Addressing Future Risks for Family Firms in the Tourism Industry* (pp. 75–102). IGI Global. https://doi.org/10.4018/978-1-7998-7352-5.ch004

Zanin, F., Comuzzi, E., & Costantini, A. (2018). The Effect of Business Strategy and Stock Market Listing on the Use of Risk Assessment Tools. In *Management Control Systems in Complex Settings: Emerging Research and Opportunities* (pp. 145–168). Hershey, PA: IGI Global. doi:10.4018/978-1-5225-3987-2.ch007

Zgheib, P. W. (2017). Corporate Innovation and Intrapreneurship in the Middle East. In P. Zgheib (Ed.), *Entrepreneurship and Business Innovation in the Middle East* (pp. 37–56). Hershey, PA: IGI Global. doi:10.4018/978-1-5225-2066-5.ch003

About the Contributors

Nadia Mansour is an assistant at The University of Sousse Tunisia, and a visiting researcher at the University of Salamanca- Spain. Her research interests focus on Banking, macroeconomic, DSGE, Big Data, Business Tourism, and Innovation. She is an academic member and ambassador of Communication Institute of Greece, a committee member of indexed conferences, editorial Board Member of Taylor & Francis, IGI GLOBAL, and Springer, a reviewer in IGI Global, Emerald, and Wiley. She has presented various scientific papers in international (France, Morocco, USA, Turkey) and national conferences. She is also a keynote speaker and session chair in several conferences in (Turkey, India UAE). She has several published articles in ranked journals and chapters (IGI Global & Palgrave Macmillan) as well as edited books (Taylor & Francis, Springer).

Salha Ben Salem is a PhD student at the Faculty of Economics and Management of Sousse, University of Sousse; and researcher at the Financial Development and Innovation Research Unit (DEFI) -Tunis. I spent three years of professional experience in the Faculty of Economics and Management of Mahdia-Tunisia, Higher Institute of Technologies, Mahdia-Tunisia, and higher institute of applied languages Moknine-Tunisia. I have national and international training and Scientific formation (Milano, Paris, Morocco, Turkey.,) I have four scientific articles and three book chapters. My field of research is on Monetary policy, banking sector vulnerability, Financial frictions, DSGE models, Financial Economics, banking system stress, Big Data.

* * *

Yakup Arı is an Assistant Professor in the Department of Economics at Alanya Alaaddin Keykubat University. Having graduated with a bachelor's degree in Mathematics, he pursued an MBA degree in Finance and a PhD degree in Financial Economics – all of which at Yeditepe University with full scholarships. He worked as a statistical consultant at several private consultancy firms in Istanbul. He teaches courses in time series analysis, mathematical economics, technical analysis, probability and statistics, biostatistics and econometrics. His primary research interest lies in the area of time series analysis, Lévy driven stochastic processes, the Bayesian approach in statistics and econometrics, in addition to statistical methods in Engineering and Social Sciences.

Manpreet Arora is an Assistant Professor of Management in the School of Commerce and Management Studies, Central University of Himachal Pradesh Dharamshala, India. With around eighteen years of teaching experience she has varied interest areas. A Gold medalist at undergraduate and postgraduate levels, she obtained her PhD in International Trade from Himachal Pradesh University, Shimla. Her areas of research interest include Accounting and Finance, Strategic Management, Entrepreneurial Leadership, Qualitative Research, Case Study Development, Communication Skills and Microfinance. She has been guiding research at the doctoral level and has worked in the area of Microfinance. As an active seminarian, she has attended more than hundred seminars/ conferences, and has visited several universities and colleges to deliver invited talks on Finance, Strategic Management, Qualitative Research, Business Communication, Interpersonal skills, Entrepreneurship and Skill Development. She is a motivational speaker and conducts workshops on communication and motivation. Having published more than 20 papers in various journals of national and international repute, she has also worked as content developer of MHRD e-PG Pathshala Project. She has written thirty book chapters in national as well as international books/handbooks. With four edited books in her credit she is a persistent researcher in the field of Management. She is an active social worker also and is working towards the protecting the rights of women.

Bechir Chenguel has a Ph.D. in Finance, and he is an associate professor of Finance at High Institute of management and computer, University of Kairouan. His research interests are: blockchain technology and crypto currencies, corporate governance, banking financial risk, and Islamic finance. Active in research, he is reviewer in many indexed peer reviewed journals (Scopus…). And he has published several papers in international peer-reviewed scopus journals indexed (Routledge, Francis & Taylor Group, Emerald).

Roshan Lal Sharma is Professor and Head in the Department of English, School of Languages, Central University of Himachal Pradesh, Dharamshala (HP). He has been a Senior Fulbright Fellow at the University of Wisconsin-Madison (USA) during 2007-08. He has authored Shorter Fiction of Raja Rao (2009), and Walt Whitman (2000); co-authored Som P. Ranchan: Dialogue Epic in Indian English Poetry (2012); and co-edited, Communication in Contemporary Scenario: Its Multiple Dimensions (2017), Mapping Diaspora Identities (2017), and Communication, Entrepreneurship and Finance: Renegotiating Diverse Perspectives (2018). Professor Sharma has more than sixty published papers and book chapters to his credit. His areas of specialization and interest include Indian Writing in English, Mystical Poetry of Diverse Literary Traditions of the World, World Literature, Comparative Literature & Translation Studies, Contemporary Literary and Cultural Theory, Communication Studies, New Media Ecology, Communication & Inter-personal Skills, Global English for Successful Communication, and Business Communication.

Harun Uçak received his PhD from Çukurova University in 2009 and he was awarded Associate Professorship in international economics by the Turkish Higher Education Council in 2012. Currently, he is full professor at the Department of Economics in Alanya Alaaddin Keykubat University. His research interests are in the areas of international economics, agricultural trade and policies, convergence analyses, development studies and water economics. He is chief editor of International Journal of Food and Agricultural Economics (ISSN 2147-8988). He was chairperson in many regular international academic events such as "International Conference on Food and Agricultural Economics" and "International Conference on Economic Research". He was visiting researcher at the Warsaw University of Life Sciences in 2008. He also gave lectures in some EU countries by short time visits teaching visits under Erasmus mobility programmes. He worked as national consultant for FAO-EBRD cooperation projects such as titled "Turkey: Premium Poultry Products-Willingness-to-pay and Investment Opportunities" and "Water along the food chain Towards water smart agrifood policies the case of red meat processing".

Esin Yelgen is an Assistant Professor in the Department of Economics at Alanya Alaaddin Keykubat University. Having graduated with a bachelor's degree in Tourism Management Education at Gazi University in Ankara, she pursued an MBA degree and a Ph.D. degree in Tourism Management at Akdeniz University in Antalya. She teaches courses in financial accounting, cost accounting, auditing, financial statements analysis, bank accounting, and firm valuation. Her primary research interest lies in the area of accounting information systems, accounting education approaches, International Financial Reporting Standards, and the new technologies, approaches and methods in accounting, accounting education and accounting reporting systems.

Index

A

access to justice 107-108, 113-114, 116
Algeria 33, 166-172, 174-183
anonymity 8, 14, 69-70, 85
Auction 174, 184

B

Big Data 1, 4, 33, 37, 41, 52, 135
Bitcoin 5-6, 9, 11-12, 14, 16-24, 26-31, 53-64, 66-70, 77-78, 83-86, 88, 99-105, 137, 141-147, 152-158
blockchain 13-16, 18, 20, 23-26, 28-31, 36, 54, 56, 60, 63-64, 71-72, 75, 79, 83, 102, 104-105, 143
business model 4, 10, 36-37, 39, 41-42, 48, 52

C

cci30 index 82, 97, 99-100, 104
CoinDesk 85, 105
CoinMarketCap 83, 88, 99, 105
conditional volatility 150, 159
connectedness 141, 151, 153, 155-156, 158-159
correlation 87, 90-91, 94, 97, 99, 143, 145-146, 151-152, 157, 159
COVID-19 1, 11, 13, 22, 34, 49, 51, 53, 61-63, 65, 71-73, 76, 107-108, 113, 115-116, 118-122, 127-139, 141-144, 150-158, 163-164
crises 24, 62, 104, 118-122, 129, 132
Cross-Border Crime 117
cryptocurrencies 8-9, 12-17, 20-28, 30-32, 53-54, 61-62, 69, 76-78, 80, 82, 104-105, 142-146, 155, 157
cryptocurrency enforcement 65-67, 70-71, 73-75, 79, 81
culture of cybersecurity 108, 110, 113-114, 116-117
cyber regulation 107
cybercrime 78, 80-81, 108-109, 111, 113-114, 116
Cyberlaw 107
cybersecurity 107-117
Cybersecurity Principles 107, 117

D

decentralized 13, 16, 20-23, 25-27, 29, 31, 66-68, 75, 78-79, 81, 83, 85, 105
Diebold-Yılmaz 141
digital 1-19, 21-24, 27-29, 31, 33-55, 60, 62-64, 66-67, 70-72, 75, 77-79, 81, 83, 85-86, 101-103, 105, 107-108, 110, 112-115, 119, 121, 132-134, 138
digital asset 19, 54, 71-72, 75, 79, 81
Digital Business 35, 38, 46, 51-52
digital currency 5-10, 12, 15-17, 21-23, 27-28, 54-55, 67, 70, 78, 81, 102-103, 105
Digital Strategy 52
digital transformation 1-3, 10-12, 33-52
Digital Wallets 31, 53
digitalization of the economy 22
Disruptive Innovation 52

E

E-business 33-34, 47
economic recovery 121, 129
energy efficiency 171, 173, 178, 183-184
enforcement actions 65-66, 70-71, 73-74, 79
entrepreneurial leaders 118, 122, 129-131
Entrepreneurial Leadership 118, 121, 129, 133, 139
entrepreneurs 9, 38, 118, 120-121, 128-132, 135, 137-138
Entrepreneurship 48, 103, 120, 132-139
Ethereum 24, 28, 84, 105, 143, 145, 158
E-Wallet (or Digital Wallet) 52

F

fraud 14, 17, 66, 69-71, 81
futures 44, 53-55, 57-63, 68, 71

G

GARCH 101, 141, 145, 147-148, 151, 155-157, 159, 161, 163-164
GDPR 111
gig economy 118, 120-121, 127, 132-133, 136-139
gig players 118, 121-122, 128, 131-132, 140
Global Crime 114, 117
global economic crisis 118, 131, 140
Global Public Awareness Related to Cybersecurity 117
Globalization 36, 44, 114, 117, 132, 134

I

ICT 11, 107-108, 113
index 82, 84, 91-92, 97, 99-100, 103-104, 141, 143-146, 148-155, 158-159
Industry 4.0 33, 36, 39, 44, 47-48, 50-52
Information Age 65, 81
innovation 4, 14, 18, 25-26, 31, 33, 36, 40-42, 47-50, 52, 63, 77, 83, 120, 134-135, 137, 139

L

Leverage Effects 159
Litecoin 23, 84, 99, 105, 143, 145

M

mining 22, 53, 56, 61, 178
money laundering 23-26, 63, 66, 69, 80-81, 103

P

pandemic 1-2, 5-6, 22-23, 46, 49, 51, 53, 61-63, 65, 67, 71-73, 107-108, 113-114, 118-122, 127-139, 142-144, 150, 157-158
partnership 76, 110, 166-168, 175-180, 182, 184
performance 5, 33, 35-36, 39-42, 44-52, 63, 84, 105, 145, 157, 182
PPP 166, 175, 184
Principal Component Analysis (PCA) 82, 88, 99, 105

R

renewable energy 166-168, 170-171, 173-184
Renewable Energy Contracts 184
renewable energy technology 166-168, 171, 173, 175-176, 179, 184
resilience 8, 11, 107-108, 113, 117-118, 121, 127-129, 131-133, 135-140
resilience strategies 118, 121, 127, 129, 131-132

S

Securities and Exchange Commission 65-66, 70-71, 73, 75, 79
security 7-9, 14, 25-26, 29, 31, 45, 63, 66, 77-78, 87, 100-101, 104, 108, 110-113, 117, 134, 167

T

tender 5, 8, 14, 23, 26-27, 67, 83, 174, 184
transformation strategies 33, 35, 38-40, 44, 48, 50
Turkish financial markets 141, 144, 150-151, 155
Typical Digital Currencies 12

V

virtual currency 11, 14, 17-18, 20, 25, 53, 66-68, 76-78, 81, 101, 104
volatility clusters 160
Volatility persistence 151, 160
volatility spillover 141, 148, 150, 152, 154, 157, 159-160

www.ingramcontent.com/pod-product-compliance
Lightning Source LLC
LaVergne TN
LVHW081326300926
849161LV00008B/1882